T0331794

Quantum Computing for Programmers

This introduction to quantum computing from a classical programmer's perspective is meant for students and practitioners alike. More than 25 fundamental algorithms are explained with full mathematical derivations and classical code for simulation, using an open-source code base developed from the ground up in Python and C++.

After presenting the basics of quantum computing, the author focuses on algorithms and the infrastructure to simulate them efficiently, beginning with quantum teleportation, superdense coding, Bernstein–Vazirani's algorithm, and Deutsc–Jozsa's algorithm. Coverage of advanced algorithms includes the quantum supremacy experiment, quantum Fourier transform, phase estimation, Shor's algorithm, Grover's algorithm with quantum counting and amplitude amplification, quantum random walks, and the Solovay–Kitaev algorithm for gate approximation. Quantum simulation is explored with the variational quantum eigensolver, quantum approximate optimization, and the NP-complete Max-Cut and Subset-Sum algorithms.

The book also discusses issues around programmer productivity, quantum noise, error correction, and challenges for quantum programming languages, compilers, and tools, with a final section on compiler techniques for transpilation.

Robert Hundt is a Distinguished Engineer at Google, where he led software development for Google's TPU supercomputers, the XLA compiler for TensorFlow, an open-source CUDA compiler, and currently the high-level synthesis toolchain XLS. He has more than 25 scientific publications, holds more than 35 patents, and is a senior member of IEEE.

Quantum Computing for Programmers

ROBERT HUNDT

CAMBRIDGE
UNIVERSITY PRESS

CAMBRIDGE
UNIVERSITY PRESS

University Printing House, Cambridge CB2 8BS, United Kingdom

One Liberty Plaza, 20th Floor, New York, NY 10006, USA

477 Williamstown Road, Port Melbourne, VIC 3207, Australia

314–321, 3rd Floor, Plot 3, Splendor Forum, Jasola District Centre,
New Delhi – 110025, India

103 Penang Road, #05–06/07, Visioncrest Commercial, Singapore 238467

Cambridge University Press is part of the University of Cambridge.

It furthers the University's mission by disseminating knowledge in the pursuit of
education, learning, and research at the highest international levels of excellence.

www.cambridge.org
Information on this title: www.cambridge.org/9781009098175
DOI: 10.1017/9781009099974

First published 2022

A catalogue record for this publication is available from the British Library.

Library of Congress Cataloging-in-Publication Data
Names: Hundt, Robert, author.
Title: Quantum computing for programmers / Robert Hundt.
Description: Cambridge, United Kingdom ; New York, NY : Cambridge
    University Press, 2022. | Includes bibliographical references and index.
Identifiers: LCCN 2021044761 (print) | LCCN 2021044762 (ebook) |
    ISBN 9781009098175 (hardback) | ISBN 9781009099974 (epub)
Subjects: LCSH: Quantum computing. | BISAC: COMPUTERS / General
Classification: LCC QA76.889 .H86 2022 (print) | LCC QA76.889 (ebook) |
    DDC 006.3/843–dc23/eng/20211105
LC record available at https://lccn.loc.gov/2021044761
LC ebook record available at https://lccn.loc.gov/2021044762

ISBN 978-1-009-09817-5 Hardback

To Mary, Thalia, and Johannes

Contents

Acknowledgments   *page* x
Introduction   xi

1   The Mathematical Minimum   1
  1.1   Complex Numbers   1
  1.2   Dirac Notation, Bras, and Kets   2
  1.3   Tensor Product   5
  1.4   Unitary and Hermitian Matrices   6
  1.5   Hermitian Adjoint of Expressions   6
  1.6   Eigenvalues and Eigenvectors   7
  1.7   Trace of a Matrix   8

2   Quantum Computing Fundamentals   9
  2.1   Tensors   9
  2.2   Qubits   13
  2.3   States   15
  2.4   Helper Functions   24
  2.5   Operators   25
  2.6   Single-Qubit Gates   33
  2.7   Controlled Gates   46
  2.8   Quantum Circuit Notation   51
  2.9   Bloch Sphere   55
  2.10   Global Phase   59
  2.11   Entanglement   60
  2.12   No-Cloning Theorem   65
  2.13   Uncomputation   66
  2.14   Reduced Density Matrix and Partial Trace   68
  2.15   Measurement   72

3   Simple Algorithms   78
  3.1   Random Number Generator   78
  3.2   Gate Equivalences   79
  3.3   Classical Arithmetic   89
  3.4   Swap Test   93

3.5   Quantum Teleportation   97
3.6   Superdense Coding   102
3.7   Bernstein–Vazirani Algorithm   105
3.8   Deutsch's Algorithm   108
3.9   Deutsch–Jozsa Algorithm   118

4   Scalable, Fast Simulation   122
4.1   Simulation Complexity   122
4.2   Quantum Registers   124
4.3   Circuits   126
4.4   Fast Gate Application   134
4.5   Accelerated Gate Application   139
4.6   Sparse Representation   145

5   Beyond Classical   149
5.1   10,000 Years, 2 Days, or 200 Seconds   150
5.2   Quantum Random Circuit Algorithm   150
5.3   Circuit Construction   152
5.4   Estimation   155
5.5   Evaluation   158

6   Complex Algorithms   160
6.1   Phase Kick   161
6.2   Quantum Fourier Transform   163
6.3   Quantum Arithmetic   172
6.4   Phase Estimation   180
6.5   Shor's Algorithm   189
6.6   Order Finding   196
6.7   Grover's Algorithm   210
6.8   Amplitude Amplification   227
6.9   Quantum Counting   230
6.10 Quantum Random Walk   234
6.11 Variational Quantum Eigensolver   240
6.12 Quantum Approximate Optimization Algorithm   253
6.13 Maximum Cut Algorithm   254
6.14 Subset Sum Algorithm   262
6.15 Solovay–Kitaev Theorem and Algorithm   266

7   Quantum Error Correction   278
7.1   Quantum Noise   278
7.2   Quantum Error Correction   284
7.3   Nine-Qubit Shor Code   289

8   **Quantum Languages, Compilers, and Tools**   292
         8.1   Challenges for Quantum Compilation   293
         8.2   Quantum Programming Model   294
         8.3   Quantum Programming Languages   294
         8.4   Compiler Optimization   303
         8.5   Transpilation   311

Appendix: Sparse Implementation   322

         References   335
         Index   343

Acknowledgments

A book like this would not be possible without the help of many people. Vincent Russo and Timofey Golubev found a large number of issues with the mathematical formulation, code, and writing. Gabriel Hannon provided valuable pointers to related physics concepts. Several of my questions were answered on the Quantum Computing Stack Exchange, a very helpful resource and community. Wes Cowley and Sarah Schedler provided line editing, Sue Klefstad produced the impressive index, and Eleanor Bolton provided outstanding copyediting services. I am grateful to Tiago Leao for pointing me to Beauregard (2003), which was key for my implementation of Shor's refactoring. Together with Rui Maia, Tiago also provides the community with a much-appreciated reference implementation (Leao, 2021).

I also want to thank many of my colleagues at Google. Dave Bennet and Michael Dorner went through the first draft of this text, which, I am certain, was not a pleasant experience. Their feedback helped to shape this work into an actual learning resource. Two of my colleagues stand out for their rigor and obsession with details: Fedor Kostritsa, who provided most detailed comments on text, math, derivations, and code; and Ton Kalker, who diligently reviewed the whole text and helped greatly in sharpening the mathematical formulation. Sergio Boixo and Benjamin Villalonga corrected many of my misunderstandings about the quantum supremacy experiment. Michael Broughton and Craig Gidney helped to improve the section on Grover's algorithm. Craig also maintains the elegant online simulator Quirk. Thanks also to Mark Heffernan, Chris Leary, Rob Springer, and Mirko Rossini. Finally, I owe gratitude to Aamer Mahmood for his extraordinary support.

Without exception, my contacts at Cambridge University Press were outstanding. First and foremost, I must thank my editor, Lauren Cowles, who did a tremendous job guiding me throughout the whole process.

Finally, and most importantly, I am incredibly thankful to my family, including my dog, Charlie, for their love, patience, and support during this all-consuming effort.

Introduction

I think I can safely say that nobody understands quantum mechanics

Feynman (1965)

I have been impressed by numerous instances of mathematical theories that are really about particular algorithms; these theories are typically formulated in mathematical terms that are much more cumbersome and less natural than the equivalent formulation today's computer scientists would use

Knuth (1974)

This book is an introduction to quantum computing from the perspective of a classical programmer. Most concepts are explained with code, based on the insight that much of the complicated-looking math typically found in quantum computing may look quite simple in code. For many programmers, reading code is faster than reading complex math notation. Coding also allows experimentation, which helps in building intuition and understanding of the fundamental mechanisms of quantum computing. I believe that this approach will make it efficient and fun to get started.

Contrary to other learning resources, we will not use available software frameworks in this book, such as the well-developed Qiskit toolkit from IBM or Google's Cirq. Instead we build our own infrastructure from the ground up, based initially on Python's numpy library. It turns out that for learning the fundamentals, only a few hundred lines of code are required. This initial code is slow, but explicit. It is easy to debug and experiment with, which makes it an excellent learning vehicle.

We then improve the infrastructure, accelerate it with C++, and detail an elegant, sparse representation. We introduce basic compiler concepts that allow transpilation of our circuits to those other platforms – Qiskit, Cirq, and others. This enables the use of these systems' advanced features, such as scale-out performance and advanced error models.

Typically, an introduction to quantum computing is prefaced by a sizeable reintroduction of complex linear algebra. We will not follow this pattern here. Many programmers do have a solid foundation in linear algebra, but others lack the background or interest in this topic. It is my goal to be an attractive learning resource for both groups, without getting into the details of linear algebra. Hence I only assume basic familiarity with complex numbers, vectors, and matrices. We review a handful of core concepts in Chapter 1. As we go along in the text we add a small number of additional mathematical concepts that are necessary to understand the algorithms. We hope that this format will be helpful to the linear algebra-challenged while not being too shallow for the cognoscenti. After the introduction of the basic mathematical concepts, the book is organized into the following major sections:

- In Chapter 2 we introduce core concepts of quantum computing and implement them with full matrices and vectors in Python. We discuss states, operators, entanglement, and measurement. We show a variety of ways to construct, describe, and analyze qubits and quantum circuits. Quantum mechanics, superposition, entanglement, and measurement are all complex and deeply philosophical topics. In this text, however, we focus exclusively on the computational aspects of the theory.
- This is followed in Chapter 3 with introductory algorithms, utilizing the infrastructure developed so far. The material is presented in an elaborate way, with detailed mathematical derivations.
- The basic infrastructure developed up to this point does not scale to a higher number of qubits, which are needed for complex algorithms. In Chapter 4, we detail techniques for faster gate application and accelerate with C++. We demonstrate how a sparse representation can produce the best performing results for a certain class of algorithms. These sections lead to building a high-performance quantum simulator. Readers not interested in infrastructure may skim or even skip this section.
- In Chapter 5 we convince ourselves that quantum computers indeed have capabilities that go *beyond classical* machines.
- With this insight, Chapter 6 on complex algorithms provides important details on several of quantum computing's core algorithms, including Grover's search, the quantum Fourier transform, phase estimation, quantum random walks, Shor's algorithm for integer factorization, and a variational quantum eigensolver with some applications. This section also details the seminal Solovay–Kitaev algorithm to approximate any unitary gate from a small universal gate set. The foundation built up in the earlier chapters is sufficient to implement and fully appreciate these marvelous algorithms.
- Chapters 7 and 8 then address practical issues around programmer productivity. We touch on quantum error correction, which is essential to the feasibility of quantum computing. We also discuss quantum programming language design, compilers, and tools to further improve programmer productivity.
- The Appendix contains additional interesting material that did not fit the main text's flow. Specifically, it contains a detailed description of the sparse simulation infrastructure.

Source Code

Much of the content in this book is explained with both math and code. To avoid turning this book into a giant code listing, however, we abbreviate less interesting or repetitive pieces of code with constructs such as `[...]`. Scaffolding code, such as Python `import` statements or C++ `#include` directives, are typically omitted. The full sources are hosted under a permissive Apache license on GitHub, along with instructions on how to download, build, and run:

```
https://github.com/qcc4cp/qcc
```

Contributions, comments, and suggestions are always welcome. Typesetting the code may have introduced errors, but the source of truth is the online repository. The code is also likely to have evolved beyond what is published here.

1   The Mathematical Minimum

In this section, we briefly discuss the minimum mathematical background that is required to fully understand this text. Readers who are familiar with the concepts may safely skip this section. Readers who are easily discouraged by even basic math may proceed to the next chapter and refer back here later.

1.1   Complex Numbers

Let us briefly recapitulate complex numbers. A complex number z is of the form

$$z = x + iy.$$

The x is called the real part of z; y is the imaginary part. The imaginary number i is defined as the solution to the equation:

$$x^2 + 1 = 0.$$

In other words, i is defined as the square root of -1. A complex number's conjugate, often denoted by $\bar{z}$ or z^*, is created by simply negating its imaginary part: $i \to -i$. For example, for $z = 5 + 2i$ the conjugate z^* would simply be $z^* = 5 - 2i$.

The conjugate of a product of complex numbers is equal to the product of the conjugates of the complex numbers:

$$(ab)^* = a^* b^*.$$

The *norm* of a complex number, denoted by $|z|$, is computed by multiplying the complex number with its conjugate:

$$|z|^2 = z^* z,$$

$$|z| = \sqrt{z^* z}.$$

Complex numbers can be drawn in the 2D plane with an x- and y-axis according to the definition. If we think of a complex number as a vector originating at $(0, 0)$, the norm of a complex number, which is then the length of the corresponding vector, is a real number and can be computed using Pythagoras' theorem as:

$$|z| = |x + iy| = \sqrt{(x - iy)(x + iy)} = \sqrt{x^2 + y^2}$$

For complex numbers, the norm is commonly referred to as the *modulus*. Note the difference between the *square* of a complex number and its squared *norm*. The square is computed as:

$$z^2 = (x + iy)^2 = (x + iy)(x + iy) = x^2 + 2ixy - y^2.$$

Complex exponentiation is defined by Euler's famous formula:

$$re^{i\phi} = r\big(\cos(\phi) + i\sin(\phi)\big).$$

Correspondingly, for complex numbers with norm $|z| = r = 1.0$:

$$z = e^{i\phi} = \cos(\phi) + i\sin(\phi).$$

The resulting complex numbers from this exponentiation are on a unit circle around the origin $(0,0)$.

In Python, complex numbers are, conveniently, part of the language. Note however, that the imaginary i is written as a j, which is customarily used in electrical engineering. An example:

```
x = 1.0 + 0.5j
```

To conjugate, you can use the built-in `conjugate()` function for the complex data types or use numpy's `conj()` function. For example:

```
x_conj = x.conjugate()    # or
x_conj = np.conj(x)
```

1.2   Dirac Notation, Bras, and Kets

In quantum computing, we think of qubits and states as column vectors of n complex numbers, where n is typically a power of 2. A vector with n elements is called n-dimensional. In the so-called *Dirac* notation, a column vector is called a *ket* and written as $|x\rangle$:

$$|x\rangle = \begin{bmatrix} x_0 \\ x_1 \\ \vdots \\ x_{n-1} \end{bmatrix}, \quad \text{with } x_i \in \mathbb{C} \text{ and } |x\rangle \in \mathbb{C}^n.$$

Remember that to *transpose* a matrix A, we take column i of A and make it row i of the transpose A^T, or $A_{ij}^T = A_{ji}$. The *Hermitian conjugate* of a column vector $|x\rangle$, denoted by a dagger $|x\rangle^\dagger$, is the transpose of the vector with each element conjugated. We write this vector as $\langle x|$, changing the direction of the angle bracket:

$$|x\rangle^\dagger = \langle x| = \begin{bmatrix} x_0^* & x_1^* & \cdots & x_{n-1}^* \end{bmatrix}.$$

In Dirac notation, such a row vector $\langle x|$ is called a *bra* or the *dual vector* for a ket $|x\rangle$. Transposition and conjugation goes both ways – applying the transformation twice results in the original ket, a property called *involutivity*.

$$|x\rangle^\dagger = \langle x|,$$
$$\langle x|^\dagger = |x\rangle,$$
$$(|x\rangle^\dagger)^\dagger = |x\rangle.$$

There is potential for confusion around the conjugates: should the conjugates be denoted explicitly, via a^* or $a^\dagger$, as in $\langle x_0^* \; x_1^* \; \cdots \; x_{n-1}^*|$, or is the fact that a vector has been converted from ket to bra sufficient? Typically, the conjugates are *not* marked explicitly.

1.2.1   Inner Product

The inner product, which is also called the *scalar product* or the *dot product*, is computed as a matrix product of a bra and a ket, which simplifies to the product between a row vector and a column vector – an element-wise vector-vector multiplication and summation. It is written in the following forms, with the dot ($\cdot$) denoting a scalar product:

$$\langle x| \cdot |y\rangle = \langle x||y\rangle = \langle x|y\rangle.$$

For kets $|x\rangle$ and $|y\rangle$, the inner product is defined as:

$$|x\rangle = \begin{bmatrix} x_0 \\ x_1 \\ \vdots \\ x_{n-1} \end{bmatrix}, \quad \langle x| = \begin{bmatrix} x_0^* & x_1^* & \cdots & x_{n-1}^* \end{bmatrix}, \quad |y\rangle = \begin{bmatrix} y_0 \\ y_1 \\ \vdots \\ y_{n-1} \end{bmatrix},$$

$$\langle x|y\rangle = x_0^* y_0 + x_1^* y_1 + \cdots + x_{n-1}^* y_{n-1}.$$

The inner product is how vectors in this notation get their names. It forms a product of a bra and a ket, a *bra(c)ket*. Naming is difficult in general and quantum computing is no exception.

Note that $\langle x|y\rangle$ does not generally equal $\langle y|x\rangle$. For example, consider two kets $|x\rangle$ and $|y\rangle$:

$$|x\rangle = \begin{bmatrix} -1 \\ 2i \\ 1 \end{bmatrix}, \quad |y\rangle = \begin{bmatrix} 1 \\ 0 \\ i \end{bmatrix}. \tag{1.1}$$

We construct the corresponding bras via transposition and negation of the imaginary parts:

$$\langle x| = \begin{bmatrix} -1 & -2i & 1 \end{bmatrix}, \quad \langle y| = \begin{bmatrix} 1 & 0 & -i \end{bmatrix}.$$

We then compute the inner products:

$$\langle x|y\rangle = -1 * 1 + 2i * 0 + i * 1 = -1 + i,$$
$$\langle y|x\rangle = 1 * -1 + 0 * 2i - i * 1 = -1 - i.$$

The second result is the conjugate of the first; the two inner products are different. This points to the important general rule:

$$\langle x|y\rangle^* = \langle y|x\rangle.$$

Two vectors are *orthogonal* if and only if their scalar product is zero. For 2D vectors, we visualize orthogonal vectors as perpendicular to each other:

$$\langle x|y\rangle = 0 \ \Rightarrow x, y \ \text{orthogonal}.$$

Similar to the way in which we compute the norm of a complex number, the norm of a vector is the scalar product of the vector with its dual vector. A vector is *normalized* if its norm is 1:

$$\left|\,|x\rangle\,\right| = \langle x|x\rangle = 1 \ \Rightarrow |x\rangle \ \text{normalized}. \tag{1.2}$$

State vectors in quantum computing represent probability distributions that must total 1.0 by definition. Hence, normalized vectors play an important role in quantum computing.

1.2.2   Outer Product

Corresponding to the inner product, we can construct an *outer* product between two kets $|x\rangle$ and $|y\rangle$, denoted as:

$$|x\rangle\langle y| = \begin{bmatrix} x_0 \\ x_1 \\ \vdots \\ x_{n-1} \end{bmatrix} \begin{bmatrix} y_0^* & y_1^* & \cdots & y_{n-1}^* \end{bmatrix} = \begin{bmatrix} x_0 y_0^* & x_0 y_1^* & \cdots & x_0 y_{n-1}^* \\ x_1 y_0^* & x_1 y_1^* & \cdots & x_1 y_{n-1}^* \\ \vdots & \vdots & \ddots & \vdots \\ x_{n-1} y_0^* & x_{n-1} y_1^* & \cdots & x_{n-1} y_{n-1}^* \end{bmatrix}.$$

In the example given by Equation (1.1), $|x\rangle$ is a 3×1 vector and $|y\rangle$ is a 1×3 vector. By the rules of matrix multiplication, their outer product will be a 3×3 matrix. Again, if the vector elements are complex, we conjugate the vector elements when converting from bra to ket and vice versa.

1.3   Tensor Product

To compute the *tensor product*[1] of two vectors, which can be either bras or kets, we use any of these notations:

$$|x\rangle \otimes |y\rangle = |x\rangle|y\rangle = |x, y\rangle = |xy\rangle. \tag{1.3}$$

And correspondingly:

$$\langle x| \otimes \langle y| = \langle x|\langle y| = \langle x, y| = \langle xy|.$$

In a tensor product, each element of the first constituent is multiplied with the whole of the second constituent. Hence, an $n \times m$ matrix tensored with an $k \times l$ matrix will result in an $nk \times ml$ matrix. For example, to compute the tensor products of the following two kets:

$$|0\rangle = \begin{bmatrix} 1 \\ 0 \end{bmatrix}, \quad |1\rangle = \begin{bmatrix} 0 \\ 1 \end{bmatrix},$$

$$|0\rangle \otimes |1\rangle = |01\rangle = \begin{bmatrix} 1\begin{bmatrix} 0 \\ 1 \end{bmatrix} \\ 0\begin{bmatrix} 0 \\ 1 \end{bmatrix} \end{bmatrix} = \begin{bmatrix} 0 \\ 1 \\ 0 \\ 0 \end{bmatrix}.$$

You can see that the tensor product of two kets is a ket. Similarly, the tensor product of two bras is a bra, and the tensor product of two diagonal matrices is a diagonal matrix. Of course, tensor products are also defined for general matrices:

$$\begin{bmatrix} a_{00} & a_{01} \\ a_{10} & a_{11} \end{bmatrix} \otimes \begin{bmatrix} b_{00} & b_{01} \\ b_{10} & b_{11} \end{bmatrix} = \begin{bmatrix} a_{00}\begin{bmatrix} b_{00} & b_{01} \\ b_{10} & b_{11} \end{bmatrix} & a_{01}\begin{bmatrix} b_{00} & b_{01} \\ b_{10} & b_{11} \end{bmatrix} \\ a_{10}\begin{bmatrix} b_{00} & b_{01} \\ b_{10} & b_{11} \end{bmatrix} & a_{11}\begin{bmatrix} b_{00} & b_{01} \\ b_{10} & b_{11} \end{bmatrix} \end{bmatrix}$$

$$= \begin{bmatrix} a_{00}b_{00} & a_{00}b_{01} & a_{01}b_{00} & a_{01}b_{01} \\ a_{00}b_{10} & a_{00}b_{11} & a_{01}b_{10} & a_{01}b_{11} \\ a_{10}b_{00} & a_{10}b_{01} & a_{11}b_{00} & a_{11}b_{01} \\ a_{10}b_{10} & a_{10}b_{11} & a_{11}b_{10} & a_{11}b_{11} \end{bmatrix}.$$

For multiplication of scalars α and β with a tensor product, these rules apply:

$$\alpha(x \otimes y) = (\alpha x) \otimes y = x \otimes (\alpha y), \tag{1.4}$$

$$(\alpha + \beta)(x \otimes y) = \alpha x \otimes y + \beta x \otimes y. \tag{1.5}$$

A key property of the the tensor product is the following – it is used in many derivations in this text:

$$(A \otimes B)(a \otimes b) = (A \otimes a)(B \otimes b). \tag{1.6}$$

---

[1] Here, we are ignoring differences between the tensor product and the Kronecker product.

The next rule is also very important for this text. Given two *composite* kets:

$$|\psi_1\rangle = |\phi_1\rangle \otimes |\chi_1\rangle \quad \text{and} \quad |\psi_2\rangle = |\phi_2\rangle \otimes |\chi_2\rangle,$$

the inner product between $|\psi_1\rangle$ and $|\psi_2\rangle$ is computed as:

$$\begin{aligned}
\langle\psi_1|\psi_2\rangle &= \left(|\phi_1\rangle \otimes |\chi_1\rangle\right)^{\dagger}\left(|\phi_2\rangle \otimes |\chi_2\rangle\right) \\
&= \left(\langle\phi_1| \otimes \langle\chi_1|\right)\left(|\phi_2\rangle \otimes |\chi_2\rangle\right) \\
&= \langle\phi_1|\phi_2\rangle\langle\chi_1|\chi_2\rangle.
\end{aligned} \tag{1.7}$$

1.4   Unitary and Hermitian Matrices

A square matrix A is *Hermitian* if it is equal to its transposed complex conjugate $A^{\dagger}$. Hence the diagonal elements must be real numbers, and the elements mirrored along the main diagonal are the complex conjugates of each other. For example:

$$A = A^{\dagger} = \begin{bmatrix} 1 & 3+i\sqrt{2} \\ 3-i\sqrt{2} & 0 \end{bmatrix}.$$

A square matrix A is *unitary* if its conjugate transpose is equal to its inverse, with $A^{\dagger}A = I$. Unitary matrices are *norm preserving* – multiplying a unitary matrix with a vector might change the vector's orientation but will not change its norm. For example, here the matrix Y is both unitary and Hermitian. The matrix S is unitary but *not* Hermitian:

$$Y = Y^{\dagger} = \begin{bmatrix} 0 & i \\ -i & 0 \end{bmatrix}, \quad \text{and} \quad S = \begin{bmatrix} 1 & 0 \\ 0 & e^{i} \end{bmatrix} \neq \begin{bmatrix} 1 & 0 \\ 0 & e^{-i} \end{bmatrix} = S^{\dagger}.$$

Similar to the way we computed Hermitian conjugates for vectors in Section 1.2, to construct the Hermitian *conjugate* of a square matrix, you have to transpose the matrix and conjugate its elements. A Hermitian conjugate is also called a Hermitian *adjoint*, or just adjoint for short. The terms adjoint and Hermitian conjugate are synonyms.

1.5   Hermitian Adjoint of Expressions

Here are the rules for how to conjugate expressions of matrices and vectors. We have already learned how to convert between bras and kets:

$$|\psi\rangle^{\dagger} = \langle\psi|,$$
$$\langle\psi|^{\dagger} = |\psi\rangle.$$

To compute the adjoint of a matrix scaled by a complex factor:

$$(\alpha A)^{\dagger} = \alpha^{*}A^{\dagger}. \tag{1.8}$$

For matrix-matrix products, the order reverses (this is an important rule used in this book):

$$(AB)^\dagger = B^\dagger A^\dagger. \tag{1.9}$$

And similarly, to compute the adjoint for products of matrices and vectors:

$$(A|\psi\rangle)^\dagger = \langle\psi|A^\dagger, \tag{1.10}$$

$$(AB|\psi\rangle)^\dagger = \langle\psi|B^\dagger A^\dagger. \tag{1.11}$$

For matrices in outer product notation, this rule is easy to derive:

$$A = |\psi\rangle\langle\phi| \quad \Rightarrow \quad A^\dagger = |\phi\rangle\langle\psi|. \tag{1.12}$$

And finally:

$$(A + B)^\dagger = A^\dagger + B^\dagger. \tag{1.13}$$

1.6 Eigenvalues and Eigenvectors

There is a special case of matrix-vector multiplication, where the following equation holds. Here, A is a square matrix, $|\psi\rangle$ is a ket, and λ is a simple (complex) scalar:

$$A|\psi\rangle = \lambda|\psi\rangle.$$

Applying A to the special vector $|\psi\rangle$ only *scales* the vector with a complex number, it does not change its orientation. We call λ an *eigenvalue* of A. There can be multiple eigenvalues for a given operator. The corresponding vectors for which this equation holds are called *eigenvectors*. In quantum mechanics, the synonym *eigenstates* is also used. Eigenvalues are allowed to be 0 by definition, but a null vector is not considered an eigenvector.

Diagonal matrices are a case for which finding the eigenvalues is trivial. Given a diagonal matrix of this form:

$$\begin{bmatrix} \lambda_0 & & & \\ & \lambda_1 & & \\ & & \ddots & \\ & & & \lambda_{n-1} \end{bmatrix},$$

we can pick the eigenvalues right off the diagonal. The corresponding eigenvectors are the computational bases $(1,0,0,\ldots)^T$, $(0,1,0,\ldots)^T$, and so on. For Hermitian matrices the eigenvalues are necessarily real.

1.7   Trace of a Matrix

The *trace* of an $n \times n$ matrix A is defined as the sum of its diagonal elements:

$$\text{tr}(A) = \sum_{i=0}^{n-1} a_{ii} = a_{00} + a_{11} + \cdots + a_{n-1 n-1}.$$

Basic properties of the trace are the following, where c is a scalar, and A and B are square matrices:

$$\text{tr}(A + B) = \text{tr}(A) + \text{tr}(B), \tag{1.14}$$

$$\text{tr}(cA) = c \, \text{tr}(A), \tag{1.15}$$

$$\text{tr}(AB) = \text{tr}(BA). \tag{1.16}$$

For tensor products, this important relation holds:

$$\text{tr}(A \otimes B) = \text{tr}(A) \, \text{tr}(B). \tag{1.17}$$

The trace of a Hermitian matrix is real because the diagonal elements of a Hermitian are real. The trace of a matrix A is the sum of its n eigenvalues λ_i:

$$\text{tr}(A) = \sum_{i=0}^{n-1} \lambda_i. \tag{1.18}$$

This next relation is important for measurements. Suppose we have two kets $|x\rangle$ and $|y\rangle$, such that

$$|x\rangle = \begin{bmatrix} x_0 \\ x_1 \\ \vdots \\ x_{n-1} \end{bmatrix} \quad \text{and} \quad |y\rangle = \begin{bmatrix} y_0 \\ y_1 \\ \vdots \\ y_{n-1} \end{bmatrix}.$$

The trace of the outer product of $|x\rangle$ and $\langle y|$ is equal to their inner product:

$$\text{tr}(|x\rangle\langle y|) = \langle y|x\rangle. \tag{1.19}$$

This is easy to see from the outer product:

$$\begin{bmatrix} x_0 \\ x_1 \\ \vdots \\ x_{n-1} \end{bmatrix} \begin{bmatrix} y_0^* & y_1^* & \cdots & y_{n-1}^* \end{bmatrix} = \begin{bmatrix} x_0 y_0^* & x_0 y_1^* & \cdots & x_0 y_{n-1}^* \\ x_1 y_0^* & x_1 y_1^* & \cdots & x_1 y_{n-1}^* \\ \vdots & \vdots & \ddots & \vdots \\ x_{n-1} y_0^* & x_{n-1} y_1^* & \cdots & x_{n-1} y_{n-1}^* \end{bmatrix}$$

$$\implies \text{tr}(|x\rangle\langle y|) = \sum_{i=0}^{n-1} x_i y_i^* = \langle y|x\rangle.$$

2 Quantum Computing Fundamentals

In this chapter, we describe the fundamental concepts and rules of quantum computing. In parallel, we develop an initial, easy-to-understand, and easy-to-debug code base for building and simulating smaller-scale algorithms.

The chapter is structured as follows. We first introduce our basic underlying data type, the Python `Tensor` type, which is derived from `numpy`'s `ndarray` data structure. Using this type we construct single qubits and quantum states composed of many qubits. We define operators, which allow us to modify states, and describe a range of important single-qubit gates. Controlled gates, which play a similar role to that of control flow in classical computing, come next. We detail how to describe quantum circuits via the Bloch sphere and in quantum circuit notation. A discussion of entanglement follows, that fascinating "spooky action at a distance," as Einstein called it. In quantum physics, measurement might be even more problematic than entanglement (Norsen, 2017). In this text, we avoid philosophy and conclude the chapter by describing a simple way to simulate measurements.

2.1 Tensors

Quantum mechanics and quantum computing are expressed in the language of linear algebra – vectors, matrices, and operations such as the dot product, outer product, and Kronecker products. As we develop the theory, we complement it with working code to allow experimentation.

We start by describing a fundamental data structure in Python. Python may be slow in general, but it also has the vectorized and accelerated `numpy` numerical library for scientific computing. We will make heavy use of this library so that we do not have to implement standard numerical linear algebra operations ourselves. In general, we follow Google's coding style guides for Python (Google, 2021b) and C++ (Google, 2021a).

The core data types, such as states, operators, and density matrices, are all vectors and matrices of complex numbers. It is good practice to base all of them on one common type abstraction, which hides the underlying implementation. This approach avoids potential problems with type mismatches and makes analysis, testing, debugging, pretty-printing, and other common functionality easier to maintain consistently. The base data type for all subsequent work will be a common `Tensor` class.

We derive `Tensor` from the `ndarray` array data structure in `numpy`. Since we derive `Tensor`, it will behave just like a `numpy` array, but we can augment it with additional convenience functions.

There are several complex ways to instantiate an `ndarray`. The proper way to derive a class from this data type is complicated but well documented.[1] The implementation is in the open-source repository in `lib/tensor.py`:

```python
import numpy as np

class Tensor(np.ndarray):
    """Tensor is a numpy array representing a state or operator."""

    def __new__(cls, input_array) -> Tensor:
        return np.asarray(input_array, dtype=tensor_type()).view(cls)

    def __array_finalize__(self, obj) -> None:
        if obj is None: return

        # np.ndarray has complex construction patterns. Because of this,
        # if new attributes are needed, add them like this:
        #     self.info = getattr(obj, 'info', None)
```

Note the use of `tensor_type()` in this code snippet: It abstracts the floating-point representation for complex numbers. Why do we do this? The choice of which complex data type to use is an interesting question, and each has its implications. Should it be complex numbers based on 64-bit doubles, 32-bit floats, or something else, for example, TPU's 16-bit bfloat format? Smaller data types are faster to simulate because of lower memory bandwidth requirements. But what level of accuracy is needed for which circuit? The `numpy` package supports `np.complex128` and `np.complex64`, so we simply define a global variable that holds this type's width. Having this information in one place makes it easy to experiment with different data types later on.

```python
# Bit width of complex data type, 64 or 128.
tensor_width = 64

# All math in this package will use this base type.
# Valid values can be np.complex128 or np.complex64
def tensor_type():
    """Return complex type."""

    if tensor_width == 64:
        return np.complex64
    return np.complex128
```

---

[1] https://numpy.org/doc/stable/user/basics.subclassing.html.

As we will see in our discussion of quantum states in Section 2.3, the Kronecker product of tensors, denoted with operator ⊗, is an important operation. This product is often referred to as *tensor product*. The *Kronecker product* describes a block product between matrices and is the correct term to use. We use the terms Kronecker product and tensor product interchangeably – *tensoring states* rolls off the tongue much more easily than *Kroneckering states*.

We implement it by adding the member function `kron` to the `Tensor` class. The function simply delegates to the function of the same name in `numpy`. We make heavy use of this operation, so for convenience we additionally overload the `*` operator to call this function.

There is the potential to confuse the `*` operator with simple matrix multiplication. However, in Python and with `numpy`, matrix multiplication is done with the `at` operator `@`. We inherit this operator from `numpy`; we don't have to implement it ourselves.

```
def kron(self, arg: Tensor) -> Tensor:
    """Return the Kronecker product of this object with arg."""

    return self.__class__(np.kron(self, arg))

def __mul__(self, arg: Tensor) -> Tensor:
    """Inline * operator maps to Kronecker product."""

    return self.kron(arg)
```

In our initial approach to quantum computing, we will often construct larger matrices by tensoring together many identical matrices, which corresponds to calling the `kron` function multiple times. For example, to tensor together n unitary matrices U, we will use the following notation:

$$\underbrace{U \otimes U \otimes \cdots \otimes U}_{n} = U^{\otimes n}.$$

This is equivalent to a power function, but instead of multiplication we want Kronecker products. Naming is hard, but this function basically names itself. We should call it Kronecker power function – or `kpow` (pronounced "Ka-Pow"). We handle cases where the exponent is 0 as a special case, as $x^0 = 1.0$. As expected, `numpy` computes the correct Kronecker product of a matrix with a scalar:

```
def kpow(self, n: int) -> Tensor:
    """Return the tensor product with itself `n` times."""

    if n == 0:
        return 1.0
    t = self
    for _ in range(n - 1):
        t = np.kron(t, self)
    return self.__class__(t)    # Necessary to return a Tensor type
```

Often, especially during testing, we want to compare a `Tensor` to a given value. We are working with complex numbers, which are based on the double or float data types. Direct comparison of values of these types is bad practice due to floating-point precision issues. Instead, for equality, we have to check that the difference between two numerical values is smaller than a given ϵ. Fortunately, `numpy` offers the function `allclose()`, which compares full tensors, so we do not have to iterate over dimensions and compare the real and imaginary parts. We use a tolerance of 10^{-6}, here and in almost all other places, and add this method to our `Tensor` type:[2]

```python
def is_close(self, arg) -> bool:
    """Check that a 1D or 2D tensor is numerically close to arg."""

    return np.allclose(self, arg, atol=1e-6)
```

Python's `math` module has an `isclose` function. However, we decided to follow Google's coding style, which requires naming those types of function with an underscore after the `is_`. This is what we have chosen to do here to keep the overall code consistent with the style guide.

In Section 1.4, we learned about Hermitian and unitary matrices. The two helper functions below check for these conditions:

```python
def is_hermitian(self) -> bool:
    """Check if this tensor is Hermitian - Udag = U."""

    if len(self.shape) != 2:
        return False
    if self.shape[0] != self.shape[1]:
        return False
    return self.is_close(np.conj(self.transpose()))


def is_unitary(self) -> bool:
    """Check if this tensor is unitary - Udag*U = I."""

    return Tensor(np.conj(self.transpose()) @ self).is_close(
            Tensor(np.eye(self.shape[0])))
```

Some of the matrices we will encounter later in the text are *permutation matrices*, which have only a single 1 in each row and column of the matrix. This routine verifies this property:

---

[2] Note that for scalars, `math.isclose` is significantly faster than `np.allclose`. We will use it in performance-critical code.

```
def is_permutation(self) -> bool:
    x = self
    return (x.ndim == 2 and x.shape[0] == x.shape[1] and
            (x.sum(axis=0) == 1).all() and
            (x.sum(axis=1) == 1).all() and
            ((x == 1) or (x == 0)).all())
```

2.2 Qubits

In classical computing, a bit can have the value 0 or 1. If we think of a bit as a switch, it is either off or on. You could say it is in the off-state (0-state) or on-state (1-state). Quantum bits, which are also called *qubits*, can be in a 0-state or a 1-state as well. What makes them quantum is that they are in a superposition of these states: They can be in the 0-state and the 1-state at the same time. What does this mean exactly?

First, we have to distinguish between a *qubit* and the *state of a qubit*. Physical qubits, developed for real quantum computers, are real physical entities, such as ions captured in an electric field, Josephson junctions on an ASIC, and so on. The state of a qubit describes some measurable property of that qubit, for example, the energy level of an electron. In quantum computing, at the level of programming abstractions, the physical implementation does not matter; instead, we are concerned with the measurable state. This is similar to classical computing, where very few people are knowledgeable about the quantum effects that enable transistors at the level of logic gates. Thus, the terms qubit and state of the qubit are used interchangeably; we typically only use the term qubit.

This state space of one or more qubits is often denoted by the Greek symbol $|\psi\rangle$ ("psi"). The standard notation for a qubit's 0-state is $|0\rangle$ in the Dirac notation. The 1-state is correspondingly written as $|1\rangle$. You can think of these as physically distinguishable states, such as the spin of an electron. These two states, $|0\rangle$ and $|1\rangle$, are known as *basis states*. We will *not* delve into the typical elaborate discussion of linear algebra and the theory of vector spaces here. All we need to know is that basis states represent orthogonal sets of vectors of dimensionality n (vectors with n components). *Any* vector of the same dimensionality can be constructed from linear combinations of basis states. In our context, we also require that basis vectors are normalized, forming an *orthonormal* set of basis vectors. Another way to say this is that the basis vectors are linearly independent and have a modulus of 1.

Superposition now simply means that the state of a qubit is a *linear combination* of orthonormal basis states, for example the $|0\rangle$ and $|1\rangle$ states:

$$|\psi\rangle = \alpha|0\rangle + \beta|1\rangle,$$

where α and β are complex numbers, called the *probability amplitudes*, with $|\alpha|^2 + |\beta|^2 = 1$.

Note that we use the square of the norm, not the square of a complex number. As will become clear later, this follows from one of the fundamental postulates of quantum mechanics: On measurement, the state collapses to either $|0\rangle$ with (real) probability $|\alpha|^2$ or $|1\rangle$ with (real) probability $|\beta|^2$. The state has to collapse to one of the two, and thus, the added probabilities must add up to 1.0. If both α and β are exactly $\sqrt{1/2}$, there is an equal $\sqrt{1/2}^2 = 1/2$ probability that the state collapses to $|0\rangle$ or $|1\rangle$ on measurement. If α is 1.0 and β is 0.0, it is certain that the state will collapse to the $|0\rangle$ state on measurement.

Let us look at a standard example. Given a qubit $|\phi\rangle$ as

$$|\phi\rangle = \frac{\sqrt{3}}{2} |0\rangle + \frac{i}{2} |1\rangle,$$

the probability of measuring $|0\rangle$ is

$$Pr_{|0\rangle}(|\phi\rangle) = \left(\frac{\sqrt{3}}{2}\right)\left(\frac{\sqrt{3}}{2}\right) = \frac{3}{4}.$$

The probability of measuring $|1\rangle$ is the following – we compute the norm squared of the factor $i/2$:

$$Pr_{|1\rangle}(|\phi\rangle) = \left|\frac{i}{2}\right|^2 = \left(\frac{-i}{2}\right)\left(\frac{i}{2}\right) = \frac{1}{4}.$$

The following code will translate these concepts into a straightforward implementation. As a forward reference, we use the type `State`, which we discuss in the next section. Put simply, a `State` is a vector of complex numbers implemented using `Tensor`.

To construct a qubit, we need either α or β, or both. If only one is provided, we can easily compute the other one, given that their squared norms must add to 1.0. To compute the norms of the complex numbers α and β, we multiply each one with its complex conjugate (hence the use of `np.conj()`). The result will be a real number. For the code not to generate a type error from `numpy`, we have to explicitly convert the result with `np.real()`. We compare the results to 1.0, and if it is within tolerance, we construct and return the qubit.

What data structure should we use to represent a qubit? We simply create an array of two complex values, fill in α and β, and return a `State` constructed from this array.

```
def qubit(alpha: Optional[np.complexfloating] = None,
          beta: Optional[np.complexfloating] = None) -> State:
    """Produce a given state for a single qubit."""

    if alpha is None and beta is None:
        raise ValueError('alpha, or beta, or both are required')

    if beta is None:
        beta = math.sqrt(1.0 - np.conj(alpha) * alpha)
```

```
if alpha is None:
    alpha = math.sqrt(1.0 - np.conj(beta) * beta)

if not math.isclose(np.conj(alpha) * alpha +
                    np.conj(beta) * beta, 1.0):
    raise ValueError('Qubit probabilities do not add to 1.')

qb = np.zeros(2, dtype=tensor.tensor_type())
qb[0] = alpha
qb[1] = beta
return State(qb)
```

From this code, you can infer what the basis states might look like – a state is just a complex vector: the $|0\rangle$ state should be $[1,0]^T$ and the $|1\rangle$ state $[0,1]^T$. With this in mind, the state of a qubit can be written in these forms:

$$|\psi\rangle = \alpha|0\rangle + \beta|1\rangle$$

$$= \alpha \begin{bmatrix} 1 \\ 0 \end{bmatrix} + \beta \begin{bmatrix} 0 \\ 1 \end{bmatrix}$$

$$= \begin{bmatrix} \alpha \\ \beta \end{bmatrix}.$$

The choice of $|0\rangle = [1,0]^T$ and $|1\rangle = [0,1]^T$ as the basis states is not the only possible one. What matters is that these vectors are orthonormal. They are orthogonal, with a mutual scalar product of $\langle 0|1\rangle = 0.0$, and normalized, with scalar products of $\langle 0|0\rangle = 1.0$ and $\langle 1|1\rangle = 1.0$.

The set of orthonormal bases $[1,0]^T$ and $[0,1]^T$ for the qubit vector space, which is also called the *computational basis*, is intuitive and simplifies the math. But other bases are possible, especially the ones resulting from rotations. Those are commonplace in quantum computing, as we will see shortly.

2.3   States

As we saw in the previous section, qubits are *states*, vectors of complex numbers representing probability amplitudes. We should use our trusty Tensor class to represent states in code. We inherit a State class from Tensor and add a moderately improved print function. The sources are in the open-source repository in lib/state.py:

```
class State(tensor.Tensor):
    """class State represents single and multi-qubit states."""

    def __repr__(self) -> str:
        s = 'State('
        s += super().__str__().replace('\n', '\n' + ' ' * len(s))
        s += ')'
        return s
```

```
def __str__(self) -> str:
    s = f'{self.nbits}-qubit state.'
    s += ' Tensor:\n'
    s += super().__str__()
    return s
```

The state of two or more qubits is defined as their tensor product. To compute it, we added the $*$ operator to the underlying `Tensor` type in the previous section (implemented as the corresponding Python `__mul__` member function). Note that the tensor product of two states, which both have a norm of 1.0, also has a norm of 1.0.

For two qubits $|\phi\rangle$ and $|\chi\rangle$, the combined state can be written as in Equation (1.3), with $\otimes$ being the symbol for the Kronecker product:

$$|\psi\rangle = |\phi\rangle \otimes |\chi\rangle = |\phi\rangle|\chi\rangle = |\phi, \chi\rangle = |\phi\chi\rangle.$$

Given this definition, the state for n qubits is a `Tensor` of 2^n complex numbers, the probability amplitudes. We could maintain this length as an extra member variable to `State`, but it is easy to compute from the length of the state vector (which is already maintained by `numpy`). We define it as a property. Because this property is required for all classes derived from `Tensor` (e.g., `States` and `Operators`), we add the `nbits` property to the `Tensor` base class, so that derived classes can inherit it:

```
@property
def nbits(self) -> int:
    """Compute the number of qubits in the state."""

    return int(math.log2(self.shape[0]))
```

Python does have a `bit_length()` function to determine how many bits are needed to represent a number. Here, using this function would be wrong. To represent eight states, $n = 3$ for a state of 2^n complex numbers. However, you would need four classical binary bits to represent the number 8. Using a value of $n - 1$ will not work for an input value of 0. Additionally, `bit_length()` returns values for negative numbers, which makes no sense in this quantum state context. For all these reasons, we decided to use the `log2` function. As a code example, let us combine two qubits:

```
psi = state.qubit(alpha=1.0)    # corresponds to |0>
phi = state.qubit(beta=1.0)     # corresponds to |1>
combo = psi * phi
print(combo)
>>
2-qubit state. Tensor:
[0.+0.j 1.+0.j 0.+0.j 0.+0.j]
```

The resulting state is a `Tensor` with the complex values $[0.0, 1.0, 0.0, 0.0]$, which is the result you would expect from tensoring $[1, 0]^T$ and $[0, 1]^T$. The index of the value

1.0 is 1, which indicates that the combination of the $|0\rangle$ state and the $|1\rangle$ state is being interpreted as binary 0b01. This will become more clear in the next section, where we discuss qubit ordering.

In all code examples that follow, states are constructed from the high order bit to the low order bit. This choice is arbitrary, and as a matter of fact, some texts have it the other way around. The important thing is to stay consistent.

A quantum state's probability amplitudes represent probabilities – the squared norms of all amplitudes must add up to 1.0. Basis states are *normalized*. As an example (which generalizes to n qubits), for two qubits there are four basis states, and we can write the state $|\psi\rangle$ as a superposition:

$$|\psi\rangle = c_0 \begin{bmatrix} 1 \\ 0 \\ 0 \\ 0 \end{bmatrix} + c_1 \begin{bmatrix} 0 \\ 1 \\ 0 \\ 0 \end{bmatrix} + c_2 \begin{bmatrix} 0 \\ 0 \\ 1 \\ 0 \end{bmatrix} + c_3 \begin{bmatrix} 0 \\ 0 \\ 0 \\ 1 \end{bmatrix}$$

$$= c_0 |\psi_0\rangle + c_1 |\psi_1\rangle + c_2 |\psi_2\rangle + c_3 |\psi_3\rangle = \sum_{i=0}^{3} c_i |\psi_i\rangle.$$

The amplitudes are complex numbers, so to compute the norm we multiply by the complex conjugates:

$$\langle\psi|\psi\rangle = c_0^* \langle\psi_0| c_0 |\psi_0\rangle + c_1^* \langle\psi_1| c_1 |\psi_1\rangle + \cdots + c_n^* \langle\psi_{n-1}| c_n |\psi_{n-1}\rangle$$
$$= c_0^* c_0 \langle\psi_0| \psi_0\rangle + c_1^* c_1 \langle\psi_1| \psi_1\rangle + \cdots + c_n^* c_n \langle\psi_{n-1}| \psi_{n-1}\rangle$$
$$= c_0^* c_0 + c_1^* c_1 + \cdots + c_{n-1}^* c_{n-1}$$
$$= 1.0.$$

For states that are products of states, we apply Equation (1.7). Note, again, that the elements in the bras are the complex conjugates:

$$|\psi\rangle = |\phi\chi\rangle$$
$$\langle\psi| = |\phi\chi\rangle^{\dagger} = \langle\phi\chi|$$
$$\langle\psi|\psi\rangle = \langle\phi\chi|\phi\chi\rangle = \langle\phi|\phi\rangle\langle\chi|\chi\rangle.$$

You can write a test like this to confirm:

```
p1 = state.qubit(alpha=random.random())
x1 = state.qubit(alpha=random.random())
psi = p1 * x1   # Tensor product.

# inner product of full state
self.assertTrue(np.allclose(np.inner(psi.conj(), psi), 1.0))

# inner product of the constituents multiplied
self.assertTrue(np.allclose(np.inner(p1.conj(), p1) *
                np.inner(x1.conj(), x1), 1.0))
```

2.3.1   Qubit Ordering

The ordering of qubits during construction, access to results, and conversion of binary strings are important and can be sources of problems if not understood properly. For this text, the key points to internalize are the following:

- As qubits are added to a circuit, they are being added from left to right (in a binary string), from the high-order qubit to the low-order qubit.
- In Dirac notation, two tensored states are written as $|x, y\rangle$, for example, $|0, 1\rangle$. Additionally, in this notation the most significant bit is the first to appear. States like this are also expressed as decimals. Here, the state is interpreted as $|1\rangle$ (binary 01) as opposed to $|2\rangle$ (binary 10) if incorrectly read from right to left:

$$\underbrace{|0\rangle}_{\text{High-order}} \otimes \cdots \otimes \underbrace{|0\rangle}_{\text{Low-order}}$$

- We will see in Section 2.8 that circuits are drawn as a vertical stack of qubits, with the top qubit being the most significant.
- We will learn soon about simple functions for constructing composite states from $|0\rangle$ and $|1\rangle$ states. In these functions, the first qubit to appear will be the most significant qubit, similar to the circuit notation. For example, the state $|\psi\rangle = |1\rangle \otimes |0\rangle \otimes 1 \otimes |0\rangle$ is constructed with

```
psi = state.bitstring(1, 0, 1, 0)
```

- When states are formatted to print, the most significant bit will also be to the left, as in binary notation.
- We have to distinguish between how bits or qubits are interpreted and how we store them in our programs. In classical computing, bit 0 is typically the rightmost bit, which is the least significant bit. When we *store* bits as an array of bits, we will store them from low index to high array index. This means the index into the array is 0 for the first stored bit. In the quantum case, this is the most significant qubit.

  This is a constant source of confusion, not just in this context but in any context that has to represent bits or qubits in an indexed, array-like data structure.

2.3.2   Binary Interpretation

We can write tensor products of $|0\rangle$ and $|1\rangle$ states as in this example:

$$|0\rangle \otimes |1\rangle \otimes |1\rangle = |011\rangle.$$

For brevity, when interpreting the bitstrings as binary numbers and numbering them in decimal, states are often written as in this example:

$$|011\rangle = |3\rangle.$$

Be aware of the potential for confusion between the state $|000\rangle$, the corresponding decimal state $|0\rangle$, and an actual one-qubit state $|0\rangle$. How does the decimal interpretation of a state relate to the state vector?

- The state $|00\rangle$ is computed as $\begin{bmatrix} 1 \\ 0 \end{bmatrix} \otimes \begin{bmatrix} 1 \\ 0 \end{bmatrix} = \begin{bmatrix} 1 \\ 0 \\ 0 \\ 0 \end{bmatrix}$. Also called $|0\rangle$.

- The state $|01\rangle$ is computed as $\begin{bmatrix} 1 \\ 0 \end{bmatrix} \otimes \begin{bmatrix} 0 \\ 1 \end{bmatrix} = \begin{bmatrix} 0 \\ 1 \\ 0 \\ 0 \end{bmatrix}$. Also called $|1\rangle$.

- The state $|10\rangle$ is computed as $\begin{bmatrix} 0 \\ 1 \end{bmatrix} \otimes \begin{bmatrix} 1 \\ 0 \end{bmatrix} = \begin{bmatrix} 0 \\ 0 \\ 1 \\ 0 \end{bmatrix}$. Also called $|2\rangle$.

- The state $|11\rangle$ is computed as $\begin{bmatrix} 0 \\ 1 \end{bmatrix} \otimes \begin{bmatrix} 0 \\ 1 \end{bmatrix} = \begin{bmatrix} 0 \\ 0 \\ 0 \\ 1 \end{bmatrix}$. Also called $|3\rangle$.

To find the probability amplitude for a given state, we can use binary addressing. The state vector for the three-qubit state $|011\rangle$ is:

$$[0, 0, 0, 1, 0, 0, 0, 0]^T.$$

Interpreting the right-most qubit in $|011\rangle$ as the least significant bit 0 with a bit value of 1, the middle one as bit 1 with a bit value of 1 and a power-of-2 value of 2, and the left-most as bit 2 with a value of 0, the state $|011\rangle$ computes the value 3 in decimal, state $|3\rangle$. We index the state vector as an array, as described above, from left to right, from 0 to n. Indeed, entry 3 of the state vector is set to 1. The amplitude for each state in the state vector can be found with this simple binary addressing scheme.

Note that the tensor product representation of this 3-qubit state contains the amplitudes for all eight possible states. Seven states have an amplitude of 0.0. This already hints at a potentially more efficient sparse representation.

2.3.3   Member Functions

We now introduce a few important member functions of the `State` type. This code uses functions from the `helper` module, which is described in Section 2.4.

Now that we understand the order of qubits and state vector indexing, we can add functions to `State` to return the amplitude and probability of a given state. The probability is a real number, but we still have to cast it to an actual real number via `np.real` to avoid warning messages on type conflicts.

```python
def ampl(self, *bits) -> np.complexfloating:
    """Return amplitude for state indexed by 'bits'."""

    idx = helper.bits2val(bits)  # in helper.py
    return self[idx]

def prob(self, *bits) -> float:
    """Return probability for state indexed by 'bits'."""

    amplitude = self.ampl(*bits)
    return np.real(amplitude.conj() * amplitude)
```

We use Python parameters that are decorated with a `*`. This means a variable number of arguments is allowed and the parameters are *packed* as a tuple. To unpack the tuple, you have to prefix the access with a `*` again, as shown in the function definitions above.

As an example, for a four-qubit state, you can get the amplitude and probability for the state $|1011\rangle$ in the following way:

```python
psi.ampl(1, 0, 1, 1)
psi.prob(1, 0, 1, 1)
```

The following snippet iterates over all possible states and prints the probabilities for each state:

```python
for bits in helper.bitprod(4):
    print(psi.prob(*bits))
```

During algorithm development, we often want to find the one state with the highest probability. For this, we add the following convenience function, which iterates over all possible states and returns the state/probability pair with the highest probability:

```python
def maxprob(self) -> (List[float], float):
    """Find state with highest probability."""

    maxbits, maxprob = [], 0.0
    for bits in helper.bitprod(self.nbits):
        cur_prob = self.prob(*bits)
        if cur_prob > maxprob:
            maxbits, maxprob = bits, cur_prob
    return maxbits, maxprob
```

As we will see later, it can become necessary to renormalize a state vector. This is done with the `normalize` member function. Note that this function assumes that the dot product is not 0.0; otherwise, this code will result in a division by zero exception:

```python
def normalize(self) -> None:
    """Renormalize the state. Sum of norms==1.0."""

    dprod = np.conj(self) @ self
    if (dprod.is_close(0.0)):
        raise AssertionError('Normalizing to zero-probability state.')
    self /= np.sqrt(np.real(dprod))
```

The *phase* of a qubit is the angle obtained when converting the qubit's complex amplitude to polar coordinates. We only use this during print-outs, so we convert the phase to degrees here.

```python
def phase(self, *bits) -> float:
    """Compute phase of a state from the complex amplitude."""

    amplitude = self.ampl(*bits)
    return math.degrees(cmath.phase(amplitude))
```

Finally, to help in debugging, it is always helpful to have a dumper function that lists all of a state's relevant information. By default, this function only prints the states with nonzero probability. (Set parameter `prob_only` to `False` to see all states). An optional description string can be passed in as well.

```python
def state_to_string(bits) -> str:
    """Convert state to string like |010>."""

    s = ''.join(str(i) for i in bits)
    return '|{:s}> (|{:d}>)'.format(s, int(s, 2))

def dump_state(psi, desc: Optional[str]=None,
               prob_only: bool=True) -> None:
    """Dump probabilities for a state, as well as local qubit state."""

    if desc:
        print('|', end='')
        for i in range(psi.nbits-1, -1, -1):
            print(i % 10, end='')
        print(f'> \'{desc}\'')

    state_list: List[str] = []
    for bits in helper.bitprod(psi.nbits):
        if prob_only and (psi.prob(*bits) < 10e-6):
            continue
        state_list.append(
            '{:s}:  ampl: {:+.2f} prob: {:.2f} Phase: {:5.1f}'
            .format(state_to_string(bits),
                    psi.ampl(*bits),
                    psi.prob(*bits),
                    psi.phase(*bits)))
```

```
    state_list.sort()
    print(*state_list, sep='\n')

def dump(self, desc: Optional[str] = None,
         prob_only: bool = True) -> None:
    dump_state(self, desc, prob_only)
```

As an example, the output from the dumper may look like the following, showing all states with nonzero probability:

```
|001> (|1>):   ampl: +0.50+0.00j prob: 0.25 Phase:   0.0
|011> (|3>):   ampl: +0.35+0.35j prob: 0.25 Phase:  45.0
|101> (|5>):   ampl: +0.00+0.50j prob: 0.25 Phase:  90.0
|111> (|7>):   ampl: -0.35+0.35j prob: 0.25 Phase: 135.0
```

2.3.4   State Constructors

Using the methods described so far, let us define standard constructors to create composite states. The first two functions are for states consisting of all $|0\rangle$ and $|1\rangle$.

```
# The functions zeros() and ones() produce the all-zero or all-one
# computational basis vector for `d` qubits, i.e.,
#     |000...0> or
#     |111...1>
#
# The result of this tensor product is
#    always [1, 0, 0, ..., 0]^T or [0, 0, 0, ..., 1]^T
#
def zeros_or_ones(d: int = 1, idx: int = 0) -> State:
    """Produce the all-0/1 basis vector for `d` qubits."""

    if d < 1:
        raise ValueError('Rank must be at least 1.')
    shape = 2**d
    t = np.zeros(shape, dtype=tensor.tensor_type())
    t[idx] = 1
    return State(t)

def zeros(d: int = 1) -> State:
    """Produce state with 'd' |0>, eg., |0000>."""
    return zeros_or_ones(d, 0)

def ones(d: int = 1) -> State:
    """Produce state with 'd' |1>, eg., |1111>."""
    return zeros_or_ones(d, 2**d - 1)
```

The function `bitstring` allows the construction of states from a defined series of $|0\rangle$ and $|1\rangle$ states. As noted above, the most significant bit comes first:

```
def bitstring(*bits) -> State:
    """Produce a state from a given bit sequence, eg., |0101>."""

    d = len(bits)
    if d == 0:
        raise ValueError('Rank must be at least 1.')
    t = np.zeros(1 << d, dtype=tensor.tensor_type())
    t[helper.bits2val(bits)] = 1
    return State(t)
```

Sometimes, in particular for testing or benchmarking, we want to generate a random combination of n $|0\rangle$ and $|1\rangle$ states:

```
def rand(n: int) -> State:
    """Produce random combination of |0> and |1>."""

    bits = [0] * n
    for i in range(n):
        bits[i] = random.randint(0, 1)
    return bitstring(*bits)
```

Finally, because the canonical single-qubit states $|0\rangle$ and $|1\rangle$ are used often, it may make sense to define constants for them. Global variables are bad style. We only added them to offer compatibility with other frameworks. Don't use them.

```
# These two are used so commonly, make them constants.
zero = zeros(1)
one = ones(1)
```

Can we initialize a state with a given normalized vector? Yes, we can. This is a pattern we will see later, in the section on phase estimation (Section 6.4), where we initialize a state directly with the eigenvector of a unitary matrix:

```
umat = scipy.stats.unitary_group.rvs(2**nbits)
eigvals, eigvecs = np.linalg.eig(umat)
psi = state.State(eigvecs[:, 0])
```

2.3.5   Density Matrix

For a given state $|\psi\rangle$, we can construct a *density matrix* by computing the outer product of a state with itself. For convenience, we add the function `density()` to our `State` class to compute this outer product. Typically, the Greek letter ρ ("rho") is used to denote a density matrix:

$$\rho = |\psi\rangle\langle\psi|.$$

In code:

```
def density(self) -> tensor.Tensor:
    return tensor.Tensor(np.outer(self, self.conj()))
```

The theory of quantum computing can be expressed in terms of density matrices. Some important concepts can *only* be expressed with the help of these matrices. We will not spend much time on this part of the theory. We mention density matrices here because they make an appearance in Section 2.15 on measurement.

One property of density matrices is important in our context. Given that these matrices are being constructed from an outer product, it means that the diagonal elements contain the probabilities of measuring one of the basis states for $|\psi\rangle = \alpha\,|0\rangle + \beta\,|1\rangle$.

$$|\psi\rangle\langle\psi| = \begin{bmatrix} \alpha \\ \beta \end{bmatrix} \begin{bmatrix} \alpha^* & \beta^* \end{bmatrix} = \begin{bmatrix} \boxed{\alpha\alpha^*} & \alpha\beta^* \\ \beta\alpha^* & \boxed{\beta\beta^*} \end{bmatrix}.$$

Because of the way we constructed this density matrix, it represents a pure state; it is not entangled or statistically mixed with anything else. Correspondingly, the trace of the density matrix is 1; it is the sum of all state probabilities.

2.4   Helper Functions

We will need a small set of helper functions. They will be used in several places, but don't seem to belong to any specific core module. Hence we collect helper functions in the open-source repository in file `lib/helper.py`.

Bit Conversions

We often have to convert between a decimal number and its binary representation as a tuple of 0s and 1s. These two helper functions make that easy:

```
def bits2val(bits: List[int]) -> int:
    """For a given enumerable 'bits', compute the decimal integer."""

    # We assume bits are given in high to low order. For example,
    # the bits [1, 1, 0] will produce the value 6.
    return sum(v * (1 << (len(bits)-i-1)) for i, v in enumerate(bits))

def val2bits(val: int, nbits: int) -> List[int]:
    """Convert decimal integer to list of {0, 1}."""

    # We return the bits in order high to low. For example,
    # the value 6 is being returned as [1, 1, 0].
    return [int(c) for c in format(val, '0{}b'.format(nbits))]
```

Iteration over Bits

There will also be times when we want to iterate over all possible combinations of 0's and 1's, which is to enumerate all binary values of length `nbits`. Note the use of Python's `yield` construct below, which allows usage of this function in Python `for` loops.

```python
def bitprod(nbits: int) -> Iterable[int]:
    """Produce the iterable cartesian of nbits {0, 1}."""

    for bits in itertools.product([0, 1], repeat=nbits):
        yield bits
```

2.5 Operators

We have discussed qubits and states. In quantum computing, how are these states *modified*? Classical bits are manipulated via logic gates, such as AND, OR, XOR, and NAND. In quantum computing, qubits and states are changed with *operators*. It seems appropriate to think of operators as the Instruction Set Architecture (ISA) of a quantum computer. It is a different ISA than that of a typical classical computer, but it is an ISA nonetheless. It enables computation.

In this section, we discuss operators, their structure, properties, and how to apply them to states. All sources are in the open-source repository, in file `lib/ops.py`.

2.5.1 Unitary Operators

Any unitary matrix of dimension 2^n can be considered a quantum operator. Operators are also called *gates*, in analogy to classical logic gates. Unitary matrices applied to state vectors do not change the modulus of the state vector; they are *norm preserving*. A state vector represents probabilities as probability amplitudes. Applying an operator to this state might change individual states' amplitudes but must not change the fact that all probabilities must still add up to 1.0. This is important enough to warrant a proof.

Proof To show that U is norm-preserving, we need to show that $\langle Uv|Uw \rangle = \langle v|w \rangle$. This is to show that if U preserves the inner product structure, it must also preserve the norm:

$$\langle Uv|Uw \rangle = (v^\dagger U^\dagger)(Uw) = v^\dagger (U^\dagger U)w.$$

Now, $v^\dagger (U^\dagger U)w = v^\dagger w = \langle v, w \rangle$ implies that $(U^\dagger U) = I$. Any operator that preserves the norm must be unitary. $\square$

An example of a single-qubit gate is the Identity gate, which, when applied, leaves a qubit unmodified:

$$\begin{bmatrix} 1 & 0 \\ 0 & 1 \end{bmatrix} \begin{bmatrix} \alpha \\ \beta \end{bmatrix} = \begin{bmatrix} \alpha \\ \beta \end{bmatrix}.$$

Another example is the X-gate (a synonym for the Pauli X-gate described in Section 2.6.2), which swaps the probability amplitudes of a qubit:

$$\begin{bmatrix} 0 & 1 \\ 1 & 0 \end{bmatrix} \begin{bmatrix} \alpha \\ \beta \end{bmatrix} = \begin{bmatrix} \beta \\ \alpha \end{bmatrix}.$$

We detail many standard gates later in this section. Note that because $UU^\dagger = I$, unitary matrices are necessarily invertible. As a result, all (unitary) quantum gates are reversible by simply using a gate's conjugate transpose.

On the other hand, Hermitian matrices are not necessarily unitary. In Section 2.15 we will see how Hermitian operators used for measurements are neither unitary nor reversible.

2.5.2   Base Class

Since operators are matrices, we derive them from our `Tensor` base class and provide the usual print functions:

```
class Operator(tensor.Tensor):
  """Operators are represented by square, unitary matrices."""

  def __repr__(self) -> str:
    s = 'Operator('
    s += super().__str__().replace('\n', '\n' + ' ' * len(s))
    s += ')'
    return s

  def __str__(self) -> str:
    s = f'Operator for {self.nbits}-qubit state space.'
    s += ' Tensor:\n'
    s += super().__str__()
    return s
```

To compute the adjoint with help of `numpy` is painless:

```
def adjoint(self) -> Operator:
  return Operator(np.conj(self.transpose()))
```

The `numpy` package has routines to print arrays, but we add another dumper function that produces a more compact output, making it easier to see the matrix structure instead of seeing values with high precision. This function can be adapted quickly to help during challenging debugging sessions.

```
def dump(self,
         description: Optional[str] = None,
         zeros: bool = False) -> None:
    res = ''
    if description:
        res += f'{description} ({self.nbits}-qubits operator)\n'
    for row in range(self.shape[0]):
        for col in range(self.shape[1]):
            val = self[row, col]
            res += f'{val.real:+.1f}{val.imag:+.1f}j  '
        res += '\n'
    if not zeros:
        res = res.replace('+0.0j', '     ')
        res = res.replace('+0.0', ' -  ')
        res = res.replace('-0.0', ' -  ')
        res = res.replace('+', ' ')
    print(res)
```

Here are examples for a two-qubit operator, printed both with this dumper function and numpy's own print[3] function.

```
# dump
0.5      0.5      0.5      0.5
0.5     -0.5      0.5     -0.5
0.5      0.5     -0.5     -0.5
0.5     -0.5     -0.5      0.5

# numpy print
Operator for 2-qubit state space. Tensor:
[[ 0.49999997+0.j  0.49999997+0.j   0.49999997+0.j   0.49999997+0.j]
 [ 0.49999997+0.j -0.49999997+0.j   0.49999997+0.j  -0.49999997+0.j]
 [ 0.49999997+0.j  0.49999997+0.j  -0.49999997+0.j  -0.49999997+0.j]
 [ 0.49999997+0.j -0.49999997+0.j  -0.49999997+0.j   0.49999997-0.j]]
```

2.5.3 Operator Application

The application of a unitary operator to a state vector is a matrix-vector multiplication (operators are matrices, states are vectors). In Python, we define the function call operator () for this purpose. If we have a gate X and a state psi, we can apply X with new_psi = ops.X(psi). The __call__ function itself just wraps the apply function, which we define next. Note that this function accepts a state as well as an operator as its argument.

---

[3] numpy has a fairly flexible way to configure prints as well; see https://numpy.org/doc/stable/reference/generated/numpy.set_printoptions.html.

```
def __call__(self,
             arg: Union[state.State, ops.Operator],
             idx: int = 0) -> state.State:
    return self.apply(arg, idx)
```

In the following, we gradually build up the function to apply an operator to a state. The initial version is fairly incomplete. We apply an operator to a state vector by using numpy's matrix multiplication function `np.matmul`:

```
def apply(self,
          arg: Union[state.State, ops.Operator],
          idx: int) -> state.State:
    """Apply operator to a state or operator."""

    [...]
    if not isinstance(arg, state.State):
        raise AssertionError('Invalid parameter, expected State.')
    [...]
    return state.State(np.matmul(self, arg))
```

We can also apply an operator to another operator. In this case, application results in matrix-matrix multiplication. What is the order of applications when multiple operators are being applied in sequence?

Assume we have an X-gate and a Y-gate (to be explained later), and we want to apply them in sequence. We can write this the following way in Python, where gates are applied to a state, and we return the updated state:

```
psi_1 = X(psi_0)
psi_2 = Y(psi_1)
```

These are assignments, not to be confused with a mathematical notation like $x = y$, which expresses an equivalence. In Python, we could omit the indices and overwrite a single state variable `psi`.

In quantum circuit notation, which we explain in more detail below, this looks like the following, with time flowing from left to right:

$$|0\rangle \; -\!\!\boxed{X}\!\!-\!\!\boxed{Y}\!\!- \; |\psi\rangle$$

In the function call notation, we would write the symbols from left to right as well. But note that function parameters are being evaluated first, which means they are being applied first:

```
# The function call should mirror this semantic
#   X(Y)
```

This already points to the fact that if we express the combined operator as the product of matrices, we have to invert their order (with @ being the matrix multiply operator in Python):

```
# But in a combined operator matrix, Y comes first:
#    (Y @ X)(psi)
```

This leads to the following, still incomplete implementation of `apply`, assuming the sizes of operator and state vector match:

```
def apply(self,
          arg: Union[state.State, ops.Operator],
          idx: int) -> Union[state.State, ops.Operator]:
  """Apply operator to a state or operator."""

  if isinstance(arg, Operator):
    if self.nbits != arg.nbits:
      raise AssertionError('Operator with mis-matched dimensions.')

    # Note: We reverse the order in this matmul. So:
    #    X(Y) == Y @ X
    #
    # This is to mirror that for a circuit like this:
    #    --- X --- Y --- psi
    #
    # Incrementally updating states we would write:
    #    psi = X(psi)
    #    psi = Y(psi)
    #
    # But in a combined operator matrix, Y comes first:
    #    (YX)(psi)
    #
    # The function call should mirror this semantic, since parameters
    # are typically evaluated first (and this mirrors the left to
    # right in the circuit notation):
    #    X(Y) = YX
    #
    return arg @ self

  if not isinstance(arg, state.State):
    raise AssertionError('Invalid parameter, expected State.')

  # Note the reversed order compared to above.
  return state.State(np.matmul(self, arg))
```

2.5.4   Multiple Qubits

The code above makes it possible to apply a gate to a single qubit. How does this work if we have a state of three qubits, which is a state of 2^3 complex numbers, and we want to apply the 2×2 gate to just one qubit in their tensor product? The key property of the tensor product that enables handling this case is Equation (1.6):

$$(A \otimes B)(\alpha \otimes \beta) = (A \otimes \alpha)(B \otimes \beta).$$

We can utilize this equation with the identity gate I, which is the matrix:

$$I = \begin{bmatrix} 1 & 0 \\ 0 & 1 \end{bmatrix}.$$

Applying I to any qubit leaves the qubit intact. The above equation allows us to, for example, apply the X-gate (discussed earlier) to the second qubit in a three-qubit state by tensoring together I, the X-gate, and another I to obtain an 8×8 matrix:

```
psi = state.bitstring(0, 0, 0)
op = ops.Identity() * ops.PauliX() * ops.Identity()
psi = op(psi)
psi.dump()
```

In Dirac notation, this is the original state:

$$\left| \psi_0 \right\rangle = |0\rangle \otimes |0\rangle \otimes |0\rangle.$$

Interpreting $|000\rangle$ as the binary number 0 (remember, the least significant bit is to the right), this means that element 0 of the state vector of 8 elements should be a 1.0, which we can confirm by dumping the state:

```
1.0   0.0   0.0   0.0   0.0   0.0   0.0   0.0
```

To apply the X-gate to qubit 1 in this way:

$$\left| \psi_1 \right\rangle = (I \otimes X \otimes I) \left| \psi_0 \right\rangle.$$

This becomes, according to Equation (1.6):

$$\left| \psi_1 \right\rangle = I|0\rangle \otimes X|0\rangle \otimes I|0\rangle.$$

The X-gate flips the probability amplitudes. Another way to say this colloquially is that it flips a state from $|0\rangle$ to $|1\rangle$ (or from $|1\rangle$ to $|0\rangle$). So, applying the gates above will result in the modified state $\left| \psi_1 \right\rangle$:

$$\left| \psi_1 \right\rangle = |0\rangle \otimes |1\rangle \otimes |0\rangle.$$

This means, interpreting $|010\rangle$ as the binary number 2, that the state vector element 2 should now have the value 1.0, and indeed it does:

```
0.0   0.0   1.0   0.0   0.0   0.0   0.0   0.0
```

To apply multiple operators in sequence, their individual expanded operators can be multiplied together to build a single, combined operator. For example, to apply the X-gate to qubit 1 and the Y-gate to qubit 2, we write:

```
psi = state.bitstring(0, 0, 0)
opx = ops.Identity() * ops.PauliX() * ops.Identity()
opy = ops.Identity() * ops.Identity() * ops.PauliY()
big_op = opx(opy)
psi = big_op(psi)
```

Note that there is a shortcut notation for this. To indicate that gate A should be applied to a qubit at a certain index i, we just write A_i. This notation means that this operator is being padded from both sides with identity matrices. For the example above, to apply the X-gate to qubit 1 and the Y-gate to qubit 2, we would write $X_1 Y_2$.

Of course, in regards to performance, constructing the full, combined operator up front for n qubits is the worst possible case, as we have to perform full matrix multiplies with matrices of size $(2^n)^2$. Matrix multiplication is of cubic[4] complexity $O(n^3)$. Since a matrix-vector product is of complexity $O(n^2)$, it can be faster to apply the gates individually, depending on the number of gates.

```
psi = state.bitstring(0, 0, 0)
opx = ops.Identity() * ops.PauliX() * ops.Identity()
psi = opx(psi)
opy = ops.Identity() * ops.Identity() * ops.PauliY()
psi = opy(psi)
```

Of course, in this particular example we could have simply combined the gates:

```
psi = state.bitstring(0, 0, 0)
opxy = ops.Identity() * ops.PauliX() * ops.PauliY()
psi = opxy(psi)
```

2.5.5   Operator Padding

Having to "pad" operators with identity matrices on the left and right is annoying and error-prone. Wouldn't it be more convenient to just apply an operator to a qubit at index idx and have the infrastructure do the rest for us? This is what *operator padding* does, which we will implement next.

---

[4] This is an approximation to make a point, which we will use in several places. More efficient algorithms are known, such as the Coppersmith–Winograd algorithm with complexity $O(2^{2.3752477})$.

To apply a given gate, say the X-gate, to a state `psi` at a given qubit index `idx`, we write:

```
X = ops.PauliX()
psi = X(psi, idx)
```

To achieve this, we augment the function call operator for `Operator`. If an index is provided as a parameter, we pad the operator up to this index with identity matrices. Then, we compute the size of the given operator, which can be larger than 2×2, and if the resulting matrix's dimension is still smaller than the state it is applied to, we pad it further with identity matrices. In above example, instead of:

```
psi = state.bitstring(0, 0, 0)
opx = ops.Identity() * ops.PauliX() * ops.Identity()
psi = opx(psi)
```

we can now write the following. Note that the first pair of parentheses to `PauliX()` returns a simple 2×2 `Operator` object. The parenthesis `(psi, 1)` are the parameters passed to the operator's function call operator `__call__`, which delegates to the `apply` function. This is where the automatic padding finally happens. This syntax may be confusing on first sight:

```
psi = state.bitstring(0, 0, 0)
psi = ops.PauliX()(psi, 1)
```

With this, we can finalize the implementation of `apply`:

```
def apply(self,
          arg: Union[state.State, ops.Operator],
          idx: int) -> Union[state.State, ops.Operator]:
    """Apply operator to a state or operator."""

    if isinstance(arg, Operator):
        arg_bits = arg.nbits
        if idx > 0:
            arg = Identity().kpow(idx) * arg
        if self.nbits > arg.nbits:
            arg = arg * Identity().kpow(self.nbits - idx - arg_bits)

        if self.nbits != arg.nbits:
            raise AssertionError('Operator(O) with mis-matched dimensions.')

        #
        # [... Comment block as shown above]
        #
        return arg @ self
```

```
if not isinstance(arg, state.State):
  raise AssertionError('Invalid parameter, expected State.')

op = self
if idx > 0:
  op = Identity().kpow(idx)  * op
if arg.nbits - idx - self.nbits > 0:
  op = op * Identity().kpow(arg.nbits - idx - self.nbits)

return state.State(np.matmul(op, arg))
```

2.6 Single-Qubit Gates

In this section, we list single-qubit gates that are commonly used in quantum computing. They are equivalent to logic gates in classical computing – understanding the basic gates helps in building up more sophisticated circuits. Quantum gates are similar. You have to understand their function in order to compose them into more interesting circuits. However, for the most part, the gates' functions are quite different from classical gates.

We start with simple gates and then discuss the more complicated roots and rotations before discussing the important Hadamard gate, which puts qubits in a superposition of basis states.

For each gate, we define a constructor function and allow passing a *dimension parameter* d, which allows the construction of multi-qubit operators from the same underlying single-qubit gates. For example, for the identity gates in the previous example, instead of having to write

```
y2 = ops.Identity() * ops.Identity() * ops.PauliY()
```

we can write the more compact

```
y2 = ops.Identity(2) * ops.PauliY()
```

that computes the following tensor product. Note the subscript in Y_2, which indicates that the Y-gate should only be applied to qubit 2:

$$Y_2 = I \otimes I \otimes Y = I^{\otimes 2} \otimes Y.$$

2.6.1 Identity Gate

We have seen the identity gate before; it is this matrix:

$$I = \begin{bmatrix} 1 & 0 \\ 0 & 1 \end{bmatrix}.$$

Applying this gate to a state leaves the state intact:

$$\begin{bmatrix} 1 & 0 \\ 0 & 1 \end{bmatrix} \begin{bmatrix} \alpha \\ \beta \end{bmatrix} = \begin{bmatrix} \alpha \\ \beta \end{bmatrix}.$$

In code it looks like this, a common pattern we use for almost all of the gate constructor functions:

```
def Identity(d: int = 1) -> Operator:
    return Operator(np.array([[1.0, 0.0], [0.0, 1.0]])).kpow(d)
```

2.6.2   Pauli Matrices

The three Pauli matrices are essential in quantum computing and have many uses, some of which we will discover as we go along. Pauli matrices are usually denoted as $\sigma_x, \sigma_y, \sigma_z$ or $\sigma_1, \sigma_2, \sigma_3$. Sometimes we want to add the identity matrix I as a first Pauli matrix σ_0.

The Pauli X-gate is also known as the X-gate, the quantum Not-gate, or just X for short. It is called a Not-gate because it seemingly "flips" basis states in the following way:

$$X \ket{0} = \ket{1} \quad \text{and} \quad X \ket{1} = \ket{0}.$$

This can look confusing, especially for beginners. To clarify, the basis states themselves remain unmodified; they represent physical states. The X-gate only swaps their probability amplitudes:

$$X \ket{\psi} = \begin{bmatrix} 0 & 1 \\ 1 & 0 \end{bmatrix} \begin{bmatrix} \alpha \\ \beta \end{bmatrix} = \begin{bmatrix} \beta \\ \alpha \end{bmatrix}.$$

So it changes $\ket{\psi} = \alpha\ket{0} + \beta\ket{1}$ to $\ket{\psi} = \beta\ket{0} + \alpha\ket{1}$. This works for all values of α and β, including the cases where either α or β is 0 and the other is 1. In code:

```
def PauliX(d: int = 1) -> Operator:
    return Operator(np.array([[0.0j, 1.0], [1.0, 0.0j]])).kpow(d)
```

The Pauli Y-gate, or just Y-gate, looks like this:

$$Y \ket{\psi} = \begin{bmatrix} 0 & -i \\ i & 0 \end{bmatrix} \begin{bmatrix} \alpha \\ \beta \end{bmatrix} = \begin{bmatrix} -i\beta \\ i\alpha \end{bmatrix}.$$

```
def PauliY(d: int = 1) -> Operator:
    return Operator(np.array([[0.0, -1.0j], [1.0j, 0.0]])).kpow(d)
```

The Pauli Z-gate, or just Z-gate, is also known as the phase-flip gate, as it inverts the sign of the second qubit component.

$$Z \ket{\psi} = \begin{bmatrix} 1 & 0 \\ 0 & -1 \end{bmatrix} \begin{bmatrix} \alpha \\ \beta \end{bmatrix} = \begin{bmatrix} \alpha \\ -\beta \end{bmatrix}.$$

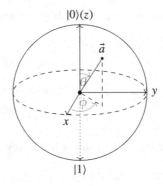

Figure 2.1 A Bloch sphere with axes x, y, and z.

In other words, it changes $|\psi\rangle = \alpha|0\rangle + \beta|1\rangle$ to $|\psi\rangle = \alpha|0\rangle - \beta|1\rangle$. Just to reiterate one more time, the basis states remain unchanged. It is the *sign* of the coefficient β that changes. The gate's constructor looks similar to the previous ones:

```
def PauliZ(d: int = 1) -> Operator:
    return Operator(np.array([[1.0, 0.0], [0.0, -1.0]])).kpow(d)
```

Together with the identity matrix, the Pauli matrices form a basis for the vector space of 2×2 Hermitian matrices. This means that all 2×2 Hermitian matrices can be constructed using a linear combination of Pauli matrices. They all have eigenvalues of 1.0 and -1.0. Pauli matrices are also involutory:

$$II = XX = YY = ZZ = I.$$

2.6.3 Rotations

Rotation operators are constructed via exponentiation of the Pauli matrices. Their impact can best be visualized as rotations around the Bloch sphere. We will discuss the Bloch sphere in more detail in Section 2.9. In short, every single qubit can be visualized as a point on a 3D sphere with a radius of 1.0 as shown in Figure 2.1. The $|0\rangle$ and $|1\rangle$ states are located at the north and south poles, respectively.

Applying a gate to a qubit moves its corresponding point from one surface point to another. This sphere lives in the 3D space, so there are x, y, and z axes with corresponding coordinates on the sphere. A qubit can reach any point on the sphere defined by spherical coordinates with $r = 1$ and the two angles θ and ϕ. The rotation around the z-axis $e^{i\phi}$ is called the *relative phase*.

$$|\psi\rangle = \cos\left(\frac{\theta}{2}\right)|0\rangle + e^{i\phi}\sin\left(\frac{\theta}{2}\right)|1\rangle.$$

We define rotations about the orthogonal axes x, y, and z, with help of the Pauli matrices as:

$$R_x(\theta) = e^{i\frac{\theta}{2}X},$$
$$R_y(\theta) = e^{i\frac{\theta}{2}Y},$$
$$R_z(\theta) = e^{i\frac{\theta}{2}Z}.$$

It can be shown that if an operator is involutory, then:

$$e^{i\theta A} = \cos(\theta)I + i\sin(\theta)A.$$

Proof If an operator function $f(A)$ has a power series expansion:

$$f(A) = c_0 I + c_1 A + c_2 A^2 + c_3 A^3 + \cdots.$$

then for the exponential function e^A we get:

$$f(A) = e^A = I + A + \frac{A^2}{2!} + \frac{A^3}{3!} + \frac{A^4}{4!} + \cdots.$$

For the function $e^{i\theta A}$ this is:

$$e^{i\theta A} = I + i\theta A - \frac{(\theta A)^2}{2!} - i\frac{(\theta A)^3}{3!} + \frac{(\theta A)^4}{4!} + \cdots.$$

If the operator is involutory and satisfies $A^2 = I$, then this becomes the following, which can be reordered into the Taylor series for $\sin(\cdot)$ and $\cos(\cdot)$:

$$e^{i\theta A} = I + i\theta A - \frac{\theta^2 I}{2!} - i\frac{\theta^3 A}{3!} + \frac{\theta^4 I}{4!} + \cdots$$
$$= \left(1 - \frac{\theta^2}{2!} + \frac{\theta^4}{4!} - \cdots\right)I + i\left(\theta - \frac{\theta^3}{3!} + \frac{\theta^5}{5!} - \cdots\right)A$$
$$= \cos(\theta)I + i\sin(\theta)A. \qquad \square$$

The Pauli matrices are involutory, with $II = XX = YY = ZZ = I$. Hence, we get rotation operators by multiplying out these expressions:

$$R_x(\theta) = e^{-i\frac{\theta}{2}X} = \cos\left(\frac{\theta}{2}\right)I - i\sin\left(\frac{\theta}{2}\right)X$$
$$= \begin{bmatrix} \cos\left(\frac{\theta}{2}\right) & -i\sin\left(\frac{\theta}{2}\right) \\ -i\sin\left(\frac{\theta}{2}\right) & \cos\left(\frac{\theta}{2}\right) \end{bmatrix},$$

$$R_y(\theta) = e^{-i\frac{\theta}{2}Y} = \cos\left(\frac{\theta}{2}\right) I - i \sin\left(\frac{\theta}{2}\right) Y$$

$$= \begin{bmatrix} \cos\left(\frac{\theta}{2}\right) & -\sin\left(\frac{\theta}{2}\right) \\ \sin\left(\frac{\theta}{2}\right) & \cos\left(\frac{\theta}{2}\right) \end{bmatrix},$$

$$R_z(\theta) = e^{-i\frac{\theta}{2}Z} = \cos\left(\frac{\theta}{2}\right) I - i \sin\left(\frac{\theta}{2}\right) Z$$

$$= \begin{bmatrix} e^{-i\frac{\theta}{2}} & 0 \\ 0 & e^{i\frac{\theta}{2}} \end{bmatrix}.$$

This also helps to explain why the Pauli Z-gate is called the phase-flip gate. Applying this gate will rotate the $|1\rangle$ part of a qubit around the z-axis by ϕ. With an angle $\phi = \pi$, the expression $e^{i\phi} = -1$, a rotation by 180°. This result is also famously known as *Euler's identity*:

$$e^{i\pi} = -1.$$

In general, rotations can be defined about *any* arbitrary axis $\hat{n} = (n_0, n_1, n_2)$:

$$R_{\hat{n}} = exp\left(-i\theta\hat{n}\frac{1}{2}\hat{\sigma}\right).$$

We learn more about general rotation and how to compute the axis and rotation angles in Section 6.15.3. For now, we can focus on the implementation of rotations about the standard Cartesian (x, y, z) axes:

```
# Cache Pauli matrices for performance reasons.
_PAULI_X = PauliX()
_PAULI_Y = PauliY()
_PAULI_Z = PauliZ()


def Rotation(v: np.ndarray, theta: float) -> np.ndarray:
    """Produce the single-qubit rotation operator."""

    v = np.asarray(v)
    if (v.shape != (3,) or not math.isclose(v @ v, 1) or
        not np.all(np.isreal(v))):
        raise ValueError('Rotation vector must be 3D real unit vector.')

    return np.cos(theta / 2) * Identity() - 1j * np.sin(theta / 2) * (
        v[0] * _PAULI_X + v[1] * _PAULI_Y + v[2] * _PAULI_Z)


def RotationX(theta: float) -> Operator:
    return Rotation([1., 0., 0.], theta)
```

```
def RotationY(theta: float) -> Operator:
    return Rotation([0., 1., 0.], theta)

def RotationZ(theta: float) -> Operator:
    return Rotation([0., 0., 1.], theta)
```

2.6.4   Phase Gate

The *phase gate*, also called the S-gate or Z90-gate, represents a phase of 90° around the z-axis for the $|1\rangle$ part of a qubit. This rotation is so common it gets its own name. In matrix form:

$$S = \begin{bmatrix} 1 & 0 \\ 0 & i \end{bmatrix}.$$

It can be derived using Euler's formula for the angle $\phi = \pi/2$:

$$e^{i\phi} = \cos(\phi) + i\sin(\phi),$$
$$e^{i\pi/2} = \cos(\pi/2) + i\sin(\pi/2) = i.$$

Note that there is an important difference between this and the `RotationZ` gate. The S-gate only affects the second component of a qubit with its imaginary i, representing a 90° rotation. It leaves the first component of a qubit intact because of the 1.0 in the operator's upper left corner. In contrast, the `RotationZ` gate affects both components of a qubit. In code:

```
# Phase gate, also called S or Z90. Rotate by 90 deg around z-axis.
def Phase(d: int = 1) -> Operator:
    return Operator(np.array([[1.0, 0.0], [0.0, 1.0j]])).kpow(d)

# Phase gate is also called S-gate.
def Sgate(d: int = 1) -> Operator:
    return Phase(d)
```

To see the difference between the `RotationZ` gate and the S-gate, you can run a few simple experiments:

```
def test_rotation(self):
    rz = ops.RotationZ(math.pi)
    rz.dump('RotationZ pi/2')
    rs = ops.Sgate()
    rs.dump('S-gate')

    psi = state.qubit(random.random())
    psi.dump('Random state')
    ops.Sgate()(psi).dump('After applying S-gate')
    ops.RotationZ(math.pi)(psi).dump('After applying RotationZ')
```

Which produces this output:

```
RotationZ pi/2 (1-qubits operator)
 -   -1.0j  -
 -           1.0j

S-gate (1-qubits operator)
 1.0         -
 -           1.0j

|0> 'Random state'
|0> (|0>):  ampl: +0.51+0.00j prob: 0.26 Phase:    0.0
|1> (|1>):  ampl: +0.86+0.00j prob: 0.74 Phase:    0.0
|0> 'After applying S-gate'
|0> (|0>):  ampl: +0.51+0.00j prob: 0.26 Phase:    0.0
|1> (|1>):  ampl: +0.00+0.86j prob: 0.74 Phase:   90.0
|0> 'After applying RotationZ'
|0> (|0>):  ampl: +0.00-0.51j prob: 0.26 Phase:  -90.0
|1> (|1>):  ampl: +0.00+0.86j prob: 0.74 Phase:   90.0
```

See how the S-gate only affects the $|1\rangle$ component of the state, while the `RotationZ` gate affects both components?

We can spot a potential source of errors – the direction of rotations, especially when porting code from other infrastructures that might interpret angle directions differently. Fortunately, for much of this text, we are shielded from this problem. However, it may be one of the first things to look out for when results do not match expectations.

Finally, remember the Z-gate and how similar it looks to the phase gate? The relationship is easy to see – applying two phase gates, each effecting a rotation of $\pi/2$, yields a rotation of π, which we get from applying the Z-gate:

$$S^2 = SS = \begin{bmatrix} 1 & 0 \\ 0 & i \end{bmatrix} \begin{bmatrix} 1 & 0 \\ 0 & i \end{bmatrix} = \begin{bmatrix} 1 & 0 \\ 0 & -1 \end{bmatrix} = Z.$$

2.6.5 Flexible Phase Gates

In the context of the quantum Fourier transform, we will encounter gates performing phase rotations by fractions of π in two different forms.

The first gate is called the *discrete phase gate* (the R_k gate, or Rk gate), a generalization of the phase gate, performing rotations around the z-axis by fractional powers of 2, as in $2\pi/2^k$, e.g., 2π, π, $\pi/2$, $\pi/4$, $\pi/8$, and so on. Because rotation by 2π is a redundant operation, this gate makes sense only for $k > 0$.

$$R_k(k) = \begin{bmatrix} 1 & 0 \\ 0 & e^{2\pi i/2^k} \end{bmatrix}.$$

```
# Rk is one of the rotation gates used in QFT.
def Rk(k: int, d: int = 1) -> Operator:
    return Operator(np.array([[(1.0, 0.0),
                    (0.0, cmath.exp(2.0 * cmath.pi * 1j / 2**k))]])).kpow(d)
```

The next form is the `U1(lambda)` gate, also known as the phase shift or phase kick gate.

$$U_1(\lambda) = \begin{bmatrix} 1 & 0 \\ 0 & e^{i\lambda} \end{bmatrix}.$$

It is similar to R_k, except arbitrary phase angles are allowed. In this text, we will only use power of 2 fractions of π. The implementation of the gate itself is straightforward:

```
def U1(lam: float, d: int = 1) -> Operator:
    return Operator(np.array([[(1.0, 0.0),
                    (0.0, cmath.exp(1j * lam))]])).kpow(d)
```

For integer powers of 2, the relationship between R_k and U_1 is the following:

$$R_k(0) = U_1\left(2\pi/2^0\right),$$

$$R_k(1) = U_1\left(2\pi/2^1\right),$$

$$R_k(2) = U_1\left(2\pi/2^2\right),$$

$$\vdots$$

You can verify this quickly:

```
def test_rk_u1(self):
    for i in range(10):
        u1 = ops.U1(2*math.pi / (2**i))
        rk = ops.Rk(i)
        self.assertTrue(u1.is_close(rk))
```

Some of the named gates are just special cases of R_k, in particular, the Identity-gate, Z-gate, S-gate, and T-gate (which we define in Section 2.6.6 below). This test code helps to clarify:

```
def test_rk(self):
    rk0 = ops.Rk(0)
    self.assertTrue(rk0.is_close(ops.Identity()))

    rk1 = ops.Rk(1)
    self.assertTrue(rk1.is_close(ops.PauliZ()))
```

```
rk2 = ops.Rk(2)
self.assertTrue(rk2.is_close(ops.Sgate()))

rk3 = ops.Rk(3)
self.assertTrue(rk3.is_close(ops.Tgate()))
```

2.6.6 Gates Square Roots

What is the square root of a classical NOT gate? There is no such thing. However, in quantum computing it is indeed possible to find a matrix $\sqrt{X}$. There are other interesting roots, some so common they also have their own names. As we will see later (Section 3.2.7), roots play an important role in constructing efficient two-qubit gates.

The root of the X-gate is the V-gate. V is unitary, with $VV^\dagger = I$, but also $V^2 = X$. It is defined in the following way:

$$V = \frac{1}{2} \begin{bmatrix} 1+i & 1-i \\ 1-i & 1+i \end{bmatrix}.$$

```
# V-gate, which is sqrt(X)
def Vgate(d: int = 1) -> Operator:
    return Operator(0.5 * np.array([[(1+1j), 1-1j),
                                    (1-1j, 1+1j)]])).kpow(d)
```

The root of a rotation is a rotation about the same axis, with the same direction, but by half the angle. This is obvious from the exponential form:

$$\sqrt{e^{i\phi}} = (e^{i\phi})^{\frac{1}{2}} = e^{i\phi/2}.$$

The root of the Phase gate (the S-gate) is called the T-gate. The S-gate represents a phase of 90° around the z-axis. Correspondingly, the T-gate is equivalent to a 45° phase around the z-axis.

$$T = \begin{bmatrix} 1 & 0 \\ 0 & e^{i\pi/4} \end{bmatrix}.$$

```
def Tgate(d: int = 1) -> Operator:
    """T-gate is sqrt(S-gate)."""

    return Operator(
        np.array([[1.0, 0.0],
                  [0.0, cmath.exp(cmath.pi * 1j / 4)]])).kpow(d)
```

The root of the Y-gate has no special name (that we know of), but it is required later in the text, so we introduce it here as Yroot. It is defined as:

$$Y_{root} = \frac{1}{2} \begin{bmatrix} 1+i & -1-i \\ 1+i & 1+i \end{bmatrix}.$$

```
def Yroot(d: int = 1) -> Operator:
    """Root of Y-gate."""

    return Operator(0.5 * np.array([[(1+1j, -1-1j),
                                     (1+1j, 1+1j)]])).kpow(d)
```

There are other interesting roots, but these are the main ones we will encounter in this text. We can test for the correct implementation of the roots with these snippets:

```
def test_t_gate(self):
    """Test that T^2 == S."""

    t = ops.Tgate()
    self.assertTrue(t(t).is_close(ops.Phase()))

def test_v_gate(self):
    """Test that V^2 == X."""

    v = ops.Vgate()
    self.assertTrue(v(v).is_close(ops.PauliX()))

def test_yroot_gate(self):
    """Test that Yroot^2 == Y."""

    yr = ops.Yroot()
    self.assertTrue(yr(yr).is_close(ops.PauliY()))
```

Finding a root in closed form can be quite cumbersome. In case of problems, you can simply use the `scipy` function `sqrtm()`. For this to work, `scipy` must be installed:

```
from scipy.linalg import sqrtm
[...]
computed_yroot = sqrtm(ops.PauliY())
self.assertTrue(ops.Yroot().is_close(computed_yroot))
```

2.6.7   Projection Operators

A projection operator for a given state, or *projector* for short, is the outer product of the state onto itself. This is also the definition of a density matrix, but projectors are usually constructed from basis states. The term projector comes from the simple fact that applying a basis state's projector to a given state extracts the amplitude of the basis state. The state is projected onto the basis state, similar to how the cosine is a projection of a 2-dimensional vector onto the x-axis. Let's see how this works. The projector is defined as:

```
def Projector(psi: state.State) -> Operator:
    """Construct projection operator for basis state."""

    return Operator(psi.density())
```

The projectors for the states $|0\rangle$ and $|1\rangle$ are:

$$P_{|0\rangle} = \begin{bmatrix} 1 \\ 0 \end{bmatrix} \begin{bmatrix} 1 & 0 \end{bmatrix} = \begin{bmatrix} 1 & 0 \\ 0 & 0 \end{bmatrix},$$

$$P_{|1\rangle} = \begin{bmatrix} 0 \\ 1 \end{bmatrix} \begin{bmatrix} 0 & 1 \end{bmatrix} = \begin{bmatrix} 0 & 0 \\ 0 & 1 \end{bmatrix}.$$

Applying the projector for the $|0\rangle$ state to a random qubit yields the probability amplitude of the qubit being found in the $|0\rangle$ state (similar for the projector to the $|1\rangle$ state):

$$P_{|0\rangle}|\psi\rangle = |0\rangle\langle 0|(\alpha|0\rangle + \beta|1\rangle) = \alpha|0\rangle.$$

Projection operators are Hermitian, hence $P = P^{\dagger}$, but note that projection operators are *not* unitary and not reversible. If a projector operator's basis states are normalized, the projection operator is equal to its own square $P = P^2$; it is *idempotent*. This is a result we will use later in the section on measurement. Similar to basis states, two projection operators are *orthogonal* if and only if their product is 0, which means that for each state:

$$P_{|0\rangle} P_{|1\rangle}|\psi\rangle = \vec{0}.$$

To generalize, you can think of the outer product $|r\rangle\langle c|$ as a 2-dimensional index $[r, c]$ into a matrix. This is called the *outer product representation* of an operator.

$$A = \begin{bmatrix} a & b \\ c & d \end{bmatrix} = a|0\rangle\langle 0| + b|0\rangle\langle 1| + c|1\rangle\langle 0| + d|1\rangle\langle 1|.$$

This also works for larger operators. For example, for this two-qubit operator U with just one nonzero element α:

$$U = \begin{array}{c} \\ |00\rangle \\ |01\rangle \\ |10\rangle \\ |11\rangle \end{array} \begin{pmatrix} |00\rangle & |01\rangle & |10\rangle & |11\rangle \\ 0 & 0 & 0 & 0 \\ 0 & 0 & 0 & 0 \\ 0 & 0 & 0 & 0 \\ 0 & \alpha & 0 & 0 \end{pmatrix}.$$

The outer product representation for the single nonzero element α in this operator would be $\alpha|11\rangle\langle 01|$, an index pattern of $|row\rangle\langle col|$. For derivations, this representation can be more convenient than having to deal with full matrices. For example, to express the application of the X-gate to a qubit, we would write:

$$X = \begin{bmatrix} 0 & 1 \\ 1 & 0 \end{bmatrix} = |0\rangle\langle 1| + |1\rangle\langle 0|,$$

$$X(\alpha|0\rangle + \beta|1\rangle)$$
$$= (|0\rangle\langle 1| + |1\rangle\langle 0|)(\alpha|0\rangle + \beta|1\rangle)$$
$$= |0\rangle\langle 1|\alpha|0\rangle + |0\rangle\langle 1|\beta|1\rangle + |1\rangle\langle 0|\alpha|0\rangle + |1\rangle\langle 0|\beta|1\rangle$$
$$= \alpha|0\rangle\underbrace{\langle 1|0\rangle}_{=0} + \beta|0\rangle\underbrace{\langle 1|1\rangle}_{=1} + \alpha|1\rangle\underbrace{\langle 0|0\rangle}_{=1} + \beta|1\rangle\underbrace{\langle 0|1\rangle}_{=0}$$
$$= \beta|0\rangle + \alpha|1\rangle.$$

2.6.8   Hadamard Gate

Finally, we have arrived at the all-important Hadamard gate, which has the following form:

$$H = \frac{1}{\sqrt{2}}\begin{bmatrix} 1 & 1 \\ 1 & -1 \end{bmatrix} = \begin{bmatrix} \frac{1}{\sqrt{2}} & \frac{1}{\sqrt{2}} \\ \frac{1}{\sqrt{2}} & -\frac{1}{\sqrt{2}} \end{bmatrix}.$$

Let us apply this gate to $|0\rangle$ and $|1\rangle$ respectively:

$$H|0\rangle = \frac{1}{\sqrt{2}}\begin{bmatrix} 1 & 1 \\ 1 & -1 \end{bmatrix}\begin{bmatrix} 1 \\ 0 \end{bmatrix} = \frac{1}{\sqrt{2}}\begin{bmatrix} 1 \\ 1 \end{bmatrix} = \frac{|0\rangle + |1\rangle}{\sqrt{2}}.$$

$$H|1\rangle = \frac{1}{\sqrt{2}}\begin{bmatrix} 1 & 1 \\ 1 & -1 \end{bmatrix}\begin{bmatrix} 0 \\ 1 \end{bmatrix} = \frac{1}{\sqrt{2}}\begin{bmatrix} 1 \\ -1 \end{bmatrix} = \frac{|0\rangle - |1\rangle}{\sqrt{2}}.$$

Both results can be stated as the sum or difference of the $|0\rangle$ and $|1\rangle$ bases, scaled by $1/\sqrt{2}$. These states are so common they get their own symbolic names, $|+\rangle$ and $|-\rangle$:

$$H|0\rangle = \frac{|0\rangle + |1\rangle}{\sqrt{2}} = |+\rangle,$$

$$H|1\rangle = \frac{|0\rangle - |1\rangle}{\sqrt{2}} = |-\rangle.$$

The Hadamard gate puts a qubit into a superposition of the two basis states. This is why the Hadamard gate is so important – it generates superposition, one of the key ingredients of quantum computation. The states in superposition form an orthonormal basis as well, called the Hadamard basis. The basis states are $|+\rangle$ and $|-\rangle$, as indicated above.

For a general state $|\psi\rangle = \alpha|0\rangle + \beta|1\rangle$, the Hadamard operator yields:

$$H|\psi\rangle = H(\alpha|0\rangle + \beta|1\rangle)$$
$$= \alpha H|0\rangle + \beta H|1\rangle$$

$$= \alpha \frac{|0\rangle + |1\rangle}{\sqrt{2}} + \beta \frac{|0\rangle - |1\rangle}{\sqrt{2}}$$

$$= \alpha|+\rangle + \beta|-\rangle$$

$$= \frac{\alpha + \beta}{\sqrt{2}}|0\rangle + \frac{\alpha - \beta}{\sqrt{2}}|1\rangle.$$

```
def Hadamard(d: int = 1) -> Operator:
    return Operator(1 / np.sqrt(2) *
            np.array([[1.0, 1.0], [1.0, -1.0]])).kpow(d)
```

Applying the Hadamard gate twice reverses the initial Hadamard gate. A Hadamard gate is its own inverse, $H = H^{-1}$, $HH = I$. It is involutory, just like the Pauli matrices:

$$HH = \frac{1}{\sqrt{2}} \begin{bmatrix} 1 & 1 \\ 1 & -1 \end{bmatrix} \frac{1}{\sqrt{2}} \begin{bmatrix} 1 & 1 \\ 1 & -1 \end{bmatrix} = \frac{1}{2} \begin{bmatrix} 2 & 0 \\ 0 & 2 \end{bmatrix} = \begin{bmatrix} 1 & 0 \\ 0 & 1 \end{bmatrix} = I.$$

A common operation is the application of Hadamard gates to several adjacent qubits. If all those qubits were in the $|0\rangle$ state, the resulting state becomes an *equal superposition* of the resulting states, all with the same amplitude of $\frac{1}{\sqrt{2^n}}$:

$$H^{\otimes n}|0\rangle^{\otimes n} = \frac{1}{\sqrt{2^n}} \sum_{x \in \{0,1\}^n} |x\rangle.$$

This construction is common for two and three qubits and used in many of the algorithms and examples. Let's spell it out explicitly:

$$(H \otimes H)(|0\rangle \otimes |0\rangle) = \frac{1}{2}(|00\rangle + |01\rangle + |10\rangle + |11\rangle),$$

$$(H \otimes H \otimes H)(|0\rangle \otimes |0\rangle \otimes |0\rangle)$$

$$= \frac{1}{\sqrt{2^3}}(|000\rangle + |001\rangle + |010\rangle + |011\rangle + |100\rangle + |101\rangle + |110\rangle + |111\rangle)$$

$$= \frac{1}{\sqrt{2^3}}(|0\rangle + |1\rangle + |2\rangle + |3\rangle + |4\rangle + |5\rangle + |6\rangle + |7\rangle)$$

$$= \frac{1}{\sqrt{2^3}} \sum_{x=0}^{7} |x\rangle \quad = \frac{1}{\sqrt{2^3}} \sum_{x \in \{0,1\}^3} |x\rangle.$$

Although we have seen single-qubit gates and learned how to construct multi-qubit states, a key ingredient to flexible computing is still missing. Where are the control flow constructs that are so common in classical computing and that seem essential for any type of algorithm? The quantum equivalents of those constructs are called *controlled gates*, which we discuss next.

2.7   Controlled Gates

Quantum computing does not have classic control flow with branches around conditionally executed parts of the code. As described earlier, all qubits are active at all times. The quantum equivalent of control-dependent execution are *controlled* qubit gates.

These are gates that are always applied but only show effect under certain conditions. At least two qubits are involved: a controller qubit and a controlled qubit. Note that 2-qubit gates of this form cannot be decomposed into single-qubit gates.

REMARK   *Before we continue, we have to agree on naming (which is hard). Shall we call a controlled not gate a, well, controlled not gate, a controlled-not gate, or Controlled-Not gate, or even a Controlled-Not-Gate?*

We will follow this convention: When we refer to an actual gate, or gate type, we will use the upper-case notation Controlled-Not, *sometimes followed by* gate, *but without a hyphen. For standard gates with single-letter names, we use a hyphen, as in* X-gate. *For gates with longer names we won't use a hyphen, such as* Swap *gate or* Hadamard *gate. In mathematical notation, gates are referred to by their symbolic names, such as* $X, Y,$ *or* Z.

Let us explain the function of controlled gates by example. Consider how the following Controlled-Not matrix (abbreviated as CNOT, or CX) from qubit 0 to qubit 1 operates on all combinations of the $|0\rangle$ and $|1\rangle$ states.

$$
CX_{0,1} = \begin{bmatrix} 1 & 0 & 0 & 0 \\ 0 & 1 & 0 & 0 \\ 0 & 0 & 0 & 1 \\ 0 & 0 & 1 & 0 \end{bmatrix}.
$$

Eagle-eyed readers will find the X-gate at the lower right side of this matrix and the identity matrix in the upper left. This can be misleading, as we show below for the controlled gate from 1 to 0. The important thing to note is that a Controlled-Not gate is a permutation matrix.

Applying this matrix to states $|00\rangle$ and $|01\rangle$ leaves the states intact:

$$
CX_{0,1} |00\rangle = \begin{bmatrix} 1 & 0 & 0 & 0 \\ 0 & 1 & 0 & 0 \\ 0 & 0 & 0 & 1 \\ 0 & 0 & 1 & 0 \end{bmatrix} \begin{bmatrix} 1 \\ 0 \\ 0 \\ 0 \end{bmatrix} = \begin{bmatrix} 1 \\ 0 \\ 0 \\ 0 \end{bmatrix} = |00\rangle.
$$

$$
CX_{0,1} |01\rangle = \begin{bmatrix} 1 & 0 & 0 & 0 \\ 0 & 1 & 0 & 0 \\ 0 & 0 & 0 & 1 \\ 0 & 0 & 1 & 0 \end{bmatrix} \begin{bmatrix} 0 \\ 1 \\ 0 \\ 0 \end{bmatrix} = \begin{bmatrix} 0 \\ 1 \\ 0 \\ 0 \end{bmatrix} = |01\rangle.
$$

Application to $|10\rangle$ *flips* the second qubit to a resulting state of $|11\rangle$.

$$CX_{0,1} |10\rangle = \begin{bmatrix} 1 & 0 & 0 & 0 \\ 0 & 1 & 0 & 0 \\ 0 & 0 & 0 & 1 \\ 0 & 0 & 1 & 0 \end{bmatrix} \begin{bmatrix} 0 \\ 0 \\ 1 \\ 0 \end{bmatrix} = \begin{bmatrix} 0 \\ 0 \\ 0 \\ 1 \end{bmatrix} = |11\rangle.$$

Application on $|11\rangle$ *flips* the second qubit to a resulting state of $|10\rangle$.

$$CX_{0,1} |11\rangle = \begin{bmatrix} 1 & 0 & 0 & 0 \\ 0 & 1 & 0 & 0 \\ 0 & 0 & 0 & 1 \\ 0 & 0 & 1 & 0 \end{bmatrix} \begin{bmatrix} 0 \\ 0 \\ 0 \\ 1 \end{bmatrix} = \begin{bmatrix} 0 \\ 0 \\ 1 \\ 0 \end{bmatrix} = |10\rangle.$$

The *CX* matrix flips the second qubit from $|0\rangle$ to $|1\rangle$, or from $|1\rangle$ to $|0\rangle$, but only if the first qubit is in state $|1\rangle$. The X-gate on the second qubit is *controlled* by the first qubit. Any 2×2 quantum gate can be controlled this way. We can have Controlled-Z gates, controlled rotations, or any other controlled 2×2 gates.

The *CX* gate is usually introduced, as we did here, by its effects on the $|0\rangle$ and $|1\rangle$ states of the second qubit. Only the amplitudes of the controlled qubit are being flipped. This is easy to see with the effects of the X-gate alone on a single qubit in superposition:

$$X|\psi\rangle = X(\alpha|0\rangle + \beta|1\rangle) = \begin{bmatrix} 0 & 1 \\ 1 & 0 \end{bmatrix} \begin{bmatrix} \alpha \\ \beta \end{bmatrix} = \begin{bmatrix} \beta \\ \alpha \end{bmatrix} = \beta|0\rangle + \alpha|1\rangle.$$

The *CX* matrix allows a first qubit to control an *adjacent* second qubit. What if the controller and controlled qubit are farther apart? The general way to construct a controlled unitary operator U with the help of projectors is the following:

$$CU_{0,1} = P_{|0\rangle} \otimes I + P_{|1\rangle} \otimes U. \tag{2.1}$$

Note that for a Controlled-Not gate $CX_{1,0}$ from 1 to 0, you cannot find the original X-gate or identity matrix in the operator. This matrix is still just a permutation matrix:

$$CX_{1,0} = \begin{bmatrix} 1 & 0 & 0 & 0 \\ 0 & 0 & 0 & 1 \\ 0 & 0 & 1 & 0 \\ 0 & 1 & 0 & 0 \end{bmatrix}.$$

If there are n qubits in between the controlling and controlled qubits, n identity matrices have to be tensored in between as well. If the index of the controlling qubit is larger than the index of the controlled qubit, the tensor products in Equation (2.1) need to be inverted. Here is an example with qubit 2 controlling gate U on qubit 0:

$$CU_{2,0} = I \otimes I \otimes P_{|0\rangle} + U \otimes I \otimes P_{|1\rangle}.$$

The corresponding code is straightforward. We have to make sure that the right number of identity matrices are being added to pad the operator:

```python
# Note on indices for controlled operators:
#
# The important aspects are direction and difference, not absolute
# values. In that regard, these are equivalent:
#   ControlledU(0, 3, U) == ControlledU(1, 4, U)
#   ControlledU(2, 0, U) == ControlledU(4, 2, U)
# We could have used -3 and +3, but felt this representation was
# more intuitive.
#
# Operator matrices are stored with all intermittent qubits
# (as Identities). When applying an operator, the starting qubit
# index can be specified.
def ControlledU(idx0: int, idx1: int, u: Operator) -> Operator:
    """Control qubit at idx1 via controlling qubit at idx0."""

    if idx0 == idx1:
      raise ValueError('Control and controlled qubit must not be equal.')

    p0 = Projector(state.zeros(1))
    p1 = Projector(state.ones(1))
    # space between qubits
    ifill = Identity(abs(idx1 - idx0) - 1)
    # 'width' of U in terms of Identity matrices
    ufill = Identity().kpow(u.nbits)

    if idx1 > idx0:
      if idx1 - idx0 > 1:
        op = p0 * ifill * ufill + p1 * ifill * u
      else:
        op = p0 * ufill + p1 * u
    else:
      if idx0 - idx1 > 1:
        op = ufill * ifill * p0 + u * ifill * p1
      else:
        op = ufill * p0 + u * p1
    return op
```

What is clear from this code is that operators larger than 2×2 can be controlled as well. We can construct Controlled-Controlled-... gates, which are required for most interesting algorithms.

This code makes one big operator matrix. This can be a problem in larger circuits, e.g., for a circuit with 20 qubits with qubit 0 controlling qubit 19 (or any other padded operator), the operator will be a matrix of size $(2^{20})^2$ * sizeof(complex), which could be 8 or 16 terabytes[5] of memory. Building such a large matrix in memory and

---

[5] tebibytes, to be precise.

applying it via matrix-vector multiplication is intractable. As this is how we express operators at this point, we are limited by the number of qubits we can experiment with. Fortunately, there are techniques to significantly improve scalability, which we will discuss detail in Chapter 4.

Also note that the controller and controlled qubits can be arbitrarily distant from each other in our simulations. In a real quantum computer, there are topological limitations on qubit interaction. Mapping an algorithm onto a concrete physical topology (IBM (2021b) shows several examples) introduces another interesting set of problems, which we will touch upon in Section 8.4.

2.7.1 Controlled-Not Gate

The Controlled-Not gates are so common that they deserve their own constructor function. We discussed the Controlled-Not (CNOT) gate at the beginning of Section 2.7. In code, its constructor looks like this:

```
def Cnot(idx0: int = 0, idx1: int = 1) -> Operator:
    """Controlled-Not between idx0 and idx1, controlled by |1>."""

    return ControlledU(idx0, idx1, PauliX())
```

The Controlled-Not-by-0 (CNOT0) gate is similar to the CNOT gate, except it is controlled by the $|0\rangle$ part of the controlling qubit. This can be accomplished by inserting an X-gate before and after the controlling qubit.

```
def Cnot0(idx0: int = 0, idx1: int = 1) -> Operator:
    """Controlled-Not between idx0 and idx1, controlled by |0>."""

    if idx1 > idx0:
        x2 = PauliX() * Identity(idx1 - idx0)
    else:
        x2 = Identity(idx0 - idx1) * PauliX()
    return x2 @ ControlledU(idx0, idx1, PauliX()) @ x2
```

Note that this construction to control a gate by $|0\rangle$ works for *any* target gate. We will see several examples of this in the later sections.

2.7.2 Controlled-Controlled-Not Gate

The full matrix construction works well in a nested fashion, extending the control to already-controlled gates. A double-controlled X-gate is also called the *Toffoli* gate, or CCX-gate for short.

This gate is interesting in classical computing because it can be shown that it is a universal gate – every classical logic function can be constructed using just this

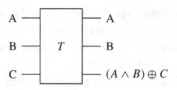

Figure 2.2 Block diagram for the Toffoli gate.

gate. Interestingly, this universality attribute does *not* hold in quantum computing. In quantum computing, there are only *sets* of universal gates (see also Section 6.15).

This is how the Toffoli gate works: if the first two inputs are $|1\rangle$ it flips the third qubit. This is often shown in form of a logic block diagram (with $\wedge$ as the logical AND), as in Figure 2.2.

In matrix form, we can describe it using block matrices, with 0_n as an $n \times n$ null matrix. Note that changing the indices of the controller and controlled qubits may destroy these patterns, but the matrix will still be a permutation matrix:

$$
\begin{bmatrix} I_4 & 0_4 \\ 0_4 & CX \end{bmatrix} = \begin{bmatrix} I_2 & 0_2 & 0_2 & 0_2 \\ 0_2 & I_2 & 0_2 & 0_2 \\ 0_2 & 0_2 & I_2 & 0_2 \\ 0_2 & 0_2 & 0_2 & X \end{bmatrix}.
$$

The constructor code is fairly straightforward and a good example of how to construct a double-controlled gate:

```
# Make Toffoli gate out of 2 controlled Cnot's.
#     idx1 and idx2 define the 'inner' cnot.
#     idx0 defines the 'outer' cnot.
#
# For a Toffoli gate to control with qubit 5
# a Cnot from 4 and 1:
#     Toffoli(5, 4, 1)
#
def Toffoli(idx0: int, idx1: int, idx2: int) -> Operator:
    """Make a Toffoli gate."""

    cnot = Cnot(idx1, idx2)
    toffoli = ControlledU(idx0, idx1, cnot)
    return toffoli
```

We observe that because we are able to construct quantum Toffoli gates, and because Toffoli gates are classical universal gates, if follows that quantum computers are at least as capable as classical computers.

2.7.3   Swap Gate

The Swap gate is another important gate. It swaps the probability amplitudes of two qubits. In matrix representation, it looks like the following:

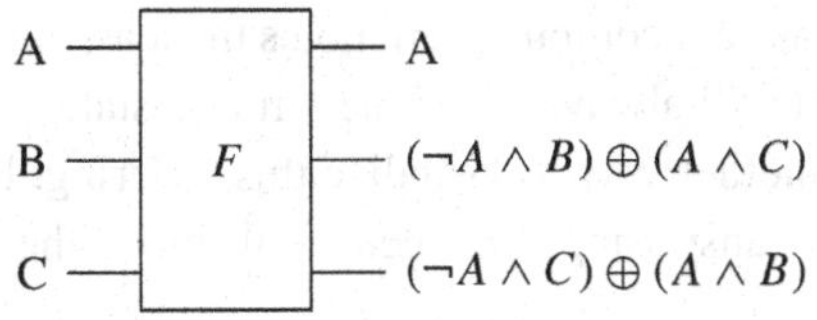

Figure 2.3 Block diagram for the Fredkin gate.

$$\begin{bmatrix} 1 & 0 & 0 & 0 \\ 0 & 0 & 1 & 0 \\ 0 & 1 & 0 & 0 \\ 0 & 0 & 0 & 1 \end{bmatrix}. \tag{2.2}$$

Our approach to construct controlled gates cannot produce this gate. However, it turns out that a sequence of three CNOT gates swaps the probability amplitudes of the basis states. For example, to swap qubit 0 and 1, you apply CX_{10} CX_{01} CX_{10}. This is analogous to classical computing, where a sequence of three XOR operations also swaps values. These techniques do not require additional temporary storage, such as a temporary variable or an additional helper qubit. There are other ways to construct Swap gates; some interesting examples are outlined in Gidney (2021b).

```
def Swap(idx0: int = 0, idx1: int = 1) -> Operator:
    """Swap qubits at idx0 and idx1 via combination of Cnot gates."""

    return Cnot(idx1, idx0) @ Cnot(idx0, idx1) @ Cnot(idx1, idx0)
```

2.7.4   Controlled Swap Gate

Like any other unitary operator, Swap gates can also be controlled. A double-controlled Swap gate is known as the *Fredkin gate*. Similar to the Toffoli gate, it is a universal gate in classical computing, but not in quantum computing. As a black box, it represents the logic shown in Figure 2.3, which may be a bit hard to reason about in isolation (with $\wedge$ as logical AND and $\neg$ as logical NOT).

The first physical quantum Fredkin gate was built relatively recently (Patel et al., 2016) and used to construct GHZ states, which we describe in Section 2.11.4.

2.8   Quantum Circuit Notation

We have learned the basics of qubits, states, operators, and gates, and how to combine them into larger circuits. We already hinted at a nice graphical way to visualize circuits. Here is how it works.

Qubits are drawn from top to bottom. Like the ordering we described earlier, the qubits are depicted from the "most significant" qubit to the "least significant" qubit. This can be confusing because you may naturally consider the top qubit as "qubit 0," which, in classical computing, denotes the least significant bit. In analytical equations, the top qubit will always be on the left of a state, such as the 1 in $|1000\rangle$.

Here is another way to visualize this ordering. If we imagine the column of qubits as a vector, transposing this vector will move the top qubit into the most significant (left-most) slot.

Graphically, the qubits' initial state is drawn to the left, and horizontal lines go to the right, indicating how the state changes over time as operators are applied. Again, note the absence of classical control flow. All gates are always active in a combined state, which could be a product state or an entangled state. Computation flows from left to right.

The initial state of three qubits appears like the following, with the initial state to the left of the circuit. It is conventional to always initialize qubits in state $|0\rangle$. However, because it is trivial to insert X-gates or Hadamard gates, we may take shortcuts and draw circuits as if these gates were present:

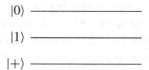

Also, note that the state of this circuit is the tensor product of the three qubits; it is a *combined* state (in the example, the state is still separable). It is tempting to reason that single, isolated qubits in the circuit diagram are in a particular state. However, the reality is that qubits are always in a combined state with other qubits, either as separable product states or entangled states.

Graphically, applying a Hadamard gate, or any other single-qubit operator, to the first qubit looks like the following. Before the operator is applied, the state is $|\psi_0\rangle = |0\rangle \otimes |0\rangle = [1, 0, 0, 0]^T$. After the operator is applied, the state is $|\psi_1\rangle$. You can think about the state $|\psi_1\rangle$ as the tensor product of the top qubit being in superposition of $|0\rangle$ and $|1\rangle$ and the bottom qubit being in state $|0\rangle$.

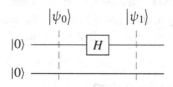

The initial state before the Hadamard gate is $|\psi_0\rangle = |0\rangle \otimes |0\rangle = |00\rangle$, the tensor product of the two $|0\rangle$ states. The Hadamard gate puts the top qubit into $1/\sqrt{2}(|0\rangle + |1\rangle) = |+\rangle$. As a result, the state $|\psi_1\rangle$ is the tensor product of the top qubit with the bottom qubit $|0\rangle$:

$$|\psi_1\rangle = |+\rangle \otimes |0\rangle = \frac{|0\rangle + |1\rangle}{\sqrt{2}} \otimes |0\rangle = \frac{1}{\sqrt{2}}\big(|00\rangle + |10\rangle\big). \qquad (2.3)$$

Applying a Z-gate after the Hadamard gate to qubit 1 results in this circuit:

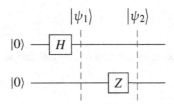

The fact that the Z-gate is to the right of the Hadamard gate indicates that this operator should be applied after the Hadamard gate. We can think of this as two separate gate applications – first the Hadamard H tensored with I, and then a second application of I tensored with Z. This is the equivalent of applying just one two-qubit operator O that has been constructed by multiplying the two tensor products (in reverse order of application, see Section 2.8.1):

$$O = (I \otimes Z)(H \otimes I).$$

Controlled-X gates are indicated with a solid dot for the controller qubit and the addition-modulo-2 symbol $\oplus$ for the controlled qubit (not to be confused with the symbol for the tensor product $\otimes$). Addition-modulo-2 behaves like the binary XOR function. If the controlled qubit is $|0\rangle$ and we apply the X-gate, the gate becomes $|1\rangle$, as in $0 \oplus 1 = 1$. If the controlled bit is $|1\rangle$, applying the X-gate will turn it into $|0\rangle$, as in $1 \oplus 1 = 0$. The XOR gives the same truth table as addition-modulo-2. In some instances, we may still want to see an X-gate, but again, these two are identical:

Any single-qubit gate can be controlled this way, for example, the Z-gate:

The Controlled-Not-by-0 gate can be built by applying an X-gate before and after the controller. It is drawn with an empty circle on the controlling qubit:

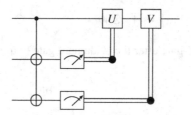

Figure 2.4 Measurement and flow of classical data after measurement, indicated with double lines.

Swap gates are marked with two connected × symbols, as in the circuit diagrams below. As discussed, like any other gate, Swap gates can also be controlled:

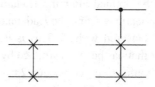

If a gate is controlled by more than one qubit, this can be indicated with multiple black or empty circles, depending on whether the gates are controlled by $|1\rangle$ or $|0\rangle$. In the example, qubits 0 and 2 must be $|1\rangle$ (have an amplitude for this base state), and qubit 1 must be $|0\rangle$ to activate the X-gate on qubit 3.

We will talk more about measurements in Section 2.15. Measurement gates produce real, classical values and are indicated with a meter symbol. Classical information flow is drawn with double lines. In the example in Figure 2.4, measurements are being made, and the real, classical measurement data may then be used to build or control other unitary gates, U and V in the example.[6]

2.8.1   Qubit Ordering Revisited

Let us reiterate the important point about ordering of gate applications. For a circuit like this following:

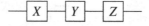

In code, we can apply the gate to the state from left to right, for example:

---

[6] All circuit diagrams in this book were created using the excellent LaTeX quantikz package.

```
psi = state.zeros(1)
psi = ops.PauliX()(psi)
psi = ops.PauliY()(psi)
psi = ops.PauliZ()(psi)
```

Or we can construct a combined ZYX operator with function call syntax:

```
psi = state.zeros(1)
op = ops.PauliX(ops.PauliY(ops.PauliZ()))
psi = op(psi)
```

But if you want to write this as an explicit matrix multiplication, the order reverses. Take note of the parentheses – in Python, the function call operator has higher precedence than the matrix multiply operator:

```
psi = state.zeros(1)
psi = (ops.PauliZ() @ (ops.PauliY() @ ops.PauliX()))(psi)
```

In mathematical notation, a good rule to remember is that the operator closest to the bar of a ket (or bra) comes first when building an operator with explicit matrix multiplications:

$$\underbrace{X}_{\text{3rd}}\ \underbrace{Y}_{\text{2nd}}\ \underbrace{Z}_{\text{1st}} |\psi\rangle. \tag{2.4}$$

2.9 Bloch Sphere

We have seen several ways to describe states and gates, including Dirac notation, matrix notation, circuit notation, and code. You may prefer one over the other in your learning journey. Another representation is especially useful for visual learners: the Bloch sphere, named after the famous physicist Felix Bloch.

A single complex number can be drawn in a 2D polar coordinate system by specifying just a radius r and an angle ϕ to the x-axis. Typically, we think of this angle as counterclockwise. Complex numbers with radius $r = 1$ are restricted to a unit circle with radius 1.

A qubit is normalized because the probabilities of measuring a basis state must add up to 1.0. A qubit also has *two* complex amplitudes. Hence, two angles will suffice[7] to describe a qubit fully – it can be placed on the surface of a sphere with radius 1.0, the *unit sphere*.

In this representation, the $|0\rangle$ state is located at the north pole along the z-axis and the $|1\rangle$ state at the south pole of a sphere with radius 1. The $|+\rangle$ state points in the positive direction of the x-axis. Typically the x-axis is drawn as pointing out

---

[7] https://en.wikipedia.org/wiki/Qubit#Bloch_sphere_representation.

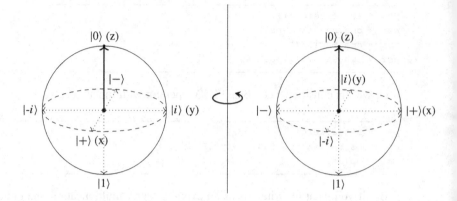

Figure 2.5 A Bloch sphere and the same sphere rotated counterclockwise by 90° about the z-axis.

of the page. The corresponding $|-\rangle$ state points in the negative x-direction into the page. The state $|i\rangle$ is on the Bloch sphere's equator on the positive y-axis, which is typically drawn to the right of the page. Correspondingly, $|-i\rangle$ is on the negative y-axis. The two spheres in Figure 2.5 are identical. The second sphere is rotated by 90° counterclockwise about the z-axis.

To see how to move about the sphere, let's start in state $|0\rangle$, the north pole of the sphere. Applying the Hadamard operator moves the state to $|+\rangle$, which is on the x-axis. This is shown in Figure 2.6a. Applying the Z-gate moves the arrow to point to state $|-\rangle$ on the negative x-axis. The relative phase is now $\pi/2$, as shown in Figure 2.6b.

It is obvious that, with rotations, you can reach any point on this sphere by using different paths or sequences of gate applications. Large rotations can also be broken down into equivalent sequences of smaller rotations.

This can also be demonstrated in code. In the example below, we start out with state $|1\rangle$ and apply the Hadamard gate to change the state to $|-\rangle$.

$$H|1\rangle = \frac{|0\rangle - |1\rangle}{\sqrt{2}} = |-\rangle.$$

Application of the X-gate changes the state to:

$$X\left(\frac{|0\rangle - |1\rangle}{\sqrt{2}}\right) = \frac{|1\rangle - |0\rangle}{\sqrt{2}}.$$

Finally, we apply the Hadamard gate again, resulting in the state $-|1\rangle$. We should wonder about the minus sign and whether $-|1\rangle = |1\rangle$. We will show in Section 2.10 that we can *ignore* this minus sign because it is a *global phase*.

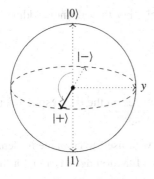

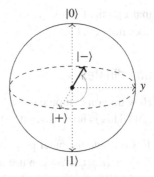

(a) Application of a H-gate   (b) Application of a Z-gate

Figure 2.6 Rotating a state about the Bloch sphere.

$$H\left(\frac{|1\rangle - |0\rangle}{\sqrt{2}}\right) = \frac{1}{\sqrt{2}}\begin{bmatrix} 1 & 1 \\ 1 & -1 \end{bmatrix}\frac{1}{\sqrt{2}}\begin{bmatrix} -1 \\ 1 \end{bmatrix}$$

$$= \frac{1}{2}\begin{bmatrix} 0 \\ -2 \end{bmatrix} = -1\begin{bmatrix} 0 \\ 1 \end{bmatrix}$$

$$= -|1\rangle.$$

```
def basis_changes():
    """Explore basis changes via Hadamard."""

    # Generate [0, 1]
    psi = state.ones(1)

    # Hadamard on |1> will result in 1/sqrt(2) [1, -1]
    #   aka |->
    psi = ops.Hadamard()(psi)

    # Simple PauliX will result in 1/sqrt(2) [-1, 1]
    # which is -1 (1/sqrt(2) [1, -1]).
    # Note that this does not move the vector on the
    # Bloch sphere!
    psi = ops.PauliX()(psi)

    # Back to computational basis will result in -|1>.
    # Global phases can be ignored.
    psi = ops.Hadamard()(psi)
    if not np.allclose(psi[1], -1.0):
        raise AssertionError("Invalid basis change.")
```

As useful as the Bloch sphere can be, it may also lead to confusion. For example, the basis states $|0\rangle$ and $|1\rangle$ are orthogonal, but on the Bloch sphere they appear on opposite poles (similarly for $|+\rangle$, $|-\rangle$, and $|i\rangle$, $|-i\rangle$). It may be tempting to think that classical rules of vector addition apply, but they do not: adding $|1\rangle$ and $-|1\rangle$ does not equal $|0\rangle$.

2.9.1   Coordinates

How do you compute the x, y, and z coordinates on the Bloch sphere for a given state $|\psi\rangle$? This is how we do it in two simple steps:

1. Compute the outer product of state $|\psi\rangle$ with itself to compute its density matrix $\rho = |\psi\rangle\langle\psi|$. We can use the convenience function `density()` for this, as described in Section 2.3.5.
2. Apply the helper function `density_to_cartesian(rho)`, shown below, which returns the corresponding x, y, z coordinates.

The function `density_to_cartesian(rho)` computes the Cartesian coordinates from a single-qubit density matrix. In the open-source repository, we add this function in file `lib/helper.py`.

How does the math[8] work? We stated in Section 2.6.2 that the Pauli matrices form a basis for the space of 2×2 Hermitian matrices. A density operator ρ is a 2×2 Hermitian matrix; we can write it as:

$$\rho = \frac{I + xX + yY + zZ}{2} = \frac{1}{2}\begin{bmatrix} 1+z & x-iy \\ x+iy & 1-z \end{bmatrix}. \tag{2.5}$$

If we think of ρ as a matrix $\begin{bmatrix} a & b \\ c & d \end{bmatrix}$, then

$$2a = 1 + z,$$

$$2c = x + iy.$$

And correspondingly, $x = 2\,\mathrm{Re}(c)$, $y = 2\,\mathrm{Im}(c)$, and $z = 2a - 1$.

```
def density_to_cartesian(rho: np.ndarray) -> Tuple[float, float, float]:
    """Compute Bloch sphere coordinates from 2x2 density matrix."""

    a = rho[0, 0]
    c = rho[1, 0]
    x = 2.0 * c.real
    y = 2.0 * c.imag
    z = 2.0 * a - 1.0
    return np.real(x), np.real(y), np.real(z)
```

[8] https://quantumcomputing.stackexchange.com/a/17180/11582.

Here is a simple test to verify the results:

```
def test_bloch(self):
  psi = state.zeros(1)
  x, y, z = helper.density_to_cartesian(psi.density())
  self.assertEqual(x, 0.0)
  self.assertEqual(y, 0.0)
  self.assertEqual(z, 1.0)

  psi = ops.PauliX()(psi)
  x, y, z = helper.density_to_cartesian(psi.density())
  self.assertEqual(x, 0.0)
  self.assertEqual(y, 0.0)
  self.assertEqual(z, -1.0)

  psi = ops.Hadamard()(psi)
  x, y, z = helper.density_to_cartesian(psi.density())
  self.assertTrue(math.isclose(x, -1.0, abs_tol=1e-6))
  self.assertTrue(math.isclose(y, 0.0, abs_tol=1e-6))
  self.assertTrue(math.isclose(z, 0.0, abs_tol=1e-6))
```

Bloch spheres are only defined for single-qubit states. You can visualize an individual qubit's Bloch sphere in a many-qubit system by *tracing out* all the other qubits in the state. This is done with with the partial trace procedure, a helpful tool which we detail in Section 2.14.

2.10 Global Phase

What do we do with the minus sign on the final state after rotating the state about the Bloch sphere? Is $|1\rangle$ different from $-|1\rangle$? The Bloch sphere does not allow simple addition, $|1\rangle$ plus $-|1\rangle$ does *not* equal $|0\rangle$! The answer is that the minus sign in $-|1\rangle$ represents a *global phase*, a rotation by π. It has no *physical* meaning and can be ignored.

This is an important insight in quantum computing. A global phase is a complex coefficient $e^{i\phi}$ to a state with norm 1.0. Multiplying a state by a complex coefficient has no physical meaning because the expectation value of the state with or without the coefficient does not change. Physicists also call this *phase invariance*.

The *expectation value* for an operator A on state $|\psi\rangle$ is this expression (which we will develop in Section 2.15 on measurement):

$$\langle\psi|A|\psi\rangle.$$

With a global phase, this turns into:

$$\langle\psi|e^{-i\phi}Ae^{i\phi}|\psi\rangle = \langle\psi|e^{-i\phi}e^{i\phi}A|\psi\rangle = \langle\psi|A|\psi\rangle.$$

The states cannot be distinguished by measurement.

We should contrast the global phase with a *relative phase*, which is the phase difference between the $|0\rangle$ and $|1\rangle$ parts of a qubit:

$$|\psi\rangle = \alpha\,|0\rangle + e^{i\phi}\beta\,|1\rangle.$$

2.11   Entanglement

The entanglement of two or more qubits is one of the most fascinating aspects of quantum physics. When two qubits (or systems) are entangled, it means that, on measurement, the results are strongly correlated, even when the states were physically separated, be it by a millimeter or across the universe! This is the effect that Albert Einstein famously called "spooky action at a distance." If we entangle two qubits in a specific way (described below), and qubit 0 is measured to be in state $|0\rangle$, qubit 1 will always be found in state $|0\rangle$ as well.

Why is this truly remarkable? What if we took two coins, placed them heads-up in two boxes, and shipped one of those boxes to Mars. When we open up the boxes, they will both show heads. So what's so special about the quantum case? In this example, coins have *hidden state*. We have placed them in the boxes *before* shipment, knowing which side to put on top in an initial, defined, nonprobabilistic state. We also know that this state will not change during shipment.

If there was hidden state in quantum mechanics, then the theory would be incomplete; the quantum mechanical wave functions would be insufficient to describe a physical state in full. This was the point that Einstein, Podolsky, and Rosen attempted to make in their famous *EPR paper* (Einstein et al., 1935).

However, a few decades later it was shown that there *cannot* be a hidden state in an entangled quantum system. A famous thought experiment, the Bell inequalities (Bell, 1964), proved this and was later experimentally confirmed.

Qubits collapse *probabilistically* during measurement to either $|0\rangle$ or $|1\rangle$.[9] This is equivalent to putting the coins in the boxes while they are twirling on their edges. Only when we open the boxes will the coins fall to one of their sides. Perfect coins would fall to each side 50% of the time. Similarly, if we prepared a qubit in the $|0\rangle$ state and applied a Hadamard gate to it, this qubit will measure either $|0\rangle$ or $|1\rangle$, with 50% probability for each outcome. The magic of quantum entanglement means that both qubits of an entangled pair will measure the same value, either $|0\rangle$ or $|1\rangle$, 100% of the time. This is equivalent to the coins falling to their same side, 100% of the time, on Earth and Mars!

There are profound philosophical arguments about entanglement, measurement, and what they tell us about the very nature of reality. Many of the greatest physicists of the last century have argued over this, for decades – Einstein, Schrödinger, Heisenberg,

---

[9] This is true as long as we measure in this basis. We talk about measurements in different bases in Section 6.11.3.

Bohr, and many others. These discussions are not settled to this day; there is no agreement. Many books and articles have been written about this topic, explaining it better than we would be able to do here. We are not even going to try. Instead, we accept the facts for what they are: rules we can exploit for computation.

This sentiment might put us in the camp of the Copenhagen interpretation of quantum mechanics (Faye, 2019). Ontology is a fancy term for questions like "What is?" or "What is the nature of reality?" The Copenhagen interpretation refuses to answer all ontological questions. To quote what David Mermin said about it (Mermin, 1989, p. 2): *If I were forced to sum up in one sentence what the Copenhagen interpretation says to me, it would be "Shut up and calculate!.".* The key here is, of course, that progress can be made, even if the ontological questions remain unanswered.

2.11.1 Product States

Let us consider two-qubit systems. Constructing the tensor product between two qubits leads to a state where each qubit can still be described without reference to the other.

There is an intuitive (though not general) way to visualize this. The state can be expressed as the result of a tensor product with result $[a,b,c,d]^T$. If two states are *not* entangled, they are said to be in a *product state*; they are *separable*. This is the case if $ad = bc$. If the states *are* entangled, this identity will *not* hold.

Proof As a quick proof, assume two qubits $q_0 = [i,k]^T$ and $q_1 = [m,n]^T$. Their Kronecker product is $q_0 \otimes q_1 = [im, in, km, kn]^T$. Multiplying the outer elements and the inner elements, corresponding to the $ad = bc$ form above, we see that

$$\underbrace{im}_{a}\ \underbrace{kn}_{d} = imkn = inkm = \underbrace{in}_{b}\ \underbrace{km}_{c}. \qquad \square$$

2.11.2 Entangler Circuit

The circuit below is the quintessential quantum entanglement circuit. We will see many uses of it in this text. Let us discuss in detail how the state changes as the gates are being applied.

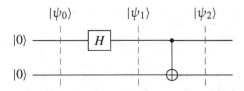

The initial state $|\psi_0\rangle$, before the Hadamard gate, is the tensor product of the two $|0\rangle$ states, which is $|00\rangle$ with a state vector of $[1,0,0,0]^T$. The Hadamard gate puts the first qubit in superposition of $|0\rangle$ and $|1\rangle$. The state $|\psi_1\rangle$ after the Hadamard gate becomes the tensor product of the superposition of the first qubit with the second qubit:

$$|\psi_1\rangle = \frac{|0\rangle + |1\rangle}{\sqrt{2}}|0\rangle = \frac{1}{\sqrt{2}}(|00\rangle + |10\rangle).$$

In code, we compute this with the following snippet. The `print` statement produces a state with nonzero entries at indices 0 and 2, corresponding to the states $|00\rangle$ and $|10\rangle$:

```
psi = state.zeros(2)
op = ops.Hadamard() * ops.Identity()
psi = op(psi)
print(psi)
>>
2-qubit state. Tensor:
[0.70710677+0.j 0.        +0.j 0.70710677+0.j 0.        +0.j]
```

Now we apply the Controlled-Not gate. The $|0\rangle$ part of the first qubit in superposition does not impact the second qubit; the $|00\rangle$ part remains unchanged. However, the $|1\rangle$ part of the superpositioned first qubit controls the second qubit and will flip it to $|1\rangle$, changing the $|10\rangle$ part to $|11\rangle$. The resulting state $|\psi_2\rangle$ after the Controlled-Not gate thus becomes:

$$|\psi_2\rangle = \frac{|00\rangle + |11\rangle}{\sqrt{2}}.$$

This state corresponds to this state vector:

$$|\psi_2\rangle = \frac{1}{\sqrt{2}}\begin{bmatrix} 1 \\ 0 \\ 0 \\ 1 \end{bmatrix} = \begin{pmatrix} a \\ b \\ c \\ d \end{pmatrix}.$$

This state is now entangled because the $ad = bc$ identity in the rule above does not hold: the product of elements 0 and 3 is $1/2$, but the product of elements 1 and 2 is 0. The state can no longer be expressed as a product state.

In code, we take the state `psi` we computed above and apply the Controlled-Not:

```
psi = ops.Cnot(0, 1)(psi)
print(psi)
```

This prints the entangled 2-qubit state, with elements 0 and 3 having values $1/\sqrt{2}$, corresponding to the binary indices of the $|00\rangle$ and $|11\rangle$ states:

```
2-qubit state. Tensor:
[0.70710677+0.j 0.        +0.j 0.        +0.j 0.70710677+0.j]
```

Entanglement also means that now only states $|00\rangle$ and $|11\rangle$ can be measured. The other two basis states have a probability of 0.0 and cannot be measured. If qubit 0 is measured as $|0\rangle$, the other qubit will be measured as $|0\rangle$ as well, since the only nonzero probability state with a $|0\rangle$ as the first qubit is $|00\rangle$. Similar logic applies for state $|1\rangle$.

This explains the correlations, the spooky action at a distance, at least mathematically. The measurement results of the two qubits are 100% correlated. We don't know why this is, what physical mechanism facilitates this effect, or what reality is. But, at least for simple circuits and their respective matrices, we now have a means to express this unreal feeling reality.

2.11.3 Bell States

Bell states are named after the great physicist John Bell, who proved in 1964 using standard probability theory that entangled qubits cannot have hidden state or hidden information (Bell, 1964). This discovery was one of the defining moments for quantum mechanics.

We saw the first of four possible Bell states above, the one that was constructed with the entangler circuit with $|00\rangle$ as input. There are a total of four Bell states, resulting from the four inputs $|00\rangle$, $|01\rangle$, $|10\rangle$, and $|11\rangle$. We denote β_{xy} as the state resulting from inputs x and y:

$$|\beta_{00}\rangle = \frac{|00\rangle + |11\rangle}{\sqrt{2}} = \frac{1}{\sqrt{2}}\begin{bmatrix} 1 \\ 0 \\ 0 \\ 1 \end{bmatrix}, \qquad |\beta_{01}\rangle = \frac{|01\rangle + |10\rangle}{\sqrt{2}} = \frac{1}{\sqrt{2}}\begin{bmatrix} 0 \\ 1 \\ 1 \\ 0 \end{bmatrix},$$

$$|\beta_{10}\rangle = \frac{|00\rangle - |11\rangle}{\sqrt{2}} = \frac{1}{\sqrt{2}}\begin{bmatrix} 1 \\ 0 \\ 0 \\ -1 \end{bmatrix}, \qquad |\beta_{11}\rangle = \frac{|01\rangle - |10\rangle}{\sqrt{2}} = \frac{1}{\sqrt{2}}\begin{bmatrix} 0 \\ 1 \\ -1 \\ 0 \end{bmatrix}.$$

Here is the code to construct these states (in file `lib/bell.py` in the open-source repository):

```
def bell_state(a: int, b: int) ->state.State:
  """Make one of the four bell states with a, b from {0,1}."""

  if a not in [0, 1] or b not in [0, 1]:
    raise ValueError('Bell state arguments are bits and must be 0 or 1.')
  psi = state.bitstring(a, b)
  psi = ops.Hadamard()(psi)
  return ops.Cnot()(psi)
```

2.11.4   GHZ States

A generalization of the Bell states are the n-qubit (maximally entangled) states of three or more qubits, named after Greenberger, Horne, and Zeilinger (GHZ) (Greenberger et al., 2008). They are constructed with this circuit, which propagates the superposition from the top qubit to all others via cascading Controlled-Not gates:

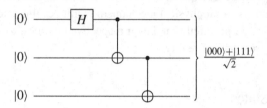

This construction can of course be extended to more than three qubits, generalizing to GHZ states $(|0000\ldots\rangle + |1111\ldots\rangle))/\sqrt{2}$. Only two possible states can be measured, each with probability $1/2$ (or amplitude $1/\sqrt{2}$). Note that instead of a cascade of Controlled-Not gates, we could just connect the Controlled-Not gates with qubit 0. In code:

```
def ghz_state(nbits: int) -> state.State:
  """Make a maximally entangled nbits state (GHZ State)."""

  # Simple construction via:
  #
  # |0> --- H --- o ---------     --- H --- o ----o----
  # |0> ----------X --- o --- or ----------X --- | ---
  # |0> ----------------X ---     ----------------X ---
  #     ...
  psi = state.zeros(nbits)
  psi = ops.Hadamard()(psi)
  for offset in range(nbits-1):
    psi = ops.Cnot(0, 1)(psi, offset)
  return psi
```

2.11.5   Maximal Entanglement

We used the term *maximally entangled* without explanation. Here is a simple definition:

A *maximally mixed* state is one where all probability amplitudes are the same. For example, applying Hadamard gates to all qubits in an n-qubit state initialized with $|0\rangle$ states leads to an equal superposition of all states.

$$(H \otimes H)|00\rangle = 1/2\big(|00\rangle + |01\rangle + |10\rangle + |11\rangle\big)$$

We then define *maximally entangled* the following way. The partial trace allows reasoning about a subspace of a state, as explained in Section 2.14. It allows *tracing out* parts of a state. What is left is a reduced density matrix, representing the reduced state, the subspace. We call a state *maximally entangled* if the remaining reduced density matrices are maximally mixed, meaning their diagonal elements are all the same.

2.12 No-Cloning Theorem

There is another profound difference between classical computing and quantum computing. In classical computing, it is always possible to copy a bit, a byte, or any memory and copy it many times. In quantum computing, this is verboten – it is generally impossible to clone the state of a given qubit. This restriction is related to the topic of measurements and the fact that it is impossible to create a measurement device that does not impact (entangle with) a state. The inability to copy is expressed with the so-called No-Cloning Theorem (Wootters and Zurek, 1982).

THEOREM 2.1 *Given a general quantum state* $|\psi\rangle = |\phi\rangle|0\rangle$, *there cannot exist a unitary operator* U *such that* $U|\psi\rangle = |\phi\rangle|\phi\rangle$.

Proof Assume state $|\phi\rangle = \alpha|0\rangle + \beta|1\rangle$, then:

$$|\psi\rangle = |\phi\rangle|0\rangle = (\alpha|0\rangle + \beta|1\rangle)|0\rangle.$$

To clone $|\phi\rangle$ we need an operator U that performs this operation:

$$U|\phi\rangle|0\rangle = |\phi\rangle|\phi\rangle. \tag{2.6}$$

Applying U to $|\psi\rangle$ would thus lead to:

$$U|\phi\rangle|0\rangle = U(\alpha|0\rangle + \beta|1\rangle)|0\rangle = \alpha|00\rangle + \beta|11\rangle.$$

But now expand the right side of Equation (2.6):

$$\begin{aligned}
U|\phi\rangle|0\rangle = |\phi\rangle|\phi\rangle &= (\alpha|0\rangle + \beta|1\rangle)(\alpha|0\rangle + \beta|1\rangle) \\
&= \alpha^2|00\rangle + \beta\alpha|10\rangle + \alpha\beta|01\rangle + \beta^2|11\rangle \\
&\neq \alpha|00\rangle + \beta|11\rangle.
\end{aligned}$$

Hence, no such U exists. A general state cannot be cloned.   □

General states can be *moved* but not *cloned*. Obviously this leads to interesting challenges in quantum algorithm design, and also the design of quantum programming languages.

Note, however, the special cases of $|0\rangle$ and $|1\rangle$. These states *can* be cloned. This is easy to see from the final form in the proof above. With one of a or b being 1.0 and the other being 0.0, only one term will remain:

$$|\phi\rangle|\phi\rangle = \alpha^2|00\rangle + \beta\alpha|10\rangle + \alpha\beta|01\rangle + \beta^2|11\rangle.$$

With the result being one of:

$$\alpha^2|00\rangle = 1.0^2|00\rangle = |00\rangle,$$

$$\beta^2|11\rangle = 1.0^2|11\rangle = |11\rangle.$$

Matching the above result, with either $\alpha = 0$ or $\beta = 0$:

$$U|\phi\rangle|0\rangle = \alpha^2|00\rangle + \beta^2|11\rangle = \alpha|00\rangle + \beta|11\rangle.$$

2.13   Uncomputation

The question of logical reversibility of computation was raised by Bennett (1973). That paper was an answer to Landauer, who is also known for Landauer's principle (Landauer, 1973). The principle states that the *erasure* of information during computing must result in heat dissipation. The fact that today's CPUs run as hot as they do is a confirmation of this principle. Truly *reversible* computing would use almost no energy, but reversing a computation would also undo any obtained result. So the question was whether it was possible to construct a reversible circuit from which it was still possible to obtain an actual result. Given that quantum computing is reversible by definition, it would be utterly useless if we failed to answer this question. Fortunately, Bennet found an elegant construction to resolve this issue.

Bennet's paper is formal and based on a three-tape Turing machine. The proposed mechanism would compute a result, then *copy* the result before uncomputing the result via reverse computation of one of the Turing machine's tapes. The goal at the time was to mitigate heat dissipation. In quantum computation, our goal is to break undesirable entanglement to *ancilla qubits*. Bennet's approach works for both.

We mentioned ancilla qubits. Let's define the relevant terms:

- For constructions like the multi-controlled gate, as we will see in Section 3.2.8, we need *additional* qubits in order to properly perform the computation. You may think of these qubits as temporary qubits, or helper qubits, that play no essential role for the algorithm. They are the equivalent of compiler-allocated stack space mitigating classical register pressure. These qubits are called *ancilla* qubits, or *ancillae*.
- Ancilla qubits may start in state $|0\rangle$ and also end up in state $|0\rangle$ after a construction like the multi-controlled gate. In other scenarios, however, ancillae may remain entangled with a state, potentially destroying a desired result. In this case, we call these ancillae *junk qubits*, or simply *junk*.

The typical structure of a quantum computation looks like that shown in Figure 2.7. All quantum gates are unitary, so we pretend we packed them all up in one giant unitary operator U_f. There is the input state $|x\rangle$ and some ancillae qubits, all initialized to $|0\rangle$. The result of the computation will be $f(|x\rangle)$ and some left over ancillae, which are now *junk*; they serve no purpose, they just hang around, intent on messing up

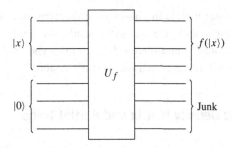

Figure 2.7 Typical structure of a quantum computation.

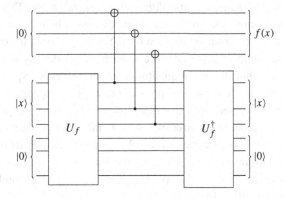

Figure 2.8 Computation, fan-out, uncomputation.

our results. The problem is that the junk qubits may still be entangled with the result, nullifying the intended effects of quantum interference, which quantum algorithms are based upon. We will not be exposed to this problem until Section 6.6, where we have to solve this problem for the order finding part of Shor's algorithm.

Here is the procedure, as shown in Figure 2.8. After computing a solution, we apply the inverse unitary operations to undo the computation completely. We can either build a giant combined unitary adjoint operator, or, if we have constructed a circuit from individual gates, we apply the inverses of the gates in reverse order. This works because operators are unitary and $U^\dagger U = I$.

The problem now is that we lost the result $f(|x\rangle)$ that we were trying to compute. Here is the "trick" to work around the problem, which is similar to Bennet's recipe. After computation, but before uncomputation, we connect the result qubits out to another quantum register via Controlled-Not gates, as shown in Figure 2.8.

With this circuit, the result of $f(|x\rangle)$ will be in the upper register, and the state of the other registers will be restored to their original state, eliminating all unwanted entanglement.

Why does this work at all? We start in the state composed of an input state $|x\rangle$ and a working register initialized with $|0\rangle$. The first U_f transforms the initial state $|x\rangle|0\rangle$ into $f(|x\rangle)g(|0\rangle)$. We add the ancillae register at the top, building a product state $|0\rangle f(|x\rangle)g(|0\rangle)$, and CNOT the register holding the result to get $f(|x\rangle)f(|x\rangle)g(|0\rangle)$.

This does *not* violate the no-cloning theorem; the two registers cannot be measured independently and give the same result. We apply $U_f^\dagger$ to the bottom two registers to uncompute U_f and obtain $f(|0\rangle)|x\rangle|0\rangle$. The final result is in the top register; the bottom registers have been successfully restored.

2.14   Reduced Density Matrix and Partial Trace

For debugging and analysis purposes, it is often desirable to inspect a subsystem of a given state. For this, we use what is called a *reduced density operator*, which we can derive with help of a procedure called a *partial trace*. This section might be a bit confusing to novices, but the technique discussed here is not used until much later in the text (see, for example, Section 6.2). You may choose to come back to it later as well.

We compute a partial trace from a state's density matrix. We briefly mentioned that the whole theory of quantum computing can be expressed using density matrices, but for simplicity, we did not elaborate on this representation. For the partial trace, however, we need to revisit this topic briefly. Two concepts are important.

First, a density matrix of a state is the outer product of the state with itself. This representation describes the whole system, including its potential entanglement with the environment. This gives rise to the notion of *pure* states, which are defined by the state vector alone, and *mixed* states, which may be entangled with something else, or are a statistical mixture of states.

Second, to apply an operator to a state as a density matrix, it applies from left and right. In state representation, we use $|\psi'\rangle = U|\psi\rangle$. To achieve the same state evolution in the density matrix representation, we apply $\rho' = U\rho U^\dagger$.

Assume we have a state $|\psi\rangle$ that is a combination of A and B with density operator $\rho^{AB} = |AB\rangle\langle AB|$. The reduced density operator ρ_A for subspace A is defined as $\rho_A = \mathrm{tr}_B(\rho^{AB})$, where tr_B is the partial trace over system B. This means that ρ_A contains the original state, but with B removed. It has been "traced out."

We want to have a mathematical tool that extracts a subspace out of the density operator. In terms of measurement, we only want to compute the trace over a subset of the full density operator, e.g., the subset describing either A or B. If ρ is the density matrix for the combined state, we want to compute either of the following:

$$\rho_B = \mathrm{tr}_A(\rho^{AB}) = \langle 0_A|\rho|0_A\rangle + \langle 1_A|\rho|1_A\rangle,$$
$$\rho_A = \mathrm{tr}_B(\rho^{AB}) = \langle 0_B|\rho|0_B\rangle + \langle 1_B|\rho|1_B\rangle.$$

$|0_A\rangle$ and $|1_A\rangle$ are the projectors on the basis states $|0\rangle$ and $|1\rangle$. Projectors are Hermitian, hence $P = P^\dagger$. Note that the partial trace is a *dimension reducing* operation. As an example, let us assume we have a system of two qubits A and B (at indices 0 and 1) with a 4×4 density matrix, and we want to trace out qubit 0.

We construct $|0_A\rangle$ and $|1_A\rangle$ by tensoring the $|0\rangle$ and $|1\rangle$ states with an identity matrix I, resulting in a matrix of size 4×2. The order depends on which specific qubit we intend to trace out. With an approach similar to that used for gate applications, we pad the $|0\rangle$ and $|1\rangle$ states with identity matrices from left and right. In our example, we want to trace out qubit 0, so the $|0\rangle$ and $|1\rangle$ states come first and are tensored with an identity matrix:

$$|0_A\rangle = \begin{pmatrix} 1 \\ 0 \end{pmatrix} \otimes \begin{pmatrix} 1 & 0 \\ 0 & 1 \end{pmatrix} = \begin{pmatrix} 1 & 0 \\ 0 & 1 \\ 0 & 0 \\ 0 & 0 \end{pmatrix}, \quad |1_A\rangle = \begin{pmatrix} 0 \\ 1 \end{pmatrix} \otimes \begin{pmatrix} 1 & 0 \\ 0 & 1 \end{pmatrix} = \begin{pmatrix} 0 & 0 \\ 0 & 0 \\ 1 & 0 \\ 0 & 1 \end{pmatrix}.$$

Multiplying the 4×4 density to the right with a 4×2 matrix results in a 4×2 matrix. Multiplying this matrix from the left with a (now transposed) 2×4 matrix results in a 2×2 matrix.

This definition of the partial trace is sufficient for implementation. The following code is written in full matrix form and will only scale to a small number of qubits.

```
def TraceOutSingle(rho: Operator, index: int) -> Operator:
    """Trace out single qubit from density matrix."""

    nbits = int(math.log2(rho.shape[0]))
    if index > nbits:
        raise AssertionError(
            'Error in TraceOutSingle, invalid index (>nbits).')

    eye = Identity()
    zero = Operator(np.array([1.0, 0.0]))
    one = Operator(np.array([0.0, 1.0]))

    p0 = p1 = tensor.Tensor(1.0)
    for idx in range(nbits):
        if idx == index:
            p0 = p0 * zero
            p1 = p1 * one
        else:
            p0 = p0 * eye
            p1 = p1 * eye

    rho0 = p0 @ rho
    rho0 = rho0 @ p0.transpose()
    rho1 = p1 @ rho
    rho1 = rho1 @ p1.transpose()
    rho_reduced = rho0 + rho1
    return rho_reduced
```

If we have a state of n qubits and are interested in the state of just one of the qubits, we have to trace out *all other* qubits. Here is a convenience function for this:

```
def TraceOut(rho: Operator, index_set: List[int]) -> Operator:
    """Trace out multiple qubits from density matrix."""

    for idx, val in enumerate(index_set):
```

```
    nbits = int(math.log2(rho.shape[0]))
    if val > nbits:
        raise AssertionError('Error TraceOut, invalid index (>nbits).')
    rho = TraceOutSingle(rho, val)

    # Tracing out a bit means that rho is now 1 bit smaller, the
    # indices right to the traced out qubit need to shift left by 1.
    # Example, to trace out bits 2, 4:
    # Before:
    #    qubit 0  1  2  3  4  5
    #          a  b  c  d  e  f
    # Trace out 2:
    #    qubit 0  1 <-  3  4  5
    #    qubit 0  1  2  3  4
    #          a  b  d  e  f
    # Trace out 4 (is now 3)
    #    qubit 0  1  2 <-  4
    #    qubit 0  1  2  3
    #          a  b  d  f
    for i in range(idx+1, len(index_set)):
        index_set[i] = index_set[i] - 1
    return rho
```

2.14.1   Experiments

Now let us see this procedure in action. We start by producing a state from two well-defined qubits.

```
q0 = state.qubit(alpha=0.5)
q1 = state.qubit(alpha=0.8660254)
psi = q0 * q1
```

Tracing out one qubit should leave the other in the resulting density matrix, with matrix element (0,0) holding the value $|\alpha|^2$ and matrix element (1, 1) holding the value $|\beta|^2$. Remember that the density matrix is the outer product of a state vector, with:

$$\begin{pmatrix} a \\ b \end{pmatrix} \begin{pmatrix} a^* & b^* \end{pmatrix} = \begin{pmatrix} aa^* & ab^* \\ ba^* & bb^* \end{pmatrix}.$$

We have seen earlier that

$$\text{tr}(|x\rangle\langle y|) = \sum_{i=0}^{n-1} x_i y_i^* = \langle y|x\rangle. \tag{2.7}$$

For an outer product of a state vector, we know that the trace must be 1.0, as the probabilities add up to 1.0. Correspondingly, density matrices also must have a trace of 1.0. This is confirmed above; the diagonal elements are the squares of the norms of the probability amplitudes.

Tracing out qubit 1 should result in a value of $0.5 * 0.5 = 0.25$ in matrix element $(0, 0)$, which is the norm squared of qubit 0's α value of 0.5:

```
reduced = ops.TraceOut(psi.density(), [1])
self.assertTrue(math.isclose(np.real(np.trace(reduced)), 1.0))
self.assertTrue(math.isclose(np.real(reduced[0, 0]),
                             0.25, abs_tol=1e-6))
self.assertTrue(math.isclose(np.real(reduced[1, 1]),
                             0.75, abs_tol=1e-6))
```

Tracing out qubit 0 should leave $0.8660254^2 = 0.75$ in matrix element $(0, 0)$:

```
reduced = ops.TraceOut(psi.density(), [0])
self.assertTrue(math.isclose(np.real(np.trace(reduced)), 1.0))
self.assertTrue(math.isclose(np.real(reduced[0, 0]),
                             0.75, abs_tol=1e-6))
self.assertTrue(math.isclose(np.real(reduced[1, 1]),
                             0.25, abs_tol=1e-6))
```

This becomes interesting for entangled states. Take, for example, the first Bell state. If we compute the density matrix and square it, the trace of the squared matrix is 1.0. If we trace out qubit 0:

```
psi = bell.bell_state(0, 0)
reduced = ops.TraceOut(psi.density(), [0])
self.assertTrue(math.isclose(np.real(np.trace(reduced)),
                             1.0, abs_tol=1e-6))
self.assertTrue(math.isclose(np.real(reduced[0, 0]),
                             0.5, abs_tol=1e-6))
self.assertTrue(math.isclose(np.real(reduced[1, 1]),
                             0.5, abs_tol=1e-6))
```

We see that the result is $I/2$, the diagonals are all the same, the state was maximally entangled. The trace of the squared, reduced density matrix is 0.5. We mentioned pure and mixed states above. The trace operation gives us a mathematical definition:

$$\text{tr}(\rho^2) < 1 : \text{Mixed State},$$

$$\text{tr}(\rho^2) = 1 : \text{Pure State}.$$

The result for the partial trace on the Bell state shows that the remaining qubit is in a mixed state:

$$\text{tr}\left((I/2)^2\right) = 0.5 < 1.$$

The joint state of the two qubits, entangled or not, is a pure state; it is known exactly, it is not entangled further with the environment. However, looking at the individual qubits of the entangled Bell state, we find that those are in a mixed state – we do not have full knowledge of their state.

2.15   Measurement

We have arrived at the end of the introductory section. What remains is to discuss measurements. This is a complex subject with many subtleties and layered theories. Here, we stick to the minimum – projective measurements.

2.15.1   Postulates of Quantum Mechanics

There are five postulates of quantum mechanics. Depending on the context, you may find them presented in a different order, with a different focus and rigor. In keeping with the spirit of our text, we present them here in an informal way that conveys just enough information to understand the essence of the postulates.

1. The state of a system is represented by a ket, which is a unit vector of complex numbers representing probability amplitudes.
2. A state evolves as the result of unitary operators operating on the state, $|\psi'\rangle = U|\psi\rangle$. This is derived from the time-independent Schrödinger equation. To describe the evolution of a system in continuous time, this postulate is expressed with the time-dependent Schrödinger equation (which we mostly ignore in this text).
3. Measurement means collapsing the probability function to a singular, measurable value, which is a real eigenvalue of the Hermitian measurement operator. This sounds scarier than it is, and it is the focus of this section.
4. The probability amplitudes and corresponding probabilities determine the likelihood of a specific measurement result.
5. After measurement, the state *collapses* to the result of the measurement. This is called the *Born rule*. We explain the implications of this postulate, in particular, the need for renormalization.

In the preceding chapters, we already *captured* postulates one and two by expressing states as full state vectors and showing how to apply unitary operators. By means of probability amplitudes, we have implicitly used postulate four and, to some degree, postulate five as well. In this section, we will focus on postulate three, measurements.

An important thing to note is that the postulates are postulates, not standard physical laws. As noted above, they are also the subject of almost a century's worth of scientific disputes and philosophical interpretation. See, for example Einstein et al. (1935), Bell (1964), Norsen (2017), Faye (2019), and Ghirardi and Bassi (2020), and many more. Nevertheless, as indicated before, we avoid philosophy and focus on how the postulates enable interesting forms of computation.

2.15.2   Projective Measurements

The class of projective measurements is easy to understand and the only method we will use in this text. Given a system that is in one of two states, e.g., an atom with an energy state high or low, the idea behind making a projective measurement is to simply determine which of those two states the atom was in. Qubits are in superposition. We may wonder whether it is in the $|0\rangle$ state or the $|1\rangle$ state, but measurement can only return one of these two states, which it does with a given probability. We know that after measurement, according to the Born rule, the state *collapses* to the measured state (postulate 5). It is now either $|0\rangle$ or $|1\rangle$ and will be found in this state for all future measurements.

Why is this called a projective measurement? In the section on single-qubit operators, we already learned about projection operators.

$$P_{|0\rangle} = |0\rangle\langle 0| = \begin{bmatrix} 1 \\ 0 \end{bmatrix} \begin{bmatrix} 1 & 0 \end{bmatrix} = \begin{bmatrix} 1 & 0 \\ 0 & 0 \end{bmatrix},$$

$$P_{|1\rangle} = |1\rangle\langle 1| = \begin{bmatrix} 0 \\ 1 \end{bmatrix} \begin{bmatrix} 0 & 1 \end{bmatrix} = \begin{bmatrix} 0 & 0 \\ 0 & 1 \end{bmatrix}.$$

Applying a projector to a qubit "extracts" a subspace. For example, for $P_{|0\rangle}$:

$$P_{|0\rangle}|\psi\rangle = |0\rangle\langle 0|(\alpha|0\rangle + \beta|1\rangle)$$

$$= \begin{bmatrix} 1 & 0 \\ 0 & 0 \end{bmatrix} \begin{bmatrix} \alpha \\ \beta \end{bmatrix} = \begin{bmatrix} \alpha \\ 0 \end{bmatrix}$$

$$= \alpha \begin{bmatrix} 1 \\ 0 \end{bmatrix} = \alpha|0\rangle.$$

We can say that the probability $Pr(i)$ of finding the ith basis state on measurement is the following, where we square the norm of the probability amplitude, as stated in the fourth postulate:

$$Pr(i) = \left(P_{|i\rangle}|\psi\rangle\right)^2.$$

Following Equation (1.2) to compute the vector norm and Equation (1.10) to compute the Hermitian adjoint of an expression, we have

$$Pr(i) = \left(P_{|i\rangle}|\psi\rangle\right)^\dagger \left(P_{|i\rangle}|\psi\rangle\right)$$

$$= \langle\psi|P_{|i\rangle}^\dagger P_{|i\rangle}|\psi\rangle.$$

Projectors are Hermitian and hence equal to their adjoint:

$$Pr(i) = \langle\psi|P_{|i\rangle} P_{|i\rangle}|\psi\rangle$$

$$= \langle\psi|P_{|i\rangle}^2|\psi\rangle.$$

We also know that for projectors of normalized basis vectors (which have 1s on the diagonal):

$$P_{|i\rangle}^2 = P_{|i\rangle},$$

which results in this final form for the probability:

$$Pr(i) = \langle\psi|P_{|i\rangle}|\psi\rangle.$$

The term $\langle\psi|P_{|i\rangle}|\psi\rangle$ is also called the *expectation value* of operator $P_{|i\rangle}$, the quantum equivalent of the *average* of $P_{|i\rangle}$. It can be written as $[P_{|i\rangle}]$.

We know from the section on the trace of a matrix (Equation (1.19)) that

$$\text{tr}\left(|x\rangle\langle y|\right) = \sum_{i=0}^{n-1} x_i y_i^* = \langle y|x\rangle. \tag{2.8}$$

By rearranging terms and using Equation (2.8), we finally arrive at the form we will use in our code:

$$Pr(i) = \langle\psi|P_{|i\rangle}|\psi\rangle = \text{tr}\left(P_{|i\rangle}|\psi\rangle\langle\psi|\right). \tag{2.9}$$

You can understand this form intuitively. The density matrix of the state $|\psi\rangle\langle\psi|$ has the probabilities $Pr(i)$ for each basis state $|x_i\rangle$ on the diagonal, as shown in Section 2.3.5. The projector zeros out all diagonal elements that are not covered by the projector's basis state. What remains on the diagonal are the probabilities of states matching the projector. The trace then adds up all these remaining probabilities off the diagonal.

After measurement, the state collapses to the measured result. Basis states that do not agree with the measured qubit values get a resulting probability of 0.0 and "disappear." As a result, the remaining states' probabilities no longer add up to 1.0 and need to be renormalized, which we achieve with the complicated-looking expression (no worries, in code, this will look quite simple):

$$|\psi\rangle = \frac{P_{|i\rangle}|\psi\rangle}{\sqrt{\langle\psi|P_{|i\rangle}|\psi\rangle}}. \tag{2.10}$$

As an example, let us assume we have this state:

$$|\psi\rangle = 1/2\left(|00\rangle + |01\rangle + |10\rangle + |11\rangle\right).$$

Each of the four basis states has equal probability $\left(\frac{1}{2}\right)^2 = 1/4$ of being measured. Let us further assume that qubit 0 is being measured as $|0\rangle$. This means that the only choices for the final, full state to be measured are $|00\rangle$ or $|01\rangle$. The first qubit is "fixed" at $|0\rangle$ after measurement. This means that the states where qubit 0 is $|1\rangle$ now have a 0% probability of ever being measured. The state collapsed to this unnormalized state:

$$|\psi\rangle_{(\neq|1\rangle)} = 1/2\left(|00\rangle + |01\rangle\right) + 0.0\left(|10\rangle + |11\rangle\right).$$

But in this form, the squares of the probability amplitudes no longer add up to 1.0. We must renormalize the state following Equation (2.10) and divide by the square root of the expectation value (which was 1/2) to get:

$$|\psi\rangle = 1/\sqrt{2}\left(|00\rangle + |01\rangle\right).$$

This step might be surprising. How does Nature know when and if to normalize? Given that we're adhering to the Copenhagen interpretation and decided to "Shut up and compute!," a possible answer is that the need for re-normalization is simply a remnant of the mathematical framework, nothing more, nothing less.

2.15.3 Implementation

The function to measure a specific qubit has the following parameters:

- The state to measure is passed as parameter `psi`.
- Which qubit to measure, indexed from the top/left, with parameter `idx`.
- Whether to measure the probability that the state collapses to $|0\rangle$ or $|1\rangle$ is controlled with parameter `tostate`.
- After measurement, whether the state should collapse or not is controlled by parameter `collapse`. In the physical world, measurement destroys superposition, but in our simulation, we can just take a peek-a-boo at the probabilities without affecting the superposition of states.

The way this function is written, if we measure and collapse to state $|0\rangle$, the state will be made to collapse to this state, *independent* of the probabilities. There are other ways to implement this, e.g., by selecting the measurement result based on the probabilities. At this early point in our exploration, the ability to force a result works quite well; it makes debugging easier. Care must be taken, though, never to force the state to collapse to a result with probability 0. This would lead to a division by 0 and likely very confusing subsequent measurement results.

The function returns two values: the probability of measuring the desired qubit state and a state. This state is either the post-measurement collapsed state, if `collapse` was set to `True`, or the unmodified state otherwise. Here is the implementation. The function first computes the density matrix and the padded operator around the projection operator:

```
def Measure(psi: state.State, idx: int,
            tostate:int=0, collapse:bool=True) -> (float, state.State):
  """Measure a qubit via a projector on the density matrix."""

  # Compute probability of qubit(idx) to be in state 0 / 1.
  rho = psi.density()
  op = Projector(state.zero) if tostate = 0 else Projector(state.one)

  # Construct full matrix to apply to density matrix:
  if idx > 0:
    op = Identity().kpow(idx) * op
  if idx < psi.nbits - 1:
    op = op * Identity().kpow(psi.nbits - idx -1)
```

The probability is computed from a trace over the matrix resulting from multiplication of the padded projection operator with the density matrix, as in Equation 2.9:

```
  # Probability is the trace.
  prob0 = np.trace(np.matmul(op, rho))
```

If state collapse is required, we update the state and renormalize it before returning the updated (or unmodified) probability and state.

```
# Collapse state (don't forget to normalize if norm != 0)
if collapse:
  mvmul = np.dot(op, psi)
  divisor = np.real(np.linalg.norm(mvmul))
  if divisor > 1e-10:
    normed = mvmul / divisor
  else:
    raise AssertionError(
            'Measure() collapsed to 0.0 probability state.')
  return np.real(prob0), state.State(normed)

# Return original state, enable chaining.
return np.real(prob0), psi
```

And just to clarify one more time, the measurement operators are projectors. They are Hermitian with eigenvalues 0 and 1, and eigenvectors $|0\rangle$ and $|1\rangle$. A measurement will produce $|0\rangle$ or $|1\rangle$, corresponding to the basis states' probabilities. Measurement will not measure, say, a value of 0.75. It will measure one of the two basis states with probability 0.75. This can be a source of confusion for beginners – in the real world we have to measure several times to find the probabilities with statistical significance.

2.15.4   Examples

Let us look at a handful of examples to see measurements in action. In the first example, let us create a 4-qubit state and look at the probabilities:

```
    psi = state.bitstring(1, 0, 1, 0)
    psi.dump()
>>
    |1010> (|10>):  ampl: +1.00+0.00j prob: 1.00 Phase:   0.0
```

There is only one state with nonzero probabilities. If we measure the second qubit to be 0, which it is:

```
    p0, _ = ops.Measure(psi, 1)
    print(p0)
>>
    1.0
```

But if we tried to measure this second qubit to be 1, which it cannot be, we will get an error, as expected:

```
      p0, _ = ops.Measure(psi, 1, tostate=1)
      print(p0)
>>

      AssertionError: Measure() collapsed to 0.0 probability state
```

Here is an example with a collapsing measurement. Let us create a Bell state:

```
      psi = bell.bell_state(0, 0)
      psi.dump()
>>

      |00> (|0>):  ampl: +0.71+0.00j prob: 0.50 Phase:   0.0
      |11> (|3>):  ampl: +0.71+0.00j prob: 0.50 Phase:   0.0
```

The state has only two possible measurement outcomes, $|00\rangle$ and $|11\rangle$. Let us measure the first qubit to be $|0\rangle$ without collapsing the state:

```
      psi = bell.bell_state(0, 0)
      p0, _ = ops.Measure(psi, 0, 0, collapse=False)
      print('Probability: ', p0)
      psi.dump()
>>

      Probability:  0.49999997
      |00> (|0>):  ampl: +0.71+0.00j prob: 0.50 Phase:   0.0
      |11> (|3>):  ampl: +0.71+0.00j prob: 0.50 Phase:   0.0
```

This shows the correct probability of 0.5 of measuring $|0\rangle$, but the state is still unmodified. Now we *collapse* the state after the measurement, which is more reflective of making an actual, physical measurement:

```
      psi = bell.bell_state(0, 0)
      p0, psi = ops.Measure(psi, 0, 0, collapse=True)
      print('Probability: ', p0)
      psi.dump()
>>

      Probability:  0.49999997
      |00> (|0>):  ampl: +1.00+0.00j prob: 1.00 Phase:   0.0
```

Now only one possible measurement outcome remains, the state $|00\rangle$, which from here on out would be measured with 100% probability.

At this point we have mastered the fundamental concepts and are ready to move on to studying our first quantum algorithms. There are two possible paths forward. You may want to explore Chapter 3 on simple algorithms next before learning more about infrastructure and high-performance simulation in Chapter 4. Or, you may prefer reading Chapter 4 on infrastructure first before exploring Chapter 3 on simple algorithms.

3 Simple Algorithms

In this section, we introduce a first set of quantum algorithms. All that is needed to follow this section is the background and infrastructure from Chapter 2. What makes the algorithms presented here *simple* compared to the *complex* algorithms in Chapter 6? A judgment call. To justify the judgement call, the algorithms in this chapter are typically shorter and require less preparation or background than those in later chapters. Additionally, the derivations are developed with great detail. Many of these techniques will be taken for granted in later sections.

In this chapter, we start with what is possibly the most simple algorithm of all: a quantum random number generator. We follow this with a range of gate equivalences – how one gate, or gate sequence, can be expressed by another. Armed with these basic tools, we implement a classical full adder but with quantum gates. This circuit does not yet exploit superposition or entanglement.

Then it gets more exciting. We describe a swap test, which allows measurement of the similarity between two states without directly measuring the states themselves. We describe two algorithms with very cool names that utilize entanglement – quantum teleportation and superdense coding.

After this we move on to three so-called oracle algorithms. These algorithms exploit superposition and compute solutions in parallel using a large unitary operator. These are the first quantum algorithms we explore that perform better than their classical counterparts.

3.1   Random Number Generator

Every programming system introduces itself with the equivalent of a "Hello World" program. In quantum computing, this may be a random number generator. It is the simplest possible quantum circuit that does something meaningful, and it does so with just one qubit and one gate:

The Hadamard gate will put the state into superposition:

$$H|0\rangle = \frac{|0\rangle + |1\rangle}{\sqrt{2}} = |+\rangle. \tag{3.1}$$

On measurement,[1] the state will collapse to either $|0\rangle$ or $|1\rangle$ with exactly 50% probability for each case. Remember that after applying the Hadamard gate, the probability amplitudes for each of the two possible resulting states are $1/\sqrt{2} = 0.707\ldots$. Recall that the probability is the square of the norm: for amplitude a, $p = |a|^2 = a^*a$. You can validate this with a simple code experiment:

```
psi = ops.Hadamard()(state.zero)
psi.dump()
>>
0.70710678+0.000000000i  |0>  50.0%
0.70710678+0.000000000i  |1>  50.0%
```

Since we can construct one single, completely random qubit, which we interpret as a classical bit after measurement, bundling multiple of these bits in parallel or sequence allows the generation of random numbers of any bit width. By *random*, we mean true, atomic-level randomness, not classical pseudo-randomness. There is a finite number of possible (enumerable) states in classical computers with a finite amount of memory. Hence all random numbers generated on a classical computer are not *truly* random; their sequence will repeat itself eventually.

This circuit can barely be called a circuit, never mind an algorithm (even though in Section 6.8 on amplitude amplification, we do call it an algorithm). It only has one gate, so it is the simplest of all possible circuits. Nevertheless, it exploits crucial quantum computing properties, namely superposition and the probabilistic collapse of the wave function on measurement. It is trivial, and it is not, both at the same time. It is a true quantum circuit.

3.2 Gate Equivalences

As we learned earlier, points on the surface of the Bloch sphere can be reached in an infinite number of ways, simply by utilizing rotations. Similarly for circuits, using only standard gates, there are many interesting equivalences for one-, two-, and many-more-qubit circuits. In this section, we describe common equivalences, mostly in the form of code. With just a little stretch of the imagination, we can consider those simple circuits as algorithms; that's why we're discussing them in this part of the book.

There are also higher-level functions that can be composed of simpler, one- or two-qubit gates, e.g., a Swap gate over larger qubit distances and the double-controlled X-gate. This aspect, the reduction to one- and two-qubit gates, is important, and in

---

[1] In the Z-basis – we talk more about this in later sections.

the remainder of this text, we will (mostly) focus on these types of gates. The main reasons for this focus are:

- Two-qubit gates are already tough to implement on a physical quantum computer. Larger ones even more so.
- One key result in quantum computing proves that any unitary gate can be approximated up to arbitrary accuracy by single- and double-qubit gates only.
- We want peak simulation performance, which can be achieved with these types of gates.

The example code in the following sections can be quite trivial. We still show it, it should encourage you to run your own experiments!

3.2.1   Root of Gate Squared = Gate

Squaring the root of a gate should result in the gate itself. The root of a rotation is a rotation by half the angle. We can check that $T^2 = S, S^2 = Z$, and $T^4 = Z$. Note that the adjoint of a rotation is a rotation in the other direction. In the code below, we also validate the root of the X-gate as $V^2 = X$:

```
def test_t_gate(self):
    """T^2 == S."""

    s = ops.Tgate() @ ops.Tgate()
    self.assertTrue(s.is_close(ops.Phase()))

def test_s_gate(self):
    """S^2 == Z."""

    x = ops.Sgate() @ ops.Sgate()
    self.assertTrue(s.is_close(ops.PauliZ()))

def test_v_gate(self):
    """V^2 == X."""

    s = ops.Vgate() @ ops.Vgate()
    self.assertTrue(s.is_close(ops.PauliX()))
```

3.2.2   Inverted Controlled-Not

We can turn a $CNOT_{a,b}$ into a $CNOT_{b,a}$ by applying a Hadamard gate to the left and right of the *CNOT* on both qubits:

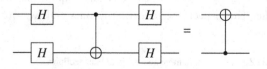

```
def test_had_cnot_had(self):
    h2 = ops.Hadamard(2)
    cnot = ops.Cnot(0, 1)
    op = h2(cnot(h2))
    self.assertTrue(op.is_close(ops.Cnot(1, 0)))
```

We can also convince ourselves of this result by looking at the operator matrices; this is a useful debugging technique. The circuit above translates to the following gate-level expression. Because this circuit is symmetric around the *CNOT* gate, we don't have to worry about the ordering of the matrix multiplications:

$$(H \otimes H)\ CNOT_{0,1}\ (H \otimes H).$$

In matrix form:

$$\frac{1}{2}\begin{bmatrix} 1 & 1 & 1 & 1 \\ 1 & -1 & 1 & -1 \\ 1 & 1 & -1 & -1 \\ 1 & -1 & -1 & 1 \end{bmatrix} \begin{bmatrix} 1 & 0 & 0 & 0 \\ 0 & 1 & 0 & 0 \\ 0 & 0 & 0 & 1 \\ 0 & 0 & 1 & 0 \end{bmatrix} \frac{1}{2}\begin{bmatrix} 1 & 1 & 1 & 1 \\ 1 & -1 & 1 & -1 \\ 1 & 1 & -1 & -1 \\ 1 & -1 & -1 & 1 \end{bmatrix}.$$

We construct this in code and find that both versions produce the same operator matrix:

```
      (ops.Hadamard(2) @ ops.Cnot(0, 1) @ ops.Hadamard(2)).dump()
>>
1.0       -          -          -
 -        -          -         1.0
 -        -         1.0         -
 -       1.0         -          -


      ops.Cnot(1, 0).dump()
>>
1.0       -          -          -
 -        -          -         1.0
 -        -         1.0         -
 -       1.0         -          -
```

3.2.3   Controlled-Z Gate

The controller and controlled qubits for a Controlled-Z gate can be swapped without affecting the results. Therefore, this controlled gate is often drawn without direction using just two black dots:

Let us confirm that the Controlled-Z is indeed symmetric. In Section 2.7 on controlled gates we learned how to construct controlled unitary gates with the help of projectors such as:

$$CU_{0,1} = P_{|0\rangle} \otimes I + P_{|1\rangle} \otimes U,$$
$$CU_{1,0} = I \otimes P_{|0\rangle} + U \otimes P_{|1\rangle}.$$

It is a good exercise to try and manually compute the tensor products for this Controlled-Z gate. In one case we add the matrices:

$$CZ_{0,1} = \begin{bmatrix} 1 & 0 & 0 & 0 \\ 0 & 1 & 0 & 0 \\ 0 & 0 & 0 & 0 \\ 0 & 0 & 0 & 0 \end{bmatrix} + \begin{bmatrix} 0 & 0 & 0 & 0 \\ 0 & 0 & 0 & 0 \\ 0 & 0 & 1 & 0 \\ 0 & 0 & 0 & -1 \end{bmatrix}.$$

In the case with the indices changed from 0, 1 to 1, 0 we add these matrices:

$$CZ_{1,0} = \begin{bmatrix} 1 & 0 & 0 & 0 \\ 0 & 0 & 0 & 0 \\ 0 & 0 & 1 & 0 \\ 0 & 0 & 0 & 0 \end{bmatrix} + \begin{bmatrix} 0 & 0 & 0 & 0 \\ 0 & 1 & 0 & 0 \\ 0 & 0 & 0 & 0 \\ 0 & 0 & 0 & -1 \end{bmatrix}.$$

In both cases the result will be this operator matrix:

$$CZ_{0,1} = CZ_{1,0} = \begin{bmatrix} 1 & 0 & 0 & 0 \\ 0 & 1 & 0 & 0 \\ 0 & 0 & 1 & 0 \\ 0 & 0 & 0 & -1 \end{bmatrix}.$$

The corresponding code for this experiment is below. Note that constructing a *Multi-Controlled-Z* results in a similar matrix with all diagonal elements being 1 except the bottom-right element, which is −1. Try it out yourself!

```
def test_controlled_z(self):
    z0 = ops.ControlledU(0, 1, ops.PauliZ())
    z1 = ops.ControlledU(1, 0, ops.PauliZ())
    self.assertTrue(z0.is_close(z1))
```

Note that all controlled phase gates are symmetric, for example:

A related gate equivalence is the following, which allows the construction of Controlled-Not gates using Hadamard gates and Controlled-Z gates:

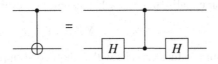

3.2.4 Negate Y-Gate

We can *negate* the Y-gate with help of two X-gates to its left and right:

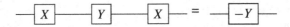

```
def test_xyx(self):
    x = ops.PauliX()
    y = ops.PauliY()
    print(y)

    op = x(y(x))
    print(op)
    self.assertTrue(op.is_close(-1.0 * y))
```

The two print statements in the code above indeed produce the expected result:

```
Operator for 1-qubit state space. Tensor:
[[ 0.+0.j -0.-1.j]
 [ 0.+1.j  0.+0.j]]
Operator for 1-qubit state space. Tensor:
[[0.+0.j 0.+1.j]
 [0.-1.j 0.+0.j]]
```

3.2.5 Pauli Matrix Relations

Placing Hadamard operators to the left and right of a Pauli matrix yields another Pauli matrix in the following ways. In general, writing operators next to each other means they follow function call syntax. So the mathematical ABC would be written as A(B(C)). The expressions below are symmetric, so the order does not matter in this instance.[2]

$$HXH = Z,$$
$$HYH = -Y = XYX,$$
$$HZH = X.$$

---

[2] Note that these equivalences are related to the *Pauli commutators*. See, for example, https://en.wikipedia.org/wiki/Pauli_matrices#Commutation_relations.

A particular equality that we will encounter in several places is the following:

$$XZ = iY. \tag{3.2}$$

You can validate these results with a short code snippet:

```python
def test_equalities(self):
    # Generate the Pauli and Hadamard matrices.
    _, x, y, z = ops.Pauli()
    h = ops.Hadamard()

    # Check equalities.
    op = h(x(h))
    self.assertTrue(op.is_close(z))

    op = h(y(h))
    self.assertTrue(op.is_close(-1.0 * y))

    op = h(z(h))
    self.assertTrue(op.is_close(x))

    op = x(z)
    self.assertTrue(op.is_close(1.0j * y))
```

3.2.6   Change Rotation Axis

The following equivalence is interesting because it shows the effects of a global phase on an operator. A T-gate represents a rotation about the z-axis by $\pi/4$. Bracketing the T-gate with Hadamard gates turns the combined unitary gate into a rotation about the x-axis by $\pi/4$:

$$HTH = R_x(\pi/4).$$

The combined HTH is this operator:

```
Operator for 1-qubit state space. Tensor:
[[0.8535533 +0.35355335j 0.14644662-0.35355335j]
 [0.14644662-0.35355335j 0.8535533 +0.35355335j]]
```

Let us compare this against a rotation by $\pi/4$ around the x-axis, which is this operator:

```
Operator for 1-qubit state space. Tensor:
[[0.9238795+0.j          0.         -0.38268343j]
 [0.        -0.38268343j 0.9238795+0.j          ]]
```

At first glance, it does not appear that these two results are equivalent. However, dividing one by the other results in a matrix with all equal elements. This means that the two operators only differ by a multiplication factor. Applying a scaled operator to a state leads to an equally scaled state. Since this is a global phase, which has no physical meaning, we can ignore it. Conversely, we can say that operators that differ only by a constant factor are equivalent. If this is true then computing the division between the two should yield a matrix with all identical elements. And indeed, it does:

```python
def test_global_phase(self):
    h = ops.Hadamard()
    op = h(ops.Tgate()(h))

    # If equal up to a global phase, all values should be equal.
    phase = op / ops.RotationX(math.pi/4)
    self.assertTrue(math.isclose(phase[0, 0].real, phase[0, 1].real,
                                 abs_tol=1e-6))
    self.assertTrue(math.isclose(phase[0, 0].imag, phase[0, 1].imag,
                                 abs_tol=1e-6))
    self.assertTrue(math.isclose(phase[0, 0].real, phase[1, 0].real,
                                 abs_tol=1e-6))
    self.assertTrue(math.isclose(phase[0, 0].imag, phase[1, 0].imag,
                                 abs_tol=1e-6))
    self.assertTrue(math.isclose(phase[0, 0].real, phase[1, 1].real,
                                 abs_tol=1e-6))
    self.assertTrue(math.isclose(phase[0, 0].imag, phase[1, 1].imag,
                                 abs_tol=1e-6))
```

3.2.7 Controlled-Controlled Gates

As long as a root $R = \sqrt{U}$ exists for a unitary gate U (it always does[3]), we can construct a double-controlled U by using two-qubit gates only. This is important for simulation performance, because two-qubit gates can be simulated very efficiently. Furthermore, for physical machines, building gates with more than two qubits is a major challenge, if not impossible.

An example of a double-controlled gate is the Toffoli gate from Section 2.7.2. It is a double-controlled X-gate, as shown on the left-hand side of Figure 3.1. It can be built with the so-called Sleator–Weinfurter construction (Barenco et al., 1995), which is illustrated on the right-hand side of Figure 3.1. Note that the circuit only uses two-qubit gates!

We know that the square root of the X-gate is the V-gate, and we also have the `adjoint()` function to compute the adjoint of this gate, or any other tensor. This construction works for any single-qubit gate and its root, so we can construct double-controlled X, Y, Z, T, and any other controlled 2×2 gates. Note that for now we are using the fixed indices 0, 1, 2 for the qubits in the code below. A general construction will follow later.

---

[3] We can prove that *any* unitary matrix has a square root. Unitary matrices are diagonalizable, so the root of the unitary matrix is just the root of the diagonal elements.

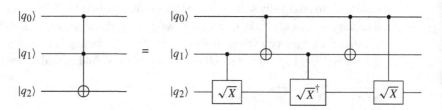

Figure 3.1 The Sleator–Weinfurter construction for a double-controlled X-gate.

```
def test_v_vdag_v(self):
  # Make Toffoli out of V = sqrt(X).
  #
  v = ops.Vgate()   # Could be any unitary, in principle!
  ident = ops.Identity()
  cnot = ops.Cnot(0, 1)

  o0 = ident * ops.ControlledU(1, 2, v)
  c2 = cnot * ident
  o2 = (ident * ops.ControlledU(1, 2, v.adjoint()))
  o4 = ops.ControlledU(0, 2, v)
  final = o4 @ c2 @ o2 @ c2 @ o0

  v2 = v @ v
  cv1 = ops.ControlledU(1, 2, v2)
  cv0 = ops.ControlledU(0, 1, cv1)
  self.assertTrue(final.is_close(cv0))
```

3.2.8   Multi-Controlled Gates

We already mentioned (Section 3.2.7) that the ability to construct double-controlled gates with only two-qubit gates is important. The logical next step is to construct multi-controlled gates.

How to go about this? There is an elegant construction for an n-way controlled gate that requires $n - 2$ ancilla qubits, all initialized to $|0\rangle$. Let's look at the first half of the circuit in Figure 3.2.

The cascading Toffoli gates build up the final predicate in the top-most ancilla qubit to control the X-gate at the bottom. Only if all predicate qubits were $|1\rangle$ will the top-most qubit be $|1\rangle$ as well.

This construction can be used to control other single-qubit gates. A potential problem is that the system's state is now entangled with the ancilla qubits. A solution for this problem, which is detailed in Section 2.13, is to *uncompute* the cascade of Toffoli gates by computing the gates' adjoints and applying them in reverse order. By doing this, as shown in the right half of Figure 3.2, the ancilla qubits are being reversed to their initial state. The state can again be expressed as a product state, and all

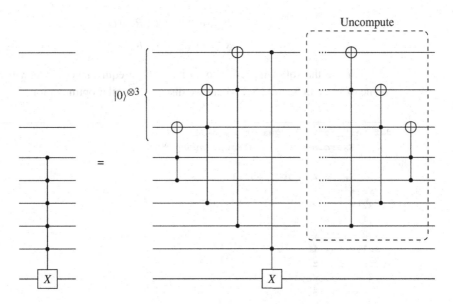

Figure 3.2 A multi-controlled X-gate.

entanglement with the ancilla qubits has been eliminated. We detail an implementation of multi-controlled gates that may have 0, 1, or many controllers and that can be controlled by $|0\rangle$ or $|1\rangle$, in Section 4.3.7.

Other constructions are possible. Mermin (2007) proposes multi-controlled gates that trade additional gates for lower numbers of ancillae, as well as circuits that don't require the ancillae to be in $|0\rangle$ states (which may save a few uncomputation gates).

3.2.9   Equivalences of Controlled Gates

In this section we list several equalities for controlled gates, using this shorthand notation:

- C_x is a Controlled-Not from qubit 0 to qubit 1.
- X_0 is the X-gate applied to qubit 0. Similar for index 1, and the Y-gate and Z-gate.

We again write ABC as a short form of $A(B(C))$[4]:

$$C_x X_0 C_x = X_0 X_1,$$
$$C_x Y_0 C_x = Y_0 X_1,$$
$$C_x Z_0 C_x = Z_0,$$
$$C_x X_1 C_x = X_1,$$
$$C_x Y_1 C_x = Z_0 Y_1,$$
$$C_x Z_1 C_x = Z_0 Z_1,$$

---

[4] But note that matrix multiplication is associative.

$$R_{z,0}(\phi)C_x = C_x R_{z,0}(\phi),$$
$$R_{x,1}(\phi)C_x = C_x R_{x,1}(\phi).$$

We can use the following code to validate these equivalences. We will also revisit some of these in Section 8.4 where we discuss compiler optimization.

```python
def test_control_equalities(self):
    """Exercise 4.31 Nielson, Chuang."""

    i, x, y, z = ops.Pauli()
    x1 = x * i
    x2 = i * x
    y1 = y * i
    y2 = i * y
    z1 = z * i
    z2 = i * z
    c = ops.Cnot(0, 1)
    theta = 25.0 * math.pi / 180.0
    rx2 = i * ops.RotationX(theta)
    rz1 = ops.RotationZ(theta) * i

    self.assertTrue(c(x1(c)).is_close(x1(x2)))
    self.assertTrue((c @ x1 @ c).is_close(x1 @ x2))
    self.assertTrue((c @ y1 @ c).is_close(y1 @ x2))
    self.assertTrue((c @ z1 @ c).is_close(z1))
    self.assertTrue((c @ x2 @ c).is_close(x2))
    self.assertTrue((c @ y2 @ c).is_close(z1 @ y2))
    self.assertTrue((c @ z2 @ c).is_close(z1 @ z2))
    self.assertTrue((rz1 @ c).is_close(c @ rz1))
    self.assertTrue((rx2 @ c).is_close(c @ rx2))
```

3.2.10   Swap Gate

For completeness, let's go over the Swap gate one more time. It is constructed with three Controlled-Not gates in series, as shown in Figure 3.3.

```python
def Swap(idx0: int = 0, idx1: int = 1) -> Operator:
    """Swap qubits at idx0 and idx1 via combination of Cnot gates."""

    return Cnot(idx1, idx0) @ Cnot(idx0, idx1) @ Cnot(idx1, idx0)
```

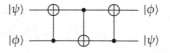

Figure 3.3 Construction of a swap gate with three Controlled-Not gates.

There are many more equivalences to be found in the literature. They are all interesting and valuable, especially in the context of optimization and compilation. An interesting (and not necessarily trivial) problem is to find them programmatically. We leave this as a challenge to you.

3.3 Classical Arithmetic

In this section we study a standard classical logic circuit, the full adder, and implement it with quantum gates. The quantum circuit does not exploit any of the quantum features – we will detail arithmetic in the quantum Fourier domain in Section 6.2. A 1-bit full adder block is usually drawn as shown in Figure 3.4.

Input bits are A and B. The carry-in from a previous, chained-in full adder is denoted by C_{in}. The outputs are the sum Sum and the potential carry-out C_{out}. Multiple full adders can be chained together (with C_{in} and C_{out}) to produce adders of arbitrary bit width. The truth table for the full adder logic circuit is shown in Table 3.1.

Classical circuits use, unsurprisingly, classical gates like AND, OR, NAND, and others. The task at hand is to construct a quantum circuit that produces the same truth table by using only quantum gates. Classical 0s and 1s are represented by the basis states $|0\rangle$ and $|1\rangle$. With some thought (and experimentation), we arrive at the circuit in Figure 3.5. Note that this circuit exploits neither superposition nor entanglement.

Table 3.1 Truth table for the full adder logic circuit.

A	B	C_{in}	C_{out}	Sum
0	0	0	0	0
0	0	1	0	1
0	1	0	0	1
0	1	1	1	0
1	0	0	0	1
1	0	1	1	0
1	1	0	1	0
1	1	1	1	1

Figure 3.4 The 1-bit full adder block diagram.

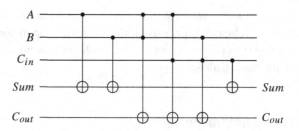

Figure 3.5 Classical full adder, implemented with quantum gates.

Let's walk through the circuit to convince ourselves that it is working properly:

- If A is 1, *Sum* will be flipped to 1 (*CNOT* from A to *Sum*).
- If B is 1, *Sum* will be flipped to 1 or flipped back to 0 if it was set to 1 already.
- If C_{in} is 1, *Sum* will be flipped one more time with the *CNOT* at the very right.
- C_{out} will be flipped if both A and B are set, or both A and C_{in} are set, or both B and C_{in} are set.
- What happens if all A, B, and C_{in} are set? *Sum* will start as 0 and go through these states: 0, 1, 0, 1. C_{out} will also start as 0 and go through these states: 0, 1, 0, 1. The final result is 1 and 1 for the two signals.

The implementation is straightforward with Controlled-Not gates and double-controlled X-gates. Measurements are probabilistic, but in this case the probability for the correct result is 100%. There is only a single state with nonzero probability.

Let us use our infrastructure to implement this circuit (the sources are in file src/arith_classic.py in the open-source repository). We apply each gate to the state in the order shown in Figure 3.5:

```
def fulladder_matrix(psi: state.State):
  """Non-quantum-exploiting, classic full adder."""

  psi = ops.Cnot(0, 3)(psi, 0)
  psi = ops.Cnot(1, 3)(psi, 1)
  psi = ops.ControlledU(0, 1, ops.Cnot(1, 4))(psi, 0)
  psi = ops.ControlledU(0, 2, ops.Cnot(2, 4))(psi, 0)
  psi = ops.ControlledU(1, 2, ops.Cnot(2, 4))(psi, 1)
  psi = ops.Cnot(2, 3)(psi, 2)
  return psi
```

We run an experiment the following way. First, we construct the state from the inputs, augmenting it with two $|0\rangle$ states for expected outputs sum and cout. Then, we apply the circuit we just constructed. We measure the probabilities of the outputs being 1, which means we will get a probability of 0.0 if the state was $|0\rangle$ and a probability of 1.0 if the state was $|1\rangle$:

```
def experiment_matrix(a: int, b: int, cin: int,
                      expected_sum: int, expected_cout: int):
  """Run a simple classic experiment, check results."""

  psi = state.bitstring(a, b, cin, 0, 0)
  psi = fulladder_classic(psi)

  bsum, _ = ops.Measure(psi, 3, tostate=1, collapse=False)
  bout, _ = ops.Measure(psi, 4, tostate=1, collapse=False)
  print(f'a: {a} b: {b} cin: {cin} sum: {bsum} cout: {bout}')
  if bsum != expected_sum or bout != expected_cout:
    raise AssertionError('invalid results')
```

We check the circuit for all inputs:

```
def add_classic():
  """Full eval of the full adder."""

  for exp_function in [experiment_matrix]:
    exp_function(0, 0, 0, 0, 0)
    exp_function(0, 1, 0, 1, 0)
    exp_function(1, 0, 0, 1, 0)
    exp_function(1, 1, 0, 0, 1)
    [...]

def main(argv):
  [...]
  add_classic()
```

This will produce the following output. The absence of error messages indicates that things went as planned:

```
a: 0 b: 0 cin: 0 sum: 0.0 cout: 0.0
a: 0 b: 1 cin: 0 sum: 1.0 cout: 0.0
a: 1 b: 0 cin: 0 sum: 1.0 cout: 0.0
a: 1 b: 1 cin: 0 sum: 0.0 cout: 1.0
[...]
```

Other classical circuits can be implemented and combined in this way to build up more powerful circuits. We show a general construction below. All these circuits point to a general statement about quantum computers: since *universal* logic gates can be implemented on quantum computers, a quantum computer is as least as capable as a classical computer. It does not mean that it performs better in the general case. The circuit presented here may be a very inefficient way to implement a simple 1-bit adder. However, we will soon see a class of algorithms that performs significantly better on quantum computers than on classical computers.

3.3.1   General Construction of Logic Circuits

Here is a general construction to express classical logic circuits with quantum gates (Williams, 2011). This method uses a small set of only three quantum gates:

$$NOT = a \longrightarrow \oplus \longrightarrow a \oplus 1$$

$$CNOT = \begin{array}{l} a \longrightarrow \bullet \longrightarrow a \\ b \longrightarrow \oplus \longrightarrow a \oplus b \end{array}$$

$$\text{Toffoli} = \begin{array}{l} a \longrightarrow \bullet \longrightarrow a \\ b \longrightarrow \bullet \longrightarrow b \\ c \longrightarrow \oplus \longrightarrow (a \wedge b) \oplus c \end{array}$$

These three gates are sufficient to construct the classical gates AND ($\wedge$), OR ($\vee$), and, of course, the NOT gate. The AND gate is a Toffoli gate with a $|0\rangle$ as third input:

$$\text{AND} = \begin{array}{l} a \longrightarrow \bullet \longrightarrow a \\ b \longrightarrow \bullet \longrightarrow b \\ |0\rangle \longrightarrow \oplus \longrightarrow a \wedge b \end{array}$$

The OR gate is slightly more involved, but it is just based on another Toffoli gate:

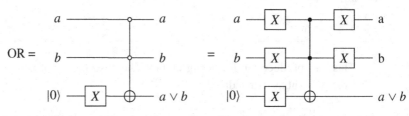

We know that with NOT and AND, we can build the universal NAND gate, which means we can construct any classical logic circuit with quantum gates. We might run into the need for fan-out to connect single wires to multiple gates for complex logic circuits. So, we need a *fan-out* circuit. Is this even possible? Doesn't fan-out violate the no-cloning theorem? The answer is no, it does not, because logical 0 and 1 are represented by qubits in states $|0\rangle$ or $|1\rangle$. For those basis states, cloning and fan-out are indeed possible, as we showed in Section 2.13.

$$\text{Fan-out} = \begin{array}{l} a \longrightarrow \bullet \longrightarrow a \\ |0\rangle \longrightarrow \oplus \longrightarrow a \end{array}$$

With these elements and knowing that any Boolean formula can be expressed as a product of sums,[5] we can build any logic circuit with quantum gates. Of course,

---

[5] https://en.wikipedia.org/wiki/Canonical_normal_form

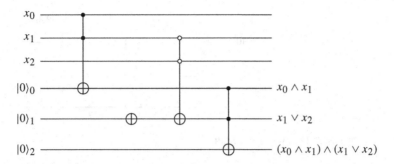

Figure 3.6 A Boolean formula, expressed with quantum gates.

making this construction efficient would require additional techniques, such as ancilla management, uncomputation, and general minimization of gates.

An example of a quantum circuit for the Boolean formula $(x_0 \land x_1) \land (x_1 \lor x_2)$ is shown in Figure 3.6. In this circuit diagram, we do not show the uncomputation following the final gate that would be required to disentangle the ancillae from the state. The ability to uncompute ancillae in a large chain of logic expressions can reduce the number of required ancillae. In this example, we could uncompute $|0\rangle_0$ and $|0\rangle_1$ and make them available again for future temporary results.

3.4   Swap Test

The quantum swap test allows measuring similarity between two quantum states without actually measuring the two states directly (Buhrman et al., 2001). If the resulting measurement probability is close to 0.5 for the basis state $|0\rangle$ of an *ancilla*, it means that the two states are very different. Conversely, a measurement probability close to 1.0 means that the two states are very similar. In the physical world, we have to run the experiment multiple times to confirm the probabilities. In our implementation, we can conveniently peek at the probabilities.

This is an instance of a quantum algorithm that allows the derivation of an *indirect* measure. It won't tell us what the two states are – that would constitute a measurement. It also does not tell us which state has the larger amplitude. However, it does tell us how similar two unknown states are without having to measure them. The circuit to measure the proximity of qubits $|\psi\rangle$ and $|\phi\rangle$ is shown in Figure 3.7.

Let's denote the state of the 3-qubit system by χ and see how it progresses going from left to right. We use this circuit as a first example to exhaustively derive the related math.

At the start of the circuit, the state is the tensor product of the three qubits:

$$|\chi_0\rangle = |0, \psi, \phi\rangle.$$

The Hadamard gate on qubit 0 superimposes the system to:

$$|\chi_1\rangle = \frac{1}{\sqrt{2}}\left(|0, \psi, \phi\rangle + |1, \psi, \phi\rangle\right).$$

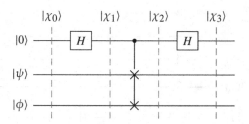

Figure 3.7 The swap test circuit.

The Controlled-Swap gate modifies the second half of this expression because of the controlling $|1\rangle$ state for qubit 0. In the part marked b, $|\phi\rangle$ and $|\psi\rangle$ switch positions:

$$|\chi_2\rangle = \frac{1}{\sqrt{2}}\Big(\underbrace{|0, \psi, \phi\rangle}_{a} + \underbrace{|1, \phi, \psi\rangle}_{b}\Big).$$

The second Hadamard now superimposes further. The first part of the state (marked as a),

$$\frac{1}{\sqrt{2}}\Big(\underbrace{|0, \psi, \phi\rangle}_{a} + \cdots\Big),$$

turns into the following (the Hadamard superposition of the $|0\rangle$ state introduces a plus sign)

$$\frac{1}{\sqrt{2}}\frac{1}{\sqrt{2}}\big(|0, \psi, \phi\rangle + |1, \psi, \phi\rangle\big) + \cdots.$$

The second part (marked as b):

$$\cdots + \underbrace{|1, \phi, \psi\rangle}_{b}\Big),$$

becomes the following state (the Hadamard superposition of $|1\rangle$ introduces a minus sign)

$$\cdots + \frac{1}{\sqrt{2}}\frac{1}{\sqrt{2}}\big(|0, \phi, \psi\rangle - |1, \phi, \psi\rangle\big).$$

Combining the two sub expressions results in state $|\chi_3\rangle$:

$$|\chi_3\rangle = \frac{1}{2}\big(|0, \psi, \phi\rangle + |1, \psi, \phi\rangle + |0, \phi, \psi\rangle - |1, \phi, \psi\rangle\big).$$

This simplifies to the following, pulling out the first qubit (qubit 0):

$$|\chi_3\rangle = \frac{1}{2}|0\rangle\big(|\psi, \phi\rangle + |\phi, \psi\rangle\big) + \frac{1}{2}|1\rangle\big(|\psi, \phi\rangle - |\phi, \psi\rangle\big).$$

Now we measure the first qubit. If it collapses to $|0\rangle$, the second term disappears (it can no longer be measured and has probability 0). We *only* consider measurements that result in state $|0\rangle$ for the first qubit and ignore all others. The probability amplitude of the state collapsing to state $|0\rangle$ is taken from the first term:

$$\frac{1}{2}|0\rangle(|\psi,\phi\rangle + |\phi,\psi\rangle).$$

The probability is computed via squaring the amplitude's norm, which is to multiply the amplitude with its complex conjugate. Here we have to be careful: to compute this square (of amplitude and its complex conjugate) we have to square the whole amplitude to the $|0\rangle$ state, which includes the two tensor products after the $|0\rangle$ itself, as well as the factor of $1/2$:

$$\frac{1}{2}(|\psi,\phi\rangle + |\phi,\psi\rangle)^\dagger \frac{1}{2}(|\psi,\phi\rangle + |\phi,\psi\rangle)$$

$$= \frac{1}{2}(\langle\psi,\phi| + \langle\phi,\psi|)\frac{1}{2}(|\phi,\psi\rangle + |\psi,\phi\rangle)$$

$$= \frac{1}{4}\langle\psi,\phi|\phi,\psi\rangle + \frac{1}{4}\underbrace{\langle\psi,\phi|\psi,\phi\rangle}_{=1} + \frac{1}{4}\underbrace{\langle\phi,\psi|\phi,\psi\rangle}_{=1} + \frac{1}{4}\langle\phi,\psi|\psi,\phi\rangle.$$

The scalar product of a normalized state with itself is 1.0, which means, in the above expression, that the second and third subterms each become $\frac{1}{4}$ and the expression simplifies to:

$$\frac{1}{2} + \frac{1}{4}\langle\psi,\phi|\phi,\psi\rangle + \frac{1}{4}\langle\phi,\psi|\psi,\phi\rangle. \tag{3.3}$$

Now recall how to compute the inner product of two tensors from Equation (1.7). Given two states:

$$|\psi_1\rangle = |\phi_1\rangle \otimes |\chi_1\rangle,$$
$$|\psi_2\rangle = |\phi_2\rangle \otimes |\chi_2\rangle,$$

we compute the inner product as:

$$\langle\psi_1|\psi_2\rangle = \langle\phi_1|\phi_2\rangle\langle\chi_1|\chi_2\rangle.$$

This means we rewrite Equation (3.3) as the following, changing the order of the scalar products; they are just complex numbers:

$$\frac{1}{2} + \frac{1}{4}\langle\psi,\phi|\phi,\psi\rangle + \frac{1}{4}\langle\phi,\psi|\psi,\phi\rangle$$

$$= \frac{1}{2} + \frac{1}{4}\langle\psi|\phi\rangle\langle\phi|\psi\rangle + \frac{1}{4}\langle\phi|\psi\rangle\langle\psi|\phi\rangle$$

$$= \frac{1}{2} + \frac{1}{4}\langle\psi|\phi\rangle\langle\phi|\psi\rangle + \frac{1}{4}\langle\psi|\phi\rangle\langle\phi|\psi\rangle$$

$$= \frac{1}{2} + \frac{1}{2}\langle\psi|\phi\rangle\langle\phi|\psi\rangle.$$

Now let us think about the square of an inner product:

$$\langle\psi|\phi\rangle^2 = \langle\psi|\phi\rangle^*\langle\psi|\phi\rangle = \langle\phi|\psi\rangle\langle\psi|\phi\rangle,$$

which means that for the swap test circuit, the final probability of measuring $|0\rangle$ will be

$$Pr(|0\rangle) = \frac{1}{2} + \frac{1}{2}\langle\psi|\phi\rangle^2.$$

This probability containing the scalar product of the two states is the key for the similarity measurement. Measuring probability for state $|0\rangle$ will give a value close to $1/2$ if the dot product of $|\psi\rangle$ and $|\phi\rangle$ is close to 0, which means that these two states are orthogonal and maximally different. The measurement will give a value close to 1.0 if the dot product is close to 1.0, which means the states are almost identical.

In code, this looks quite simple. In each experiment, we construct the circuit:

```
def run_experiment(a1: np.complexfloating, a2: np.complexfloating,
                   target: float) -> None:
    """Construct swap test circuit and measure."""

    # |0> --- H --- o --- H --- Measure
    #               |
    # a1  --------- x ---------
    #               |
    # a2  ----------x ---------
    psi = state.bitstring(0) * state.qubit(a1) * state.qubit(a2)
    psi = ops.Hadamard()(psi, 0)
    psi = ops.ControlledU(0, 1, ops.Swap(1, 2))(psi)
    psi = ops.Hadamard()(psi, 0)
```

We perform the usual measurement by peek-a-boo and find the probability of qubit 0 to be in state $|0\rangle$:

```
# Measure qubit 0 once.
p0, _ = ops.Measure(psi, 0)
```

That's all there is to it. The variable p0 will be the probability of qubit 0 to be found in the $|0\rangle$ state. What's left to do now is to compare this probability against a target to check that the result is valid. We allow a 5% error margin (0.05):

```
if abs(p0 - target) > 0.05:
    raise AssertionError(
        'Probability {:.2f} off more than 5 pct from target {:.2f}'
        .format(p0, target))
print('Similarity of a1: {:.2f}, a2: {:.2f} ==>   \%: {:.2f}'
        .format(a1, a2, 100.0 * p0))
```

and run a few experiments

```
def main(argv):
    [...]
    print('Swap test. 0.5 means different, 1.0 means similar')
    run_experiment(1.0, 0.0, 0.5)
    run_experiment(0.0, 1.0, 0.5)
    run_experiment(1.0, 1.0, 1.0)
    run_experiment(0.0, 0.0, 1.0)
    run_experiment(0.1, 0.9, 0.65)
    [...]
```

This should produce output similar to the following:

```
Swap test to compare state. 0.5 means different, 1.0 means similar
Similarity of a1: 1.00, a2: 0.00 ==>  %: 50.00
Similarity of a1: 0.00, a2: 1.00 ==>  %: 50.00
Similarity of a1: 1.00, a2: 1.00 ==>  %: 100.00
Similarity of a1: 0.00, a2: 0.00 ==>  %: 100.00
Similarity of a1: 0.10, a2: 0.90 ==>  %: 63.71
[...]
```

3.5   Quantum Teleportation

This section describes the quantum algorithm with one of the most intriguing names of all time – quantum teleportation (Bennett et al., 1993). It is a small example from the fascinating field of quantum information, which includes encryption and error correction. This type of algorithm exploits entanglement to communicate information across spatially separate locations.

The algorithmic story begins, as always, with Alice and Bob, placeholders for the distinct systems A and B. At the beginning of the story, they are together in a lab on Earth and create an entangled pair of qubits, for example, the Bell state $|\beta_{00}\rangle$. Let us mark the first qubit as Alice's and the second one as Bob's:

$$|\beta_{00}\rangle = \frac{|0_A 0_B\rangle + |1_A 1_B\rangle}{\sqrt{2}}$$

```
def main(argv):
    [...]

    # Step 1: Alice and Bob share an entangled pair, and separate.
    psi = bell.bell_state(0, 0)
```

After creating the state, they each take one of the qubits and physically separate – Alice goes to the Moon and Bob ships off to Mars. Let's not worry about how they are getting their super-cooled quantum qubits across the solar system. Nobody said teleportation was easy.

Sitting there on the Moon, Alice happens to be in possession of this other qubit $|x\rangle$, which is in a specific state with probability amplitudes α and β:

$$|x\rangle = \alpha|0\rangle + \beta|1\rangle.$$

Alice does not know what the values of α and β are, and measuring the qubit would destroy the superposition. But Alice wants to communicate α and β to Bob, so that when he measures, he will obtain the basis states of $|x\rangle$ with the corresponding probabilities. How can Alice "send" or "teleport" the state of $|x\rangle$ to Bob? She can do this by exploiting the entangled qubit she already has in her hands from the time before the Moon travel.

In code, let's create the qubit $|x\rangle$ with defined values for α and β so we can check later whether Alice has teleported the correct values to Bob:

```
# Step 2: Alice wants to teleport a qubit |x> to Bob,
#         which is in the state:
#           |x> = a|0> + b|1> (with a^2 + b^2 == 1)
a = 0.6
b = math.sqrt(1.0 - a * a)
x = state.qubit(a, b)
print('Quantum Teleportation')
print('Start with EPR Pair a={:.2f}, b={:.2f}'.format(a, b))
```

Here comes the key "trick": Alice combines the new qubit $|x\rangle$ with the qubit she brought with her from Earth, the one that is entangled with Bob's qubit. We don't concern ourselves with how this might be accomplished in the physical world; we just assume it is possible:

```
# Produce combined state 'alice'.
alice = x * psi
```

Abusing notation a little bit, the combined state is now $|xAB\rangle$, with A representing Alice's entangled qubit on the Moon and B being Bob's entangled qubit on Mars. She now explicitly entangles $|x\rangle$ with the usual technique of applying a Controlled-Not gate:

```
# Alice lets qubit 0 (|x>) interact with qubit 1, which is her
# part of the entangled state with Bob.
alice = ops.Cnot(0, 1)(alice)
```

Finally, she applies a Hadamard gate to $|x\rangle$. Note that the application of an entangler circuit in reverse, with a first Controlled-Not gate followed by a Hadamard gate, is also called making a *Bell measurement*.

```
# Now she applies a Hadamard to qubit 0. Bob still owns qubit 2.
alice = ops.Hadamard()(alice, idx=0)
```

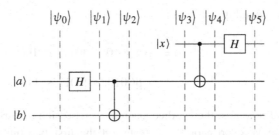

Figure 3.8 Quantum teleportation in circuit notation.

The whole procedure in circuit notation is shown in Figure 3.8. Let us analyze how the state progresses from left to right and spell out the math in great detail. Starting in the lab, before the first Hadamard gate, the state is just the tensor product of the two qubits:

$$|\psi_0\rangle = |0\rangle_A \otimes |0\rangle_B = |0_A 0_B\rangle.$$

The first Hadamard gate creates a superposition of qubit $|0\rangle_A$:

$$|\psi_1\rangle = \frac{|0\rangle_A + |1\rangle_A}{\sqrt{2}} \otimes |0\rangle_B.$$

The Controlled-Not entangles the two qubits and generates a Bell state. We discussed this mechanism in Section 2.11.2 on entanglement. Note that up to this point, Bob and Alice are at the same location: the lab on Earth.

$$|\psi_2\rangle = \frac{|0_A 0_B\rangle + |1_A 1_B\rangle}{\sqrt{2}}.$$

Alice has now traveled to the Moon, where she tensors together her new qubit $|x\rangle$ with the qubit she brought with her from Earth, resulting in state $|\psi_3\rangle$:

$$|\psi_3\rangle = (\alpha|0\rangle + \beta|1\rangle) \otimes \frac{|0_A 0_B\rangle + |1_A 1_B\rangle}{\sqrt{2}}$$

$$= \frac{\alpha|0\rangle(|0_A 0_B\rangle + |1_A 1_B\rangle) + \beta|1\rangle(|0_A 0_B\rangle + |1_A 1_B\rangle)}{\sqrt{2}}.$$

Now we apply the Controlled-Not from $|x\rangle$ to Alice's qubit (this is now qubit 1). This means that the $|1\rangle$ part of the superimposed $|x\rangle$ will flip the controlled qubit. As a result, qubits $|0\rangle_A$ and $|1\rangle_A$ flip in the right-hand side of the expression:

$$|\psi_4\rangle = \frac{\alpha|0\rangle(|0_A 0_B\rangle + |1_A 1_B\rangle) + \beta|1\rangle(|1_A 0_B\rangle + |0_A 1_B\rangle)}{\sqrt{2}}.$$

Finally, we apply the Hadamard gate to $|x\rangle$, which puts $|x\rangle$'s parts $\alpha|0\rangle$ and $\beta|1\rangle$ in superposition:

$$|\psi_5\rangle = \frac{\alpha(|0\rangle + |1\rangle)(|0_A 0_B\rangle + |1_A 1_B\rangle) + \beta(|0\rangle - |1\rangle)(|1_A 0_B\rangle + |0_A 1_B\rangle)}{2}$$

We now multiply this out:

$$|\psi_5\rangle = \frac{1}{2}\big(\alpha(|000\rangle + |011\rangle + |100\rangle + |111\rangle\big)$$
$$+ \beta(|010\rangle + |001\rangle - |110\rangle - |101\rangle)\big)$$

We're almost there. Alice has in her possession the first two qubits. If we regroup the above expression and isolate out the first two qubits, we arrive at our target expression:

$$|\psi_5\rangle = \frac{1}{2}\big(|00\rangle(\alpha|0\rangle + \beta|1\rangle)$$
$$+ |01\rangle(\beta|0\rangle + \alpha|1\rangle)$$
$$+ |10\rangle(\alpha|0\rangle - \beta|1\rangle)$$
$$+ |11\rangle(-\beta|0\rangle + \alpha|1\rangle)\big).$$

Remember that the first two qubits are Alice's, and the third qubit is Bob's. Alice's four basis states have probabilities determined by combinations of α and β. She can measure her first two qubits, while leaving the superposition of Bob's third qubit intact. The probability amplitudes changed, but Bob's qubit remains in superposition.

As Alice measures her two qubits, the state collapses and leaves only one probability combination for Bob's qubit. The final trick is now that Alice *tells* Bob over a classic communication channel what she has measured:

- If she measured $|00\rangle$, we know that Bob's qubit is in the state $\alpha|0\rangle + \beta|1\rangle$.
- If she measured $|01\rangle$, we know that Bob's qubit is in the state $\beta|0\rangle + \alpha|1\rangle$.
- If she measured $|10\rangle$, we know that Bob's qubit is in the state $\alpha|0\rangle - \beta|1\rangle$.
- If she measured $|11\rangle$, we know that Bob's qubit is in the state $-\beta|0\rangle + \alpha|1\rangle$.

Alice succeeded in teleporting the probability amplitudes of $|x\rangle$ to Bob. She still has to classically communicate her measurement results, so there is no faster than light communication. However, the spooky action at a distance "modified" Bob's entangled qubit on Mars to obtain the probability amplitudes from Alice's qubit $|x\rangle$, which she created on the Moon. This spooky action is truly spooky, and also astonishing.

The final step is, depending on Alice's classical communication, to apply gates to Bob's qubit to put it in the actual state of $\alpha|0\rangle + \beta|1\rangle$:

- If she sends 00, nothing needs to be done.
- If she sends 01, Bob needs to flip the amplitudes by applying the X-gate.
- If she sends 10, Bob flips the phase by applying the Z-gate.
- Correspondingly, for 11, Bob applies a Z-gate and a X-gate.

After this, Bob's qubit on Mars will be in the state of Alice's original qubit $|x\rangle$ on the Moon. Teleportation completed. Minds blown.

In code (in file `src/teleportation.py` in the open source repository), we run four experiments, corresponding to the four possible measurement results:

```python
# Alice measures and communicates the result |00>, |01>, ... to Bob.
alice_measures(alice, a, b, 0, 0)
alice_measures(alice, a, b, 0, 1)
alice_measures(alice, a, b, 1, 0)
alice_measures(alice, a, b, 1, 1)
```

For each experiment, we pretend that Alice measured a specific result and apply the corresponding decoder gates to Bob's qubit:

```python
def alice_measures(alice: state.State,
                   expect0: np.complexfloating, expect1: np.complexfloating,
                   qubit0: np.complexfloating, qubit1: np.complexfloating):
  """Force measurement and get teleported qubit."""

  # Alices measure her state and gets a collapsed |qubit0 qubit1>.
  # She let's Bob know which one of the 4 combinations she obtained.
  # We force measurement here, collapsing to a state with the
  # first two qubits collapsed. Bob's qubit is still unmeasured.
  _, alice0 = ops.Measure(alice, 0, tostate=qubit0)
  _, alice1 = ops.Measure(alice0, 1, tostate=qubit1)

  # Depending on what was measured and communicated, Bob has to do
  # one of these things to his qubit2:
  if qubit0 == 0 and qubit1 == 0:
    pass
  if qubit0 == 0 and qubit1 == 1:
    alice1 = ops.PauliX()(alice1, idx=2)
  if qubit0 == 1 and qubit1 == 0:
    alice1 = ops.PauliZ()(alice1, idx=2)
  if qubit0 == 1 and qubit1 == 1:
    alice1 = ops.PauliX()(ops.PauliZ()(alice1, idx=2), idx=2)
```

Then, we measure Bob's qubit and confirm that it matches expectations:

```python
# Now Bob measures his qubit (2) (without collapse, so we can
# 'measure' it twice. This is not necessary, but good to double check
# the maths).
p0, _ = ops.Measure(alice1, 2, tostate=0, collapse=False)
p1, _ = ops.Measure(alice1, 2, tostate=1, collapse=False)

# Alice should now have 'teleported' the qubit in state 'x'.
# We sqrt() the probability, we want to show (original) amplitudes.
bob_a = math.sqrt(p0.real)
bob_b = math.sqrt(p1.real)
```

```
print('Teleported (|{:d}{:d}>)    a={:.2f}, b={:.2f}'.format(
    qubit0, qubit1, bob_a, bob_b))

if (not math.isclose(expect0, bob_a, abs_tol=1e-6) or
    not math.isclose(expect1, bob_b, abs_tol=1e-6)):
    raise AssertionError('Invalid result.')
```

This should result in the following output:

```
Quantum Teleportation
Start with EPR Pair a=0.60, b=0.80
Teleported (|00>)    a=0.60, b=0.80
Teleported (|01>)    a=0.60, b=0.80
Teleported (|10>)    a=0.60, b=0.80
Teleported (|11>)    a=0.60, b=0.80
```

The core idea of exploiting entanglement is found in other algorithms of this type. An interesting example is *superdense coding*, which we discuss next. *Entanglement swapping* would be another representative of this class of algorithms (Berry and Sanders, 2002), but we won't discuss it further here. A sample implementation can be found in file `src/entanglement_swap.py` in the open source repository.

3.6　　Superdense Coding

Superdense coding, another algorithm with a very cool name, takes the core idea from quantum teleportation and turns it on its head. Alice and Bob again share an entangled pair of qubits. Alice takes hers to the Moon, while Bob takes his to Mars. Sitting on the Moon, Alice wants to communicate two classical bits to Bob. Superdense coding encodes two classical bits and sends them to Bob by physically transporting just a single qubit. Two qubits are still needed in total, but the communication is done with just a single qubit.

There exists no other classical compression scheme that would allow the compression of two classical bits into one. Of course, here we are dealing with qubits, which have two degrees of freedom (two angles define the position on a Bloch sphere). The challenge is how to exploit this fact in order to compress information. To understand how this works, we again begin with an entangled pair of qubits (the corresponding code is in file `src/superdense.py`):

```
# Step 1: Alice and Bob share an entangled pair, and separate.
psi = bell.bell_state(0, 0)
```

Alice manipulates her qubit 0 on the Moon according to the rules of how to encode two classical bits into a single qubit, as shown below. In a twist of events, she will classically ship her qubit to Bob's Mars station. There, Bob will disentangle and

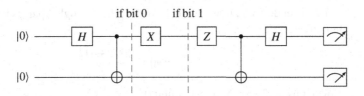

Figure 3.9 Superdense coding in circuit notation.

measure both qubits. Based on the results of the measurement, he can derive Alice's original two classical bits. Alice sent just one qubit to allow Bob to restore two classical bits.

To start the process, Alice manipulates her qubit, which is qubit 0, in the following way.

- If classical bit 0 is set, she applies the X-gate.
- If classical bit 1 is set, she applies the Z-gate.
- Of course, if both bit 0 and bit 1 are set, both the X-gate and Z-gate are being applied.

The whole procedure in circuit notation is shown in Figure 3.9. In code, the two classical bits encode four possible cases (00, 01, 10, and 11). We iterate over these four combinations to drive our experiments:

```
# Alice manipulates her qubit and sends her 1 qubit back to Bob,
# who measures. In the Hadamard basis he would get b00, b01, etc.
# but we're measuring in the computational basis by reverse
# applying Hadamard and Cnot.

for bit0 in range(2):
  for bit1 in range(2):
    psi_alice = alice_manipulates(psi, bit0, bit1)
    bob_measures(psi_alice, bit0, bit1)
```

Here is the routine where Alice manipulates the qubits.

```
def alice_manipulates(psi: state.State,
                      bit0: int, bit1: int) -> state.State:
  """Alice encodes 2 classical bits in her 1 qubit."""

  # Note: This logic applies the Z-gate and X-gate to qubit 0.
  ret = ops.Identity(2)(psi)
  if bit0:
    ret = ops.PauliX()(ret)
  if bit1:
    ret = ops.PauliZ()(ret)
  return ret
```

Let us understand how the math works. The entangled pair is in the Bell state $|\beta_{00}\rangle$ initially:

$$|\beta_{00}\rangle = \frac{|00\rangle + |11\rangle}{\sqrt{2}}.$$

Now let us apply the X-gate to qubit 0:

$$(X \otimes I)|\beta_{00}\rangle = \begin{bmatrix} 0 & 0 & 1 & 0 \\ 0 & 0 & 0 & 1 \\ 1 & 0 & 0 & 0 \\ 0 & 1 & 0 & 0 \end{bmatrix} \frac{1}{\sqrt{2}} \begin{bmatrix} 1 \\ 0 \\ 0 \\ 1 \end{bmatrix} = \frac{1}{\sqrt{2}} \begin{bmatrix} 0 \\ 1 \\ 1 \\ 0 \end{bmatrix} = |\beta_{01}\rangle.$$

Or, in short:

$$(X \otimes I)|\beta_{00}\rangle = \frac{|10\rangle + |01\rangle}{\sqrt{2}} = |\beta_{01}\rangle.$$

Applying the X-gate changes the state and turns it into a different Bell state – it flips the second subscript of the Bell state. This corresponds to setting the classical bit 0 to 1 in Alice's encoding.

Applying the Z-gate changes the state and flips the first subscript of the Bell state, which corresponds to setting classical bit 1 to 1 in Alice's encoding:

$$(Z \otimes I)|\beta_{00}\rangle = \frac{|00\rangle - |11\rangle}{\sqrt{2}} = |\beta_{10}\rangle.$$

Applying both the X-gate and the Z-gate will change the state to $|\beta_{11}\rangle$, indicating that both classical bits 0 and 1 were set to 1. Analogously, as we saw earlier with Equation (3.2), we *could* explicitly apply iY to $|\beta_{00}\rangle$ to yield $|\beta_{11}\rangle$. Of course, this step is not needed here because the prior applications of the X-gate and Z-gate already compound to this effect.

$$(iY \otimes I)|\beta_{00}\rangle = \frac{|01\rangle - |10\rangle}{\sqrt{2}} = |\beta_{11}\rangle.$$

Bob measures in the Hadamard basis, which is another way of saying that before measurement, he converts the state to the computational basis by applying the entangler's Hadamard and Controlled-Not gates in reverse order.

Going through the entangler circuit in reverse uncomputes the entanglement and changes the state to one of the defined basis states $|00\rangle, |01\rangle, |10\rangle$, or $|11\rangle$, depending on the value of the original classical bits. The probability for each possible case is 100%. We will find the classic bit values as they were set by Alice.

```python
def bob_measures(psi: state.State, expect0: int, expect1: int) -> None:
    """Bob measures both bits (in computational basis)."""

    # Change Hadamard basis back to computational basis.
    psi = ops.Cnot(0, 1)(psi)
    psi = ops.Hadamard()(psi)
```

```
p0, _ = ops.Measure(psi, 0, tostate=expect1)
p1, _ = ops.Measure(psi, 1, tostate=expect0)

if (not math.isclose(p0, 1.0, abs_tol=1e-6) or
    not math.isclose(p1, 1.0, abs_tol=1e-6)):
  raise AssertionError(f'Invalid Result p0 {p0} p1 {p1}')

print(f'Expected/matched: {expect0}{expect1}.')
```

This confirms results with 100% probability for the $|0\rangle$ and $|1\rangle$ states, depending on how the qubit was manipulated by Alice. Here is the expected output:

```
Expected/matched: 00
Expected/matched: 01
Expected/matched: 10
Expected/matched: 11
```

3.7   Bernstein–Vazirani Algorithm

The Bernstein–Vazirani algorithm is an example for which the equivalent classical algorithm is of complexity $O(n)$, while the quantum algorithm only requires a single invocation (please note the subtle difference).

Assume we have an input state of n qubits. Also, assume there is another secret string s of the same length consisting of 0s and 1s with the property that the scalar product of the input and output bits equals 1. In other words, if the inputs are b_i and the secret string has bits s_i, then this scalar product should hold:

$$b_0 s_0 + b_1 s_1 + \cdots + b_{n-1} s_{n-1} = 1. \tag{3.4}$$

The goal is to find the secret string s. On a classical computer, we would have to try n times. Each experiment would have an input string of all 0s, except for a single 1. Each iteration where Equation (3.4) holds identifies a 1-bit in s at position t for trial $t \in [0, n-1]$.

In the quantum formulation, we construct a circuit. After the circuit has been applied, the outputs will be in states $|0\rangle$ and $|1\rangle$, corresponding to the secret string's bits, which we encode into a big unitary operator U_f. In the example below, the secret string is 001.

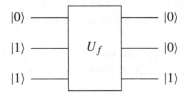

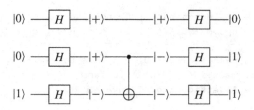

Figure 3.10 Applying Controlled-Not gates to $|+\rangle$ and $|-\rangle$.

To see how this works, we need to understand the mechanics of basis changes. Remember how the $|0\rangle$ and $|1\rangle$ states are put in superposition with Hadamard gates:

$$H|0\rangle = \frac{|0\rangle + |1\rangle}{\sqrt{2}} = |+\rangle, \tag{3.5}$$

$$H|1\rangle = \frac{|0\rangle - |1\rangle}{\sqrt{2}} = |-\rangle. \tag{3.6}$$

As a first step, we create an input state of length n, initialized with all $|0\rangle$, with an additional ancilla qubit in state $|1\rangle$. The main trick of this circuit and algorithm is the following.

If we apply a Controlled-Not from a controlling qubit in the $|+\rangle$ state to a qubit in the $|-\rangle$ state, this has the effect of flipping the controlling qubit into the $|-\rangle$ state! This is the crucial trick because now applying another Hadamard gate will rotate the bases from $|+\rangle$ back to $|0\rangle$ and from $|-\rangle$ to $|1\rangle$. In other words, the qubits on which we applied the Controlled-Not will have the resulting state $|1\rangle$.

We can visualize this effect with the circuit in Figure 3.10, where we symbolically inline the states. Let us write this in code (in file `src/bernstein.py` in the open source repository). First, we create the secret string:

```python
def make_c(nbits: int) -> Tuple[bool]:
  """Make a random constant c from {0,1}, the c we try to find."""

  constant_c = [0] * nbits
  for idx in range(nbits-1):
    constant_c[idx] = int(np.random.random() < 0.5)
  return tuple(constant_c)
```

Next, we construct the circuit, which is also called an *oracle*. The construction is simple – we apply a Controlled-Not for each of the qubits corresponding to 1s in the secret string. For example, for the secret string `1010`, we would construct the circuit in Figure 3.11.

We construct the corresponding circuit as one big unitary operator matrix U. This limits the number of qubits we can use but is still sufficient for exploring the algorithm.

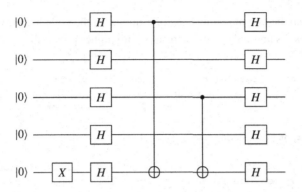

Figure 3.11 The quantum circuit for the Bernstein–Vazirani algorithm with secret string 1010.

```
def make_u(nbits: int, constant_c: Tuple[bool]) -> ops.Operator:
    """Make general Bernstein oracle."""

    op = ops.Identity(nbits)
    for idx in range(nbits-1):
        if constant_c[idx]:
            op = ops.Identity(idx) * ops.Cnot(idx, nbits-1) @ op

    if not op.is_unitary():
        raise AssertionError('Constructed non-unitary operator.')
    return op
```

For the full circuit, we perform the following steps. First we create a secret string of length `nbits-1` and construct the big unitary. Then we build a state consisting of `nbits` states initialized as $|0\rangle$, tensored with an ancilla qubit initialized as $|1\rangle$. We follow this with the big unitary, which we sandwiched between Hadamard gates. As a final step, we measure and compare the results:

```
def run_experiment(nbits: int) -> None:
    """Run full experiment for a given number of bits."""

    c = make_c(nbits-1)
    u = make_u(nbits, c)

    psi = state.zeros(nbits-1) * state.ones(1)
    psi = ops.Hadamard(nbits)(psi)
    psi = u(psi)
    psi = ops.Hadamard(nbits)(psi)
    check_result(nbits, c, psi)
```

To check the results, we measure the probability for all possible states and ensure the state with nonzero probability ($p > 0.1$) matches the secret string. There should only be one matching state of n qubits. In the code below, we iterate over all possible results and only print the results with higher probability.

```python
def check_result(nbits: int, nbits: int, c: Tuple[bool],
                 psi: state.State) -> None
  """Check expected vs. achieved results."""

  print(f'Expected: {c}')

  # The state with the 'flipped' bits will have probability 1.0.
  # It will be found on the very first try.
  for bits in helper.bitprod(nbits):
    if psi.prob(*bits) > 0.1:
      print('Found    : {}, with prob: {:.1f}'
      .format(bits[:-1], psi.prob(*bits)))
      if bits[:-1] != c:
        raise AssertionError('invalid result')
```

That's it! Running this program will produce something like the following output, showing the bit settings and the resulting probabilities:

```
Expected: (0, 1, 0, 1, 0, 0)
Found   : (0, 1, 0, 1, 0, 0), with prob: 1.0
```

3.8   Deutsch's Algorithm

Deutsch's algorithm is another, somewhat contrived, algorithm with no apparent practical use (Deutsch, 1985). However, it was one of the first to showcase the potential power of quantum computers, and therefore it is always one of the first algorithms to be discussed in textbooks. Never fight the trend, let's discuss it right away.

As with the previous section on Bernstein–Vazirani, Deutsch's algorithm is in the class of "oracle" algorithms, where a larger black-box unitary operator performs a critical function. As we discuss the algorithm, it is not clear *how* the oracle is being implemented, but its function can be described, which is sufficient to show the advantages of quantum computing. The impression you get is that there is some "trick" to construct the oracle, a magical quantum way of doing this, which allows the unitary operator to answer specific algorithmic questions. This can be confusing for beginners. It is important to understand that to construct the oracle we need to visit all possible input states and explicitly construct the actual oracle to give the right answers. The oracle can be a circuit or a big permutation matrix.

The oracle is thus not a magical oracle, perhaps more *oracle adjacent*. What really makes the oracle oracle-ish is that we can feed it states in superposition. This leads to quantum parallelism, where all answers are computed in parallel. The ingenuity of a particular algorithm is then to extract some meaningful information from the resulting states, which may be entangled with junk qubits.

There are a handful of oracle algorithms to be found in the literature. We will visit 2.5 of them. First, we will discuss the fundamental Deutsch algorithm, and then, later in this chapter, its extension to more than two input qubits. That's two algorithms, so we add another 1/2 algorithm by showing how to formulate the previously discussed Bernstein–Vazirani algorithm in oracle form as well, using the oracle constructor we develop in this section.

3.8.1 Problem: Distinguish Two Types of Functions

Assume we have a function f that maps a single 0 or 1 to a single 0 or 1:

$$f : \{0, 1\} \rightarrow \{0, 1\}$$

There are four possible cases for this function, which we call *constant* or *balanced*:

$$
\begin{aligned}
f(0) &= 0, & f(1) &= 0 & \Rightarrow \text{constant,} \\
f(0) &= 0, & f(1) &= 1 & \Rightarrow \text{balanced,} \\
f(0) &= 1, & f(1) &= 0 & \Rightarrow \text{balanced,} \\
f(0) &= 1, & f(1) &= 1 & \Rightarrow \text{constant.}
\end{aligned}
$$

Deutsch's algorithm answers the following question: *Given one of these four functions f, which type of function is it: balanced or constant?*

To answer this question with a classical computer, you have to evaluate the function for all possible inputs. In the quantum model, we assume we have an oracle that, given two input qubits $|x\rangle$ and $|y\rangle$, changes the state to Equation 3.7. Note that XOR, denoted by $\oplus$, is equivalent to addition modulo 2, hence the plus sign in the circle:

$$|x, y\rangle \rightarrow |x, y \oplus f(x)\rangle \tag{3.7}$$

The input $|x\rangle$ remains unmodified, $|y\rangle$ is being XOR'ed with $f(|x\rangle)$. This is a formulation that we will see in other oracle algorithms as well – there is always an ancilla $|y\rangle$, and the result of the evaluated function is XOR'ed with that ancilla. Remember that quantum operators must be reversible; this is one of the ways to achieve this.

Assuming we have oracle U_f representing and applying the unknown function $f(x)$, then the Deutsch algorithm can be drawn as the circuit shown in Figure 3.12.

As discussed, it is a convention to start every circuit with all qubits in state $|0\rangle$. The algorithm requires the ancilla qubit to be in state $|1\rangle$, which can be achieved easily by adding an X-gate to the lower qubit. Let us look at the detailed math again. Initially, after the X-gate on qubit 1, the state is:

$$|\psi_0\rangle = |01\rangle.$$

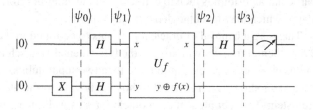

Figure 3.12 The circuit representation of Deutsch's algorithm.

After the first Hadamard gates, the state is in superposition:

$$|\psi_1\rangle = \frac{|0\rangle + |1\rangle}{\sqrt{2}} \otimes \frac{|0\rangle - |1\rangle}{\sqrt{2}}.$$

Applying U_f to this state's second qubit (note the operator $\oplus$ is an XOR in the right side of the equation):

$$|\psi_2\rangle = \frac{|0\rangle + |1\rangle}{\sqrt{2}} \otimes \frac{|0 \oplus f(x)\rangle - |1 \oplus f(x)\rangle}{\sqrt{2}}.$$

If $f(x) = 0$, then $|\psi_2\rangle = |\psi_1\rangle$:

$$|\psi_2\rangle = \frac{|0\rangle + |1\rangle}{\sqrt{2}} \otimes \frac{|0 \oplus 0\rangle - |1 \oplus 0\rangle}{\sqrt{2}}$$

$$= \frac{|0\rangle + |1\rangle}{\sqrt{2}} \otimes \frac{|0\rangle - |1\rangle}{\sqrt{2}}.$$

But if $f(x) = 1$, then

$$|\psi_2\rangle = \frac{|0\rangle + |1\rangle}{\sqrt{2}} \otimes \frac{|0 \oplus 1\rangle - |1 \oplus 1\rangle}{\sqrt{2}}$$

$$= \frac{|0\rangle + |1\rangle}{\sqrt{2}} \otimes \frac{|1\rangle - |0\rangle}{\sqrt{2}}.$$

We can combine the two results into a single expression:

$$|\psi_2\rangle = (-1)^{f(x)} \frac{|0\rangle + |1\rangle}{\sqrt{2}} \otimes \frac{|0\rangle - |1\rangle}{\sqrt{2}}.$$

The first qubit x is in a superposition, so we multiply in the constant factor:

$$|\psi_2\rangle = \frac{(-1)^{f(x)}|0\rangle + (-1)^{f(x)}|1\rangle}{\sqrt{2}} \otimes \frac{|0\rangle - |1\rangle}{\sqrt{2}}.$$

Or, with substituting in the corresponding value for x:

$$|\psi_2\rangle = \frac{(-1)^{f(0)}|0\rangle + (-1)^{f(1)}|1\rangle}{\sqrt{2}} \otimes \frac{|0\rangle - |1\rangle}{\sqrt{2}}. \qquad (3.8)$$

Finally, applying the final Hadamard to the top qubit takes the state from the Hadamard basis back to the computational basis. To see how this works, let us remind ourselves that the Hadamard operator is its own inverse:

$$H|0\rangle = \frac{|0\rangle + |1\rangle}{\sqrt{2}} \quad \text{and} \quad H\frac{|0\rangle + |1\rangle}{\sqrt{2}} = |0\rangle,$$

$$H|1\rangle = \frac{|0\rangle - |1\rangle}{\sqrt{2}} \quad \text{and} \quad H\frac{|0\rangle - |1\rangle}{\sqrt{2}} = |1\rangle.$$

If we look at Equation (3.8) and take $f(0) = f(1) = 0$, we get:

$$
\begin{aligned}
|\psi_2\rangle &= \frac{(-1)^{f(0)}|0\rangle + (-1)^{f(1)}|1\rangle}{\sqrt{2}} \otimes \frac{|0\rangle - |1\rangle}{\sqrt{2}} \\
&= \frac{(-1)^0|0\rangle + (-1)^0|1\rangle}{\sqrt{2}} \otimes \frac{|0\rangle - |1\rangle}{\sqrt{2}} \\
&= \frac{|0\rangle + |1\rangle}{\sqrt{2}} \otimes \frac{|0\rangle - |1\rangle}{\sqrt{2}}.
\end{aligned}
$$

And then, applying the final Hadamard gate to reach state $|\psi_3\rangle$:

$$|\psi_3\rangle = H\frac{|0\rangle + |1\rangle}{\sqrt{2}} \otimes \frac{|0\rangle - |1\rangle}{\sqrt{2}} = |0\rangle \otimes \frac{|0\rangle - |1\rangle}{\sqrt{2}}.$$

For $f(0) = f(1) = 1$ we get the same expression, but with a minus sign in front of the first qubit.

$$|\psi_3\rangle = -|0\rangle \otimes \frac{|0\rangle - |1\rangle}{\sqrt{2}}.$$

For a balanced function, $f(0) = 0$ and $f(1) = 1$, and we get:

$$
\begin{aligned}
|\psi_2\rangle &= \frac{(-1)^{f(0)}|0\rangle + (-1)^{f(1)}|1\rangle}{\sqrt{2}} \otimes \frac{|0\rangle - |1\rangle}{\sqrt{2}} \\
&= \frac{(-1)^0|0\rangle + (-1)^1|1\rangle}{\sqrt{2}} \otimes \frac{|0\rangle - |1\rangle}{\sqrt{2}} \\
&= \frac{|0\rangle - |1\rangle}{\sqrt{2}} \otimes \frac{|0\rangle - |1\rangle}{\sqrt{2}}.
\end{aligned}
$$

And then, applying the final Hadamard gate to reach state $|\psi_3\rangle$:

$$|\psi_3\rangle = H\frac{|0\rangle - |1\rangle}{\sqrt{2}} \otimes \frac{|0\rangle - |1\rangle}{\sqrt{2}} = |1\rangle \otimes \frac{|0\rangle - |1\rangle}{\sqrt{2}}.$$

And similarly, for $f(0) = 1$ and $f(1) = 0$, we get a similar expression, just with a minus sign in front:

$$|\psi_3\rangle = -|1\rangle \otimes \frac{|0\rangle - |1\rangle}{\sqrt{2}}.$$

Table 3.2 Truth table for $f(0) = f(1) = 0$.

x	y	$f(x)$	$y \oplus f(x)$	new state
0	0	0	0	0,0
0	1	0	1	0,1
1	0	0	0	1,0
1	1	0	1	1,1

For a constant function f, we always have a $|0\rangle$ in the front, and in the balanced case the first qubit will always be in state $|1\rangle$. This means that after a single run of the circuit, we can determine the type of f simply by measuring the first qubit.

The superposition allows the computation of the results for both basis states $|0\rangle$ and $|1\rangle$ simultaneously. This is also called *quantum parallelism*. The XOR'ing to the ancilla qubit allows the math to add up in a smart way such that a result can be obtained with high probability. The result does not tell us which specific function it is out of the four possible cases, but it does tell us which of the two classes it belongs to. Because the algorithm is able to exploit superposition to compute the result in parallel, it has a true advantage over the classical equivalent.

3.8.2   Construct U_f

The math in Subsection 3.8.1 is a bit abstract, but things may become clearer when considering how to construct U_f. To reiterate, for a combined state of two qubits, the basis states are:

$$|00\rangle = [1,0,0,0]^T,$$
$$|01\rangle = [0,1,0,0]^T,$$
$$|10\rangle = [0,0,1,0]^T,$$
$$|11\rangle = [0,0,0,1]^T.$$

We want to construct an operator that takes any linear combination of these input states to one with the condition that the second qubit flips to:

$$|x,y\rangle \rightarrow |x, y \oplus f(x)\rangle.$$

We show this by example, followed by the code to compute the oracle operator.

$f(0) = f(1) = 0$

The function f only modifies the second qubit as a function of the first qubit. For the case where $f(0) = f(1) = 0$ the truth table is shown in Table 3.2. The columns x and y represent the input qubits $f(x)$ is constant 0 in this case. The next column shows the result of XOR'ing the function's return value with y, which is $y \oplus f(x)$. The last column finally shows the resulting new state, which leaves the first qubit unmodified and changes the second qubit to the result of the previous XOR.

Table 3.3 Truth table for $f(0) = 0$, $f(1) = 1$.

x	y	$f(x)$	$y \oplus f(x)$	new state
0	0	0	0	0,0
0	1	0	1	0,1
1	0	1	1	1,1
1	1	1	0	1,0

We can express this with a 4×4 permutation matrix, where the rows and columns are marked with the four basis states. We use the combination of x and y as row index, and the new state as column index. In this example, old state and new state are identical, and the resulting U_f matrix is the identity matrix I:

$$
\begin{array}{c c}
 & \begin{array}{cccc} |00\rangle & |01\rangle & |10\rangle & |11\rangle \end{array} \\
\begin{array}{c} |00\rangle \\ |01\rangle \\ |10\rangle \\ |11\rangle \end{array} &
\left(\begin{array}{cccc}
1 & 0 & 0 & 0 \\
0 & 1 & 0 & 0 \\
0 & 0 & 1 & 0 \\
0 & 0 & 0 & 1
\end{array} \right).
\end{array}
$$

Note that this has to be a permutation matrix in order to make this a *reversible* operator.

$f(0) = 0, f(1) = 1$

The construction follows the same pattern as above, with a truth table as shown in Table 3.3. The table translates into this matrix:

$$
\begin{array}{c c}
 & \begin{array}{cccc} |00\rangle & |01\rangle & |10\rangle & |11\rangle \end{array} \\
\begin{array}{c} |00\rangle \\ |01\rangle \\ |10\rangle \\ |11\rangle \end{array} &
\left(\begin{array}{cccc}
1 & 0 & 0 & 0 \\
0 & 1 & 0 & 0 \\
0 & 0 & 0 & 1 \\
0 & 0 & 1 & 0
\end{array} \right).
\end{array}
$$

$f(0) = 1, f(1) = 0$

We apply the same approach for this flavor of $f(x)$, with the truth table as shown in Table 3.4. It translates into this matrix:

$$
\begin{array}{c c}
 & \begin{array}{cccc} |00\rangle & |01\rangle & |10\rangle & |11\rangle \end{array} \\
\begin{array}{c} |00\rangle \\ |01\rangle \\ |10\rangle \\ |11\rangle \end{array} &
\left(\begin{array}{cccc}
0 & 1 & 0 & 0 \\
1 & 0 & 0 & 0 \\
0 & 0 & 1 & 0 \\
0 & 0 & 0 & 1
\end{array} \right).
\end{array}
$$

Table 3.4 Truth table for $f(0) = 1$, $f(1) = 0$.

x	y	$f(x)$	$y \oplus f(x)$	new state
0	0	1	1	0,1
0	1	1	0	0,0
1	0	0	0	1,0
1	1	0	1	1,1

Table 3.5 Truth table for $f(0) = f(1) = 1$.

x	y	$f(x)$	$y \oplus f(x)$	new state
0	0	1	1	0,1
0	1	1	0	0,0
1	0	1	1	1,1
1	1	1	0	1,0

$f(0) = f(1) = 1$

For the final case, the truth table is in Table 3.5. It corresponds to this matrix:

$$
\begin{array}{c}
 \\
|00\rangle \\
|01\rangle \\
|10\rangle \\
|11\rangle
\end{array}
\begin{array}{cccc}
|00\rangle & |01\rangle & |10\rangle & |11\rangle \\
\left(\begin{array}{cccc}
0 & 1 & 0 & 0 \\
1 & 0 & 0 & 0 \\
0 & 0 & 0 & 1 \\
0 & 0 & 1 & 0
\end{array} \right).
\end{array}
$$

3.8.3 Computing the Operator

We can compute this matrix for all cases with the help of the following code snippet (the full implementation is in `src/deutsch.py`), which mirrors how we computed the tables above. Note the `x + xor` construction for the second index below, which is a bit clumsy. We will improve upon this later.

```
def make_uf(f: Callable[[int], int]) -> ops.Operator:
  """Simple way to generate the 2-qubit, 4x4 Deutsch Oracle."""

  u = np.zeros(16).reshape(4, 4)
  for col in range(4):
    y = col & 1
    x = col & 2
    fx = f(x >> 1)
```

```
        xor = y ^ fx
        u[col][x + xor] = 1.0

    op = ops.Operator(u)
    if not op.is_unitary():
        raise AssertionError('Produced non-unitary operator.')
    return op
```

Now we check the four cases/matrices:

```
for i in range(4):
    f = make_f(i)
    u = make_uf(f)
    print(f'Flavor {i:02b}: {u}')
```

which produces output like the following:

```
Flavor 00: Operator for 2-qubit state space. Tensor:
[[1.+0.j 0.+0.j 0.+0.j 0.+0.j]
 [0.+0.j 1.+0.j 0.+0.j 0.+0.j]
 [0.+0.j 0.+0.j 1.+0.j 0.+0.j]
 [0.+0.j 0.+0.j 0.+0.j 1.+0.j]]
Flavor 01: Operator for 2-qubit state space. Tensor:
[[1.+0.j 0.+0.j 0.+0.j 0.+0.j]
 [0.+0.j 1.+0.j 0.+0.j 0.+0.j]
 [0.+0.j 0.+0.j 0.+0.j 1.+0.j]
 [0.+0.j 0.+0.j 1.+0.j 0.+0.j]]

[...] similar for flavors 10 and 11
```

3.8.4 Experiments

To run an experiment, we construct the circuit and measure the first qubit. If it collapses to $|0\rangle$, $f(\cdot)$ was a balanced function, according to the math above. If it collapses to $|1\rangle$, $f(\cdot)$ was a constant function.

First, we define a function `make_f` which returns a function object according to one of the four possible function flavors. We can call the returned function object as $f(0)$ or $f(1)$, it will return 0 or 1:

```
def make_f(flavor: int) -> Callable[[int], int]:
    """Return a 1-bit constant or balanced function f. 4 flavors."""

    # The 4 versions are:
    #   f(0) -> 0, f(1) -> 0   constant
    #   f(0) -> 0, f(1) -> 1   balanced
```

```
#     f(0) -> 1, f(1) -> 0   balanced
#     f(0) -> 1, f(1) -> 1   constant
flavors = [[0, 0], [0, 1], [1, 0], [1, 1]]

def f(bit: int) -> int:
  """Return f(bit) for one of the 4 possible function types."""
  return flavors[flavor][bit]

return f
```

The full experiment first constructs this function object, then the oracle. Hadamard gates are applied to each qubit in an initial state $|0\rangle \otimes |1\rangle$, followed by the oracle operator and a final Hadamard gate on the top qubit:

```
def run_experiment(flavor: int) -> None:
  """Run full experiment for a given flavor of f()."""

  f = make_f(flavor)
  u = make_uf(f)
  h = ops.Hadamard()

  psi = h(state.zeros(1)) * h(state.ones(1))
  psi = u(psi)
  psi = (h * ops.Identity())(psi)
  p0, _ = ops.Measure(psi, 0, tostate=0, collapse=False)

  print('f(0) = {:.0f} f(1) = {:.0f}'
        .format(f(0), f(1)), end='')
  if math.isclose(p0, 0.0):
    print('  balanced')
    if flavor == 0 or flavor == 3:
      raise AssertionError('Invalid result, expected balanced.')
  else:
    print('  constant')
    if flavor == 1 or flavor == 2:
      raise AssertionError('Invalid result, expected constant.')
```

Finally, we check that we get the right answer for all four function flavors:

```
def main(argv):
  if len(argv) > 1:
    raise app.UsageError('Too many command-line arguments.')

  run_experiment(0)
  run_experiment(1)
  run_experiment(2)
  run_experiment(3)
```

which should result in output like this:

```
f(0) = 0 f(1) = 0  constant
f(0) = 0 f(1) = 1  balanced
f(0) = 1 f(1) = 0  balanced
f(0) = 1 f(1) = 1  constant
```

3.8.5   General Oracle Operator

The code above to construct the operator is *almost* general and only depends on the function f to be provided as input. A combination of basis states is being taken to another combination of basis states via a permutation matrix (only a single 1 per row and column), and the process is controlled by the function and XOR operation. In the example above, we only considered one single input qubit and one ancilla qubit (and it had that clumsy addition for the second index), but this can be easily generalized and extended to any number of input bits.

This type of oracle can be used for other algorithms. For reuse, we add this constructor function to the list of operator constructors in `lib/ops.py`.

```python
def OracleUf(nbits: int, f: Callable[[List[int]], int]):
  """Make an n-qubit Oracle for function f (e.g. Deutsch, Grover)."""

  # This Oracle is constructed similar to the implementation in
  # ./deutsch.py, just with an n-bit x and a 1-bit y
  #
  dim = 2**nbits
  u = np.zeros(dim**2).reshape(dim, dim)
  for row in range(dim):
    bits = helper.val2bits(row, nbits)
    fx = f(bits[0:-1])   # f(x) without the y.
    xor = bits[-1] ^ fx

    new_bits = bits[0:-1]
    new_bits.append(xor)

    # Construct new column (int) from the new bit sequence.
    new_col = helper.bits2val(new_bits)
    u[row][new_col] = 1.0

  op = Operator(u)
  if not op.is_unitary():
    raise AssertionError('Constructed non-unitary operator.')
  return op
```

3.8.6   Bernstein–Vazirani in Oracle Form

As promised, we present the Bernstein–Vazirani algorithm in oracle form. Much of the implementation remains the same, but instead of constructing a circuit explicitly with

Controlled-Not gates to represent the secret number, we write an oracle function and call the `OracleUf` constructor above. This also demonstrates how a multi-qubit input can be used to build the oracle. This implementation only supports a single ancilla qubit.

First, we construct the function to compute the dot product between the state and the secret string:

```python
# Alternative way to achieve the same result, using the
# Deutsch Oracle Uf.
#
def make_oracle_f(c: Tuple[bool]) -> ops.Operator:
  """Return a function computing the dot product mod 2 of bits, c."""

  const_c = c
  def f(bit_string: Tuple[int]) -> int:
    val = 0
    for idx in range(len(bit_string)):
      val += const_c[idx] * bit_string[idx]
    return val % 2
  return f
```

And then we repeat much of the original algorithm, but with an oracle:

```python
def run_oracle_experiment(nbits: int) -> None:
  """Run full experiment for a given number of bits."""

  c = make_c(nbits-1)
  f = make_oracle_f(c)
  u = ops.oracleUf(nbits, f)

  psi = state.zeros(nbits-1) * state.ones(1)
  psi = ops.Hadamard(nbits)(psi)
  psi = u(psi)
  psi = ops.Hadamard(nbits)(psi)

  check_result(nbits, c, psi)
```

We run the code to convince ourselves that we implemented all this correctly:

```
Expected: (0, 1, 0, 1, 0, 0)
Found    : (0, 1, 0, 1, 0, 0), with prob: 1.0
```

3.9   Deutsch–Jozsa Algorithm

The Deutsch–Jozsa algorithm is a generalization of the Deutsch algorithm to multiple input qubits (Deutsch and Jozsa, 1992). The function to evaluate is still balanced or constant, but over an expanded domain with multiple input bits:

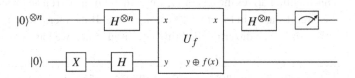

Figure 3.13 The Deutsch–Jozsa algorithm as a circuit diagram.

$$f: \{0,1\}^n \to \{0,1\}.$$

The mathematical treatment of this case parallels the two-qubit Deutsch algorithm. The key result is that we will measure a state of n qubits in the end. If we only find qubits in state $|0\rangle$ then the function is constant; if we find anything else, the function is balanced. The circuit, shown in Figure 3.13, looks similar to the two-qubit case, except that multiple qubits are being handled on both the input and output. The single ancilla qubit at the bottom will still be the key to the answer:

3.9.1   Implementation

Let us focus on the code (in file `src/deutsch_jozsa.py`), which looks quite compact with our U_f operator. First, we create the many-qubit function as either a constant function (all 0s or all 1s with equal probability) or a balanced function (the same number of 0s and 1s, randomly distributed over the length of the input bitstring). We create an array of bits and fill it with 0s and 1s accordingly. Finally, we return a function object that returns one of the values from this prepopulated array, thus representing one of the two function types:

```
def make_f(dim: int = 1,
           flavor: int = exp_constant) -> Callable[[List[int]], int]:
  """Return a constant or balanced function f over 2**dim bits."""

  power2 = 2**dim
  bits = np.zeros(power2, dtype=np.uint8)
  if flavor == exp_constant:
    bits[:] = int(np.random.random() < 0.5)
  else:
    bits[np.random.choice(power2, size=power2//2, replace=False)] = 1

  def f(bit_string:List[int]) -> int:
    """Return f(bits) for one of the 2 possible function types."""

    idx = helper.bits2val(bit_string)
    return bits[idx]

  return f
```

This function drives the rest of the implementation. To run an experiment, we construct the circuit shown in Figure 3.13 and measure. If the measurement finds that only state $|00\ldots0\rangle$ has a nonzero probability amplitude, then we have a constant function.

```python
def run_experiment(nbits: int, flavor: int):
  """Run full experiment for a given flavor of f()."""

  f = make_f(nbits-1, flavor)
  u = ops.OracleUf(nbits, f)

  psi = (ops.Hadamard(nbits-1)(state.zeros(nbits-1)) *
         ops.Hadamard()(state.ones(1)))
  psi = u(psi)
  psi = (ops.Hadamard(nbits-1) * ops.Identity(1))(psi)

  # Measure all of |0>. If all close to 1.0, f() is constant.
  for idx in range(nbits - 1):
    p0, _ = ops.Measure(psi, idx, tostate=0, collapse=False)
    if not math.isclose(p0, 1.0, abs_tol=1e-5):
      return exp_balanced
  return exp_constant
```

Finally, we run the experiments on numbers of qubits ranging from 2 to 7 and ensure that the results match the expectations. Note that we still generate operators and oracles as full matrices, limiting the number of qubits we can handle. We will learn shortly how to expand this number by quite a bit:

```python
def main(argv):
  [...]
  for qubits in range(2, 8):
    result = run_experiment(qubits, exp_constant)
    print('Found: {} ({} qubits) (expected: {})'
          .format(result, qubits, exp_constant))
    if result != exp_constant:
      raise AssertionError('Error, expected {}'.format(exp_constant))

    result = run_experiment(qubits, exp_balanced)
    print('Found: {} ({} qubits) (expected: {})'
          .format(result, qubits, exp_balanced))
    if result != exp_balanced:
      raise AssertionError('Error, expected {}'.format(exp_balanced))

if __name__ == '__main__':
  app.run(main)
```

This should result in output like the following:

```
Found: constant (2 qubits) (expected: constant)
Found: balanced (2 qubits) (expected: balanced)
Found: constant (3 qubits) (expected: constant)
Found: balanced (3 qubits) (expected: balanced)
[...]
Found: constant (7 qubits) (expected: constant)
Found: balanced (7 qubits) (expected: balanced)
```

Other algorithms of this nature are *Simon's algorithm* and *Simon's generalized algorithm* (Simon, 1994). We won't discuss them here, but implementations can be found in the open-source repository in files `simon.py` and `simon_general.py`.

At this point, notice how the execution speed slows down as we increase the number of qubits in this algorithm. Once we reach 10, 11, or 12 qubits, the corresponding operator matrices become very large. Adding a few more qubits makes simulation intractable. To remedy this, we develop ways to make gate application much faster in Chapter 4, increasing our ability to simulate many more qubits.

4   Scalable, Fast Simulation

The concepts and basic infrastructure consisting of tensors, states, and operators, implemented as big matrices and state vectors, are sufficient to implement many small-scale quantum algorithms. All the algorithms in Chapter 3 on simple algorithms were implemented this way.

This basic infrastructure is great for learning and experimenting with the basic concepts and mechanisms of quantum computing. However, for complex algorithms, which typically consist of much larger circuits with many more qubits, this matrix-based infrastructure becomes unwieldy, error-prone, and does not scale. In this chapter we address the scalability problem by developing an improved infrastructure that scales easily to much larger problems. We recommend at least skimming this content before exploring the complex algorithms in Chapter 6. Ultimately, we are building the foundation for a high-performance quantum simulator. You don't want to miss it!

In this chapter, we first give an overview of the various levels of infrastructure that will be developed, with the corresponding computational complexities and levels of performance. We introduce *quantum registers*, which are named groups of qubits. We describe a *quantum circuit model*, where most of the complexity of the base infrastructure is hidden away in an elegant way. To handle the larger circuits of advanced algorithms, we need faster simulation speeds. We detail an approach to apply an operator with linear complexity rather than the $O(n^2)$ method that we started with in Section 2.5.3. We then further accelerate this method with C++, attaining a performance improvement of up $100\times$ over the Python version. For some specific algorithms we can do even better. We describe a sparse state representation, which will be the best-performing implementation for many circuits.

4.1   Simulation Complexity

This book focuses on algorithms and how efficiently simulate them on a classical computer. Quantum simulation can be implemented in a multitude of ways. The key attributes of the various implementation strategies are computational complexity, the resulting performance, and the maximal number of qubits that can be simulated in a *reasonable* amount of time with *reasonable* resource requirements.

The size of the quantum state vector (as described so far) grows exponentially with the number of qubits. For a single qubit, we only need to store two complex numbers, amounting to 8 bytes when using `float` or 16 bytes when using `double` as the underlying data type. Two qubits require four complex numbers; n qubits require 2^n complex numbers. Simulation speed, or the ability to fit a state into memory, is typically measured by the number of qubits at which a given methodology is still tractable. By tractable, we mean that a result that can be obtained in roughly less than an hour. At the time of this writing, the world record in storing and simulating a full wave function stood at 48 qubits (De Raedt et al., 2019).

Because of the exponential nature of the problem, improving performance by a factor of $8\times$ means that we can only handle three more qubits. If we see a speedup of $100\times$, this means we can handle six or seven additional qubits. The following are the five different approaches we describe in this book:

- **Worst**. We have seen this approach already. Implementing gates as potentially very large matrices and constructing operators via matrix-matrix products is of complexity $O(n^3)$. This is the worst case; avoid it if at all possible. It becomes intractable even at relatively small numbers of qubits; performance starts to suffer at $N \sim 8$.
- **Bad**. Instead of constructing big-matrix operators, you can apply gates to the state vector one at a time as matrix-vector products. This leads to complexity $O(n^2)$, which is already a substantial improvement and reaches a number of qubits $N \sim 12$ before becoming intractable.
- **Good**. In Section 4.4, we will learn that one- and two-qubit gates can be applied with a linear traversal over the state, resulting in complexity $O(n)$, a massive improvement over the first two approaches, reaching $N \sim 16$ before becoming intractable.
- **Better**. We started our journey with Python, but we can go faster by using C++. With this approach, in Section 4.5 we will implement the previous `apply` functions in C++, extending Python with its foreign function interface (FFI). Although this approach still has complexity $O(n)$ as above, the performance gain of C++ over Python is about $100\times$ and can reach $N \sim 25$ qubits, depending on the problem.
- **Best**. Using this approach, in Section 4.6 we will change the underlying representation to a sparse one, saving memory and reducing iterations. Additionally, gate application is efficient. This approach is $O(n)$ in the worst case but can win over other implementations by a significant factor. The improvements are possible because for many circuits, the number of nonzero probability states is less than 3%, often even lower. With this, we may reach $N \sim 30$ qubits, or even more for some algorithms.

We could improve our proposed techniques (which are also called *Schröedinger full-state simulations*) further with vectorization (perhaps add one or two qubits), parallelization (64 cores might add $\log_2(64) = 6$ additional qubits), or even by using TPU SuperPODs with 4,096 TensorCores. We could employ machine clusters with 128 or more machines, and corresponding additional qubits, to reach simulation capability of around 45 qubits, utilizing 512 TB of memory. Today's supercomputers would add another handful of qubits (if they were fully dedicated to a simulation job, including all their secondary storage).

These aforementioned techniques are mostly standard High-Performance Computing (HPC) techniques. Since they don't add much to the exposition here, we will not discuss them further. We list a range of open-source solutions in Section 8.5.10, several of which do support distributed simulation (the transpilation techniques detailed in Section 8.5 allow the targeting of several of these simulators). What these numbers demonstrate is how quickly simulation hits limits. Improving performance or scalability by $1,000\times$ only gains about 10 qubits. Adding 20 qubits results in $1,000,000\times$ higher resource requirements.

There are other important simulation techniques. For example, the Schrödinger–Feynman simulation technique, which is based on path history (Rudiak-Gould, 2006; Frank et al., 2009). This technique trades performance for reduced memory requirements. Other simulators work efficiently on restricted gate sets, such as the Clifford gates (Anders and Briegel, 2006; Aaronson and Gottesman, 2004). Furthermore, there is ongoing research on improving simulation of specific circuit types (Markov et al., 2018; Pan and Zhang, 2021). As exciting as these efforts are, they are beyond the scope of this book.

4.2   Quantum Registers

For larger and more complex circuits, we want to make the formulation of algorithms more readable by addressing qubits in named groups. For example, the circuit in Figure 4.1 has a total of eight qubits. We want to name the first four `data`, the next three `ancilla`, and the bottom one `control`. In the example, the gates are just random. On the right side, it shows the global qubit index as g_x, as well as the index into the named groups; for example, global qubit g_5 corresponds to register $ancilla_1$.

These named groups of adjacent qubits are called *quantum registers*. In classical machines, a register typically holds a single value (ignoring vector registers for a moment). A group of registers, or the full physical implementation of registers in hardware, is what is typically called a register file. In that sense, because a quantum register is a named group of qubits, it is more akin to a classical register file, like a group of pipes in a church organ register.

The state of the system is still the tensor product of all eight (global) qubits, numbered from 0 to 7 (g_0 to g_7). At the same time, we want to address `data` with indices ranging from 0 to 3, which should produce the global qubit indices 0 to 3 in the combined state; we want to address `ancilla` from 0 to 2, resulting in global qubit indices 4 to 6; and we want to address `control` with index 0, resulting in global qubit index 7. In code, a simple lookup table will do the trick.

The initial implementation is a bit rough. No worries, we will wrap this up nicely in the next section. We introduce a Python class `Reg` (for "Register") and initialize it by passing the size of the register file we want to create *and* the current global offset,

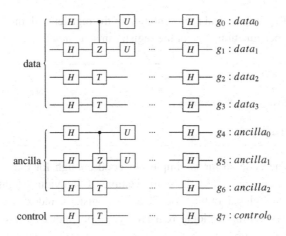

Figure 4.1 Quantum registers *data*, *ancilla*, and *control*.

which has to be manually maintained for this interface. In the example above, the first global offset is 0, for the second register it is 4, and for the last register it is 7.

By default, the states are assumed to be all $|0\rangle$, but an initializer, it, can be passed as well. If it is an integer, it is converted to a string with the number's binary representation. If it is a string (including after the previous step), tuple, or list, the lookup table is initialized with 0s and 1s according to the binary numbers passed. Again, the ordering is from most significant to least significant qubit.

```
class Reg():
  def __init__(self, size: int, it=0, global_reg: int = None):
    self.size = size
    self.global_idx = list(range(global_reg,
                                  global_reg + size))
    self.val = [0] * size

    if it:
      if isinstance(it, int):
        it = format(it, '0{}b'.format(size))
      if isinstance(it, (str, tuple, list)):
        for idx, val in enumerate(it):
          if val == '1' or val == 1:
            self.val[idx] = 1
```

For example, to create and initialize data with $|1011\rangle$ and ancilla with $|111\rangle$, which is the binary representation of decimal 7, and to access global qubit 5, we write:

```
data = state.Reg(4, (1, 0, 1, 1), 0)    # 0b1011
ancilla = state.Reg(3, 7, 4)    # 0b111

# Access global qubit 5 as:
. . . = ancilla[1]
```

To give a textual representation of the register with the initial state, we write a short dumper function to print the register in state notation:

```python
def __str__(self) -> str:
    s = '|'
    for _, val in enumerate(self.val):
        s += f'{val}'
    return s + '>'
```

The code so far is simple but good enough for our next use cases. It does not, for example, allow the initialization of individual registers in superposition. To get the global qubit index from a register's index, we use this function, which allows getting a global register by simply indexing into the register, for example, `greg = ancilla[1]`:

```python
def __getitem__(self, idx: int) -> int:
    return self.global_idx[idx]
```

To initialize a specific qubit (with 0 or 1) at a register index:

```python
def __setitem__(self, idx: int, val: int) -> None:
    self.val[idx] = val
```

To get the size of a register, we also add this standard function:

```python
@property
def nbits(self) -> int:
    return self.size
```

After all this setup, we still have to create an actual state from the register, with:

```python
def psi(self) -> State:
    return bitstring(*self.val)
```

We must only call this function once per initialized register, as a final step. Modifying the initialization value of a register after the state has been created has no effect on the created state. This may not be the most elegant way to do this, but it is compact and sufficient for our purposes. We do not show any code examples here, because we are going to develop a much nicer interface next.

4.3 Circuits

So far we have used full state vectors and operator matrices to implement the initial algorithms. This infrastructure is easy to understand and works quite well for algorithms with a small number of qubits. It is helpful for learning, but the representation is explicit. It exposes the underlying data structures, and that can cause problems:

- Describing states and operators explicitly at a very low level of abstraction requires a lot of typing, which is error-prone.
- The representation exposes the implementation details. Changing aspects of the implementation would be difficult – all users of the base infrastructure would have to be updated.
- A minor point to make is that this style of representation differs from that commonly found in existing frameworks such as Qiskit (Gambetta et al., 2019) or Cirq (Google, 2021c).

The second problem is especially important in our context, as we want to develop faster ways to apply gates, both in Python and C++-accelerated Python. We might want to change the representation of states themselves from storing a full state vector to a sparse representation. The current level of abstraction does not allow that without changing all dependent client code.

In order to remedy these problems, we create a data structure we call a quantum circuit qc. It wraps up and nicely packages all the functions we have discussed so far. The naming convention is all lowercase to distinguish from the explicit representation discussed in Chapters 2 and 3.

A circuit's constructor accepts a string argument to assign a name to a circuit. This name is consequently used in printouts. The circuit has an internally stored quantum state that we initialize to the scalar value of 1.0, indicating that there is no qubit in this circuit right after creation. Here is the constructor:

```
class qc:
  """Wrapper class to maintain state + operators."""

  def __init__(self, name=None):
    self.name = name
    self.psi = 1.0
    state.reset()
```

4.3.1   Qubits

The circuit class supports quantum registers, which immediately add a register's qubits to the circuit's full state. This is the place where the global register count is maintained, hiding away the rough earlier interface of the underlying Reg class:

```
def reg(self, size: int, it, *, name: str = None):
  ret = state.Reg(size, it, self.global_reg)
  self.global_reg = self.global_reg + size
  self.psi = self.psi * ret.psi()
  return ret
```

To add individual qubits to the circuit, we wrap the various constructor functions discussed earlier with corresponding member functions of qc. Each of these generator functions immediately combines the newly generated qubits with the internal state. In order to allow mixing of qubits and registers, we have to update the global register count as well.

```python
def qubit(self,
          alpha: np.complexfloating = None,
          beta: np.complexfloating = None) -> None:
    self.psi = self.psi * state.qubit(alpha, beta)
    self.global_reg = self.global_reg + 1

def zeros(self, n: int) -> None:
    self.psi = self.psi * state.zeros(n)
    self.global_reg = self.global_reg + n

def ones(self, n: int) -> None:
    self.psi = self.psi * state.ones(n)
    self.global_reg = self.global_reg + n

def bitstring(self, *bits) -> None:
    self.psi = self.psi * state.bitstring(*bits)
    self.global_reg = self.global_reg + len(bits)

def arange(self, n: int) -> None:
    self.zeros(n)
    for i in range(0, 2**n):
        self.psi[i] = float(i)
    self.global_reg = self.global_reg + n

def rand(self, n: int) -> None:
    self.psi = self.psi * state.rand(n)
    self.global_reg = self.global_reg + n
```

Of course, we have to have the ubiquitous nbits property, which we forward to the state's function of the same name:

```python
@property
def nbits(self) -> int:
    return self.psi.nbits
```

4.3.2   Gate Application

In order to apply gates to qubits, assume for now that there are two functions to do that, one each for single gates and for controlled gates. We will detail their implementation in the following sections. For now, let us pretend that these functions will apply gates at index idx, while updating the internal state.

```
def apply1(self, gate: ops.Operator, idx: int,
          name: str  = None, *, val: float = None):
    [...]

def applyc(self, gate: ops.Operator, ctl: int, idx: int,
          name: str = None, *, val: float = None):
    [...]
```

The function `apply1` applies the single-qubit gate `gate` to the qubit at `idx`. The gate to be applied may get a name. Some gates require parameters, e.g., the rotation gates, which can be specified with the named parameter `val`.

The function `applyc` operates the same way, but it additionally gets the index of the controlling qubit `ctl`.

4.3.3   Gates

With these two apply functions in place, we can now wrap all standard gates as member functions of the circuit. This is mostly a straightforward wrapping, except for the double-controlled X-gate and the corresponding `ccx` member function, which uses the special construction we saw earlier in Section 3.2.7.

```
def cv(self, idx0: int, idx1: int) -> None:
    self.applyc(ops.Vgate(), idx0, idx1, 'cv')

def cv_adj(self, idx0: int, idx1: int) -> None:
    self.applyc(ops.Vgate().adjoint(), idx0, idx1, 'cv_adj')

def cx(self, idx0: int, idx1: int) -> None:
    self.applyc(ops.PauliX(), idx0, idx1, 'cx')

def cu1(self, idx0: int, idx1: int, value) -> None:
    self.applyc(ops.U1(value), idx0, idx1, 'cu1', val=value)

# [... similar for cy, cz, crk]

def ccx(self, idx0: int, idx1: int, idx2: int) -> None:
    """Sleator-Weinfurter Construction."""

    self.cv(idx0, idx2)
    self.cx(idx0, idx1)
    self.cv_adj(idx1, idx2)
    self.cx(idx0, idx1)
    self.cv(idx1, idx2)

def toffoli(self, idx0: int, idx1: int, idx2: int) -> None:
    self.ccx(idx0, idx1, idx2)

def h(self, idx: int) -> None:
    self.apply1(ops.Hadamard(), idx, 'h')
```

```
def t(self, idx: int) -> None:
  self.apply1(ops.Tgate(), idx, 't')

# [... similar for u1, v, x, y, z, s, yroot]

def rx(self, idx: int, theta: float) -> None:
  self.apply1(ops.RotationX(theta), idx, 'rx')

# [... similar for ry, rz]

# This doesn't go through the apply functions. Don't use.
def unitary(self, op, idx: int) -> None:
  self.psi = ops.Operator(op)(self.psi, idx, 'u')
```

All these gates can be applied with our still-hypothetical two apply functions, except the `unitary` function. This function allows the application of an arbitrarily sized operator, falling back to the full matrix implementation. In the context of qc, this function is an abomination. As a matter of fact, we don't use it for any of the examples and algorithms in this book. We only added it for generality. Don't use it.

4.3.4   Adjoint Gates

We have wrapped operators as member functions of the qc class. But what about adjoints? There appear to be two obvious design choices.

Explicit wrapping. For each gate, offer the apply function as above, as well as a function to apply the adjoint. For example, for the CV-gate, we would offer a member function `qc.cv(...)` as well as `qc.cv_adj(...)`.

Alternatively, we could *add two static functions*:

```
def id(gate: ops.Operator) -> ops.Operator:
  return gate
def adjoint(gate: ops.Operator) -> ops.Operator:
  return gate.adjoint()
```

And add the `id` function as a default parameter to each gate application function. For example, for the S-gate:

```
def s(self, idx: int, trans: Callable = id)  -> None:
  self.apply1(trans(ops.Sgate()), idx, 's')
```

And to apply the adjoint function, call the function with the `adjoint` function as parameter:

```
qc.s(0, circuit.adjoint)
```

This is certainly elegant, especially for compiled languages, which can optimize away the overhead from this construction. Python is relatively slow as is, and we don't want to further slow it down, so we go with the first alternative – we add individual apply functions for adjoint gates, as needed for the code examples.

4.3.5 Measurement

We wrap the measurement operator in a straightforward way:

```
def measure_bit(self, idx: int, tostate: int = 0,
                collapse: bool = True) -> (float, state.State):
  return ops.Measure(self.psi, idx, tostate, collapse)
```

Note that we construct a full-matrix measurement operator, which means this way of measuring won't scale. Fortunately, in many cases we don't have to perform an actual measurement to determine a most likely measurement outcome. We can just look at the state vector and find the one state with the highest probability – we can do *measurement by peek-a-boo*.

For convenience, we also add a statistical sampling function. Its parameter is the probability of measuring $|0\rangle$. For example, we could provide the value 0.25. The function picks a random number in the range of 0.0 to 1.0. If the probability of measuring $|0\rangle$ is lower than this random number, it means that we happened to measure a state $|1\rangle$.

```
def sample_state(self, prob_state0: float):
  if prob_state0 < random.random():
    return 1  # corresponds to |1>
  return 0  # corresponds to |0>
```

To a degree this is silly, as in our infrastructure we know the probabilities for any given state. We don't have to sample over the probabilities to obtain probabilities we already know. Nevertheless, some code might be written in a way as if it would run on an actual quantum computer, and that would make sampling necessary. To mimic this, and also to mirror code that can be found in other infrastructures, we offer this function.

4.3.6 Swap Operations

We also add implementations of the Swap gate (swap) and Controlled Swap gate (cswap), as described earlier in Sections 2.7.3 and 2.7.4. The cswap gate, specifically,

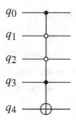

Figure 4.2 A multi-controlled X-gate.

will be used later in Shor's algorithm (Section 6.6). It is easy to implement by simply changing the `cx` gates in a Swap gate to double-controlled `ccx` gates:

```
def swap(self, idx0: int, idx1: int) -> None:
    self.cx(idx1, idx0)
    self.cx(idx0, idx1)
    self.cx(idx1, idx0)

def cswap(self, ctl: int, idx0: int, idx1: int) -> None:
    self.ccx(ctl, idx1, idx0)
    self.ccx(ctl, idx0, idx1)
    self.ccx(ctl, idx1, idx0)
```

4.3.7   Multi-Controlled Gates

To build multi-controlled gates as outlined in Section 3.2.8, we use the following code. We make it quite fancy:

- For the controlling gates, we allow 0, 1, or 2 or more controllers. This makes this implementation quite versatile in several scenarios.
- We allow for Controlled-By-1 gates and Controlled-By-0 gates. To mark a gate as Controlled-By-0, the index `idx` of the controller is passed as a single element list item `[idx]`.

For the example in Figure 4.2, for the X-gate on qubit q_4, which is controlled by By-1 and By-0 control qubits, we make the following function call. Of course, we have to make sure we have reserved enough space for the ancillae in the `aux` register:

```
qc.multi_control([0, [1], [2], 3], 4, aux, ops.PauliX(), 'multi-X'))
```

Here is the full implementation. We also modified the function `applyc` to enable Controlled-By-0 gates by emitting an X-gate before and after the controller qubit (not shown here).

```python
def multi_control(self, ctl, idx1, aux, gate, desc: str):
  """Multi-Controlled gate, using aux as ancilla."""

  # This is a simpler version that requires n-1 ancillae, instead
  # of n-2. The benefit is that the gate can be used as a
  # single-controlled gate, which means we don't need to take the
  # root (no need to include scipy). This construction also makes
  # the Controlled-By-0 gates a little bit easier, those controllers
  # are being passed as single-element lists, eg.:
  #   ctl = [1, 2, [3], [4], 5]
  #
  # This can be optimized (later) to turn into a space-optimized
  # n-2 version.
  #
  # We also generalize to the case where ctl is empty or only has 1
  # control qubit. This is very flexible and practically any gate
  # could be expressed this way. This would make bulk control of
  # whole gate sequences straightforward, but changes the trivial
  # IR we're working with here. Something to keep in mind.
  with self.scope(self.ir, f'multi({ctl}, {idx1}) # {desc})'):
    if len(ctl) == 0:
      self.apply1(gate, idx1, desc)
      return
    if len(ctl) == 1:
      self.applyc(gate, ctl[0], idx1, desc)
      return

    # Compute the predicate.
    self.ccx(ctl[0], ctl[1], aux[0])
    aux_idx = 0
    for i in range(2, len(ctl)):
      self.ccx(ctl[i], aux[aux_idx], aux[aux_idx+1])
      aux_idx = aux_idx + 1

    # Use predicate to single-control qubit at idx1.
    self.applyc(gate, aux[aux_idx], idx1, desc)

    # Uncompute predicate.
    aux_idx = aux_idx - 1
    for i in range(len(ctl)-1, 1, -1):
      self.ccx(ctl[i], aux[aux_idx], aux[aux_idx+1])
      aux_idx = aux_idx - 1
    self.ccx(ctl[0], ctl[1], aux[0])
```

4.3.8   Example

To show an example of how to use the circuit model, here is the classical arithmetic adder circuit using the matrix-based infrastructure:

```
def fulladder_matrix(psi: state.State) -> state.State:
    """Non-quantum-exploiting, classic full adder."""

    psi = ops.Cnot(0, 3)(psi, 0)
    psi = ops.Cnot(1, 3)(psi, 1)
    psi = ops.ControlledU(0, 1, ops.Cnot(1, 4))(psi, 0)
    psi = ops.ControlledU(0, 2, ops.Cnot(2, 4))(psi, 0)
    psi = ops.ControlledU(1, 2, ops.Cnot(2, 4))(psi, 1)
    psi = ops.Cnot(2, 3)(psi, 2)
    return psi
```

And here is the formulation using the quantum circuit. It is considerably more compact. It also hides the implementation details, which means we will be able to accelerate the circuit later (in Sections 4.4 and 4.5) by providing fast implementations of the `apply` functions.

```
def fulladder_qc(qc: circuit.qc) -> None:
    """Non-quantum-exploiting, classic full adder."""

    qc.cx(0, 3)
    qc.cx(1, 3)
    qc.ccx(0, 1, 4)
    qc.ccx(0, 2, 4)
    qc.ccx(1, 2, 4)
    qc.cx(2, 3)
```

As we will see later in Section 8.5, this wrapper class makes it easy to augment the implementations of the gate application functions to add functionality for transpilation of a circuit to other forms, e.g., QASM (Cross et al., 2017), Cirq (Google, 2021c), or Qiskit (Gambetta et al., 2019).

But wait – we have not yet detailed the `apply` functions! They will be the topic of the next sections.

4.4   Fast Gate Application

Up to this point, we have applied a gate by first tensoring it with identity matrices and then applying the resulting large matrix to a full state vector. As described in the introductory notes in Section 4.1, this does not scale well beyond a small number of qubits. For ten qubits, the augmented matrix is already a 1024×1024 matrix, requiring 1024^2 multiplications and additions. Can we devise a more efficient way to apply gates? Yes, we can.

Let's analyze what happens during gate application. To start the analysis, we create a pseudo state vector which is *not* normalized, but allows the visualization of what happens to it as gates are applied to individual qubits.

```
qc = circuit.qc('test')
qc.arange(4)
print(qc.psi)
>>
4-qubit state. Tensor:
[ 0.+0.j  1.+0.j  2.+0.j  3.+0.j  4.+0.j  5.+0.j  6.+0.j  7.+0.j  8.+0.j
  9.+0.j 10.+0.j 11.+0.j 12.+0.j 13.+0.j 14.+0.j 15.+0.j]
```

Now we apply the X-gate to qubits 0 to 3, one by one, always starting with a freshly created vector. The X-gate is interesting in that it multiplies state vector entries by 0 and 1, causing values to swap. This is similar to how applying the X-gate to a regular qubit "flips" $|0\rangle$ and $|1\rangle$.

```
# Let's try this for qubits 0 to 3.
for idx in range(4):
    qc = circuit.qc('test')

    # Populate vector with values 0 to 15.
    qc.arange(4)

    # Apply X-gate to qubit at index `idx`.
    qc.x(idx)
    print('Applied X to qubit {}: {}'.format(idx, qc.psi))
```

First we apply the X-gate to qubit 0 to get this result:

```
Applied X to qubit 0: 4-qubit state. Tensor:
[ 8.+0.j  9.+0.j 10.+0.j 11.+0.j 12.+0.j 13.+0.j 14.+0.j 15.+0.j
  0.+0.j  1.+0.j  2.+0.j  3.+0.j  4.+0.j  5.+0.j  6.+0.j  7.+0.j]
```

It appears the right half of the vector was swapped with the left half. Let's try the next qubit index. Applying the X-gate to qubit 1 results in:

```
Applied X to qubit 1: 4-qubit state. Tensor:
[ 4.+0.j  5.+0.j  6.+0.j  7.+0.j  0.+0.j  1.+0.j  2.+0.j  3.+0.j
 12.+0.j 13.+0.j 14.+0.j 15.+0.j  8.+0.j  9.+0.j 10.+0.j 11.+0.j]
```

Now it appears that chunks of four vector elements are being swapped. The elements 4–7 swap position with elements 0–3, and the elements 12–15 swap position with elements 8–11. A pattern is emerging. Let us apply the X-gate to qubit 2:

```
Applied X to qubit 2: 4-qubit state. Tensor:
[ 2.+0.j   3.+0.j   0.+0.j   1.+0.j   6.+0.j   7.+0.j   4.+0.j   5.+0.j
 10.+0.j  11.+0.j   8.+0.j   9.+0.j  14.+0.j  15.+0.j  12.+0.j  13.+0.j]
```

The pattern continues: now groups of two elements are swapped. And finally, for qubit 3 we see that individual qubits are being swapped:

```
Applied X to qubit 3: 4-qubit state. Tensor:
[ 1.+0.j   0.+0.j   3.+0.j   2.+0.j   5.+0.j   4.+0.j   7.+0.j   6.+0.j   9.+0.j
  8.+0.j  11.+0.j  10.+0.j  13.+0.j  12.+0.j  15.+0.j  14.+0.j]
```

We recognize a clear "power-of-2" pattern. The vector has $2^4 = 16$ elements, corresponding to four qubits. To express numbers from 0–15, we need four classical bits: $b_3 b_2 b_1 b_0$. Remember that we enumerate qubits from left to right and classical bits from right to left. Also, remember that we are using the X-gate, which multiplies by 0s and 1s, leaving the impression of swapping elements.

- **Qubit 0**. Applying the X-gate to qubit 0 swaps the first half of the state vector with the second half.

   If we interpret vector indices in binary, the state elements with indices that had bit 3 set (most significant bit) switched position with the indices that did not have bit 3 set. Positions 8–15 had bit 3 set and switched positions with 0–7, which did not have bit 3 set. One block of eight elements got switched.

- **Qubit 1**. Applying the X-gate to qubit 1 swaps the second quarter of the state vector with the first, and the fourth quarter with the third.

   Correspondingly, the vector elements with indices that had bit 2 set switched with the ones that have bit 2 not set, "bracketed" by the bit pattern in bit 3. What does it mean that an index is bracketed by a higher-order bit? It simply means that the higher-order bit did not change, it remained 0 or 1. Only the lower order bits switch between 0 and 1. Blocks of four elements were switched at a time and there are two brackets for qubit index 1.

- **Qubit 2**. Applying the X-gate to qubit 2 swaps the second eighth of the state vector with the first, the fourth with the third, the sixth with the fifth, and so on.

   Similar to above, the vector elements with indices that had bit 1 set switched with the ones that didn't have bit 1 set. This swapping is bracketed by the bit pattern in bit 2 and further bracketed by the bit patterns of bit 3.

- **Qubit 3**. Finally, and again similar to above, applying the X-gate to qubit 3 now swaps single elements: element 0 swaps with element 1, element 3 swaps with element 2, and so on.

We can put this pattern in a closed form by looking at the binary bit pattern for the state vector indices (Smelyanskiy et al., 2016). Let us introduce this *bit index* notation for a state with a classical binary bit representation (where we omit the state brackets $|\cdot\rangle$ for ease of notation):

$$\psi_{\beta_{n-1}\beta_{n-2}...\beta_0}$$

If we expect a specific 0 or 1 at a given bit position k, we specify this bit value in the notation:

$$\psi_{\beta_{n-1}\beta_{n-2}...0_k...\beta_0}$$
$$\psi_{\beta_{n-1}\beta_{n-2}...1_k...\beta_0}$$

As an example, the state $|01101\rangle$ can be written as decimal $|13\rangle$ or ψ_{01101} in this notation.

Applying a single-qubit gate on qubit k in an n-qubit state (qubits 0 to $n-1$) applies the gate to a pair of amplitudes whose indices differ in bit $(n-1-k)$ in binary representation. In our first example, we have four qubits. Qubit 0 translates to classical bit 3 in this notation, and qubit 3 corresponds to classical bit 0. We apply the X-gate to the probability amplitudes that correspond to the states where the bit index switches between 0 and 1, thus swapping chunks of the state vector. The swapping happens because we applied the X-gate. Again, the same approach will work for all gates; it just becomes visual and easy to understand for the X-gate.

In general, we want to apply a gate G to a qubit of a system in state $|\psi\rangle$, where G is a 2×2 matrix. Let us name the four matrix elements G_{00}, G_{01}, G_{10}, and G_{11}, corresponding to left-top, right-top, left-bottom, and right-bottom.

Applying a gate G to the kth qubit corresponds to the following recipe. This notation indicates looping over the full state vector. All vector elements whose indices match the specified bit patterns are being multiplied with the gate elements G_{00}, G_{01}, G_{10}, and G_{11}, as specified in this recipe.

$$\psi_{\beta_{n-1}\beta_{n-2}...0_k...\beta_0} = G_{00}\,\psi_{\beta_{n-1}\beta_{n-2}...0_k...\beta_0} + G_{01}\,\psi_{\beta_{n-1}\beta_{n-2}...1_k...\beta_0}$$

$$\psi_{\beta_{n-1}\beta_{n-2}...1_k...\beta_0} = G_{10}\,\psi_{\beta_{n-1}\beta_{n-2}...0_k...\beta_0} + G_{11}\,\psi_{\beta_{n-1}\beta_{n-2}...1_k...\beta_0}$$

For controlled gates, the pattern can be extended. We have to ensure that the control bit c is set to 1 and only apply the gates to states for which this is the case:

$$\psi_{\beta_{n-1}\beta_{n-2}...1_c...0_k...\beta_0} = G_{00}\,\psi_{\beta_{n-1}\beta_{n-2}...1_c...0_k...\beta_0} + G_{01}\,\psi_{\beta_{n-1}\beta_{n-2}...1_c...1_k...\beta_0}$$

$$\psi_{\beta_{n-1}\beta_{n-2}...1_c...1_k...\beta_0} = G_{10}\,\psi_{\beta_{n-1}\beta_{n-2}...1_c...0_k...\beta_0} + G_{11}\,\psi_{\beta_{n-1}\beta_{n-2}...1_c...1_k...\beta_0}$$

In the implementation, we have to be mindful of the qubit ordering. Qubit 0 is the topmost qubit, but for the bit patterns, as is common, classical bit 0 is the least significant bit. So in our implementation, we have to reverse the bit indices.

To apply a single gate, we add this function to our implementation of states in file lib/state.py (with 1<<n as an optimized version of 2**n):

```python
def apply(self, gate: ops.Operator, index: int) -> None:
  """Apply single-qubit gate to this state."""

  # To maintain qubit ordering in this infrastructure,
  # index needs to be reversed.
  #
  index = self.nbits - index - 1
  pow_2_index = 1 << index
  g00 = gate[0, 0]
  g01 = gate[0, 1]
  g10 = gate[1, 0]
  g11 = gate[1, 1]
  for g in range(0, 1 << self.nbits, 1 << (index+1)):
    for i in range(g, g + pow_2_index):
      t1 = g00 * self[i] + g01 * self[i + pow_2_index]
      t2 = g10 * self[i] + g11 * self[i + pow_2_index]
      self[i] = t1
      self[i + pow_2_index] = t2
```

The implementation for controlled gates is very similar, but note the additional if statement in the code, checking whether or not the control bit is set:

```python
def applyc(self, gate: ops.Operator, ctrl: int, target: int) -> None:
  """Apply a controlled 2-qubit gate via explicit indexing."""

  # To maintain qubit ordering in this infrastructure,
  # index needs to be reversed.
  qbit = self.nbits - target - 1
  pow_2_index = 2**qbit
  ctrl = self.nbits - ctrl - 1
  g00 = gate[0, 0]
  g01 = gate[0, 1]
  g10 = gate[1, 0]
  g11 = gate[1, 1]
  for g in range(0, 1 << self.nbits, 1 << (qbit+1)):
    idx_base = g * (1 << self.nbits)
    for i in range(g, g + pow_2_index):
      idx = idx_base + i
      if idx & (1 << ctrl):
        t1 = g00 * self[i] + g01 * self[i + pow_2_index]
        t2 = g10 * self[i] + g11 * self[i + pow_2_index]
        self[i] = t1
        self[i + pow_2_index] = t2
```

4.4.1   Benchmarking

The complexity of this method is now $O(n)$, compared to $O(n^2)$ for matrix-vector multiplication. To see how quickly one outperforms the other, we write a quick test. This is not "rocket surgery," but the effects are too pleasing to ignore.

```python
def single_gate_complexity() -> None:
  """Compare times for full matmul vs single-gate."""

  nbits = 12
  qubit = random.randint(0, nbits-1)
  gate = ops.PauliX()

  def with_matmul():
    psi = state.zeros(nbits)
    op = ops.Identity(qubit) * gate * ops.Identity(nbits - qubit - 1)
    psi = op(psi)

  def apply_single():
    psi = state.zeros(nbits)
    psi = apply_single_gate(gate, qubit, psi)

  print('Time with full matmul: {:.3f} secs'
        .format(timeit.timeit(with_matmul, number=1)))
  print('Time with single gate: {:.3f} secs'
        .format(timeit.timeit(apply_single, number=1)))
```

Using mildly unscientific methodology, we see a significant performance difference of over $100\times$ for 12 qubits already:

```
Time with full matmul: 0.627 secs
Time with single gate: 0.004 secs
```

We could now add these routines to the quantum circuit class, but wait – we can do even better and accelerate these routines with C++. This will be the topic of the next section.

4.5   Accelerated Gate Application

We now understand how to apply gates to a state vector with linear complexity, but the code was in Python, which is known to execute slower than C++. In order to add a few more qubits to our simulation capabilities and accelerate gate application, we implement the gate application functions in C++ and import them into Python using standard extension techniques.

This section contains a lot of C++ code. The core principles were shown in Section 4.4; there is not much new here, except some fun observations about performance at the end. We still detail this code as it might be of value for readers with no experience extending Python with fast C++. The actual open-source code is about 150 lines long and available in the open-source repository.

The key routines are in a file xgates.cc for "accelerated gates". The <path> to numpy must be set correctly to point to a local setup. The open-source repository will have the latest instructions on how to compile and use this Python extension. We also want to support both float and double complex numbers, so we templatize the code accordingly.

```cpp
// Make sure this header can be found:
#include <Python.h>

#include <stdio.h>
#include <stdlib.h>
#include <complex>

// Configure the path, likely in the BUILD file:
#include "<path>/numpy/core/include/numpy/ndarraytypes.h"
#include "<path>/numpy/core/include/numpy/ufuncobject.h"
#include "<path>/numpy/core/include/numpy/npy_3kcompat.h"

typedef std::complex<double> cmplxd;
typedef std::complex<float> cmplxf;

// apply1 applies a single gate to a state.
//
// Gates are typically 2x2 matrices, but in this implementation they
// are flattened to a 1x4 array:
//     a b
//     c d   -> a b c d
//
template <typename cmplx_type>
void apply1(cmplx_type *psi, cmplx_type gate[4],
            int nbits, int tgt) {
  tgt = nbits - tgt - 1;
  int q2 = 1 << tgt;
  for (int g = 0; g < 1 << nbits; g += (1 << (tgt+1))) {
    for (int i = g; i < g + q2; ++i) {
      cmplx_type t1 = gate[0] * psi[i] + gate[1] * psi[i + q2];
      cmplx_type t2 = gate[2] * psi[i] + gate[3] * psi[i + q2];
      psi[i] = t1;
      psi[i + q2] = t2;
    }
  }
}
```

```
// applyc applies a controlled gate to a state.
template <typename cmplx_type>
void applyc(cmplx_type *psi, cmplx_type gate[4],
            int nbits, int ctl, int tgt) {
  //[... similar to above, but for controlled gates]
}
```

The code above mirrors the Python implementation very closely. To now extend Python and make this extension loadable as a shared module, we add standard Python bindings code for single-qubit gates:

```
template <typename cmplx_type, int npy_type>
void apply1_python(PyObject *param_psi, PyObject *param_gate,
                   int nbits, int tgt) {
  PyObject *psi_arr =
    PyArray_FROM_OTF(param_psi, npy_type, NPY_IN_ARRAY);
  cmplx_type *psi = ((cmplx_type *)PyArray_GETPTR1(psi_arr, 0));

  PyObject *gate_arr =
    PyArray_FROM_OTF(param_gate, npy_type, NPY_IN_ARRAY);
  cmplx_type *gate = ((cmplx_type *)PyArray_GETPTR1(gate_arr, 0));

  apply1<cmplx_type>(psi, gate, nbits, tgt);

  Py_DECREF(psi_arr);
  Py_DECREF(gate_arr);
}

static PyObject *apply1_c(PyObject *dummy, PyObject *args) {
  PyObject *param_psi = NULL;
  PyObject *param_gate = NULL;
  int nbits;
  int tgt;
  int bit_width;

  if (!PyArg_ParseTuple(args, "OOiii", &param_psi, &param_gate,
                        &nbits, &tgt, &bit_width))
    return NULL;
  if (bit_width == 128) {
    apply1_python<cmplxd, NPY_CDOUBLE>(param_psi,
                                       param_gate, nbits, tgt);
  } else {
    apply1_python<cmplxf, NPY_CFLOAT>(param_psi,
                                      param_gate, nbits, tgt);
  }
  Py_RETURN_NONE;
}
```

There is, of course, similar code for the controlled gates in the open-source repository. The following are the functions the Python interpreter will call when importing a module. We register the Python wrappers in a module named xgates with standard boilerplate code:

```
// Python boilerplate to expose above wrappers to programs.
static PyMethodDef xgates_methods[] = {
    {"apply1", apply1_c, METH_VARARGS,
     "Apply single-qubit gate, complex double"},
    {"applyc", applyc_c, METH_VARARGS,
     "Apply controlled qubit gate, complex double"},
    {NULL, NULL, 0, NULL}};

static struct PyModuleDef xgates_definition = {
  PyModuleDef_HEAD_INIT,
  "xgates",
  "Python extension to accelerate quantum simulation math",
  -1,
  xgates_methods
};

PyMODINIT_FUNC PyInit_xgates(void) {
  Py_Initialize();
  import_array();
  return PyModule_Create(&xgates_definition);
}
```

In order for Python to be able to find this extension, we typically set an environment variable. For example, on Linux:

```
export PYTHONPATH=path_to_xgates.so
```

Alternatively, you can extend Python's module search path programmatically with code like this:

```
import sys
sys.path.append('/path/to/search')
```

4.5.1   Circuits Finally Finalized

With our accelerated implementation, we can finally finish the apply function in the quantum circuit qc class. Both single-qubit gates and controlled gates can be applied to qubits, but, for convenience, single-qubit gates can also be applied to whole registers:

```
import xgates

def apply1(self, gate: ops.Operator, idx: int,
          name: str = None, *, val: float = None):
  if isinstance(idx, state.Reg):
    for reg in range(idx.nbits):
      xgates.apply1(self.psi, gate.reshape(4), self.psi.nbits,
                    idx[reg], tensor.tensor_width)
    return
  xgates.apply1(self.psi, gate.reshape(4), self.psi.nbits, idx,
                tensor.tensor_width)

def applyc(self, gate: ops.Operator, ctl: int, idx: int,
          name: str = None, *, val: float = None):
  if isinstance(idx, state.Reg):
    raise AssertionError('controlled register not supported')
  xgates.applyc(self.psi, gate.reshape(4), self.psi.nbits, ctl,
                idx, tensor.tensor_width)
```

4.5.2 Premature Optimization, First Act

Looking at the standard gates, we find a lot of 0s and 1s, which means that several gate applications should run faster if we optimized for these special cases. Emphasis on *should*. Let us run an experiment to verify this assumption.

We construct a benchmark to compare the general gate application routines with ones that are specialized for the X-gate, which has two 0s and two 1s. This should enable us to save a total of four multiplies, two additions, and perhaps some memory accesses per single qubit. In other words, for this original inner loop:

```
for (int i = g; i < g + q2; ++i) {
  cmplx t1 = gate[0][0] * psi[i] + gate[0][1] * psi[i + q2];
  cmplx t2 = gate[1][0] * psi[i] + gate[1][1] * psi[i + q2];
  psi[i] = t1;
  psi[i + q2] = t2;
}
```

This is a modified and seemingly faster variant of the inner loop, which avoids at least four multiplications:

```
for (int i = g; i < g + q2; ++i) {
  cmplx t1 = psi[i + q2];
  cmplx t2 = psi[i];
  psi[i] = t1;
  psi[i + q2] = t2;
}
```

In the code below, we only show the implementation of the noncontrolled gates, but we benchmark both single gates and controlled gates. At the time of writing, the specific benchmarking infrastructure BENCHMARK_BM was not open-sourced, but there are countless other ways available in open-source for this type of benchmarking.

```cpp
typedef std::complex<double> cmplx;
static const int nbits = 22;
static cmplx* psi;

void apply_single(cmplx* psi, cmplx gate[2][2], int nbits, int qubit) {
  int q2 = 1 << qubit;
  for (int g = 0; g < 1 << nbits; g += 1 << (qubit+1)) {
    for (int i = g; i < g + q2; ++i) {
      cmplx t1 = gate[0][0] * psi[i] + gate[0][1] * psi[i + q2];
      cmplx t2 = gate[1][0] * psi[i] + gate[1][1] * psi[i + q2];
      psi[i] = t1;
      psi[i + q2] = t2;
    }
  }
}

void apply_ctl(cmplx* psi, cmplx gate[2][2], int nbits,
               int ctl, int tgt) {
  [...]
}

// --- Benchmark full gates ---
void BM_apply_single(benchmark::State& state) { [...] }
BENCHMARK(BM_apply_single);

void BM_apply_controlled(benchmark::State& state) { [...] }
BENCHMARK(BM_apply_controlled);

// --- "Optimized Gates" ---
void apply_single_opt(cmplx* psi, int nbits, int qubit) {
  int q2 = 1 << qubit;
  for (int g = 0; g < 1 << nbits; g += 1 << (qubit + 1)) {
    for (int i = g; i < g + q2; ++i) {
      cmplx t1 = psi[i + q2];
      cmplx t2 = psi[i];
      psi[i] = t1;
      psi[i + q2] = t2;
    }
  }
}

void apply_ctl_opt(cmplx* psi, int nbits, int ctl, int tgt) {
  [... similar to apply_single_opt, but controlled version]
}
```

Table 4.1 Benchmark results (program output), comparing hand-optimized and nonoptimized gate application routines.

Benchmark	Time(ns)	CPU(ns)	Iterations
BM_apply_single	116403527	116413785	24
BM_apply_single_opt	132820169	132829412	21
BM_apply_controlled	81595871	81600200	34
BM_apply_controlled_opt	89064964	89072559	31

```
// --- Benchmark optimized gates ---
void BM_apply_single_opt(benchmark::State& state) { [...] }
BENCHMARK(BM_apply_single_opt);
void BM_apply_controlled_opt(benchmark::State& state) { [...] }
BENCHMARK(BM_apply_controlled_opt);
```

The performance results are shown in Table 4.1. Remember our hypothesis that the optimized version would be faster, because it executes fewer multiplications and additions. Column Iterations shows iterations per second; higher is better.

The specialized version runs about 10% *slower*! For the given x86 platform, the compiler was able to vectorize the nonspecialized version, leading to a slightly higher overall throughput. Intuition is good, validation is better.

In summary, we found a way to apply gates with linear complexity and accelerated it by another significant factor with C++. Performance comparison to the Python version shows a speedup of about 100×. This should add six or seven additional qubits to our simulation capabilities. This infrastructure is sufficient for all remaining algorithms in this book.

There are other ways to simulate quantum computing (Altman et al., 2021), as we discussed at the end of Section 4.1. There is one specific, interesting way to represent states *sparsely*. For many circuits this is a very efficient data structure. We give a brief overview of it in Section 4.6 and provide full implementation details in the Appendix.

4.6 Sparse Representation

So far, our data structure for representing quantum states is a dense array holding all probability amplitudes for all superimposed states, where the amplitude for a specific state can be found via binary indexing. However, for many circuits and algorithms, there can be a high percentage of states with close to zero probability. Storing these 0-states and applying gates to them will have no effect and is wasteful. This fact can be exploited with a sparse representation. An excellent reference implementation of this principle can be found in the venerable, open source libquantum library (Butscher and Weimer, 2013).

We re-implement the core ideas of that library as they pertain to this book; libquantum addresses other aspects of quantum information, which we do not cover. We therefore name our implementation libq to distinguish it from the original. The original library is in plain C, but our implementation was moderately updated with C++ for improved readability and performance. We maintain some of the C naming conventions for key variables and functions to help with direct comparisons.

Here is the core idea: assume we have a state of N qubits, all initialized to be in the state $|0\rangle$. The dense representation stores 2^N complex numbers, where only the very first entry is a 1.0 and all other values are 0.0, corresponding to state $|00\ldots0\rangle$.

Our library libq turns this on its head. States are stored as bitmasks (currently up to 64 qubits, but this can be extended), where 0s and 1s correspond to states $|0\rangle$ and $|1\rangle$. Each of these bit combinations is then paired with a probability amplitude. In the above example, libq would store the tuple (0x00...0, 1.0), indicating that the only state with nonzero probability is $|00\ldots0\rangle$. For 53 qubits, the full state representation would require 72 petabytes of memory, while the sparse representation only requires a total of 16 bytes if the amplitude is stored as a double precision value, 12 bytes if we use 4-byte floats.

Applying a Hadamard gate to the least significant qubit will put it in superposition. In libq, this means that there are now two states with nonzero probability:

- $|000\ldots00\rangle$ with probability 50%.
- $|000\ldots01\rangle$ with probability 50%.

Correspondingly, libq stores only two tuples, each with a probability amplitude of $1/\sqrt{2}$, using 32 bytes (or 24 bytes for 4-byte floats).

While a circuit is running, superposition is generated and destroyed. States become probable and no longer probable. A key aspect of libquantum is that gates are recognized as producing or destroying superposition and handled accordingly. Furthermore, it filters out all states with close to 0.0 probability after application of superpositioning gates. This reduces the number of stored tuples and accelerates future gate applications.

Gate application itself becomes very fast. For example, assume we need to apply the X-gate to the least significant qubit. In the dense case, the whole state vector needs to be traversed and modified, as outlined in Section 4.5 on accelerated gate application. In the libq case, only a bit-flip is needed. In the example above, assuming an initial state of all $|0\rangle$, applying the X-gate to the least significant qubit means we only have to flip the least significant bit in the bitmask; the tuple (0x00...00, 1.0) becomes (0x00...01, 1.0). This is dramatically faster than having to traverse and modify a potentially very large state vector, especially if the number of nonzero probability states is low.

To maintain the state tuples, we need to support two main operations:

- Iterate over all available state tuples.
- Find or create a specific state tuple.

libquantum implements a hash table to manage the tuples, and, as we will later see, despite the favorable performance characteristics of hash tables, it ultimately remains the performance bottleneck in the implementation. Our `libq` moderately improves this data structure.

The implementation is about 500 lines of C++ code. A detailed, annotated description, which also includes optimization wins and fails, can be found in the Appendix.

There are also downsides to this design, which may prevent it from scaling to very large numbers of qubits or circuits with a high percentage of nonzero probabilities. Individual states are encoded efficiently as tuples of a bitmask to encode a state and probability amplitude. But there are additional data structures, such as the hash table to maintain existing states. The memory requirement per state is higher than in a full-state representation. This means that there is a crossover point where the sparse representation becomes *less* efficient than the full-state representation. In particular, it does not appear to do well on the quantum random algorithms that we discuss in Section 5.2.

Another problem might arise from the way the hash table is used to store the states. At some size threshold, the hash table's random memory accesses will be outperformed by linear memory accesses, which benefit from caches and can be prefetched effectively. Furthermore, in a distributed computing environment, hash table entries might be distributed unpredictably across machines. Gate application might thus incur prohibitively high communication costs.

4.6.1   Benchmarking

We only provide anecdotal evidence for the efficiency of the sparse representation. A full performance evaluation is ill-advised in a book like this – the results will be out of date and no longer relevant by the time you read this.

The most complex algorithm in this book is Shor's integer factorization algorithm (Section 4.6). The quantum part of the algorithm is called order finding. To factor the number 15, it requires 18 qubits and 10,533 gates; to factor 21, it requires 22 qubits and 20,671 gates, and to factor 35, it requires 26 qubits and 36,373 gates. We run this circuit in two different ways:

- Run it as is, using the accelerated quantum circuit implementation.
- Transpile the circuit directly to `libq` without executing it. We describe transpilation in Section 8.5. The output is a C++ source file, which is compiled and linked with the `libq` library to produce an executable.

Both versions will compute the same result; the textual output only differs marginally. To factor 21 with 22 qubits, we get the following result. Note that a maximum of only 1.6% of all possible states ever obtain a nonzero probability at one point or the other during execution:

```
# of qubits       : 22
# of hash computes : 2736
Maximum # of states: 65536, theoretical: 4194304, 1.562%
States with nonzero probability:
 0.499966 +0.000000i|4> (2.499658e-01) (|00 0000 0000 0000 0000 0100>)
```

```
 0.000001 -0.000000i|32772> (6.148556e-13) (|00 0000 1000 0000 0000
 ↪   0100>)
-0.499970 +0.000000i|65536> (2.499696e-01) (|00 0001 0000 0000 0000
 ↪   0000>)
 0.499966 +0.000000i|65540> (2.499658e-01) (|00 0001 0000 0000 0000
 ↪   0100>)
 0.000001 -0.000000i|98308> (6.148556e-13) (|00 0001 1000 0000 0000
 ↪   0100>)
 0.499970 -0.000000i|0> (2.499696e-01) (|00 0000 0000 0000 0000 0000>)
real    0m4.225s
```

The libq version runs in under five seconds on a modern workstation, while the circuit version takes about 2.5 minutes, a speedup of roughly 25×. To factor the number 35 with 26 qubits, the libq version runs for about 3 minutes, while the full state simulation takes about an hour. Again, a solid speedup, this time of about 20×. We do ignore the compile times for the generated C++ versions. We would have to include these in an actual scientific evaluation, which this is not.

5 Beyond Classical

The term *Beyond Classical* is now the preferred term over *Quantum Advantage*, which was the preferred term over the unfortunate term *Quantum Supremacy*. That term was originally coined by Prof. John Preskill to describe a computation that can be run efficiently on a quantum computer but would be intractable to run on a classical computer (Preskill, 2012; Harrow and Montanaro, 2017).

Computational complexity theory is a pillar of computer science. A good introduction, along with extensive literature references, can be found in Dean (2016). There exists a large set of complexity classes. The best known big categories are the following:

- Class P, the class of decision problems (with a yes or no answer) with problem size n that run in polynomial time (n^x).
- Class NP, decision problems with exponential run time (x^n) which can be *verified* in polynomial time.
- Class NP-complete, which is a somewhat technical construction. It is a class of NP problems that other NP-complete problems can be mapped to in polynomial time. Finding a single example from this class falling into P would mean that all members of this class are in P as well.
- Class NP-hard, the class of problems that are at least as hard as the hardest problems in NP. To simplify a little bit, this is the class of NP problems that may not be a decision problem, such as integer factorization, or for which there is no known polynomial-time algorithm for verification, such as the traveling salesman problem (Applegate et al., 2006).

There are dozens of complexity classes with various properties and inter-relationships. The famous question of whether $P = NP$ remains one of the great challenges in computer science today (and can be answered jokingly with *yes* – if $N = 1$ or $P = 0$).

The interest in quantum computing arises from the belief that quantum algorithms fall into class BQP, the complexity class of algorithms that can be solved by a quantum Turing machine in polynomial time with an error probability of less than 1/3. This group is believed to be more powerful than class BPP, the class of algorithms that can be solved in polynomial time by a probabilistic Turing machine with a similar error rate. Stated simply, there is a class of algorithms that can run exponentially faster on quantum machines than on classical machines.

From a complexity-theoretic point of view, since BQP *contains* BPP, this would mean that quantum computers can efficiently simulate classical computers. However, would we run a word processor or video game on a quantum computer? Classical and quantum computing appear complementary. The term *beyond* seems well chosen to indicate that there is a complexity class for algorithms that run tractably only on quantum computers.

To establish the quantum advantage, we will not take a complexity-theoretic approach in this book. Instead, we will try to estimate and validate the results of the quantum supremacy paper by Arute et al. (2019) to convince ourselves that quantum computers indeed reach capabilities beyond those of classical machines.

5.1   10,000 Years, 2 Days, or 200 Seconds

In 2019, Google published a seminal paper claiming to finally have reached quantum advantage on their 53-qubit Sycamore chip (Arute et al., 2019). A quantum random algorithm was computed and sampled 1,000,000 times in just 200 seconds, a result that was estimated to take the world's fastest supercomputer 10,000 years to simulate classically.

Shortly thereafter, IBM, a competitor in the field of quantum computing, followed up by estimating that a similar result could be achieved in just a few days, with higher accuracy, on a classical supercomputer (Pednault et al., 2019). A few days versus 200 seconds is a factor of about $1,000\times$. A few days versus 10,000 years is another factor of $1,000\times$. Disagreements of this magnitude are exciting. How is it that these two great companies disagree to the tune of a combined $1,000,000\times$?

5.2   Quantum Random Circuit Algorithm

In order to make claims about performance, you first need a proper benchmark. Typical benchmark sets are SPEC (www.spec.org) for CPU performance and the recent MLPerf benchmarks (http://mlcommons.org) for machine learning systems. It is also known that as soon as benchmarks are published, large groups of people embark on efforts to optimize and tune their various infrastructures towards the benchmarks. When these efforts cross into an area where optimizations *only* work for benchmarks, these efforts are called *benchmark gaming*.

The challenge, therefore, is to build a benchmark that is meaningful, general, yet hard to game. Google suggested the methodology of using quantum random circuits (QRC) and cross entropy benchmarking (XEB) (Boixo et al., 2018). XEB observes that the measurement probabilities of a random circuit follow certain patterns, which would be destroyed if there were errors or chaotic randomness in the system. XEB samples the resulting bitstrings and uses statistical modeling to confirm that the chip indeed performed a nonchaotic computation. The math is beyond the scope of this text, so we defer to Boixo et al. (2018) for further details.

How do you construct a random circuit? Initially Google used a set of 2×2 operators and Controlled-Z gates. The choice of this particular set of gates, as well as the corresponding constraints on connectivity, were influenced by the capabilities of the Sycamore chip (Google, 2019).

The problem size with a 53-qubit random circuit is very large. Assuming complex numbers of size 2^3 bytes, traditional Schrödinger full-state simulation would require 2^{56} bytes, or 72 PB of storage; twice that for 16-byte complex numbers. Assuming that a full-state simulation would not be realistic, the Google team used a hybrid simulation technique combining full-state simulation with a simulation technique based on Schrödinger–Feynman path history (Rudiak-Gould, 2006). This method trades exponential space requirements for exponential runtime. The hybrid technique breaks the circuit into two (or more) chunks. It simulates each half using the Schrödinger full-state method, and for gates spanning the divided hemispheres, it uses path history techniques. The performance overhead for those gates is very high, but their numbers are comparatively small. Based on benchmarking of the hybrid technique, as well as evaluation of full-state simulation on a supercomputer (Häner and Steiger, 2017), it was estimated that a full simulation for 53 qubits would take thousands of years, even when run on 1,000,000 server-class machines.

Soon after publication, ways were indeed found to game the benchmark with targeted simulation techniques for this specific circuit type, exploiting some unfortunate patterns in how the circuits were constructed. The benchmark needed to be refined. Fortunately, relatively simple changes, such as the introduction of new gate types, seemed to counter these techniques. Details can be found in Arute et al. (2020).

There are, of course, concerns that this choice of benchmark is a somewhat artificial proposition – an algorithm of no practical use for which no other classically equivalent algorithm exists other than quantum simulation. To play devil's advocate, let's take a pendulum with a magnetic weight and have it swing right over an opposite magnetic pole. The movement will be highly chaotic. Simulating this behavior from some assumed starting conditions can theoretically be done in polynomial time but an enormous amount of computing resources are required to model the motion with accuracy over a prolonged period of time. And even then, it is not possible to model *all* starting conditions – the proverbial flap of a butterfly wing on the other side of earth will eventually influence the motion. If we ran the simulations n times and sampled the final positions, the results would come out as chaotically random, and differ from equivalent physical experiments.

On the other hand, just letting the pendulum swing as a physical system "performs" the problem in real time, using practically no computational resources, and resulting in an equally chaotic, random outcome. Have we really proven the pendulum-swing computer advantage?

This is an intriguing argument, but it is flawed. The pendulum-swing computer is a chaotic, physical, analog, and, most importantly, a nonrepeatable process. The most insignificant changes in the initial conditions will lead to different, unpredictable, and nonrepeatable outcomes. As such, it does not perform a computation (which is why we used the term *performs* above).

A random quantum circuit, on the other hand, is a digital computation. A significant change in the setup, such as modified sequences of different gates or starting from a different initial state, will change the outcome chaotically. However, small changes to parameterized gates, different levels of noise, or modest exposure to errors will not cause the resulting probabilities to change meaningfully; the deviations are bounded. In future machines, quantum error correction will make outcomes even more robust and repeatable.

The key argument stands: A nonchaotic calculation can be computed efficiently on a quantum computer. It runs dramatically less efficiently on a classical machine to the tune of thousands of years, thus proving a quantum advantage.

In all cases, it is just a matter of time until we will be able to run something big *and* meaningful on a quantum computer – perhaps Shor's algorithm utilizing millions of qubits with error correction. In the meantime, let's take a closer look at Google's quantum circuit and estimate how long it would take to simulate it in *our* infrastructure.

5.3   Circuit Construction

There are specific constraints for the gates on the Google chip, and they cannot be placed at random. We follow the original construction rules from Boixo et al. (2018).

The supremacy experiment uses three types of gates, each a rotation by $\pi/2$ around an axis on a Bloch sphere's equator. Note that the definitions of the gates is slightly different from those we presented earlier:

$$X^{1/2} \equiv R_X(\pi/2) = \frac{1}{\sqrt{2}} \begin{bmatrix} 1 & -i \\ -i & 1 \end{bmatrix},$$

$$Y^{1/2} \equiv R_Y(\pi/2) = \frac{1}{\sqrt{2}} \begin{bmatrix} 1 & -1 \\ 1 & 1 \end{bmatrix},$$

$$W^{1/2} \equiv R_{X+Y}(\pi/2) = \frac{1}{\sqrt{2}} \begin{bmatrix} 1 & -\sqrt{i} \\ \sqrt{-i} & 1 \end{bmatrix}.$$

There is a list of specific constraints for circuits:

- For each qubit, the very first and last gates must be Hadamard gates. This is reflected in a notation for circuit depth as *1-n-1*, indicating that n steps, or gate levels, are to be sandwiched between Hadamard gates.
- Apply *CZ* gates in the patterns shown in Figure 5.1, alternating between horizontal and vertical layouts.
- Apply single-qubit operators $X^{1/2}$, $Y^{1/2}$, and T (or $W^{1/2}$) to qubits that are not affected by the *CZ* gates, using the criteria below. For our simulation (using our infrastructure, which does not specialize for specific gates), the choice of gates actually does *not* matter in regards to computational complexity: they are all 2×2 gates, and we can use any of the standard gates. For more sophisticated methodology, like tensor networks, the choice of gates can make a difference.

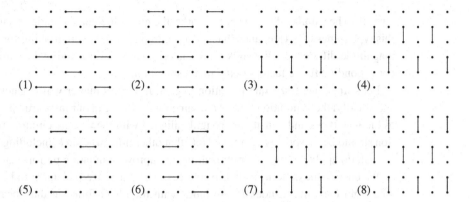

Figure 5.1 Patterns for applying controlled gates on the Sycamore chip.

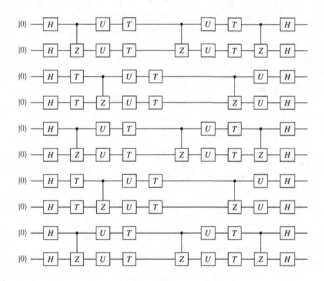

Figure 5.2 A smaller-scale, semi-random supremacy circuit.

- If the previous cycle had a *CZ* gate, apply any of three single-qubit unitary gates.
- If the previous cycle had a nondiagonal unitary gate, apply the T-gate.
- If the previous cycle had no unitary gate (except Hadamard), apply the T-gate.
- Else, don't apply a gate.
- Repeat above steps for a given number of steps (which we call *depth* in our implementation).
- Apply the final Hadamard and measure.

This interpretation of the rules produces a circuit like the one shown in Figure 5.2. Note that there have been refinements since first publication; Arute et al. (2020) has the details. The main motivation for making changes was to make it harder for the new circuits to be simulated by tensor networks, the most efficient simulation technique for this type of network (Pan and Zhang, 2021). In our case, we are looking for orders of magnitude differences. We stick with this original definition and make sure to apply corresponding fudge factors in the final estimation.

Let's implement this interpretation. Again, it doesn't matter which gates to apply specifically; the simulation time is the same for each gate in our infrastructure. As long as the gate types and density are roughly aligned with the Google circuit, our estimation should be reasonably accurate. Note that other infrastructures, including Google's qsimh, do apply a range of optimizations to improve simulation performance.

We encode the patterns as lists of indices, where a nonzero element indicates a *CZ* gate from the current index to the index with the offset found at that location. The eight patterns are then encoded like this:

```
# The paper suggests 8 patterns of size 6*6 of CZ gates. To fully
# encode the patterns one would need at least 36 qubits, but that's
# hard to simulate. We make a compromise and try to apply as many
# gates as possible. The patterns are encoded as simple lists, where
# a non-zero element at index i serves as the control and has
# the offset to the target qubit. To go right, the offset is 1, to
# go down the offset is 6.
#
pattern1 = [0, 0, 1, 0, 0, 0,
            1, 0, 0, 0, 1, 0] * 3

pattern2 = [1, 0, 0, 0, 1, 0,
            0, 0, 1, 0, 0, 0] * 3

[...] # similar for the remaining patterns

patterns = [pattern1, pattern2, pattern3, pattern4,
            pattern5, pattern6, pattern7, pattern8]
```

Gates are represented by a simple enumeration (H, T, U, CZ). With this, we are ready to build the circuit. We start from the horizontal and vertical patterns and then proceed to apply the rules as stated above. Note, again, for our simulation the actual gates do not matter:

```
def build_circuit(nbits, depth):
    """Construct the full circuit."""

    def apply_pattern(pattern):
        bits_touched = []
        for i in range(min(nbits, len(pattern))):
            if pattern[i] != 0 and i + pattern[i] < nbits:
                bits_touched.append((i, i + pattern[i]))
        return bits_touched

    print('\nBuild smaller circuit ({} qubits, depth {})\n'.
          format(nbits, depth))
```

```
state0 = [Gate.H] * nbits
states = []
states.append(state0)

for _ in range(depth - 1):
  state1 = [Gate.UNK] * nbits
  touched = apply_pattern(patterns[random.randint(0, 7)])
  for idx1, idx2 in touched:
    state1[idx1] = Gate.CZ
    state1[idx2] = Gate.CZ
  for i in range(len(state0)):
    if state0[i] == Gate.CZ and state1[i] != Gate.CZ:
      state1[i] = Gate.U
    if state0[i] == Gate.U and state1[i] != Gate.CZ:
      state1[i] = Gate.T
    if state0[i] == Gate.H and state1[i] != Gate.CZ:
      state1[i] = Gate.T
  state0 = state1
  states.append(state0)

state0 = [Gate.H] * nbits
states.append(state0)
return states
```

Let's print a sample circuit with 12 qubits and depth of *1-10-1*:

```
def print_state(states, nbits, depth):
  [...]
>>
      0  1  2  3  4  5  6  7  8  9 10 11 12
 0: h  cz cz u  t                          h
 1: h  t  cz u  t              cz cz h
 2: h  cz u  t           cz u  t  cz h
 3: h  t     cz u  t  cz cz cz cz cz u  h
 4: h  cz cz cz u  t  cz cz u  cz u  t  h
 5: h  t  cz u  t              cz u  h
 6: h  cz u  t           cz u  t     h
 7: h  t     cz u  t  cz cz cz cz cz u  h
 8: h  cz cz cz u  t  cz cz u  cz u  t  h
 9: h  t  cz u  t              cz cz h
10: h  cz u  t           cz u  t  cz h
11: h  t              cz u  cz u  h
```

5.4　Estimation

So far, so good: We have implemented functionality to construct circuits for a given number of qubits and circuit depths. For a bottom-up estimation, we construct a circuit with a smaller, tractable dimension, simulate it, and from the simulation results we extrapolate to a 53-qubit circuit.

We make several simplifying assumptions, most notably, that communication between machines is free. At the end of the estimation, we should apply appropriate factors to account for such overheads.

Simulation is done with an eager execution function, which iterates over the depth of the circuit, simulating each gate one by one:

```python
def sim_circuit(states, nbits, depth, target_nbits, target_depth):
  """Simulate the generated circuit."""

  [...]
  qc = circuit.qc('Supremacy Circuit')
  qc.reg(nbits)

  for d in range(depth):
    s = states[d]
    for i in range(nbits):
      if s[i] == Gate.UNK:
        continue
      ngates += 1
      if s[i] == Gate.T:
        qc.t(i)
      [... similar for H, U/V, U/Yroot]
      if s[i] == Gate.CZ:
        ngates += 1  # This is just an estimate of the overhead
        if i < nbits - 1 and s[i + 1] == Gate.CZ:
          qc.cz(i, i+1)
          s[i+1] = Gate.UNK
        if i < nbits - 6 and s[i + 6] == Gate.CZ:
          qc.cz(i, i+6)
          s[i+6] = Gate.UNK
  [...]
```

To estimate the time it would take to execute this circuit at 53 qubits, we make the following assumptions:

- We assume that one-qubit and two-qubit gate application time is linear over the size of the state vector.
- Performance is memory-bound.
- We know we'd have to distribute the computation over multiple machines, but we ignore the communication cost.
- We assume a number of machines and a number of cores on those machines. We know that a small number of cores on a high-core machine can saturate the available memory bandwidth, so we take a guess on what the number of reasonably utilized cores would be (16, but this number can be adjusted).

With these assumptions, the metric *Time per gate per byte in the state vector* is the one we'll use to extrapolate results. It is remarkably stable across qubits and depth and thus can be used to estimate approximate performance of bigger circuits. In order to estimate how many gates there would be in a larger circuit, we compute a gate ratio, which is the number of gates found in a circuit divided by (nbits * depth). In code:

```
print('\nEstimate simulation time on larger circuit:\n')
gate_ratio = ngates / nbits / depth
print('Simulated circuit:')
print('  Qubits                 : {:d}'.format(nbits))
print('  Circuit Depth          : {:d}'.format(depth))
print('  Gates                  : {:.2f}'.format(ngates))
print('  State Memory           : {:.4f} MB'.format(
    2 ** (nbits-1) * 16 / (1024 ** 2)))
print('Estimated Circuit Qubits : {}'.format(target_nbits))
print('Estimated Circuit Depth  : {}'.format(target_depth))
print('Estimated State Memory   : {:.5f} TB'.format(
    2 ** (target_nbits-1) * 16 / (1024 ** 4)))
print('Machines used            : {}'.format(flags.FLAGS.machines))
print('Estimated cores per server: {}'.format(flags.FLAGS.cores))
print('Estimated gate density   : {:.2f}'.format(gate_ratio))

estimated_sim_time_secs = (
    # time per gate per byte
    (duration / ngates / (2**(nbits-1) * 16))
    # gates
    * target_nbits
    # gate ratio scaling factor to circuit size
    * gate_ratio
    # depth
    * target_depth
    # memory
    * 2**(target_nbits-1) * 16
    # number of machines
    / flags.FLAGS.machines
    # Active core per machine
    / flags.FLAGS.cores)

print('Estimated for {} qbits: {:.2f} y or {:.2f} d or ({:.0f} sec)'
    .format(target_nbits,
            estimated_sim_time_secs / 3600 / 24 / 365,
            estimated_sim_time_secs / 3600 / 24,
            estimated_sim_time_secs))
```

Let's look at a specific result. We assume the target circuit has 53 qubits and is run on 100 machines, each one having 16 fully available cores. The number of gates in our simulation (475) seems to roughly align with the published number of gates from the Google publication, though not exactly. (Google quoted 1,200 gates, while extrapolating the 475 would yield about 2,000 gates.) For these parameters, the estimation results are:

```
Estimate simulation time on larger circuit:
Simulated circuit:
   Qubits               : 25
   Circuit Depth        : 20
   Gates                : 412.00
   State Memory         : 256.0000 MB
Estimated Circuit Qubits   : 53
Estimated Circuit Depth    : 20
Estimated State Memory     : 65536.00000 TB
Machines used              : 100
Estimated cores per server: 255
Estimated gate density     : 0.82
Estimated for 53 qbits: 0.01 y or 2.81 d or (242490 sec)
```

Of course, these parameters are hopelessly naive – how would we provision 72 PB of memory on just 100 machines? Assuming we can provision 1 TB per server, we'd need at least 72K hosts. At this scale, we can no longer ignore communication costs. You may want to experiment with more realistic settings.

5.5   Evaluation

For comparison, let's look at the massive Summit supercomputer (Oak Ridge National Laboratory, 2021). It is theoretically capable of performing up to 10^{17} single precision floating point operations per second. To compute 2^{53} equivalents of 2×2 matrix multiplications is of complexity 2^{56}. At 100 percent utilization, it would take Summit just a few seconds to compute a full simulation!

To store a full state of 53 qubits, we need 72 PB bytes of storage. Summit has an estimated 2.5 PB of RAM on all sockets, and 250 PB of secondary storage. This means we should expect that the simulation encounters high communication overhead moving data from permanent storage into RAM. Much of the permanent storage would have to be reserved for this experiment as well. The researchers at IBM found an impressive way to minimize data transfers, which is a major contribution by Pednault et al. (2019). With this technique, a slow-down of about 500× was anticipated, which led to the estimate that a full simulation could run in about two days.

Now let's try to answer the question that started this section: Where does the discrepancy of 10,000 years versus days come from? This is a factor of about 1,000×, after all.

The Google Quantum X team based their estimations on a different simulator architecture (Markov et al., 2018), assuming that a full-state simulation is not realistic.

The simulation techniques were benchmarked at smaller scale. Full-state simulation results were evaluated on a supercomputer. From these data points, the computational costs were extrapolated to 1,000,000 machines, arriving at the estimate of 10,000 years of simulation time for 53 qubits and a circuit depth of 20.

The IBM researchers, on the other hand, found an elegant way to squeeze the problem onto one of the biggest supercomputers in the world. The results are only estimated—an experiment was not performed. It is difficult to determine how realistic the estimates are in practice because at petabyte scale, other factors have to be taken into account, for example, disk error rates. This also assumes that most of the machine's secondary storage was committed to the experiment.

Is there a right or wrong? The answer is *no* because we are comparing apples to oranges. The evaluated simulation techniques are different based on different assumptions of what can realistically run on a supercomputer. The supremacy experiment was physically run, the Summit paper was estimated. Even if physical simulation took just a day on Summit, adding a handful of additional qubits will exhaust its storage capacity. The simulation technique would have to change and trade storage requirements for simulation time, similar to the Schrödinger-Feynman path history technique (Rudiak-Gould, 2006). At that point, and only at that point, would we be able to make a more fair, apples-to-apples comparison.

It is safe to anticipate that other smart simulation techniques will emerge. However, as long as $BPP \subset BQP$ is true, it is also safe to assume that additional qubits or moderately modified benchmarks will again defeat attempts to simulate these circuits classically.

6 Complex Algorithms

Now that we have convinced ourselves that quantum computers can indeed reach capabilities *beyond classical*, at least on a semi-random circuit, we move on to discuss more meaningful algorithms. The previous sections on simple algorithms prepared us well to explore the complex algorithms in this chapter. We will still use a mix of full matrix and accelerated circuit implementations, depending on which seems best in context. It is recommended that you at least skim Chapter 4 on infrastructure before exploring this chapter.

In this chapter, we develop the quantum Fourier transform (QFT), an important technique used by many complex algorithms, and show it in action by performing arithmetic in the quantum Fourier domain. We discuss phase estimation next, another essential tool, especially when used together with QFT. Armed with these tools, we embark on implementing Shor's famous factorization algorithm.

After this, we switch gears and discuss Grover's search algorithm, along with some derivatives and improvements. We show how combining Grover and phase estimation leads to the interesting quantum counting algorithm. A short interlude on the topic of quantum random walks follows. Quantum walks are a complex topic; we only discuss and implement basic principles.

At a high level, quantum computing appears to have a computational complexity advantage over classical computing for several classes of algorithms and their derivatives. These are algorithms utilizing quantum search, algorithms based on the quantum Fourier transform, algorithms utilizing quantum random walks, and a fourth class, the simulation of quantum systems. We detail the variational quantum eigensolver algorithm (VQE), which allows finding minimum eigenvalues of a Hamiltonian. As an application, we develop a graph maximum cut algorithm by framing the problem as a Hamiltonian. This algorithm was introduced as part of the quantum approximate optimization algorithm (QAOA), which we briefly touch upon. We further explore the Subset Sum problem using a similar mechanism.

We conclude this chapter with an in-depth discussion of the elegant Solovay–Kitaev algorithm for gate approximation, another seminal result in quantum computing.

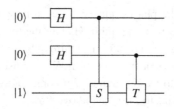

Figure 6.1 A phase kick circuit.

6.1   Phase Kick

In this section we discuss the *phase kick* mechanism, which is the basis for the quantum Fourier transform.

The controlled rotation gates have the interesting property that they can be used in an additive fashion. The basic principle is best explained with a circuit that is commonly known as a *phase kick* circuit. An example is shown in Figure 6.1.

Any number of qubits (the two top qubits in this example circuit) are initialized as $|0\rangle$ and put into superposition with Hadamard gates. A third ancilla qubit starts out in state $|1\rangle$. We apply the controlled S-gate and T-gate, but remember that these gates only add a phase to the $|1\rangle$ part of a state.

Each of the top qubits then connects a controlled rotation gate to the ancilla. In the example above:

- The top qubit controls a 90° rotation gate, the S-gate.
- The second qubit controls a 45° gate, the T-gate.

To express this in code:

```
psi = state.bitstring(0, 0, 1)
psi = ops.Hadamard(2)(psi)
psi = ops.ControlledU(0, 2, ops.Sgate())(psi)
psi = ops.ControlledU(1, 2, ops.Tgate())(psi, 1)
psi.dump()
```

Because of the superposition, the $|1\rangle$ part of each of the top qubits' superpositioned states will activate the rotation of the controlled gate. Using this, we can perform addition of phases. For the example, these are the resulting probability amplitudes and phases:

```
|001> (|1>):  ampl: +0.50+0.00j prob: 0.25 Phase:   0.0
|011> (|3>):  ampl: +0.35+0.35j prob: 0.25 Phase:  45.0
|101> (|5>):  ampl: +0.00+0.50j prob: 0.25 Phase:  90.0
|111> (|7>):  ampl: -0.35+0.35j prob: 0.25 Phase: 135.0
```

Note how the phases add up because they are controlled by a (superpositioned) $|1\rangle$ in the corresponding qubit. Having the top qubit as $|1\rangle$ adds 90°, and having the second qubit as $|1\rangle$ adds 45°. The third qubit is an ancilla. Also, note that we could use arbitrary rotations or fractions of π. We can use this type of circuit and corresponding rotation gates to express numerical computations in terms of phases. Of course, we have to normalize to 2π to avoid overflows.

The ability to add phases in a controlled fashion is powerful and is the foundation of the quantum Fourier transformation, which we will explore in the next section. In preparation for this section, let us briefly look at how to express the rotations mathematically.

- A rotation by 180° as a fraction of 2π is $e^{2\pi i/2^1}$. Expressed as a phase angle this is -1.
- A rotation by 90° as a fraction of 2π is $e^{2\pi i/2^2}$, a phase of i.
- A rotation by 45° as a fraction of 2π is $e^{2\pi i/2^3}$.
- Finally, a rotation by $135° = 90° + 45°$ as a fraction of 2π is $e^{2\pi i(1/2^2+1/2^3)}$.

So why is this circuit called a phase *kick* circuit? To understand this, let us look at a simpler version of the circuit and the corresponding math.

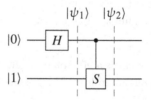

The state $|\psi_1\rangle$ after the Hadamard is:

$$|+\rangle \otimes |1\rangle = \frac{1}{\sqrt{2}}\big(|0\rangle|1\rangle + |1\rangle|1\rangle\big).$$

With the Controlled-S operation, the state $|\psi_2\rangle$ becomes

$$|\psi_2\rangle = \frac{1}{\sqrt{2}}\big(|0\rangle|1\rangle + |1\rangle S|1\rangle\big)$$

$$= \frac{1}{\sqrt{2}}\big(|0\rangle|1\rangle + |1\rangle e^{i\pi/2}|1\rangle\big).$$

We pull out the $|1\rangle$ on the right:

$$|\psi_2\rangle = \frac{1}{\sqrt{2}}\big(|0\rangle + e^{i\pi/2}|1\rangle\big)|1\rangle.$$

We observe that the second qubit $|1\rangle$ remains *unmodified*. The trick here is that $|1\rangle$ is an eigenstate of the S-gate. We will elaborate further on eigenvalues in Section 6.4 on phase estimation, but in summary, we found a way to *kick* the phase from qubit 1 to the controlling qubit 0.

This mechanism also enabled the Bernstein–Vazirani algorithm, covered in Section 3.7. We did not use rotation gates in our implementation, but rather Controlled-Not gates on states in the Hadamard basis. A Controlled-Not gate in this basis corresponds to a simple Z-gate (see also Section 8.4.5), a 180° rotation about the z-axis.

6.2 Quantum Fourier Transform

The quantum Fourier transform (QFT) is one of the foundational algorithms of quantum computing. It is important to note that although it does not speed up classical Fourier analysis of classical data, it does enable other important algorithms, such as phase estimation, which is the approximation of the eigenvalues of an operator. Phase estimation is a key ingredient in Shor's factoring algorithm and others. Let us discuss a few preliminaries first.

6.2.1 Binary Fractions

In Section 6.3 we will learn how to interpret qubits measured as $|0\rangle$ and $|1\rangle$ as bits in a binary number, with the most significant bit being on the left or at the top in circuit diagrams. To convert a binary representation to a decimal number, we added the `bits2val` routine to `lib/helpers.py`.

However, we can also interpret the bits as constituents of a *binary fraction*. We have a choice to interpret the bit order from left to right or right to left and decide which bit should be the least significant qubit, for example:

$$|\psi\rangle = |x_0 x_1 \cdots x_{n-2} x_{n-1}\rangle.$$

The x_i should be interpreted as binary bits, with values of either 0 or 1. This looks natural in the following mathematical notation:

$$\frac{x_0}{2^1} = x_0 \frac{1}{2^1} = 0.x_0,$$

$$\frac{x_0}{2^1} + \frac{x_1}{2^2} = x_0 \frac{1}{2^1} + x_1 \frac{1}{2^2} = 0.x_0 x_1,$$

$$\frac{x_0}{2^1} + \frac{x_1}{2^2} + \frac{x_2}{2^3} = x_0 \frac{1}{2^1} + x_1 \frac{1}{2^2} + x_2 \frac{1}{2^3} = 0.x_0 x_1 x_2,$$

$$\vdots$$

We can define this the other way around, with x_0 being least significant fractional part of a binary fraction, as in $0.x_{n-1} \cdots x_1 x_0$. It is important to note that this is just a notational difference. We will encounter an example of this in the derivation of phase estimation in Section 6.4.

In our code below, the most significant bit represents the largest part of the fraction, for example, 0.5 for the first bit, 0.25 for the second bit, 0.125 for the third, and so on. Again, we can easily revert the order. Given a binary string of states, we use the following routine from file `lib/helpers.py` to compute binary fractions:

```python
def bits2frac(bits: Iterable) -> float:
    """For given bits, compute the binary fraction."""

    return sum(bits[i] * 2**(-i-1) for i in range(len(bits)))
```

Computing the fraction from a single 0 will result in:

```python
val = helper.bits2frac((0,))
print(val)
>> 0
```

The fraction from a single 1:

```python
val = helper.bits2frac((1,))
print(val)
>> 0.5
```

For two bits, the first one will represent the 0.5 part of the fraction, the second part will represent the 0.25 part of the fraction:

```python
val = helper.bits2frac((0, 1))
print(val)
>> 0.25
val = helper.bits2frac((1, 0))
print(val)
>>0.5
val = helper.bits2frac((1, 1))
print(val)
>>0.75
```

6.2.2 Phase Gates

We already learned about two different phase gates in Section 2.6.5 on single-qubit gates. We saw the discrete phase gate R_k and the U_1 gate:

$$R_k = \begin{bmatrix} 1 & 0 \\ 0 & e^{2\pi i/2^k} \end{bmatrix} \quad \text{and} \quad U_1(\lambda) = \begin{bmatrix} 1 & 0 \\ 0 & e^{i\lambda} \end{bmatrix},$$

with:

$$R_k(0) = U_1(2\pi/2^0),$$

$$R_k(1) = U_1(2\pi/2^1),$$
$$R_k(2) = U_1(2\pi/2^2),$$
$$\vdots$$

Remember Euler's formula, which represents rotation as complex exponentiation:

$$e^{i\phi} = \cos(\phi) + i\sin(\phi). \tag{6.1}$$

Applying one of these gates to a state means only the $|1\rangle$ basis state gets a phase. To reiterate, the angles (with cw meaning clockwise and ccw meaning counterclockwise) are:

$$e^{i\frac{\pi}{2}} = i \Rightarrow 90°\,ccw,$$
$$e^{i\pi} = -1 \Rightarrow 180°\,ccw,$$
$$e^{i\frac{3\pi}{2}} = -i \Rightarrow 270°\,ccw = 90°\,cw.$$

You might have noticed that the S-gate and T-gate we used in Section 6.1 are also of this form, except they have their rotation angles at the fixed values of $\pi/2$ and $\pi/4$.

6.2.3 Quantum Fourier Transform

We now have all ingredients necessary for the QFT, which we will implement with Hadamard gates and controlled discrete phase gates R_k. Later, for example in Section 6.3 and 6.6, we will also see versions of QFT being implemented with U_1 gates. QFT takes a state $|\psi\rangle$, where each qubit should be interpreted as part of a binary fraction:

$$|\psi\rangle = |x_0\,x_1\,\cdots\,x_{n-1}\rangle.$$

And converts it to a form where fractional values are encoded as fractional phases. Since we use the phase gates, only the $|1\rangle$ basis state gets a phase. This is how the state looks after we apply a QFT circuit. A detailed derivation for how this state comes about is presented later, in Section 6.4.

$$QFT|x_0\,x_1\,\cdots\,x_{n-1}\rangle = \frac{1}{2^{n/2}}\left(|0\rangle + e^{2\pi i\,0.x_0}|1\rangle\right)$$
$$\otimes\left(|0\rangle + e^{2\pi i\,0.x_0x_1}|1\rangle\right)$$
$$\vdots$$
$$\otimes\left(|0\rangle + e^{2\pi i\,0.x_0x_1x_2\cdots x_{n-1}}|1\rangle\right).$$

If we interpret the binary fractions in the reverse order, we'd get this state:

$$\frac{1}{2^{n/2}} \left(|0\rangle + e^{2\pi i \, 0.x_{n-1}} |1\rangle \right)$$

$$\otimes \left(|0\rangle + e^{2\pi i \, 0.x_{n-1}x_{n-2}} |1\rangle \right)$$

$$\vdots$$

$$\otimes \left(|0\rangle + e^{2\pi i \, 0.x_{n-1}x_{n-2}\cdots x_1 x_0} |1\rangle \right).$$

Note that the *QFT* is a unitary operation, as it is made up of other unitary operators. Since it is unitary, it has an inverse, and we should explicitly state this important inverse relation:

$$QFT^{\dagger} \frac{1}{2^{n/2}} \left(|0\rangle + e^{2\pi i \, 0.x_0} |1\rangle \right)$$

$$\otimes \left(|0\rangle + e^{2\pi i \, 0.x_0 x_1} |1\rangle \right)$$

$$\vdots$$

$$\otimes \left(|0\rangle + e^{2\pi i \, 0.x_0 x_1 x_2 \cdots x_{n-1}} |1\rangle \right)$$

$$= |x_0 \, x_1 \, \cdots \, x_{n-1}\rangle. \tag{6.2}$$

This mathematical formulation gives us the blueprint for constructing the circuit. We have to put the qubits into superposition, and we have to apply controlled rotation gates to rotate qubits around according to the scheme of binary fractions.

We can construct the QFT in two directions, depending on our interpretation of the input qubits. We can draw it from top to bottom:

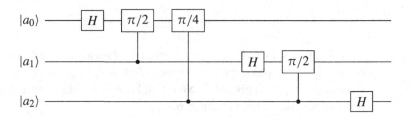

Or from bottom to top:

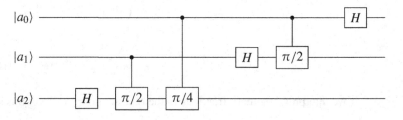

Or we can implement it one way and add an optional Swap gate to get both possible directions with just one implementation. We will see examples of all of these styles in the remainder of this book. Note how we can also switch the controlling and controlled phase gates in the following diagram. Phase gates are symmetric, as shown in Section 3.2.3

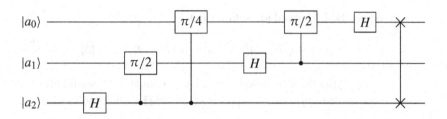

An interesting question is that of accuracy. How many fractions do we need in order to achieve a reliable result for a specific algorithm? This is an interesting metric to play around with. Early work on approximate quantum Fourier transform indicates that for Shor's algorithm, you can stop adding rotation gates as the rotation angles become smaller than π/n^2 (Coppersmith, 2002).

6.2.4   Two-Qubit QFT

It can be helpful to explore the QFT on two qubits. There are only four basis states, which may help to develop intuition. We should start with a simple QFT circuit and the input $|00\rangle$. Note that, as with the Controlled-Z gates from Section 3.2, the direction of the Controlled-S gate does *not* matter. Try it out!

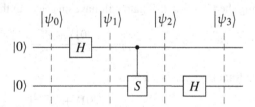

We construct this in code with this snippet:

```
psi = state.bitstring(0, 0)
psi = ops.Hadamard()(psi)
psi = ops.ControlledU(0, 1, ops.Sgate())(psi)
psi = ops.Hadamard()(psi, 1)
psi.dump()
```

All states are equally likely with the same probability:

```
|00> (|0>):  ampl: +0.50+0.00j prob: 0.25 Phase:    0.0
|01> (|1>):  ampl: +0.50+0.00j prob: 0.25 Phase:    0.0
|10> (|2>):  ampl: +0.50+0.00j prob: 0.25 Phase:    0.0
|11> (|3>):  ampl: +0.50+0.00j prob: 0.25 Phase:    0.0
```

Let us briefly look at how to compute the results of this circuit. We start with the tensor product of two inputs set to $|0\rangle$ initially.

$$|\psi_0\rangle = |0\rangle \otimes |0\rangle.$$

Apply the Hadamard to the first qubit:

$$|\psi_1\rangle = (H \otimes I)(|0\rangle \otimes |0\rangle) = (H \otimes |0\rangle)(I \otimes |0\rangle) = \frac{|0\rangle + |1\rangle}{\sqrt{2}}|0\rangle.$$

Applying the Controlled-S gate has no effect, as it would affect the $|1\rangle$ part of a state, hence $|\psi_2\rangle = |\psi_1\rangle$. Applying the final Hadamard will yield:

$$|\psi_3\rangle = (I \otimes H)\left(\frac{|0\rangle + |1\rangle}{\sqrt{2}}|0\rangle\right)$$
$$= \frac{1}{2}(|00\rangle + |01\rangle + |10\rangle + |11\rangle).$$

Now let's do these calculations with $|0\rangle \otimes |1\rangle = |01\rangle$ as input.

$$|\psi_0\rangle = |0\rangle \otimes |1\rangle,$$
$$|\psi_1\rangle = (H \otimes I)(|0\rangle \otimes |1\rangle)$$
$$= \frac{|0\rangle + |1\rangle}{\sqrt{2}}|1\rangle$$
$$= \frac{|01\rangle + |11\rangle}{\sqrt{2}}.$$

Applying the Controlled-S gate will have an effect in this case:

$$|\psi_2\rangle = \frac{|01\rangle + e^{i\pi/2}|11\rangle}{\sqrt{2}}.$$

And the final Hadamard leads to:

$$|\psi_3\rangle = (I \otimes H)\left(\frac{|01\rangle + e^{i\pi/2}|11\rangle}{\sqrt{2}}\right)$$
$$= \frac{1}{2}\left(|0\rangle(|0\rangle - |1\rangle) + e^{i\pi/2}|1\rangle(|0\rangle - |1\rangle)\right).$$

As $e^{i\pi/2} = i$, this results in:

$$|\psi_3\rangle = \frac{1}{2}(|00\rangle - |01\rangle + i|10\rangle - i|11\rangle).$$

Now let's look the four different inputs in matrix form. Remember that applying the operators in a circuit means we have to multiply the matrices in reverse order:

$$(I \otimes H)\,CS\,(H \otimes I) = \frac{1}{2}\begin{bmatrix} 1 & 1 & 1 & 1 \\ 1 & -1 & i & -i \\ 1 & 1 & -1 & -1 \\ 1 & -1 & -i & i \end{bmatrix}.$$

Applying this gate to the $|0, 0\rangle$ base state pulls out the first row, and, correspondingly, $|0, 1\rangle$ pulls out the second, matching our results above. Similarly, for the other three basis states and columns 2 and 3:

$$\frac{1}{2}\begin{bmatrix} 1 & 1 & 1 & 1 \\ 1 & -1 & i & -i \\ 1 & 1 & -1 & -1 \\ 1 & -1 & -i & i \end{bmatrix}\begin{bmatrix} 1 \\ 0 \\ 0 \\ 0 \end{bmatrix} = \begin{bmatrix} 1 \\ 1 \\ 1 \\ 1 \end{bmatrix}$$

$$= \frac{1}{2}(|00\rangle + |01\rangle + |10\rangle + |11\rangle).$$

And indeed, the other three cases produce amplitudes that correspond to rows 1, 2, and 3 of the above matrix:

```
Input: |01>
|00> (|0>):  ampl: +0.50+0.00j prob: 0.25 Phase:    0.0
|01> (|1>):  ampl: -0.50+0.00j prob: 0.25 Phase:  180.0
|10> (|2>):  ampl: +0.00+0.50j prob: 0.25 Phase:   90.0
|11> (|3>):  ampl: +0.00-0.50j prob: 0.25 Phase:  -90.0
Input: |10>
|00> (|0>):  ampl: +0.50+0.00j prob: 0.25 Phase:    0.0
|01> (|1>):  ampl: +0.50+0.00j prob: 0.25 Phase:    0.0
|10> (|2>):  ampl: -0.50+0.00j prob: 0.25 Phase:  180.0
|11> (|3>):  ampl: -0.50+0.00j prob: 0.25 Phase:  180.0
Input: |11>
|00> (|0>):  ampl: +0.50+0.00j prob: 0.25 Phase:    0.0
|01> (|1>):  ampl: -0.50+0.00j prob: 0.25 Phase:  180.0
|10> (|2>):  ampl: +0.00-0.50j prob: 0.25 Phase:  -90.0
|11> (|3>):  ampl: +0.00+0.50j prob: 0.25 Phase:   90.0
```

In summary, QFT encodes the binary fractional encoding of a state into phases representing the fractions for the basis states. It "rotates around" the states according to the binary fractional parts of each qubit. In the Section 6.3, we will see an immediate application of this: quantum arithmetic. We will combine two states in an additive fashion to enable addition and subtraction in the Fourier domain.

One very important aspect of QFT is that while it enables encoding of (binary) states with phases, on measurement the state would collapse to just one of the basis states. All other information will be lost. The challenge for QFT-based algorithms is to apply transformations such that, on measurement, you can find an algorithmic solution to the problem at hand. In practically all cases, we will apply the inverse QFT to get the state out of superposition to measure a result, following Equation (6.2).

6.2.5   QFT Operator

Here is an implementation of the QFT operator in full matrix form. We put all the input qubits in superposition, then apply controlled rotations for each fractional part to each qubit. There are many different ways to encode this, and all implementations must get the indices into the right order. It usually helps to transpile a circuit into a textual format, such as QASM (defined in Section 8.3.1) or similar, to inspect the indices.

```
def Qft(nbits: int) -> Operator:
  """Make an n-bit QFT operator."""

  op = Identity(nbits)
  h = Hadamard()

  for idx in range(nbits):
    # Each qubit first gets a Hadamard
    op = op(h, idx)

    # Each qubit now gets a sequence of Rk(2), Rk(3), ..., Rk(nbits)
    # controlled by qubit (1, 2, ..., nbits-1).
    for rk in range(2, nbits - idx + 1):
      controlled_from = idx + rk - 1
      op = op(ControlledU(controlled_from, idx, Rk(rk)), idx)

  # Now the qubits need to change their order.
  for idx in range(nbits // 2):
    op = op(Swap(idx, nbits - idx - 1), idx)

  if not op.is_unitary():
    raise AssertionError('Constructed non-unitary operator.')
  return op
```

Computing the inverse of the QFT operator is trivial. QFT is a unitary operator, so the inverse is being computed trivially as the adjoint:

```
Qft = ops.Qft(nbits)
[...]
InvQft = Qft.adjoint()
```

If the QFT is computed via explicit gate applications in a circuit, then the inverse has to be implemented as the application of the inverse gates in reverse order, as outlined in Section 2.13 on reversible computing. We will see examples of this explicit construction shortly.

6.2.6   Online Simulation

It can be helpful to use one of the available online simulators to verify results. We have to be aware that the simulators might not agree on the qubit ordering. For experiments, we can always add Swap gates at the end of a circuit to follow online simulators' qubit ordering. Alternatively, we can also add the Swap gates to the circuits in the online simulators themselves.

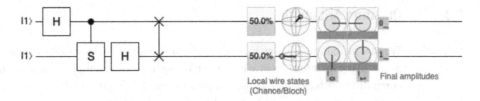

Figure 6.2 A partial screenshot from https://algassert.com/quirk.

A widely used online simulator is Quirk (Gidney, 2021a). Let us construct a simple two-qubit QFT circuit in Quirk, as shown in Figure 6.2. If we look to the very right and reconstruct the phases from the gray circles (blue on the website), we see that state $|00\rangle$ (top left) has a phase of 0 (the direction of the x-axis). The state $|01\rangle$ (top right) has a phase of 180°, the state $|10\rangle$ (bottom left) has a phase of −90°, and the state $|11\rangle$ has a phase of 90°. So it appears that Quirk agrees with our qubit ordering (or we agree with Quirk).

Quirk also shows the state of individual qubits on a Bloch sphere. How does this work, as we are dealing with a two-qubit tensored state, and Bloch spheres only represent single qubits? We talked about the partial trace in Section 2.14, which allows *tracing out* qubits from a state. The result after a trace-out operation is a density matrix. Since it only represents a partial state, it is called a reduced density matrix. In Section 2.9, we showed how to compute the Bloch sphere coordinates from a density matrix. Note that for systems of more than two qubits, all qubits that are not of interest must be traced out, such that only a 2×2 density matrix remains.

Let's give this a try. From the state as shown in Figure 6.2, we trace out qubit 0 and qubit 1 individually and compute the Bloch sphere coordinates:

```
psi = state.bitstring(1, 1)
psi = ops.Qft(2)(psi)

rho0 = ops.TraceOut(psi.density(), [1])
rho1 = ops.TraceOut(psi.density(), [0])

x0, y0, z0 = helper.density_to_cartesian(rho0)
x1, y1, z1 = helper.density_to_cartesian(rho1)

print('x0: {:.1f} y0: {:.1f} z0: {:.1f}'.format(x0, y0, z0))
print('x1: {:.1f} y1: {:.1f} z1: {:.1f}'.format(x1, y1, z1))

>>
x0: -1.0 y0: 0.0 z0: -0.0
x1: -0.0 y1:-1.0 z1: -0.0
```

This result seems to agree with Quirk as well. The first qubit is located at −1 on the x-axis of the Bloch sphere (going from the back of the page to the front of the page), and the second qubit is located at −1 on the y-axis (going from left to right).

6.3　　Quantum Arithmetic

We saw in Section 3.3 how a quantum circuit could be used to emulate a classical full adder, using quantum gates without exploiting any of the unique features of quantum computing, such as superposition or entanglement. It is fair to say that this was a nice exercise demonstrating the universality of quantum computing, but otherwise, a fairly inefficient way to construct a full adder.

In this section, we discuss another algorithm that performs addition and subtraction. This time the math is being developed in the Fourier domain with a technique that was first described by Draper (2000).

To perform addition, we will apply a QFT, some magic, and a final inverse QFT to obtain a numerical result. We explain this algorithm with just a hint of math and lots of code. This implementation uses a different direction from the controller to the controlled qubit as our early QFT operator. This is not difficult to follow; simply inverting the qubits in a register leads to identical implementations. We use explicit angles and the Controlled-U1 gate. The code can be found in the file `src/arith_quantum.py` in the open-source repository.

The first thing we need to specify is the bit width of the inputs a and b. If we want to do n-bit arithmetic, we need to store results as $(n + 1)$ bits to account for overflow.

Our entry point's signature will get the bit width as n and the two initial integer values `init_a` and `init_b`, which must fit into the available bits. The parameter `factor` will be 1.0 for addition and -1.0 for subtraction. We'll see shortly how this factor is applied.

```
def arith_quantum(n: int, init_a: int, init_b: int,
                  factor: float = 1.0, dumpit: bool = False) -> None:
```

We instantiate two registers with bitwidth $n + 1$. Because we interpret the bits in reverse order in this example, we have to invert the bits when initializing the registers:

```
a = qc.reg(n+1, helper.val2bits(init_a, n)[::-1], name='a')
b = qc.reg(n+1, helper.val2bits(init_b, n)[::-1], name='b')
```

The algorithm performs three basic operations:

- Apply the QFT over the qubits representing a. This encodes the bits as phases on states.
- Evolve a by b. This cryptic sounding step basically performs another set of QFT-like rotations on a using the same controlled-rotation mechanism as with regular QFT. It is not a full QFT though. There are also no initial Hadamard gates as the states are already in superposition. We detail the steps below.
- Perform inverse QFT to decode phases back to bits.

Here is the high level in code:

```
for i in range(n+1):
    qft(qc, a, n-i)
for i in range(n+1):
    evolve(qc, a, b, n-i, factor)
for i in range(n+1):
    inverse_qft(qc, a, i)
```

Let us look at these three steps in detail, using the example of two-qubit additions. We can insert dumpers after each of the loops to dump and visualize the circuit, as described in Section 8.5.6. After the first loop, we produced this circuit, in QASM format (Cross et al., 2017):

```
OPENQASM 2.0;
qreg a[3];
qreg b[3];

h a[2];
cu1(pi/2) a[1],a[2];
cu1(pi/4) a[0],a[2];
h a[1];
cu1(pi/2) a[0],a[1];
h a[0];
```

This sequence corresponds to a standard three-qubit QFT circuit. We can choose to enumerate the qubits from 0 to 2, or 2 to 0; it does not make a real difference, as long as we stay consistent. After the first loop, we constructed a standard QFT circuit.

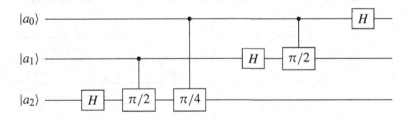

The middle loop in Figure 6.3 is where the magic happens – the evolve step produces this circuit in QASM format. We explain how this works below.

```
cu1(pi) b[2],a[2];
cu1(pi/2) b[1],a[2];
cu1(pi/4) b[0],a[2];
cu1(pi) b[1],a[1];
cu1(pi/2) b[0],a[1];
cu1(pi) b[0],a[0];
```

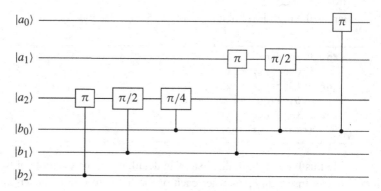

Figure 6.3 The evolve step of quantum arithmetic in the Fourier domain.

The construction of the inverse QFT circuit happens in the third loop. All of the first QFT's gates are inverted and applied in reverse order. Remember that the inverse of the Hadamard gate is another Hadamard gate, and the inverse of a rotation is a rotation by the same angle in the opposite direction.

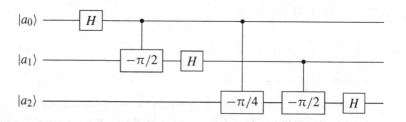

This is how the combined circuit looks. The gates are too small to read, but the elegant, melodic structure of the whole circuit becomes apparent:[1]

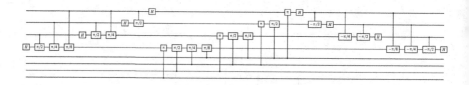

Why and how does this work? Let us first try to explain this mathematically, before explaining it by looking at the state vector. First, remember that QFT takes this state:

$$|\psi\rangle = |x_{n-1}\, x_{n-2}\, \cdots\, x_1\, x_0\rangle,$$

and changes it into this form again; depending on bit ordering, two forms are possible:

---

[1] This circuit was generated with our LaTeX transpiler, explained in Section 8.5.

$$\frac{1}{2^{n/2}} \left(|0\rangle + e^{2\pi i\ 0.x_{n-1}} |1\rangle \right)$$

$$\otimes \left(|0\rangle + e^{2\pi i\ 0.x_{n-1}x_{n-2}} |1\rangle \right)$$

$$\vdots$$

$$\otimes \left(|0\rangle + e^{2\pi i\ 0.x_{n-1}x_{n-2}\cdots x_1 x_0} |1\rangle \right).$$

Applying the rotations of the `evolve` step adds the binary fractions of b to a. For example, the first part of above state for a:

$$\left(|0\rangle + e^{2\pi i\ 0.a_{n-1}} |1\rangle \right),$$

becomes:

$$\left(|0\rangle + e^{2\pi i\ 0.(a_{n-1}+b_{n-1})} |1\rangle \right).$$

And so on for all fractional parts. The "trick" for quantum arithmetic is to interpret the qubits not as binary fractions, but as bits of full binary numbers. When interpreted this way, the net result is a full binary addition.

Another way to explain this is to look at the state vector and the evolve circuit itself. Let's assume we want to add 1 in register a and 1 in register b. Before we enter the main loops, the state looks like the following. The first three qubits belong to a, with the qubit 0 now in the role of the least significant qubit. The next three qubits belong to b. This is how we initialize the state, and, as a result, only one state has a nonzero probability:

```
|100100> (|34>):  ampl: +1.00+0.00j prob: 1.00 Phase:   0.0
```

After the initial QFT, we get this state vector:

```
|543210> after qft
|000100> (|4>):   ampl: +0.35+0.00j prob: 0.12 Phase:    0.0
|001100> (|12>):  ampl: +0.25+0.25j prob: 0.12 Phase:   45.0
|010100> (|20>):  ampl: +0.00+0.35j prob: 0.12 Phase:   90.0
|011100> (|28>):  ampl: -0.25+0.25j prob: 0.12 Phase:  135.0
|100100> (|36>):  ampl: -0.35+0.00j prob: 0.12 Phase:  180.0
|101100> (|44>):  ampl: -0.25-0.25j prob: 0.12 Phase: -135.0
|110100> (|52>):  ampl: -0.00-0.35j prob: 0.12 Phase:  -90.0
|111100> (|60>):  ampl: +0.25-0.25j prob: 0.12 Phase:  -45.0
```

Since we only apply QFT to the first three qubits, we now have eight superimposed states, all with the same probability. Let's now look at the circuit diagram for the evolve phase. The least significant qubit for b is global qubit 3, corresponding to b_0 in the diagram. Because it is set, the evolve circuit controls rotations of a full π to qubit a_0, a rotation of $\pi/2$ to qubit a_1, and a rotation of $\pi/4$ to qubit a_2.

This works like clockwork, as in, how a clock *actually* works, where smaller gears drive the larger ones. Here we deal with rotations; the higher-order qubits are made to rotate slower than the lower-order qubits:

- The least significant qubit gets a full rotation by π. If it was not set, it will have a phase of π now. If it was set, it will now have a phase of 0.
- For qubit 1 of register a, it gets a rotation of $\pi/2$.
- The most significant qubit of register a rotates by $\pi/4$.

This means, for example, that when adding a number 1 twice, the least significant qubit flip flops between 0 and π, qubit 1 runs in increments of $\pi/2$, and qubit 2 in increments of $\pi/4$. The same scheme works for the higher order qubits in register b. For our example of $1 + 1$, the following are the phases on the state vector after the evolve step:

```
|543210> after evolve
|000100> (|4>):    ampl: +0.35+0.00j prob: 0.12 Phase:    0.0
|001100> (|12>):   ampl: -0.00+0.35j prob: 0.12 Phase:   90.0
|010100> (|20>):   ampl: -0.35+0.00j prob: 0.12 Phase:  180.0
|011100> (|28>):   ampl: -0.00-0.35j prob: 0.12 Phase:  -90.0
|100100> (|36>):   ampl: +0.35-0.00j prob: 0.12 Phase:   -0.0
|101100> (|44>):   ampl: -0.00+0.35j prob: 0.12 Phase:   90.0
|110100> (|52>):   ampl: -0.35+0.00j prob: 0.12 Phase:  180.0
|111100> (|60>):   ampl: -0.00-0.35j prob: 0.12 Phase:  -90.0
```

How does this compare if we initialize a with the value 2 instead of 1? Here is that state after initialization. Note the first three qubits are now in state $|010\rangle$:

```
|010100> (|20>):   ampl: +1.00+0.00j prob: 1.00 Phase:    0.0
```

Here is the state after the initial QFT. We see that the phases are identical to the $1 + 1$ state above after evolving:

```
|543210> after qft
|000100> (|4>):    ampl: +0.35+0.00j prob: 0.12 Phase:    0.0
|001100> (|12>):   ampl: +0.00+0.35j prob: 0.12 Phase:   90.0
|010100> (|20>):   ampl: -0.35+0.00j prob: 0.12 Phase:  180.0
|011100> (|28>):   ampl: -0.00-0.35j prob: 0.12 Phase:  -90.0
|100100> (|36>):   ampl: +0.35+0.00j prob: 0.12 Phase:    0.0
|101100> (|44>):   ampl: +0.00+0.35j prob: 0.12 Phase:   90.0
|110100> (|52>):   ampl: -0.35+0.00j prob: 0.12 Phase:  180.0
|111100> (|60>):   ampl: -0.00-0.35j prob: 0.12 Phase:  -90.0
```

Back to our $1 + 1$ example. After evolve and the inverse QFT, the state corresponding to value $a = 2$ is the only state with nonzero probability, the addition worked.

Remember that the first three qubits correspond to the register a, with qubit 0 acting as the least significant bit.

```
|543210> after inv
|000100> (|4>):    ampl: +0.00+0.00j prob: 0.00 Phase:   90.0
|001100> (|12>):   ampl: +0.00-0.00j prob: 0.00 Phase:  -26.6
|010100> (|20>):   ampl: +1.00+0.00j prob: 1.00 Phase:    0.0
|011100> (|28>):   ampl: -0.00-0.00j prob: 0.00 Phase: -180.0
|100100> (|36>):   ampl: -0.00-0.00j prob: 0.00 Phase: -112.5
|101100> (|44>):   ampl: -0.00+0.00j prob: 0.00 Phase:  157.5
|110100> (|52>):   ampl: -0.00+0.00j prob: 0.00 Phase:  112.5
|111100> (|60>):   ampl: -0.00-0.00j prob: 0.00 Phase: -157.5
```

The code for the QFT and evolve functions is straightforward using the `cu1` gate. The indices are hard to follow. It is a good exercise to dump the circuit textually, for example as QASM, and check that the gates are applied in the correct order (as we have done above):

```
def qft(qc: circuit.qc, reg: state.Reg, n: int) -> None:
  qc.had(reg[n])
  for i in range(n):
    qc.cu1(reg[n-(i+1)], reg[n], math.pi/float(2**(i+1)))


def evolve(qc: circuit.qc, reg_a: state.Reg, reg_b: state.Reg,
           n: int, factor: float) -> None:
  for i in range(n+1):
    qc.cu1(reg_b[n-i], reg_a[n], factor * math.pi/float(2**(i)))


def inverse_qft(qc: circuit.qc, reg: state.Reg, n: int) -> None:
  for i in range(n):
    qc.cu1(reg[i], reg[n], -1*math.pi/float(2**(n-i)))
  qc.had(reg[n])
```

Given the insight that rotations in the Fourier domain facilitate addition, it is almost too easy to implement subtraction – we add a factor to b, and, for subtraction, we evolve the state in the opposite direction. This is already implemented in the code above in the `evolve` function.

With the same line of reasoning, multiplication of the form $a + cb$, with c being a constant other than ± 1, also just applies the factor c to the rotations. We have to be careful with overflow because we only accounted for one overflow bit.

You could argue that this is a bit disingenuous, as the rotations are fixed to a given classical factor c. The algorithm does not implement an actual multiplication (as recently proposed in Gidney (2019)) where the factor c is another quantum register used as input to the algorithm. Argued this way, it is true that this multiplication is not purely quantum. Nevertheless, performing multiplication this way has a valid use case. In Section 6.5 on Shor's algorithm, we will deal with known integer values. We can classically compute multiplication results before performing multiplication as above with an unknown quantum state. Perhaps we should call this *semi*-quantum multiplication? Naming is difficult.

In the upcoming discussion on the order-finding algorithm, we will see that for certain, more complex computations, you do indeed have to implement full arithmetic functions in the quantum domain.

To test our code, we check the results with a routine that performs a measurement. We don't actually measure, we just find the state with the highest probability. The input state with the bit pattern representing a has a probability of 1.0. After the rotations and coming out of superposition, the state $a + b$ will also have a probability close to 1.0. Note how we invert the bit order again to get to a valid result.

```python
def check_result(psi: state.State, a, b,
                 nbits: int, factor: float = 1.0) -> None:
  """Find most likely result, dump it, compare against expected."""

  maxbits, _ = psi.maxprob()
  result = helper.bits2val(maxbits[0:nbits][::-1])
  if result != a + factor * b:
    print(f'{a} + ({factor} * {b}) != {result}')
    raise AssertionError('Incorrect addition.')
```

Our test program drives this with a few loops, passing `factor` through to `arith_quantum` and `evolve` to allow testing of subtraction and (pseudo) multiplication.

```python
def main(argv):
  print('Check quantum addition...')
  for i in range(7):
    for j in range(7):
      arith_quantum(6, i, j, +1.0)

  print('Check quantum subtraction...')
  for i in range(8):
    for j in range(i):  # Note: Results can be 2nd complements.
      arith_quantum(6, i, j, -1.0)

  print('Check quantum multiplication...')
  for i in range(7):
    for j in range(7):
      arith_quantum(6, 0, i, j)
```

Since we're using the circuit implementation with accelerated gates, we can easily handle up to 14 qubits, hence we test with bit widths of 6 (plus one overflow bit per input) for the individual inputs.

6.3.1   Adding a Constant

Adding a *known constant* to a quantum register does not require a second quantum register, as it did for the general case. We can simply precompute the rotation angles and directly apply them, as they would have, if they were controlled by a second register. To precompute the required angles:

```
def precompute_angles(a: int, n: int) -> List[float]:
    """Precompute angles used in the Fourier Transform, for fixed a."""

    # Convert 'a' to a string of 0's and 1's.
    s = bin(int(a))[2:].zfill(n)

    angles = [0.] * n
    for i in range(n):
        for j in range(i, n):
            if s[j] == '1':
                angles[n-i-1] += 2**(-(j-i))
        angles[n-i-1] *= math.pi
    return angles
```

We also have to modify the `evolve` step in the quantum addition. Instead of adding controlled gates, we simply add the rotation gates directly. This is the method we will use later in Shor's algorithm as well.

```
    for i in range(n+1):
        qft(qc, a, n-i)

    angles = precompute_angles(c, n)
    for i in range(n):
        qc.u1(a[i], angles[i])

    for i in range(n+1):
        inverse_qft(qc, a, i)
```

For a three-qubit addition of $1 + 1$, the circuit no longer needs the *b* register and turns into:

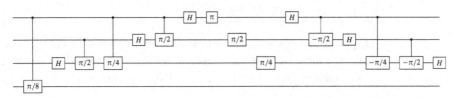

This is the same circuit for addition of $1 + 2$, but notice the modified rotation angles in the evolve step:

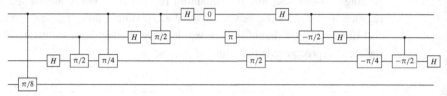

6.4   Phase Estimation

Quantum phase estimation (QPE) is a key building block for the advanced algorithms presented in this chapter. QPE cannot be discussed without the concepts of eigenvalues and eigenvectors. Let us briefly reiterate what we already know about them.

6.4.1   Eigenvalues and Eigenvectors

We have seen how operators are applied to matrices via matrix-vector multiplication. In the introductory Section 1.6, we also briefly mentioned eigenvalues and eigenvectors, for which the following equation holds, where A is an operator, $|\psi\rangle$ is a state, and λ is a simple (complex) scalar:

$$A|\psi\rangle = \lambda|\psi\rangle.$$

For example, the identity matrix I has the eigenvalue 1.0. It leaves any vector it is applied to unmodified. Correspondingly, every nonzero, size-compatible vector is an eigenvector of I. Another example would be the Pauli matrices, which have eigenvalues of $+1$ and -1. Note that any multiple of an eigenvector is also an eigenvector. Eigenvalues for a given matrix are found by solving the characteristic equation:[2]

$$\det(A - \lambda I) = 0.$$

In this text, we keep it simple and find eigenvalues of a given matrix with the help of numpy:

```
import numpy as np
[...]
umat = ... # some matrix
eigvals, eigvecs = np.linalg.eig(umat)
```

Diagonal matrices are a special case for which finding of eigenvalues is trivial – we can take them right off the diagonal, with the corresponding eigenvectors being the computational bases $(1, 0, 0, \ldots)^T$, $(0, 1, 0, \ldots)^T$, and so on. If you are an attentive

---

[2] With det being the determinant of a matrix. See, for example: https://en.wikipedia.org/wiki/Determinant.

reader, you will have noticed that the gates we used for phase rotations during quantum Fourier transforms are of similar form:

$$R_k = \begin{bmatrix} 1 & 0 \\ 0 & e^{2\pi i/2^k} \end{bmatrix} \quad \text{and} \quad U_1(\lambda) = \begin{bmatrix} 1 & 0 \\ 0 & e^{i\lambda} \end{bmatrix}.$$

6.4.2   Phase Estimation

The definition of *phase estimation* is as follows. *Given a unitary matrix U with an eigenvector $|u\rangle$ and an eigenvalue $e^{2\pi i\phi}$, estimate the value of ϕ.*

The ϕ in this eigenvalue is a factor in the range of 0.0 to 1.0 that computes a fraction of 2π. At a high level, the procedure works in two steps:

1. Encode the unknown phase with a circuit that produces a result that is identical to the result of the QFT discussed earlier in Section 6.2. We interpret the resulting qubits as parts of a binary fraction.
2. Apply $QFT^\dagger$ to compute the phase ϕ.

To detail step one, we define a register with t qubits, where t is determined by the precision we want to achieve. Just as with QFT, we will interpret the qubits as parts of a binary fraction; the more qubits, the more fine-grained fractions of powers of 2 we will be able to add up to the final result. We initialize the register with $|0\rangle$ and put it in superposition with Hadamard gates.

We add a second register representing the eigenvector $|u\rangle$. We then connect this register to a sequence of t instances of the unitary gate U, each one taken to increasing powers of 2 ($1, 2, 4, 8, \ldots, 2^{t-1}$). Similar to QFT, we connect the t register's qubits as controlling gates to the unitary gates. To achieve the powers of 2, we multiply U with itself and accumulate the results. The whole procedure is shown in Figure 6.4 in circuit notation.

Now, the relation to the quantum Fourier rotation gates becomes apparent – higher powers of 2 of U will result in the fractional phase angle being multiplied by increasing powers of 2. Please note the ordering of the qubits and their corresponding powers of 2.

A question to ask is this: Why does $|u\rangle$ have to be initialized with an eigenvector? Wouldn't this procedure work for any normalized state vector $|x\rangle$? The answer is no. This equation holds true only for eigenvectors:

$$A|u\rangle = \lambda|u\rangle.$$

This means we can apply U and any power of U to $|u\rangle$ as often as we want to. Since $|u\rangle$ is an eigenvector, it will only be scaled by a number: the complex eigenvalue ϕ with modulus 1 (as we will prove below). Let's develop the details in the next section. If you are not interested in the math, you may jump to Section 6.4.4 on implementation.

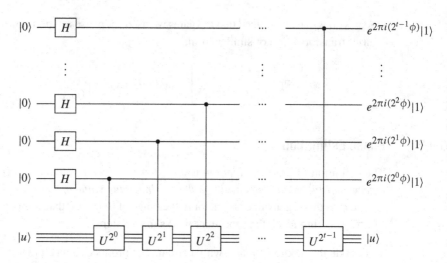

Figure 6.4 The phase estimation circuit.

6.4.3   Detailed Derivation

The first thing to know is that the eigenvalues of a unitary matrix have a modulus of 1, which is easy to prove.

Proof   We know that eigenvalues are defined as

$$U|x\rangle = \lambda|x\rangle.$$

Squaring the equation yields:

$$\langle xU^\dagger|Ux\rangle = \langle x\lambda^*|\lambda x\rangle.$$

We know that $UU^\dagger = I$, and λ^2 is a factor that we can pull in front of the inner product. State vectors are also normalized with an inner product of 1.0:

$$\langle xU^\dagger|Ux\rangle = (\lambda^*\lambda)\langle x|x\rangle,$$
$$\langle x|x\rangle = |\lambda|^2\langle x|x\rangle,$$
$$1 = |\lambda|^2 = |\lambda|. \qquad \square$$

Since $|\lambda| = 1$, we know that the eigenvalues are of this form, with ϕ being a factor between 0 and 1:

$$\lambda = e^{2\pi i\phi}.$$

In Section 6.2, we used the following notation for binary fractions with t bits of resolution, with ϕ_i being binary bits with values 0 or 1:

$$\phi = 0.\phi_0\phi_1\ldots\phi_{t-1}$$
$$= \phi_0\frac{1}{2^1} + \phi_1\frac{1}{2^2} + \cdots + \phi_{t-1}\frac{1}{2^t}.$$

With these preliminaries, let's see what happens to a state in the following circuit, which is a first small part of the phase estimation circuit. The lower qubits are in state $|\psi\rangle$, which must be an eigenstate of U.

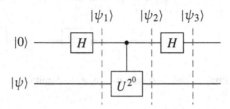

We start by limiting the precision for the eigenvalue of U to just one fractional bit. Once we understand how this works for a single fractional bit, we expand to two, which then makes it easy to generalize.

Let start with U having eigenvalue $\lambda = e^{2\pi i\ 0.\phi_0}$, with only one binary fractional part, corresponding to 2^{-1}. The phase can thus only have a value of 0.0 or 0.5. The state $|\psi_1\rangle$ after the first Hadamard gate is:

$$|\psi_1\rangle = |+\rangle \otimes |\psi\rangle = \frac{1}{\sqrt{2}} \left(|0\rangle|\psi\rangle + |1\rangle|\psi\rangle \right).$$

After the Controlled-U operation, the state $|\psi_2\rangle$ will be:

$$|\psi_2\rangle = \frac{1}{\sqrt{2}} \left(|0\rangle|\psi\rangle + |1\rangle U|\psi\rangle \right)$$

$$= \frac{1}{\sqrt{2}} \left(|0\rangle|\psi\rangle + e^{2\pi i 0.\phi_0}|1\rangle|\psi\rangle \right)$$

$$= \frac{1}{\sqrt{2}} \left(|0\rangle + e^{2\pi i 0.\phi_0}|1\rangle \right) |\psi\rangle.$$

We observe that $|\psi\rangle$ remains unmodified, as it should be, since it is an eigenstate of U. We can apply U as often as we want, $|\psi\rangle$ remains unmodified. However, the eigenvalue has turned into a phase of the $|1\rangle$ part of the first qubit. We *kicked* the phase to qubit 0, as described in Section 6.1.

There is still the problem that, on measuring the first qubit, the state might still collapse to $|0\rangle$ or $|1\rangle$ with equal probability of $1/2$, independently of whether the phase value is 0.0 or 0.5. Kicking the phase up does not change the probabilities. To resolve this, we apply another Hadamard gate to the top qubit and obtain state $|\psi_3\rangle$ (omitting the trailing qubit $|\psi\rangle$ for simplicity):

$$|\psi_3\rangle = \frac{1}{\sqrt{2}} H \left(|0\rangle + e^{2\pi i 0.\phi_0}|1\rangle \right)$$

$$= \frac{1}{2} \left(1 + e^{2\pi i 0.\phi_0} \right) |0\rangle + \frac{1}{2} \left(1 - e^{2\pi i 0.\phi_0} \right) |1\rangle.$$

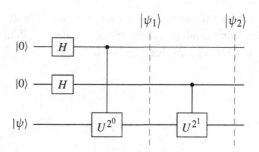

Figure 6.5 Phase estimation with two digits and unitaries.

The term ϕ_0 is a binary digit and can only be 0 or 1. If it is 0, the fraction $0(2^{-1}) = 0$. The factor $e^{2\pi i 0.\phi_0} = e^0$ becomes 1, and $|\psi_3\rangle$ becomes:

$$|\psi_3\rangle = \frac{1}{2}|0\rangle + \frac{1}{2}|0\rangle + \frac{1}{2}|1\rangle - \frac{1}{2}|1\rangle = |0\rangle.$$

If, on the other hand, the digit $\phi_0 = 1$, then $1(2^{-1}) = 1/2$. The factor $e^{2\pi i 0.\phi_0}$ becomes $e^{2\pi i/2} = -1$ and $|\psi_3\rangle$ becomes:

$$|\psi_3\rangle = \frac{1}{2}|0\rangle - \frac{1}{2}|0\rangle + \frac{1}{2}|1\rangle + \frac{1}{2}|1\rangle = |1\rangle.$$

We will now measure either $|0\rangle$ or $|1\rangle$ with certainty, depending on whether ϕ was 0.0 or 0.5.

Now let's move on and consider two (or more) fractional binary parts for the phase $\phi = 0.\phi_0\phi_1$, which can now have values $0.0, 0.25, 0.5$, and 0.75. The corresponding circuit also has two exponentiated U gates and is shown in Figure 6.5. From above, we know that $|\psi_1\rangle$ will have this form:

$$|\psi_1\rangle = \frac{1}{\sqrt{2^3}} \underbrace{\left(|0\rangle + e^{2\pi i 0.\phi_0\phi_1}\right)|1\rangle}_{\text{qubit 0}} \otimes \underbrace{(|0\rangle + |1\rangle)}_{\text{qubit 1}} \otimes \underbrace{|\psi\rangle}_{\text{qubit 2}}.$$

Now let's study the effect of the controlled U^{2^1} on qubit 1. We know that squaring a rotation means doubling the rotation angle:

$$U^2|\psi\rangle = e^{2\pi i(2\phi)}|\psi\rangle.$$

Looking at the fractional representation and the effects of U^2, we see that the binary point shifts by one digit:

$$2\phi = 2(0.\phi_0\phi_1)$$
$$= 2\left(\phi_0 2^{-1} + \phi_1 2^{-2}\right)$$
$$= \phi_0 + \phi_1 2^{-1} = \phi_0.\phi_1.$$

We split the fraction at the decimal point:

$$e^{2\pi i(2\phi)} = e^{2\pi i(\phi_0.\phi_1)}$$
$$= e^{2\pi i(\phi_0 + 0.\phi_1)}$$
$$= e^{2\pi i(\phi_0)} e^{2\pi i(0.\phi_1)}.$$

The term ϕ_0 corresponds to a binary digit; it can only be 0 or 1. This means the first factor corresponds to a rotation by 0 or 2π, which has no effect. The final result is:

$$e^{2\pi i(2\phi)} = e^{2\pi i(0.\phi_1)}.$$

which we can generalize to:

$$e^{2\pi i(2^k\phi)} = e^{2\pi i\, 0.\phi_k}.$$

For our three-qubits circuit above, the final state becomes:

$$|\psi_2\rangle = \frac{1}{\sqrt{2^3}} \underbrace{\left(|0\rangle + e^{2\pi i 0.\phi_0\phi_1}|1\rangle \right)}_{\text{qubit 0}} \otimes \underbrace{\left(|0\rangle + e^{2\pi i 0.\phi_1}|1\rangle \right)}_{\text{qubit 1}} \otimes \underbrace{|\psi\rangle}_{\text{qubit 2}}$$

This is the form that results from applying the QFT operator to two qubits! This means we can apply the two-qubit adjoint $QFT^\dagger$ operator to retrieve the binary fractions of $\phi = 0.\phi_0\phi_1$ as qubit states $|0\rangle$ or $|1\rangle$:

$$QFT_{0,1}^\dagger |\psi_2\rangle = |\phi_1\rangle \otimes |\phi_0\rangle \otimes |\psi\rangle.$$

To summarize, we connected the 0th power of 2 to the last qubit in register t and the $(t-1)$'s power of 2 to the first qubit (or the other way around, depending on how we want to interpret the binary fractions). The final state thus becomes:

$$\frac{1}{2^{t/2}} \left(|0\rangle + e^{i\pi 2^{t-1}\phi}|1\rangle \right)$$
$$\otimes \left(|0\rangle + e^{i\pi 2^{t-2}\phi}|1\rangle \right)$$
$$\vdots$$
$$\otimes \left(|0\rangle + e^{i\pi 2^0\phi}|1\rangle \right).$$

Similar to a QFT, we express ϕ in t bits in the fractional notation as the following:

$$\phi = 0.\phi_{t-1}\phi_{t-2}\cdots\phi_0.$$

Multiplying this angle with the powers of two as shown above will shift the digits of the binary representation to the left, and the state after the circuit will be:

$$\frac{1}{2^{t/2}} \left(|0\rangle + e^{i2\pi 0.\phi_{t-1}} |1\rangle \right)$$

$$\otimes \left(|0\rangle + e^{i2\pi 0.\phi_{t-1}\phi_{t-2}} |1\rangle \right)$$

$$\vdots$$

$$\otimes \left(|0\rangle + e^{i2\pi 0.\phi_{t-1}\phi_{t-2}\cdots\phi_1\phi_0} |1\rangle \right).$$

The form above is similar to the result of a QFT, where the rotations come out according to how the input qubits were initialized in binary representation. The bit indices are reversed from what we usually see, but this is just a renaming or ordering issue. The final step of phase estimation reverses the QFT. It applies $QFT^\dagger$ to allow reconstruction of the input, which, in our case, was the representation of ϕ in binary fractions. The complete circuit layout is shown in Figure 6.6.

It is important not to confuse the ordering in code and notation. As usual, all textbooks disagree on notation and ordering. This is not that important in our case as we can interpret the binary fraction in the proper order to obtain the desired result.

We can now measure the qubits, interpret them as binary fractions, and combine them to approximate ϕ, as we will show in the implementation. Remember how we used $|1\rangle$ to initialize the ancilla qubit in the phase kick circuit? The underlying mechanism is the same. State $|1\rangle$ is an eigenstate for both the S-gate and T-gate.

6.4.4   Implementation

In code, this may look simpler than the math above. The full implementation can be found in file `src/phase_estimation` in the open source repository. We drive this algorithm from `main()`, reserving six qubits for t and three qubits for the unitary operator. It is instructive to experiment with the numbers. We run ten experiments:

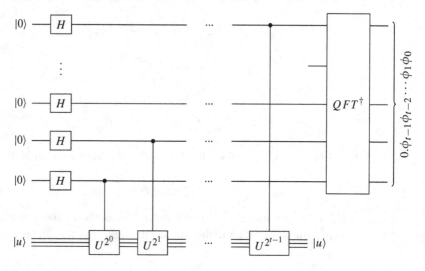

Figure 6.6 Full quantum phase estimation circuit.

```
def main(argv):
  nbits = 3
  t = 6
  print('Estimating {} qubits random unitary eigenvalue '
        .format(nbits) + 'with {} bits of accuracy.'.format(t))
  for i in range(10):
    run_experiment(nbits, t)
```

In each experiment, we create a random operator and obtain its eigenvalues and eigenvectors to ensure that our estimates below are close.

```
def run_experiment(nbits: int, t: int = 8):
  """Run single phase estimation experiment."""

  # Make a unitary and find eigenvalue/vector to estimate.
  # We use functions from scipy for this purpose.
  umat = scipy.stats.unitary_group.rvs(2**nbits)
  eigvals, eigvecs = np.linalg.eig(umat)
  u = ops.Operator(umat)
```

We pick eigenvector 0 to use as an example here, but the procedure works for all other pairs of eigenvectors and eigenvalues. To check whether the algorithm works, we compute the to-be-estimated angle phi upfront. Since we are assuming the eigenvalue to be of the form $e^{2\pi i\phi}$, as discussed in Section 6.4.2, we divide by 2j*np.pi. Also, we don't want to deal with negative values. Again, this angle does not participate in the algorithm; we just compute it upfront to confirm later that we indeed computed a correct approximation:

```
# Pick eigenvalue at eigen_index
# (any eigenvalue / eigenvector pair will work).
eigen_index = 0
phi = np.real(np.log(eigvals[eigen_index]) / (2j*np.pi))
if phi < 0:
  phi += 1
```

For the overall circuit, note how we initialize the state psi with t qubits in state $|0\rangle$ tensored with another state that is initialized with an eigenvector.

```
# Make state + circuit to estimate phi.
# Pick eigenvector 'eigen_index' to match the eigenvalue.
psi = state.zeros(t) * state.State(eigvecs[:, eigen_index])
```

After we have this initialized state, we connect it with exponentiated operators, "unpacking" the binary fractions from the phase. We then run the inverse QFT on the resulting state.

```
psi = expo_u(psi, u, t)
psi = ops.Qft(t).adjoint()(psi)
```

The heart of this circuit is the controlled connection of the operators taken to powers of 2, which is implemented in `expo_u` (naming is difficult):

```
def expo_u(psi: state.State, u: ops.Operator, t: int) -> state.State:
  """Exponentiate U."""

  psi = ops.Hadamard(t)(psi)
  for idx, inv in enumerate(range(t-1, -1, -1)):
    u2 = u
    for _ in range(idx):
      u2 = u2(u2)
    psi = ops.ControlledU(inv, t, u2)(psi, inv)
  return psi
```

All that is left to do is to simulate a measurement by picking the state with the highest probability, computing the binary fraction from this state, and comparing the result against the target value. Since we have limited bits to represent the result, we allow an error margin of 2%. More bits for t will make the circuit run slower but also improve the error margins.

```
# Find state with highest measurement probability and show results.
maxbits, maxprob = psi.maxprob()
phi_estimate = sum(maxbits[i] * 2**(-i-1) for i in range(t))

delta = abs(phi - phi_estimate)
print('Phase    : {:.4f}'.format(phi))
print('Estimate: {:.4f} delta: {:.4f} probability: {:5.2f}%'
      .format(phi_estimate, delta, maxprob * 100.0))
if delta > 0.02 and phi_estimate < 0.98:
  print('*** Warning: Delta is large')
```

There is the potential of `delta` to be larger than two percent, especially when not enough bits were reserved for `t`. Another interesting error case is when the eigenvalue rounds to 1.0. In this case, all digits after the dot are 0. As a result, the estimated value from the binary fractions will also be 0.0 instead of the correct value of 1.0. The code warns about this case.

The result should look similar to the following output. Note that the highest probability found may not be close to 1.0. This means that when measured on a real, probabilistic quantum computer, we would obtain a fairly noisy result, with the correct solution hopefully showing enough distinction from other measurements.

```
Estimating 3 qubits random unitary eigenvalue with 6 bits of accuracy
Phase    : 0.5180
Estimate: 0.5156 delta: 0.0024 probability: 31.65%
```

```
Phase    : 0.3203
Estimate: 0.3125 delta: 0.0078 probability:  7.30%
[...]
Phase    : 0.6688
Estimate: 0.6719 delta: 0.0030 probability: 20.73%
```

6.5   Shor's Algorithm

Shor's algorithm for number factorization is the one algorithm that has sparked a tremendous amount of interest in quantum computing (Shor, 1994). The internet's RSA (Rivest, Shamir, Adlemen) encryption algorithm (Rivest et al., 1978) is based on the assumption that number factoring is an intractable problem. If quantum computers could crack this code, it would have severe implications.

Shor's algorithm is complex to implement, at least with the background of the material presented so far. To factor numbers like 15 or 21, it requires a large number of qubits and a very large number of gates, in the order of many thousands.

This looks like a great challenge, so let's dive right in. The algorithm has two parts:

1. It has a classical part, grounded in number theory, which relies on modular arithmetic and a process called order finding.
2. Order finding is intractable when done classically but can be mapped efficiently to a probabilistic quantum algorithm.

Correspondingly, we split the description of the algorithm into two parts. The classical part is discussed in this section, and the quantum part will be discussed in Section 6.6 on order finding.

6.5.1   Modular Arithmetic

Modular arithmetic is a complete arithmetic over integers that wrap around a given number, called the modulus, and considers the remainder. The modulus *mirrors* the C++ or Python percent operators, but it is not quite the same. One definition is,

$$a \equiv b \bmod N \Rightarrow b \equiv qN + a, \text{for some } q.$$

Or, equivalently,

$$a \equiv b \bmod N \Rightarrow a \bmod N \equiv b \bmod N.$$

Two numbers are *congruent* mod N if their modulus is the same, in which case they are in the same equivalence class. Here are examples for a modulus of 12:

$$15 \equiv 3 \bmod 12,$$
$$15 \equiv -9 \bmod 12.$$

The numbers $15, 3$, and -9 are in the same mod 12 equivalence class. Note that in Python, applying the % operator would yield `-9 % 12 = 3`. Simple algebraic rules hold:

$$(x + y) \bmod N \equiv x \bmod N + y \bmod N,$$
$$(xy) \bmod N \equiv (x \bmod N)(y \bmod N).$$

We can use these rules to simplify computation with large numbers, for example:

$$(121 + 241) \bmod 12 \equiv 1 + 1 = 2,$$
$$(121 \cdot 241) \bmod 12 \equiv 1 \cdot 1 = 1.$$

## 6.5.2	Greatest Common Divisor

We will need to compute the *greatest common divisor* (GCD) of two integers. To reiterate, for two numbers, we break the numbers down into their prime factors and find the largest common factor. For example, the GCD of the integers 15 and 21 is 3:

$$15 = 3 \cdot 5,$$
$$21 = 3 \cdot 7.$$

Of course, we compute the GCD with the famous Euclidean algorithm:

```python
def gcd(a: int, b: int) -> int:
    while b != 0:
        t = b
        b = a % b
        a = t
    return a
```

## 6.5.3	Factorization

Now we shall see how to use modular arithmetic and the GCD to factor a large number into two primes. We are only considering numbers that have two prime factors. Why is this important? In general, any number can be factored into several prime factors p_i:

$$N = p_0^{e_0} p_1^{e_1} \cdots p_{n-1}^{e_{n-1}}.$$

But the factoring is most difficult if N has just two prime factors of roughly equal length. This is why this mechanism is used in RSA encryption. Hence, we assume that

$$N = pq.$$

We can rephrase this problem in an interesting way. The problem of factoring a large number N into two primes is equivalent to solving this equation

$$x^2 \equiv 1 \bmod N. \tag{6.3}$$

There are two trivial solutions to this equation: $x = 1$ and $x = -1$. Are there other solutions? In the following, the typical examples for N are 15 and 21. As we will see later, this is mostly determined by the number of qubits we will be able to simulate.

Let us pick 21 as our example integer. We will iterate over all values from 0 to N and see whether we find another x for which above Equation (6.3) holds:

```
1*1 =  1 =  1 mod N
2*2 =  4 =  4 mod N
3*3 =  9 =  9 mod N
4*4 = 16 = 16 mod N
5*5 = 25 =  4 mod N
6*6 = 36 = 15 mod N
7*7 = 49 =  8 mod N
8*8 = 64 =  1 mod N
[...]
```

Indeed, we found another x for which this equation holds, $x = 8$. We can turn the search around and, instead of looking for the n in $n^2 = 1 \bmod N$, we search for the n with a given constant c in $c^n = 1 \bmod N$. This is the mechanism we will use during order finding. Here is an example with $c = 2$:

```
2^0 =  1 =  1 mod N
2^1 =  2 =  2 mod N
2^2 =  4 =  4 mod N
2^3 =  8 =  8 mod N
2^4 = 16 = 16 mod N
2^5 = 32 = 11 mod N
2^6 = 64 =  1 mod N
```

Since:

$$x^2 \equiv 1 \bmod N,$$
$$x^2 - 1 \equiv 0 \bmod N.$$

We can factor this via the quadratic formula into:

$$(x + 1)(x - 1) \equiv 0 \bmod N.$$

The modulo 0 means that N divides this product. We can therefore find the prime factors by computing:

```
factor1 = gcd(N, x+1)
factor2 = gcd(N, x-1)
```

This looks easy but suffers from the "little technical problem" of having to find that number x. In the classical case, our only options are to either iterate over all numbers or pick random values, square them, and check whether we hit a modulo 1 number.

Picking random values means that the birthday paradox applies,[3] and the probability of finding the right value for an N-bit number is roughly $\sqrt{2N}$. The is completely intractable for the large numbers used in internet encryption and numbers with lengths of 1024 bits, 4096 bits, and higher. What now?

6.5.4   Period Finding

We apply the following, and somewhat unexpected, three next steps; later we will find an efficient quantum algorithm for step 2.

Step 1 – Select Seed Number

We pick a random number $a < N$ that does not have a nontrivial factor in common with N. We also say that a and N are *coprime*. This can be tested with the help of the GCD. If their GCD is 1, the two numbers do not have a common factor and are coprime. If a does divide N, we got lucky and have found a factor already.

Step 2 – Find Order

Find the *powers modulo N*, with this sequence:

$$a^0 \bmod N = 1,$$
$$a^1 \bmod N = \ldots,$$
$$a^2 \bmod N = \ldots,$$
$$\vdots$$

With the help of this function of a, N, and x (with a and N known, x unknown):

$$f_{a,N}(x) = a^x \bmod N.$$

Number theory guarantees that for any coprime a of N, this function will compute a result of 1 for some $x < N$. Once the sequence produces the 1 (for $x > 0$), the sequence of numbers computed so far will repeat itself. Remember that the sequence starts with the exponent of 0, resulting in $a^x = 1$. The length of the sequence, typically named r, is called the *order*, or period, of the function:

$$f_{a,N}(s + r) = f_{a,N}(s).$$

We will see how to construct a quantum algorithm to find the order in the next section. For now, let's just pretend we have an efficient way to compute it.

---

[3] https://en.wikipedia.org/wiki/Birthday_problem.

Step 3 – Factor

Once we have the order, how does it help us to get the factors of N?

If we find an order r that is an odd number, we give up, throw the result away, and try a different initial value of a in step 1.

If we find an order r that is an even number, we can use what we discovered earlier, namely, we can get the factors if we can find the x in this equation:

$$x^2 \equiv 1 \bmod N.$$

We just found in step 2 above that:

$$a^r \equiv 1 \bmod N.$$

Which we can rewrite as the following, if r is even:

$$\left(a^{r/2}\right)^2 \equiv 1 \bmod N.$$

This means we can now compute the factors similar to above, (with $r = $ order) as:

```
factor1 = gcd(N, a ** (order // 2) + 1)
factor2 = gcd(N, a ** (order // 2) - 1)
```

There is another little (as in, actually little) caveat – we do not know whether a given initial value of a will result in an even or odd order. It can be shown that the probability of getting an even order is $1/2$. We might have to run the algorithm multiple times.

These three steps, select seed number, find ordering, and factor, are the core of Shor's algorithm, minus the quantum parts. Let us write some code to explore the concepts this far before explaining quantum order finding in Section 6.6.

6.5.5 Playground

In this section, we will pick random numbers and apply the ideas from above. We still compute the order and derive the prime factors classically. Since our numbers are small, this is still tractable. Let us write a few helper functions first (the full source code is in file `src/shor_classic.,py`).

When picking a random number to play with, we must make sure that it is, indeed, factorizable and not prime:

```
def is_prime(num: int) -> bool:
  """Check to see whether num can be factored at all."""

  for i in range(3, num // 2, 2):
    if num % i == 0:
      return False
  return True
```

The algorithm requires picking a random number to seed the process. This number must not be a relative prime of the larger number, or the process might fail:

```python
def is_coprime(num: int, larger_num: int) -> bool:
    """Determine if num is coprime to larger_num."""

    return math.gcd(num, larger_num) == 1
```

Find a random, odd, nonprime number in the range of numbers from `fr` to `to` and also find a corresponding coprime:

```python
def get_odd_non_prime(fr: int, to: int) -> int:
    """Get a non-prime number in the range."""

    while True:
        n = random.randint(fr, to)
        if n % 2 == 0:
            continue
        if not is_prime(n):
            return n

def get_coprime(larger_num: int) -> int:
    """Find a number < larger_num which is coprime to it."""

    while True:
        val = random.randint(3, larger_num - 1)
        if is_coprime(val, larger_num):
            return val
```

And finally, we will need a routine to compute the order of a given modulus. This routine is, of course, classical and iterates until it finds the result of 1 that is guaranteed to exist.

```python
def classic_order(num: int, modulus: int) -> int:
    """Find the order classically via simple iteration."""

    order = 1
    while True:
        newval = (num ** order) % modulus
        if newval == 1:
            return order
        order += 1
    return order
```

Here is the main algorithm, which we execute many times over randomly chosen numbers. We first select a random a and N, as described above. N is the number we want to factorize, so it must not be prime. The value *a* must not be a coprime. Once we have those, we compute the order:

```python
def run_experiment(fr: int, to: int) -> (int, int):
    """Run the classical part of Shor's algorithm."""

    n = get_odd_non_prime(fr, to)
    a = get_coprime(n)
    order = classic_order(a, n)
```

All that's left is to compute the factors from the even order and to print and check the results:

```python
    factor1 = math.gcd(a ** (order // 2) + 1, n)
    factor2 = math.gcd(a ** (order // 2) - 1, n)
    if factor1 == 1 or factor2 == 1:
        return None

    print('Found Factors: N = {:4d} = {:4d} * {:4d} (r={:4})'.
          format(factor1 * factor2, factor1, factor2, order))
    if factor1 * factor2 != n:
        raise AssertionError('Invalid factoring')

    return factor1, factor2
```

We run some 25 tests and should see results like the following. For random numbers up to 9,999, the order can already reach values of up to almost 4,000:

```python
def main(argv):
    print('Classic Part of Shor\'s Algorithm.')
    for i in range(25):
        run_experiment(21, 9999)

[...]
Classic Part of Shor's Algorithm.
Found Factors: N = 3629 =  191 *   19 (r=1710)
Found Factors: N = 4295 =    5 *  859 (r=1716)
[...]
Found Factors: N = 2035 =    5 *  407 (r= 180)
Found Factors: N = 9023 = 1289 *    7 (r=3864)
Found Factors: N = 1781 =  137 *   13 (r= 408)
```

In summary, we have learned how to factor a number *N* into two prime factors based on order finding and modular arithmetic. Order finding for very large numbers is intractable classically, but in the next section we will learn an efficient quantum algorithm for this task. The whole algorithm is quite magical, and it becomes even more so when considering the quantum parts!

6.6   Order Finding

In the last section, we learned how finding the order of a specific function classically lets us efficiently factor a number into its two prime factors. In this section, we discuss an effective quantum algorithm to replace this classical task. We start by stating an objective – finding the phase of a particular operator. Initially, it might not be apparent how this relates to finding the order, but no worries, we develop all the details in the next few sections.

Quantum order finding is phase estimation applied to this operator U:

$$U|y\rangle = |xy \bmod N\rangle. \tag{6.4}$$

Phase estimation needs an eigenvector in order to run correctly. Let us first find the eigenvalues of this operator. We know that eigenvalues are defined as:

$$U|v\rangle = \lambda|v\rangle.$$

We use a process similar to the power iteration process. We know that the eigenvalues must be of norm 1; otherwise, the probabilities in the state vector would not add up to 1. Thus we can state:

$$U^k|v\rangle = \lambda^k|v\rangle,$$

and substitute this into the operator of Equation (6.4). This is a key step that is, unfortunately, often omitted in the literature:

$$U^k|y\rangle = |x^k y \bmod N\rangle.$$

If r is now the order of $x \bmod N$, with $x^r = 1 \bmod N$, then we get this result:

$$U^r|v\rangle = \lambda^r|v\rangle = |x^r y \bmod N\rangle = |v\rangle.$$

From this we can derive:

$$\lambda^r = 1.$$

This means the eigenvalues of U are the rth *roots of unity*. A root of unity is a complex number that, when raised to some integer power n, yields 1.0. It is defined as:

$$\lambda = e^{2\pi is/r} \quad \text{for } s = 0, \dots, r-1.$$

With this result, we will show below that the eigenvectors of this operator are the following for order r and a value s with $0 \le s < r$:

$$|v_s\rangle = \frac{1}{\sqrt{r}} \sum_{k=0}^{r-1} e^{2\pi iks/r} |a^k \bmod N\rangle.$$

With phase estimation, we can find the eigenvalues $e^{2\pi i s/r}$. The final trick will be to get to the order from the fraction s/r.

There is, of course, a big problem – for the phase estimation circuit, we needed to know an *eigenvector*. Because we do not know the order r, we cannot know any of the eigenvectors. Here comes another smart trick. We do know that the operator in Equation (6.4) is a permutation operator. Following the pattern of modular arithmetic, states are uniquely mapped to other states with order r. In this context, we should interpret states as integers, with state $|1\rangle$ representing decimal 1, and state $|1001\rangle$ representing decimal 9. For all values less than r, this mapping is a 1:1 mapping. For our operator:

$$U|y\rangle = |xy \bmod N\rangle .$$

We see that state $|y\rangle$ is multiplied by $x \bmod N$. As we iterate over exponents, this becomes:

$$U^n|y\rangle = |x^n y \bmod N\rangle .$$

For our example above, with $a = 2$ and $N = 21$, each application multiplies the state of the input register by $2 \bmod N$. We started with $2^0 = 1 = 1 \bmod N$, corresponding to state $|1\rangle$. Then:

$$U|1\rangle = |2\rangle,$$
$$U^2|1\rangle = UU|1\rangle = U|2\rangle = |4\rangle,$$
$$U^3|1\rangle = |8\rangle,$$
$$U^4|1\rangle = |16\rangle,$$
$$U^5|1\rangle = |11\rangle,$$
$$U^6|1\rangle = U^r|1\rangle = |1\rangle.$$

We can deduce that the first eigenvector of this operator is the *superposition of all states*. This is easy to understand from a simpler example.[4] Assume a unitary gate only permutes between the two states $|0\rangle$ and $|1\rangle$, with:

$$U|0\rangle = |1\rangle \quad \text{and} \quad U|1\rangle = |0\rangle.$$

Applying U to the superposition of both these states leads to the following result with an eigenvalue of 1:

$$U\left(\frac{|0\rangle + |1\rangle}{\sqrt{2}}\right) = \frac{U|0\rangle + U|1\rangle}{\sqrt{2}}$$
$$= \frac{|1\rangle + |0\rangle}{\sqrt{2}} = \frac{|0\rangle + |1\rangle}{\sqrt{2}}$$
$$= 1.0 \frac{|0\rangle + |1\rangle}{\sqrt{2}}.$$

[4] https://quantumcomputing.stackexchange.com/a/15590/11582.

For the operator in Equation (6.4), we can generalize to multiple basis states. The superposition of the basis states is an eigenvector of U with eigenvalue 1.0:

$$|u_1\rangle = \frac{1}{\sqrt{r}} \sum_{k=0}^{r-1} |a^k \bmod N\rangle.$$

We also deduced above that the other eigenvalues are of the form:

$$\lambda = e^{2\pi i s/r} \quad \text{for } s = 0, \ldots, r-1.$$

Let's look at the eigenstates where the phase of the kth basis state is proportional to k:

$$|u_1\rangle = \frac{1}{\sqrt{r}} \sum_{k=0}^{r-1} e^{2\pi i k/r} |a^k \bmod N\rangle. \tag{6.5}$$

For our example, applying the operator to this eigenvector follows the permutation rules of the operator U ($|1\rangle \rightarrow |2\rangle, |2\rangle \rightarrow |4\rangle, \ldots$):

$$|u_1\rangle = \frac{1}{6}\left(|1\rangle + e^{2\pi i/6}|2\rangle + e^{4\pi i/6}|4\rangle + e^{6\pi i/6}|8\rangle + e^{8\pi i/6}|16\rangle + e^{10\pi i/6}|11\rangle\right),$$

$$U|u_1\rangle = \frac{1}{6}\left(|2\rangle + e^{2\pi i/6}|4\rangle + e^{4\pi i/6}|8\rangle + e^{6\pi i/6}|16\rangle + e^{8\pi i/6}|11\rangle + e^{10\pi i/6}|1\rangle\right).$$

We can pull out the factor $e^{-2\pi i/6}$ to arrive at:

$$U|u_1\rangle = \frac{1}{6}e^{-2\pi i/6}\left(e^{\frac{2\pi i}{6}}|2\rangle + e^{\frac{4\pi i}{6}}|4\rangle + e^{\frac{6\pi i}{6}}|8\rangle + e^{\frac{8\pi i}{6}}|16\rangle + e^{\frac{10\pi i}{6}}|11\rangle + \underbrace{e^{\frac{12\pi i}{6}}}_{=1}|1\rangle\right)$$

$$= e^{-2\pi i/6}|u_1\rangle.$$

Note how the order $r = 6$ now appears in the denominator. To make this general for all eigenvectors, we multiply in a factor s:

$$|u_s\rangle = \frac{1}{\sqrt{r}} \sum_{k=0}^{r-1} e^{2\pi i k s/r} |a^k \bmod N\rangle.$$

As a result, for our operator, we now get a unique eigenvector for each integer $s = 0, \ldots, r-1$, with the following eigenvalues (note that if we added the minus sign to Equation (6.5) above, the minus sign here would disappear; we can ignore it):

$$e^{-2\pi i s/r}|u_s\rangle.$$

Furthermore, there is another important result from this: if we add up all these eigenvectors, the phases cancel out except for $|1\rangle$ (not shown here; it is voluminous, but not challenging). This helps us because now we can use $|1\rangle$ as the eigenvector input to the phase estimation circuit. Phase estimation will give us the following result:

$$\phi = \frac{s}{r}.$$

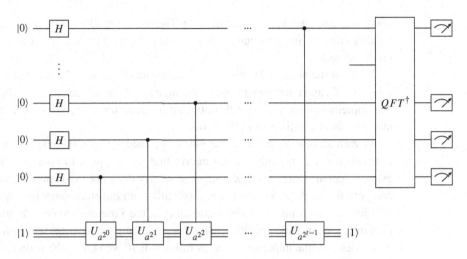

Figure 6.7 Order finding circuit.

But why is it that can we use $|1\rangle$ to initialize the phase estimation? Here[5] is an answer: Phase estimation should work for one eigenvector/eigenvalue pair. But in this case, we initialize the circuit with the sum of all eigenvectors, which we can consider as the *superposition* of all eigenstates. On measurement, the state will collapse to one of them. Which one? We do not know, but we do know from above that it will have a phase $\phi = s/r$. This is all we need to find the order with the method of continued fractions.

With all these preliminaries, we can now construct a phase estimation circuit as shown in Figure 6.7. For a given to-be-factored N, we define the number of bits necessary to represent N as $L = \log_2(N)$. The output of this circuit will be less than N, and we may need up to L output bits. We need to evaluate the unitary operation for at least N^2 values of x to be able to sample the order reliably, so we need $2L$ input bits:

$$\log_2 N^2 = 2 \log_2 N = 2L.$$

When we implement the algorithm, we will also use an ancilla register to store intermediate results from additions with a bit width of $L + 2$. (Typically you reserve a single bit for addition overflow, but we implement controlled addition, which requires an additional ancilla.) In summary, in order to factor a number fitting in L classical bits, we need $L + 2L + L + 2 = 4L + 2$ qubits. To factor 15, which fits into four classical bits, we will need 18 qubits. To factor 21, which fits in five classical bits, we will need 22 qubits. This number differs from what is typically quoted in the literature, which is theoretically closer to $2L + 1$. This discrepancy appears to be an artifact of the implementation details.

The big practical challenge for this circuit is how to implement the large unitary operator U. Our solution is based on a paper from Stephane Beauregard (Beauregard,

---

[5] https://quantumcomputing.stackexchange.com/q/15589/11582

2003) and a reference implementation by Tiago Leao and Rui Maia (Leao, 2021). It is a rather complex implementation, but, fortunately, we have seen most of the building blocks already.

To factor the number 21, we need 22 qubits and more than 20,000 gates. There are lots of QFTs and uncomputations, so the number of gates increases quickly. With our fast implementation, we can still simulate this circuit tractably. The overall implementation is about 250 lines of Python code.

As with all oracles or high-level unitary operators, you might expect some sort of quantum trick, a specially crafted matrix that just happens to compute the modulo exponentiation. Unfortunately, a magical matrix does not exist. Instead, we have to compute the modulo exponentiation explicitly with quantum gates by implementing addition and multiplication (by a constant) in the Fourier domain. We also have to implement the modulo operation, which is something we have not seen before.

We describe the implementation as follows: first, we outline the main routine driving the whole process. Then, we describe the helper routines, e.g., for addition. We have seen most of these before in other sections. Finally, we describe the code that builds the unitary operators and connects them to compute the phase estimate. We then get actual experimental results from the estimated phase with help of continued fractions.

6.6.1   Main Program

The implementation can be found in file `src/order_finding.py` in the open source repository. We get the numbers N and a from command line parameters. With these values, we compute the required bit width and construct three registers:

- `aux` for ancillae.
- `up` is the top register in the circuit shown in Figure 6.7. We will compute the inverse QFT on this register to get the phase estimation.
- `down` is the register that we will connect to the unitary operators. We also initialize it to $|1\rangle$.

```
def main(argv):
print('Order finding.')

number = flags.FLAGS.N
a = flags.FLAGS.a

# Test some of the basic routines.
test_preliminaries(a, number)

# The classical part are handled in 'shor_classic.py'
nbits = number.bit_length()
print('Shor: N = {}, a = {}, n = {} -> qubits: {}'
      .format(number,        a, nbits, nbits*4 + 2))
```

```
qc = circuit.qc('order_finding')

# Aux register for addition and multiplication.
aux = qc.reg(nbits+2, name='q0')

# Register for QFT. This reg will hold the resulting x-value.
up = qc.reg(nbits*2, name='q1')

# Register for multiplications.
down = qc.reg(nbits, name='q2')
```

We follow this with a one-to-one implementation of the circuit diagram in Figure 6.7. We apply Hadamard gates to all of the up register qubits and apply the X-gate to the down register to initialize it with |1⟩. Note that in order to stay closer to the reference implementation (Leao, 2021), we interpret down in a reversed order. Then, we iterate over the number of up bits (nbits * 2) and create and connect the unitary gates with the Controlled-Multiply-Modulo (by power of 2) routine cmultmodn, which we show below. All of this is then followed by a final $QFT^\dagger$:

```
qc.had(up)
qc.x(down[0])
for i in range(nbits*2):
    cmultmodn(qc, up[i], down, aux, int(a**(2**i)), number, nbits)
inverse_qft(qc, up, 2*nbits, with_swaps=1)
```

Finally, we check the results. For the numbers given ($N = 15$, $a = 4$), we expect a result of 128 or 0 in the up register, corresponding to interpretations as binary fractions of 0.5 and 0.0. We will detail the next steps on how to get to the factors at the end of this section. This code snippet differs from the final implementation. Note again that we inverted the bit order with [::-1]:

```
# -- Results. An x-value of 128 would result in
#    the correct continuous fractions later.
print('Measurement...')
total_prob = 0.0
for bits in helper.bitprod(nbits*4 + 2):
    prob = qc.psi.prob(*bits)
    if prob > 0.01:
        print('Final x-value. Got: {:3d} Want: 128, probability: {:.3f}'
            .format(
                helper.bits2val(bits[nbits+2 : nbits+2 + nbits*2][::-1]),
                prob.real))
        total_prob += qc.psi.prob(*bits)
        if total_prob > 0.999:
            break

print(qc.stats())
```

And indeed, we will get this result with 50% probability. This is the reality of this algorithm – it is probabilistic. On a real machine, we might find only 1 and N and have to run the algorithm multiple times until we find at least one prime factor. In our infrastructure, of course, we can just peek at the resulting probabilities, no need to run multiple times.

```
[...]
Swap...
Uncompute...
Measurement...
Final x-value. Got:   0 Want: 128, probability: 0.250
Final x-value. Got:   0 Want: 128, probability: 0.250
Final x-value. Got: 128 Want: 128, probability: 0.250
Final x-value. Got: 128 Want: 128, probability: 0.250
Circuit Statistics
   Qubits: 18
   Gates : 10553
```

6.6.2   Support Routines

We use the variable a to compute a modulo number. Since we have to do uncomputation, we need the *modulo inverse* of this number. The modulo inverse of $x \bmod N$ is the number x_{inv}, such that $x x_{inv} = 1 \bmod N$. We can compute this number with the help of the extended Euclidean algorithm (Wikipedia, 2021c):

```python
def modular_inverse(a: int, m: int) -> int:
  """Compute Modular Inverse."""

  def egcd(a: int, b: int) -> (int, int, int):
    """Extended Euclidian algorithm."""

    if a == 0:
      return (b, 0, 1)
    else:
      g, y, x = egcd(b % a, a)
    return (g, x - (b // a) * y, y)

  # Modular inverse of x mod m is the number x^-1 such that
  #   x * x^-1 = 1 mod m
  g, x, _ = egcd(a, m)
  if g != 1:
    raise Exception(f'Modular inverse ({a}, {m}) does not exist.')
  else:
    return x % m
```

We will run a large number of QFTs and inverse QFTs. Many of these operations are part of adding a quantum register with a known constant value. As we saw in

Section 6.3 on quantum arithmetic, this makes the implementation of quantum addition easier. We precompute the angles to apply them directly to the target register:

```python
def precompute_angles(a: int, n: int) -> List[float]:
    """Pre-compute angles used in the Fourier transform, for a."""

    # Convert 'a' to a string of 0's and 1's.
    s = bin(int(a))[2:].zfill(n)

    angles = [0.] * n
    for i in range(0, n):
        for j in range(i, n):
            if s[j] == '1':
                angles[n-i-1] += 2**(-(j-i))
        angles[n-i-1] *= math.pi
    return angles
```

We will need circuitry to compute addition, controlled addition, and double-controlled addition. The basic code is similar to quantum arithmetic with a constant that we have seen earlier in Section 6.3.1. We implement constant addition in `add` and controlled addition in `cadd` with `u1` and `cu1`. For the double-controlled addition in `ccadd`, we use the `ccphase` gate outlined below.

```python
def add(qc, q, a: int, n: int, factor: float) -> None:
    """Add in fourier space."""

    angles = precompute_angles(a, n)
    for i in range(n):
        qc.u1(q[i], factor * angles[i])

def cadd(qc, q, ctl, a: int, n: int, factor: float -> None):
    """Controlled add in Fourier space."""

    angles = precompute_angles(a, n)
    for i in range(n):
        qc.cu1(ctl, q[i], factor * angles[i])

def ccadd(qc, q, ctl1: int, ctl2: int, a: int, n: int,
          factor: float) -> None:
    """Double-controlled add in Fourier space."""

    angles = precompute_angles(a, n)
    for i in range(n):
        ccphase(qc, factor*angles[i], ctl1, ctl2, q[i])
```

We need a double-controlled phase gate for the double-controlled `ccadd` above. In Section 3.2.7, we learned how to construct a double-controlled gate with the help of their controlled root and adjoint. For rotations around an angle x, the root is just a rotation by $x/2$, and the adjoint of a rotation is a rotation in the other direction:

```python
def ccphase(qc, angle: float, ctl1: int, ctl2: int, idx: int) -> None:
    """Controlled controlled phase gate."""

    qc.cu1(ctl1, idx,  angle/2)
    qc.cx(ctl2, ctl1)
    qc.cu1(ctl1, idx, -angle/2)
    qc.cx(ctl2, ctl1)
    qc.cu1(ctl2, idx,  angle/2)
```

Using the adjoint of the addition circuit, we get $(b-a)$ if $b \geq a$, and $(2^{n-1}-(a-b))$ if $b < a$. So we can use this to subtract and compare numbers. If $b < a$, then the most significant qubit will be $|1\rangle$. We utilize this qubit to control other gates later.

$$b - \boxed{QFT} - \boxed{Add^\dagger(a)} - \boxed{QFT^\dagger} \quad = \quad \begin{cases} |b-a\rangle & \text{if } b \geq a, \\ |2^{n-1}-(a-b)\rangle & \text{if } b < a. \end{cases}$$

We implement QFT and $QFT^\dagger$ on the up register, this time with an option for swaps (which we actually don't use for this algorithm).

```python
def qft(qc, up_reg, n: int, with_swaps: bool = False) -> None:
    """Apply the H gates and Cphases."""

    for i in range(n-1, -1, -1):
      qc.h(up_reg[i])
      for j in range(i-1, -1, -1):
        qc.cu1(up_reg[i], up_reg[j], math.pi/2**(i-j))

    if with_swaps:
      for i in range(n // 2):
        qc.swap(up_reg[i], up_reg[n-1-i])


def inverse_qft(qc, up_reg, n: int, with_swaps: bool = False) -> None:
    """Function to create inverse QFT."""

    if with_swaps == 1:
      for i in range(n // 2):
        qc.swap(up_reg[i], up_reg[n-1-i])

    for i in range(n):
      qc.had(up_reg[i])
      if i != n-1:
```

```
j = i+1
for y in range(i, -1, -1):
    qc.cu1(up_reg[j], up_reg[y], -math.pi / 2**(j-y))
```

6.6.3 Modular Addition

At this point, we know how to add numbers and to check whether a value has turned negative by checking the sign qubit. This means we should have all necessary ingredients for *modular* addition: we compute $a + b$, and subtract N if $a + b > N$.

We achieve this by adding an ancilla qubit in the initial state $|0\rangle$. We start by adding a and b as before. We also reserve an overflow bit. Then we use the adjoint of the adder to subtract N (a fancy way of saying that we apply a negative factor in the addition routines above). In order to get to the most significant qubit and determine if this result was negative, we have to perform $QFT^{\dagger}$. We connect the most significant qubit and the ancilla with a Controlled-Not gate. It will only be set to $|1\rangle$ if $a + b - N$ is negative.

After this, we go back into the Fourier domain with another QFT. If $a + b - N$ is negative, we use the ancilla qubit to control the addition of N to make the result positive again. The circuit is shown in Figure 6.8.

There is a resulting problem that is not easy to solve – the ancilla qubit is still entangled. It has turned into a junk qubit. We have to find a way to return it to its original state of $|0\rangle$, else it will mess up our results, as junk qubits make a habit of doing.

To resolve this, we use the almost identical circuit again, but with a twist. We observe the following, with register b in the state after the prior modulo operation:

$$(a + b) \bmod N \geq a \Rightarrow a + b < N.$$

This time we run an inverse addition to subtract a from the result above and compute $(a+b) \bmod N - a$. The most significant bit is going to be $|0\rangle$ if $(a+b) \bmod N \geq a$.

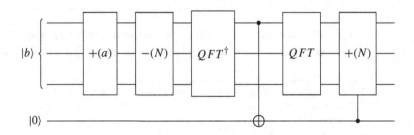

Figure 6.8 First half of the modular addition circuit.

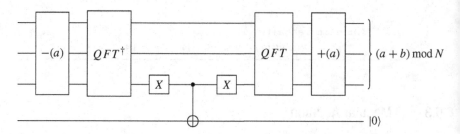

Figure 6.9 Second half of the modulo addition circuit, disentangling the ancilla.

We apply a NOT gate and use it as the controller for a Controlled-Not to the ancilla. With this, the ancilla has been restored. Now we have to undo what we just did. We apply another NOT gate to the most significant qubit, followed by a QFT and an addition of a to revert the initial subtraction. The end result is a clean computation of $(a + b) \bmod N$. In circuit notation, the second half of the circuit is shown in Figure 6.9. In code:

```
def cc_add_mod_n(qc, q, ctl1, ctl2, aux, a, number, n):
    """Circuit that implements doubly controlled modular addition by a."""

    ccadd(qc, q, ctl1, ctl2, a, n, factor=1.0)
    add(qc, q, number, n, factor=-1.0)
    inverse_qft(qc, q, n, with_swaps=0)
    qc.cx(q[n-1], aux)
    qft(qc, q, n, with_swaps=0)
    cadd(qc, q, aux, number, n, factor=1.0)

    ccadd(qc, q, ctl1, ctl2, a, n, factor=-1.0)
    inverse_qft(qc, q, n, with_swaps=0)
    qc.x(q[n-1])
    qc.cx(q[n-1], aux)
    qc.x(q[n-1])
    qft(qc, q, n, with_swaps=0)
    ccadd(qc, q, ctl1, ctl2, a, n, factor=1.0)
```

We will also need the inverse of this procedure. As before, and as explained in the section on uncomputation, we simply apply the inverse gates in the reverse order:

```
def cc_add_mod_n_inverse(qc, q, ctl1, ctl2, aux, a, number, n):
    """Inverse of the double controlled modular addition."""

    ccadd(qc, q, ctl1, ctl2, a, n, factor=-1.0)
    inverse_qft(qc, q, n, with_swaps=0)
    qc.x(q[n-1])
    qc.cx(q[n-1], aux)
    qc.x(q[n-1])
```

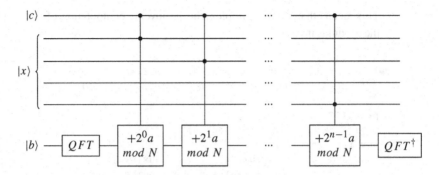

Figure 6.10 Circuit for controlled modular multiplication.

```
qft(qc, q, n, with_swaps=0)
ccadd(qc, q, ctl1, ctl2, a, n, factor=1.0)

cadd(qc, q, aux, number, n, factor=-1.0)
inverse_qft(qc, q, n, with_swaps=0)
qc.cx(q[n-1], aux)
qft(qc, q, n, with_swaps=0)
add(qc, q, number, n, factor=1.0)
ccadd(qc, q, ctl1, ctl2, a, n, factor=-1.0)
```

Uncomputing circuits like this is tedious. In Section 8.5.5 we show how to automate uncomputation in an elegant way.

6.6.4 Controlled Modular Multiplication

The next step is now to build a controlled modular multiplier from the modular adders we just constructed. Our circuit will be controlled by a qubit $|c\rangle$ and take the state $|c, x, b\rangle$ to the state $|c, x, b + (ax) \bmod N\rangle$, if $|c\rangle = |1\rangle$, else it will leave the original state intact.

We perform successive applications of the controlled modular addition gate, as controlled by the individual bits x_i of x. The bit positions correspond to powers of 2 using this identity:

$$(ax) \bmod N =$$
$$(\ldots(((2^0 ax_0) \bmod N + 2^1 ax_1) \bmod N) + \cdots + 2^{n-1} ax_{n-1}) \bmod N.$$

The circuit to compute this expression is shown in Figure 6.10.

As described in the section on uncomputation, in order to eliminate the entanglement with $|b\rangle$, we swap out $|x\rangle$ and uncompute the circuit after the swap. In code, we see three sections. In the first section, it computes the multiplication modulo N. In the second block, it connects the results with controlled gates to swap out $|x\rangle$ to the aux register (the cswap was introduced in Section 4.3 on quantum circuits). Finally, it uncomputes the results, as we have seen in Section 2.13 on reversible computing.

This means that we must implement the inverse computation of the first block using the modular inverse.

```python
def cmultmodn(qc, ctl, q, aux, a, number, n):
    """Controlled Multiply of q by number, with n bits."""

    print('Compute...')
    qft(qc, aux, n+1, with_swaps=0)
    for i in range(n):
        cc_add_mod_n(qc, aux, q[i], ctl, aux[n+1],
                     ((2**i)*a) % number, number, n+1)
    inverse_qft(qc, aux, n+1, with_swaps=0)

    print('Swap...')
    for i in range(n):
        qc.cswap(ctl, q[i], aux[i])
    a_inv = modular_inverse(a, number)

    print('Uncompute...')
    qft(qc, aux, n+1, with_swaps=0)
    for i in range(n-1, -1, -1):
        cc_add_mod_n_inverse(qc, aux, q[i], ctl, aux[n+1],
                             ((2**i)*a_inv) % number, number, n+1)
    inverse_qft(qc, aux, n+1, with_swaps=0)
```

In summary, the modular multiplication circuit performs:

$$|x\rangle|0\rangle \rightarrow |ax \bmod N\rangle|0\rangle.$$

We shall name this circuit CU_a. There is still a problem – the phase estimation algorithm requires powers of this circuit. Does this mean that we have to multiply this circuit n times with itself to get to $(CU_a)^n$ for each power of 2 as required by phase estimation? Fortunately, we don't. We simply compute a^n classically with:

$$(CU_a)^n = CU_{a^n}.$$

This can be seen at the top level in the code where we iterate over the calls to the modular arithmetic circuit (those expressions containing $2**i$).

6.6.5   Continued Fractions

We are very close to the final result. We mentioned in Section 6.6.1 that an expected result for the up register was 128. This was an interpretation of this register as an integer. However, we performed phase estimation, so we have to interpret the bits of the register as binary fractions. A value of 0 corresponds to a phase of 0.0, and a value of 128 corresponds to a phase of 0.5. We also know that phase estimation will give a phase of the following form with order r:

$$\phi = \frac{s}{r}.$$

Shouldn't this mean that if we could find a fraction of integers approximating this phase, we would have an initial guess for the order r?

To approximate a fractional value to an arbitrary degree of accuracy, we can use the technique of *continued fractions*.[6] Fortunately for us, an implementation of it already exists in the form of a Python library. We include the module:

```
import fractions
```

When we decode the x-register we have to interpret it as a binary fraction (note, again, how we interpret the register bits in a reversed order):

```
phase = helper.bits2frac(
    bits[nbits+2 : nbits+2 + nbits*2][::-1], nbits*2)
```

We get the lowest denominator from the continued fractions algorithm. We also want to limit the accuracy via `limit_denominator` to ensure we get reasonably sized denominators:

```
r = fractions.Fraction(phase).limit_denominator(number).denominator
```

With this `r`, we can then follow the explanations on the nonquantum part of Shor's algorithm and seek to compute the factors. We might get 1s, or we might get Ns, which are both useless. With a little luck and by following actual probabilities, we might just find one or two of the real factors.

```
guesses = [math.gcd(a**(r//2)-1, number),
           math.gcd(a**(r//2)+1, number)]

print('Final x: {:3d} phase: {:3f} prob: {:.3f} factors: {}'.
      format(intval, phase, prob.real, guesses))
```

6.6.6   Experiments

Let us run just a few examples to demonstrate that this machinery works. To factorize 15 with a value of a of 4, we run a circuit with 10,553 gates and obtain two sets of factors, the trivial ones with 1 and 15, but, Eureka! also the real factors of 3 and 5:

```
.../order_finding -- --a=4 --N=15
Final x-value int:   0 phase: 0.000000 prob: 0.250 factors: [15, 1]
Final x-value int: 128 phase: 0.500000 prob: 0.250 factors: [3, 5]
Circuit Statistics
   Qubits: 18
   Gates : 10553
```

---

[6] https://en.wikipedia.org/wiki/Continued_fraction.

To factor 21 with an a value of 5, the required number of qubits grows from 18 to 22, thus increasing the number of gates to over 20,000 and the runtime by roughly a factor of $8\times$. Other than the trivial factors, the routine finds one of the real factors with the value 3.

```
Final x-value int:    0 phase: 0.000000 prob: 0.028 factors: [21, 1]
Final x-value int: 512 phase: 0.500000 prob: 0.028 factors: [1, 3]
Final x-value int: 853 phase: 0.833008 prob: 0.019 factors: [1, 21]
Final x-value int: 171 phase: 0.166992 prob: 0.019 factors: [1, 21]
Final x-value int: 683 phase: 0.666992 prob: 0.019 factors: [1, 3]
Circuit Statistics
  Qubits: 22
  Gates : 20671
```

Finally, factoring 35 with an initial a value of 4, uses over 36,000 gates and a runtime of approximately 60 minutes:

```
Final x-value int:     0 phase: 0.000000 prob: 0.028 factors: [35, 1]
Final x-value int: 2048 phase: 0.500000 prob: 0.028 factors: [1, 5]
Final x-value int: 1365 phase: 0.333252 prob: 0.019 factors: [1, 5]
Final x-value int: 3413 phase: 0.833252 prob: 0.019 factors: [7, 5]
Final x-value int:  683 phase: 0.166748 prob: 0.019 factors: [7, 5]
Final x-value int: 2731 phase: 0.666748 prob: 0.019 factors: [1, 5]
Circuit Statistics
  Qubits: 26
  Gates : 36373
```

You may want to experiment and perhaps convert this code to libq with the transpilation facilities described in Section 8.5. The code runs significantly faster in libq, which allows experimentation with much larger numbers of qubits. As a rough and unscientific estimate – factorization with 22 qubits runs for about two minutes on a standard workstation. After compilation to libq, it accelerates because of the sparse representation and takes less than five seconds to complete, a speedup factor of over $25\times$. Factoring 35 with 26 qubits takes about an hour, but with libq it takes about three minutes, a still significant speedup of about $20\times$.

To summarize, the algorithm as a whole – from the classical parts to the quantum parts and finding the order with continued fraction – is truly magical. No wonder it has gotten so much attention and stands out as one of the key contributors to today's interest in quantum computing.

6.7   Grover's Algorithm

Grover's algorithm is one of the fundamental algorithms of quantum computing (Grover, 1996). It allows searching over N elements in a domain in $O(\sqrt{N})$ time. By "searching" we mean that there is a function $f(x)$ and one (or more) special inputs x' for which:

$$f(x) = 0 \quad \forall x \neq x',$$
$$f(x) = 1 \quad x = x'.$$

The classical algorithm to find x' is of complexity $O(N)$ in the worst case. It needs to evaluate all possible inputs to f. Strictly speaking, $N-1$ steps are required, because once all the elements, including the penultimate one, have returned 0, we know that the last element must be the elusive x'. Being able to do this with complexity $O(\sqrt{N})$ is, of course, an exciting prospect.

To understand and implement the algorithm, we first describe the algorithm at a high level in fairly abstract terms. We need to learn two new concepts – *phase inversion* and *inversion about the mean*. Once these concepts are understood, we detail several variants of their implementation. We finally combine all the pieces into Grover's algorithm and run a few experiments.

6.7.1 High-Level Overview

At the high level, the algorithm performs the following steps:

1. Create an equal superposition state $|+ + \cdots +\rangle$ by applying Hadamard gates to an initial state $|00\ldots0\rangle$.
2. Construct a *phase inversion* operator U_f around the special input $|x'\rangle$, defined as:

$$U_f = I^{\otimes n} - 2|x'\rangle\langle x'|.$$

3. Construct an *inversion about the mean* operator $U_\perp$, defined as:

$$U_\perp = 2(|+\rangle\langle+|)^{\otimes n} - I^{\otimes n}.$$

4. Combine $U_\perp$ and U_f into the Grover operator G (in this notation, U_f is applied first):

$$G = U_\perp U_f.$$

5. Iterate k times and apply G to the state. We derive the iteration count k below. The resulting state will be close to the special state $|x'\rangle$:

$$G^k |+\rangle^{\otimes n} \sim |x'\rangle.$$

This basically explains the whole procedure. Some of you may look at this, shrug, and understand it right away. For the rest of us, the next sections explain this procedure in great detail, sometimes in multiple different ways. Grover's algorithm is foundational, so we want to make sure we understand and appreciate it fully.

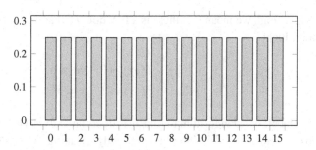

Figure 6.11 Equally distributed probability amplitudes.

6.7.2   Phase Inversion

The first new concept we need to learn about it phase inversion. Let's assume a given state $|\psi\rangle$ with probability amplitudes c_x:

$$|\psi\rangle = \sum_x c_x |x\rangle.$$

For simplicity, let's assume all c_i are equal $1/\sqrt{N}$ (remember that $N = 2^n$ for n qubits). Figure 6.11 shows a bar graph where the x-axis enumerates the states $|x_i\rangle$, and the y-axis plots the height of the corresponding probability amplitudes c_i. It is safe to ignore the *actual* values; we are just trying to make a point.

Let's now further assume that we want to consider one of these input states as special, corresponding to the element $|x'\rangle$ mentioned above. Phase inversion converts the original state into a state where the phase has been *negated* for the special element $|x'\rangle$:

$$|\psi\rangle = \sum_x c_x |x\rangle \quad \rightarrow \quad |\psi\rangle = \sum_{x \neq x'} c_x |x\rangle - c_{x'} |x'\rangle.$$

In the chart in Figure 6.12, we negated the phase of state $|4\rangle$, which should serve as our special state $|x'\rangle$.

To relate this back to the function $f(x)$ we are trying to analyze, we use phase inversion to negate the phase for the special elements only, which we can express with this closed form:

$$|\psi\rangle = \sum_x c_x |x\rangle \quad \rightarrow_{inv} \quad |\psi\rangle = \sum_x c_x (-1)^{f(x)} |x\rangle. \tag{6.6}$$

A key aspect of this procedure is that the function f has to be known. Because how else can we implement and perform this operation? There is an important distinction: Even though an implementation has to know the function, observers who try to reconstruct and measure the function would still have to go through N steps in the classical case, but only $\sqrt{N}$ in the quantum case. This is still different from, say, finding an element meeting certain criteria in a database.

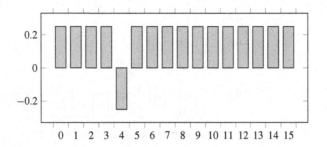

Figure 6.12 Probability amplitudes after phase inversion.

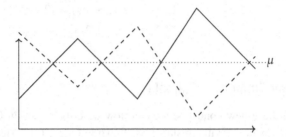

Figure 6.13 An example of (solid line) random data and (dashed line) its inversion about the mean.

6.7.3   Inversion About the Mean

The second new concept is *inversion about the mean*. We can compute the mean μ ("mu") of the probability amplitudes c_x of the original state:

$$\mu = \left(\sum_x c_x \right) / N.$$

Inversion about the mean is the process of mirroring each c_x across the mean. To achieve this, we take each value's distance from the mean, which is $\mu - c_x$, and add it to the mean. For values that were above the mean, $\mu - c_x$ is negative, and the value is reflected below the mean. Conversely, for values that were below the mean, $\mu - c_x$ is positive, and the values are being reflected up. An example with a random set of values is shown in Figure 6.13 (solid line).

For each c_i we compute:

$$c_i \rightarrow \mu + (\mu - c_i) = (2\mu - c_i).$$

This reflects each value about the mean. For the example in Figure 6.13, the reflected values are shown with a dashed line. Each amplitude c_i has been reflected about the mean of all amplitudes.

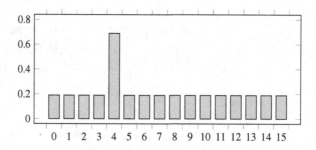

Figure 6.14 Distribution of amplitudes after phase and mean inversion.

$$c_x \rightarrow \mu + (\mu - c_x) = (2\mu - c_x),$$

$$\sum_x c_x |x\rangle \rightarrow \sum_x (2\mu - c_x)|x\rangle. \tag{6.7}$$

6.7.4   Simple Numerical Example

With these new concepts, we can now describe a step in Grover's algorithm with a simple example with 16 states, as shown in Figure 6.11. Here is how it works:

1. **Initialization.** As seen in Section 6.7.1, we put states in superposition and start with all states being equally likely with amplitude $1/\sqrt{N}$.
2. **Phase inversion.** Apply phase inversion as shown above in Equation (6.6). The phase of the special element becomes negative, thus pushing the mean of all amplitudes down. In our example with 16 states and amplitude $1/\sqrt{16} = 0.25$, the overall mean is roughly pushed down to $(0.25 * 15 - 0.25)/16 = 0.22$.
3. **Inversion around the mean.** This will push down amplitudes of 0.25 to $0.22 + (0.22 - 0.25) = 0.19$, but amplify the special element to a value of $0.22 + (0.22 + 0.25) = 0.69$.

Now rinse and repeat steps 2 and 3. For our artificial amplitude example above, a single step would turn the initial state into the state shown in Figure 6.14.

6.7.5   Two-Qubit Example

Let's make this more concrete and visualize the procedure using an example with two qubits. A geometrical interpretation is shown in Figure 6.15. In a two-qubit system, our special element x' and its corresponding outer product shall be:

$$|x'\rangle = |11\rangle = \begin{bmatrix} 0 \\ 0 \\ 0 \\ 1 \end{bmatrix} \quad \text{and} \quad |x'\rangle\langle x'| = \begin{bmatrix} 0 & 0 & 0 & 0 \\ 0 & 0 & 0 & 0 \\ 0 & 0 & 0 & 0 \\ 0 & 0 & 0 & 1 \end{bmatrix}.$$

The solution $|x'\rangle$ corresponds to the solution space $|\beta\rangle$ in Figure 6.15. The phase inversion operator U_f from step 2 in Section 6.7.1 then becomes the following (note that in the implementation below, we use a different methodology to get this operator):

$$U_f = I - 2|x'\rangle\langle x'| = \begin{bmatrix} 1 & 0 & 0 & 0 \\ 0 & 1 & 0 & 0 \\ 0 & 0 & 1 & 0 \\ 0 & 0 & 0 & -1 \end{bmatrix}.$$

We know how to create an equal superposition state $|s\rangle = |++\rangle$. The state $|x^\perp\rangle$ *orthogonal* to $|x'\rangle$ is very close to $|s\rangle$; $|s\rangle$ is *almost* orthogonal to $|x'\rangle$.

$$|s\rangle = H^{\otimes 2}|00\rangle = |++\rangle = \frac{1}{2}\begin{bmatrix} 1 \\ 1 \\ 1 \\ 1 \end{bmatrix} \quad |x^\perp\rangle = \frac{1}{\sqrt{3}}\begin{bmatrix} 1 \\ 1 \\ 1 \\ 0 \end{bmatrix}.$$

Note that $|x^\perp\rangle = |s\rangle - |x'\rangle$ is the equal superposition state $|s\rangle$ with $|x'\rangle$ removed; it corresponds to the axis $|a\rangle$ in Figure 6.15. The state $|\psi\rangle$ in the figure corresponds to the initial $|s\rangle$. It is easy to see how applying the operator U_f inverts the phase of the $|x'\rangle$ component in $|s\rangle$:

$$U_f|s\rangle = \frac{1}{2}\begin{bmatrix} 1 \\ 1 \\ 1 \\ -1 \end{bmatrix}.$$

In Figure 6.15, this corresponds to a reflection of the state $|\psi\rangle$ (which is our $|s\rangle$) about the α-axis. The inversion about the mean operator $U_\perp$, as defined in step 3) above, is:

$$U_\perp = 2(|+\rangle\langle+|)^{\otimes 2} - I^{\otimes 2}$$
$$= 2|s\rangle\langle s| - I^{\otimes 2}.$$

The operator $U_\perp$ reflects $U_f|\psi\rangle$ about the original state $|s\rangle$ into the new state $U_\perp U_f|\psi\rangle = |11\rangle$. For our example with just two qubits, a single iteration is all that is needed to move state $|s\rangle$ to $|x'\rangle$. In code:

```
x = state.bitstring(1, 1)
s = ops.Hadamard(2)(state.bitstring(0, 0))

Uf = ops.Operator(ops.Identity(2) - 2 * x.density())
Ub = ops.Operator(2 * s.density() - ops.Identity(2))
(Ub @ Uf)(s).dump()
>>
|11> (|3>):  ampl: +1.00+0.00j prob: 1.00 Phase:   0.0
```

The iteration count of 1 agrees with Equation (6.11), which we will derive next.

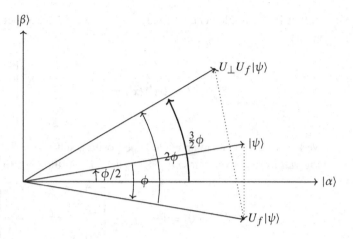

Figure 6.15 Geometric interpretation of a Grover rotation.

6.7.6   Iteration Count

How many iterations k should we perform? How do we know when to stop? It turns out we need exactly k iterations, where:

$$k = \frac{\pi}{4}\sqrt{N}.$$

How do we arrive at this number? First, we define two subspaces: the space of all the states that do not contain a solution and the space of states that are special. Note that in the implementation, we search for just one special element $|x'\rangle$, but here we generalize this derivation to search for M solutions in a population of N elements.

$$|\alpha\rangle = \frac{1}{\sqrt{N-M}}\sum_x |x\rangle,$$

$$|\beta\rangle = \frac{1}{\sqrt{M}}\sum_{x'} |x'\rangle.$$

We can define the whole state as a composite of these two subspaces:

$$|\psi\rangle = \sqrt{\frac{N-M}{N}}|\alpha\rangle + \sqrt{\frac{M}{N}}|\beta\rangle. \tag{6.8}$$

We can visualize this space in two dimensions, where the x-axis corresponds to state space $|\alpha\rangle$ and the y-axis to solution space $|\beta\rangle$, as shown in Figure 6.15.

Application of phase inversion (let's call the corresponding operator U_f, as before) reflects the state about $|\alpha\rangle$. This, in essence, negates the second part of the superposition, similar to the effect of a Z-gate on a single qubit, where a and b are the probability amplitudes for the subspaces α and β:

$$U_f(a|\alpha\rangle + b|\beta\rangle) = a|\alpha\rangle - b|\beta\rangle.$$

The inversion around the mean (let's again call this operator $U_\perp$) then performs another reflection about the vector $|\psi\rangle$. The two reflections amount to a rotation, which means the state remains in the space spanned by $|\alpha\rangle$ and $|\beta\rangle$. Furthermore, the state incrementally rotates towards the solution space $|\beta\rangle$. We have seen in (6.8) above that:

$$|\psi\rangle = \sqrt{\frac{N-M}{N}}|\alpha\rangle + \sqrt{\frac{M}{N}}|\beta\rangle.$$

We can geometrically position the state vector with simple trigonometry. We define the initial angle between $|\psi\rangle$ and $|\alpha\rangle$ as $\phi/2$. Equation (6.9) is important; we will use it in Section 6.9 on quantum counting:

$$\cos\left(\frac{\phi}{2}\right) = \sqrt{\frac{N-M}{N}},$$

$$\sin\left(\frac{\phi}{2}\right) = \sqrt{\frac{M}{N}}, \tag{6.9}$$

$$|\psi\rangle = \cos\left(\frac{\phi}{2}\right)|\alpha\rangle + \sin\left(\frac{\phi}{2}\right)|\beta\rangle.$$

From Figure 6.16, we can see that after phase inversion and inversion around the mean, the state has rotated by ϕ towards $|\beta\rangle$. The angle between $|\alpha\rangle$ and $|\psi\rangle$ is now $3\phi/2$. We call the combined operator the Grover operator $G = U_\perp U_f$:

$$G|\psi\rangle = \cos\left(\frac{3\phi}{2}\right)|\alpha\rangle + \sin\left(\frac{3\phi}{2}\right)|\beta\rangle.$$

From this, we see that repeated application of the Grover operator G takes the state to:

$$G^k|\psi\rangle = \cos\left(\frac{2k+1}{2}\phi\right)|\alpha\rangle + \sin\left(\frac{2k+1}{2}\phi\right)|\beta\rangle.$$

In order to maximize the probability of measuring $|\beta\rangle$, the term $\sin\left(\frac{2k+1}{2}\phi\right)$ ought to be as close to 1.0 as possible. Taking the arcsin of the expression yields:

$$\sin\left(\frac{2k+1}{2}\phi\right) = 1$$

$$\frac{2k+1}{2}\phi = \pi/2$$

$$k = \frac{\pi}{2\phi} - \frac{1}{2} = \frac{\pi}{4\frac{\phi}{2}} - \frac{1}{2}. \tag{6.10}$$

Note that the iteration number must be an integer, so the question we face now is what to do with the $-1/2$. We could ignore it, use it for rounding up, or for rounding down. In our implementation, we chose to ignore it. For our examples below, the probabilities for finding the solutions are around 40% or higher, and this term has no impact.

Now let's solve for k. From Equation (6.9), we know that:

$$\sin\left(\frac{\phi}{2}\right) = \sqrt{\frac{M}{N}}.$$

We use the approximation that for small angles, $\sin(x) \approx x$. Substituting in $\frac{\phi}{2} = \sqrt{M/N}$ and $M = 1$ into Equation (6.10), we find the final result for the number of iterations k:

$$k = \frac{\pi}{4}\sqrt{\frac{N}{M}} = \frac{\pi}{4}\sqrt{N}. \tag{6.11}$$

6.7.7   Implementation of Phase Inversion

We will present three different ways to implement phase inversion. We have already seen the mathematical way, which simply computes the operator $U_f = I - 2|x'\rangle\langle x'|$. But how do we construct an actual circuit for this? A second strategy will use an oracle operator, which we suspect can be implemented as a circuit (we also want to demonstrate the utility of the oracle operator one more time). Finally, we develop an actual quantum circuit for phase inversion.

Our second implementation strategy uses a mechanism we have seen before: the oracle operator! The oracle structure is similar to the Deutsch–Jozsa oracle – the input is a whole register of (initially $|0\rangle$, then equal superposition) states:

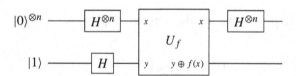

It is important to note that the bottom ancilla qubit is initialized as $|1\rangle$. The Hadamard gate puts it into state $|-\rangle$. This is important because it means that the input state is transformed by U_f into the desired state:

$$|\psi\rangle = \sum_x c_x |x_i\rangle \quad \rightarrow_{inv} \quad |\psi\rangle = \sum_x c_x (-1)^{f(x)} |x\rangle.$$

How so? State $|-\rangle$ is:

$$|-\rangle = \frac{|0\rangle - |1\rangle}{\sqrt{2}}.$$

Since we use an oracle, all input values are computed in parallel. If $f(x) = 0$, the bottom qubit in state $|-\rangle$ is XOR'ed with 0, which means the state of the qubit remains unmodified:

$$|-\rangle \rightarrow |-\rangle.$$

If $f(x) = 1$, the bottom qubit in state $|-\rangle$ is XOR'ed with 1, which means the state changes to:

$$\frac{|1\rangle - |0\rangle}{\sqrt{2}}.$$

This means it gets a phase:

$$|-\rangle \rightarrow -|-\rangle.$$

For the ancilla, the output is now:

$$(-1)^{f(x)}|-\rangle.$$

The combination of input bits plus the ancilla becomes:

$$\sum_x c_x |x\rangle (-1)^{f(x)}|-\rangle.$$

We can slightly rearrange the terms, ignore the ancilla, and arrive at the exact form we were looking for:

$$|\psi\rangle = \sum_x c_x (-1)^{f(x)}|x\rangle.$$

6.7.8   Phase Inversion Operator

We constructed the phase inversion operator as a giant matrix, which is inefficient for larger numbers of qubits. Here is a more efficient construction with a multi-controlled X-gate. It will be of higher performance, despite the fact that $n - 2$ ancilla qubits are required, as outlined in Section 3.2.8. We are trying to compute a unitary operator U such that:

$$U_f |x\rangle |y\rangle = |x\rangle |y \oplus f(x)\rangle \text{ where } \begin{cases} f(x) = 0 & \forall x \neq x', \\ f(x) = 1 & x = x'. \end{cases}$$

We only want to apply the XOR for the special state $|x'\rangle$ for which $f(x) = 1$. This means we can multi-control the final qubit as shown in Figure 6.16, ensuring that all control bits are $|1\rangle$.

6.7.9   Implementation of Inversion about the Mean

To reiterate, inversion about the mean is this procedure:

$$\sum_x c_x |x\rangle \rightarrow \sum_x (2\mu - c_x)|x\rangle.$$

In matrix form, we can accomplish this by multiplying the state vector with a matrix that has $2/N$ at each element, except for the diagonal elements, which are

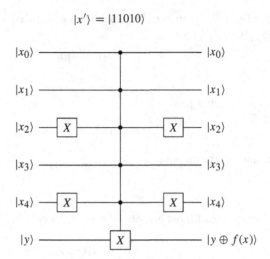

Figure 6.16 Phase inversion circuit.

$2/N - 1$. Note that this matrix is the desired end result of the derivation in the next few paragraphs. It represents this expression, as shown in the introduction of this section:

$$U_\perp = 2(|+\rangle\langle+|)^{\otimes n} - I^{\otimes n}. \tag{6.12}$$

This matrix is also called the *diffusion operator* because its form is similar to the discretized version of the diffusion equation, but we can safely ignore this fun fact here. This is the operator we hope to construct:

$$U_\perp = \begin{pmatrix} 2/N - 1 & 2/N & \cdots & 2/N \\ 2/N & 2/N - 1 & \cdots & 2/N \\ \vdots & \vdots & \ddots & \vdots \\ 2/N & 2/N & \cdots & 2/N - 1 \end{pmatrix}. \tag{6.13}$$

Why do we look for this specific operator? Remember Equation 6.10. We want to construct an operator that performs this transformation.

$$\sum_x c_x |x\rangle \rightarrow \sum_x (2\mu - c_x)|x\rangle.$$

Why does this work? Each row multiplies and adds up each state vector element by $2/N$ before subtracting the one element corresponding to the diagonal. This is the exact definition of the closed form inversion procedure shown in Equation (6.12) above.

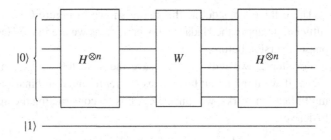

Figure 6.17 Inversion about the mean circuit.

$$
\begin{pmatrix}
2/N - 1 & 2/N & \cdots & 2/N \\
2/N & 2/N - 1 & \cdots & 2/N \\
\vdots & \vdots & \ddots & \vdots \\
2/N & 2/N & \cdots & 2/N - 1
\end{pmatrix}
\begin{pmatrix}
c_0 \\
c_1 \\
\vdots \\
c_{n-1}
\end{pmatrix}
$$

$$
=
\begin{pmatrix}
(2c_0/N + 2c_1/N + \cdots + 2c_{n-1}/N) - c_0 \\
(2c_0/N + 2c_1/N + \cdots + 2c_{n-1}/N) - c_1 \\
\vdots \\
(2c_0/N + 2c_1/N + \cdots + 2c_{n-1}/N) - c_{n-1}
\end{pmatrix}
$$

$$
=
\begin{pmatrix}
2\mu - c_0 \\
2\mu - c_1 \\
\vdots \\
2\mu - c_{n-1}
\end{pmatrix}.
$$

How would we arrive at this matrix from what we've learned so far? We've seen the geometrical interpretation above – we can think of inversion about the mean as a reflection around a subspace. Hence, a possible derivation consists of three steps:

1. Ideally, we would want to rotate around the space in equal superposition $|++\cdots+\rangle$. But it is hard to construct an operator to do this reflection in this basis. Therefore, we use Hadamard gates to get into the computational basis and construct the reflection there.
2. Coming out of the Hadamard basis, $|++\cdots+\rangle$ turns into $|00\ldots0\rangle$. It seems obvious to reflect about $|00\ldots0\rangle$. We could pick another state for reflection, as long as that state is still almost orthogonal to subspace α, but for state $|00\ldots0\rangle$, the inversion operator has an elegant construction (which we show in Section 6.7.10).
3. Transform the basis back to the X-basis with Hadamard gates.

These three steps define the circuit shown in Figure 6.17. For steps 1 and 3, it is sufficient to apply the Hadamard operators, as we are in the Hadamard basis from the phase inversion before.

For step 2, we will want to leave the state $|00\ldots0\rangle$ alone but reflect all other states. If we think about how states are represented in binary and how matrix-vector multiplication works, we can achieve this by constructing the matrix W, which is easy to derive:

$$W = \begin{pmatrix} 1 & & & \\ & -1 & & \\ & & \ddots & \\ & & & -1 \end{pmatrix}$$

$$= 2(P_{|0\rangle})^{\otimes n} - I^{\otimes n} = \begin{pmatrix} 2 & & & \\ & 0 & & \\ & & \ddots & \\ & & & 0 \end{pmatrix} - \begin{pmatrix} 1 & & & \\ & 1 & & \\ & & \ddots & \\ & & & 1 \end{pmatrix}.$$

Again, we could pick any state as the axis to reflect about, but the math is elegant and simple when picking the state $|00\ldots0\rangle$. This will become more clear with the derivation immediately below.

Only the first bit in the state vector remains unmodified, and that first bit corresponds to the state $|00\ldots0\rangle$. Remember that the state vector for this state is all 0s, except the very first element, which is a 1. All other states are therefore being negated. In combination, we want to compute the following:

$$H^{\otimes n} W H^{\otimes n} = H^{\otimes n} \begin{pmatrix} 1 & & & \\ & -1 & & \\ & & \ddots & \\ & & & -1 \end{pmatrix} H^{\otimes n}$$

$$= H^{\otimes n} \left[\begin{pmatrix} 2 & & & \\ & 0 & & \\ & & \ddots & \\ & & & 0 \end{pmatrix} - I \right] H^{\otimes n}$$

$$= H^{\otimes n} \begin{pmatrix} 2 & & & \\ & 0 & & \\ & & \ddots & \\ & & & 0 \end{pmatrix} H^{\otimes n} - H^{\otimes n} I H^{\otimes n}.$$

Since the Hadamard is its own inverse, the second term reduces to just the identity matrix I. Multiplying in the left and right Hadamard gates:

$$= \begin{pmatrix} 2/\sqrt{N} & 0 & \cdots & 0 \\ 2/\sqrt{N} & 0 & \cdots & 0 \\ \vdots & \vdots & \ddots & \vdots \\ 2/\sqrt{N} & 0 & \cdots & 0 \end{pmatrix} H^{\otimes n} - I$$

$$= \begin{pmatrix} 2/N & 2/N & \cdots & 2/N \\ 2/N & 2/N & \cdots & 2/N \\ \vdots & \vdots & \ddots & \vdots \\ 2/N & 2/N & \cdots & 2/N \end{pmatrix} - I.$$

Finally, subtracting the identity I yields a matrix where all elements are $2/N$, except the diagonal elements, which are $2/N - 1$:

$$U_\perp = \begin{pmatrix} 2/N - 1 & 2/N & \cdots & 2/N \\ 2/N & 2/N - 1 & \cdots & 2/N \\ \vdots & \vdots & \ddots & \vdots \\ 2/N & 2/N & \cdots & 2/N - 1 \end{pmatrix}. \tag{6.14}$$

This is the matrix $U_\perp$ we were looking for. Applying this matrix to a state turns each element c_x into $2\mu - c_x$, which is exactly what we wanted from the inversion about the mean procedure, as shown in Equation (6.9)!

6.7.10 Inversion About the Mean Operator

As a third implementation strategy, we can construct a quantum circuit for the inversion about the mean using similar reasoning as for the phase inversion operator (Mermin, 2007).

The main "trick" for constructing an operator for mean inversion is to realize that the direction of the rotation for amplitude amplification does not matter, it can be negative or positive. This means that instead of constructing $W = 2(P_{|0\rangle})^{\otimes n} - I^{\otimes n}$ as before, we construct:

$$W' = I^{\otimes n} - 2(P_{|0\rangle})^{\otimes n} = I^{\otimes n} - 2|00\ldots0\rangle\langle00\ldots0|.$$

Not to foreshadow the implementation below, but we can verify this by changing this line in `src/grover.py`:

```
<<
  reflection = op_zero * 2.0 - ops.Identity(nbits)
>>
  reflection = ops.Identity(nbits) - op_zero * 2.0
```

We want to build a gate that leaves every state untouched, except $|00\ldots0\rangle$, which should get its phase negated. A Z-gate will do this for us. Because the Z-gate must be

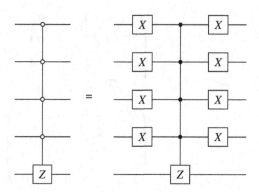

Figure 6.18 Inversion about the mean circuit (omitting leading and trailing Hadamard gates applied to *all* qubits).

controlled to only apply to $|00\ldots 0\rangle$, we expect all inputs to be $|0\rangle$. Hence, to control the Z-gate, we sandwich it between X-gates (omitting the left and right Hadamard gates from the construction in Equation (6.13)), as shown in Figure 6.18.

As a result, for the big inversion operator $U_\perp$ from Equation (6.13), the circuit in Figure 6.18 corresponds to the closed form below, which yields $-U_\perp$:

$$H^{\otimes n} X^{\otimes n} (CZ)^{n-1} X^{\otimes n} H^{\otimes n} = -U_\perp.$$

6.7.11   Implementation of Grover's Algorithm

Now let's put all the pieces together (the source code can be found in file `src/grover.py`). The full Grover iteration circuit is shown in Figure 6.19. In code, we first define the function f that we intend to analyze. The `make_f` function creates an array of all 0s, except for one special element set to 1, which corresponds to $|x'\rangle$. The function also creates a function object `func` to convert its parameter, a sequence of address bits, to a decimal index and return the array value at that index. Finally, the function is returned as a callable function object:

```
def make_f(d: int = 3):
    """Construct function that will return 1 for only one bitstring."""

    num_inputs = 2**d
    answers = np.zeros(num_inputs, dtype=np.int32)
    answer_true = np.random.randint(0, num_inputs)

    bit_string = format(answer_true, '0{}b'.format(d))
    answers[answer_true] = 1

    def func(*bits):
        return answers[helper.bits2val(*bits)]

    return func
```

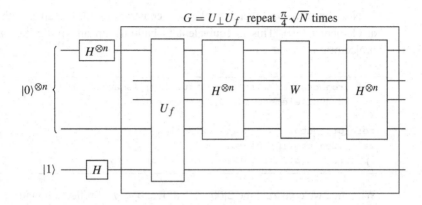

Figure 6.19 Full circuit for Grover iteration.

The circuit's initial state is a register of $|0\rangle$ qubits with an additional ancilla qubit in state $|1\rangle$. Applying the Hadamard gate to all of the qubits puts the ancilla into the state $|-\rangle$:

```
# State initialization:
psi = state.zeros(nbits) * state.ones(1)
for i in range(nbits + 1):
  psi.apply(ops.Hadamard(), i)
```

In order to implement phase inversion, we generate an oracle with the function object we created above. To create the oracle itself, we use our trusty `OracleUf` operator and pass it the function object. Note that using an oracle this way is quite slow, as it utilizes the full matrix implementation. Of course, any given operator can be implemented with quantum gates, but this can become cumbersome. Fortunately for us, this is not the case here, as we showed for the elegant phase inversion operator in Figure 6.18.

```
# Make f and uf. Note:
# We reserve space for an ancilla 'y', which is unused in
# Grover's algorithm. This allows reuse of the Deutsch Uf builder.
#
# We use the Oracle construction for convenience. It is rather
# slow (full matrix) for larger qubit counts. One can construct
# a 'regular' function for the Grover search algorithm, but this
# function is different for each bitstring and that quickly gets
# confusing.
#
f = make_f(nbits)
uf = ops.OracleUf(nbits+1, f)
```

Now on to mean inversion. We first construct an all-0 matrix with a single 1.0 at element $(0, 0)$. This is equivalent to building up an `nbits`-dimensional $|0\rangle\langle0|$ projector:

```
# A projector of all |00...0><0...00| is an all-0 matrix
# with just element (0, 0) set to 1:
#
zero_projector = np.zeros((2**nbits, 2**nbits))
zero_projector[0, 0] = 1
op_zero = ops.Operator(zero_projector)
```

With this, we construct the $2|00\ldots0\rangle\langle00\ldots0| - I^{\otimes n}$ reflection matrix:

```
reflection = op_zero * 2.0 - ops.Identity(nbits)
```

The full inversion operator $U_\perp$ consists of the Hadamard gates bracketing the reflection matrix W. We add an identity gate to account for the ancilla we added earlier for the phase inversion oracle. Finally, we build the full Grover operator $G =$ `grover` as the combination of mean inversion `inversion` with the phase inversion operator `uf`:

```
# Build Grover operator, note Identity() for the ancilla.
# The Grover operator is the combination of:
#    - phase inversion via the uf unitary operator
#    - inversion about the mean (see matrix above)
#
hn = ops.Hadamard(nbits)
reflection = op_zero * 2.0 - ops.Identity(nbits)
inversion = hn(reflection(hn)) * ops.Identity()
grover = inversion(uf)
```

We finally iterate the desired number of times based on the size of the state as discussed above (see Equation (6.10)):

```
iterations = int(math.pi / 4 * math.sqrt(2**nbits))

for _ in range(iterations):
  psi = grover(psi)
```

To check whether we have computed the right result, we perform measurement by peek-a-boo and compare the state with the highest probability to the desired output:

```
# Measurement - pick element with highest probability.
#
# Note: We constructed the oracle with n+1 qubits, to allow
# for the 'XOR-ancilla'. To check the result, we need to
```

```
# ignore this ancilla.
#
maxbits, maxprob = psi.maxprob()
result = f(maxbits[:-1])
print('Got f({}) = {}, want: 1, #: {:2d}, p: {:6.4f}'
      .format(maxbits[:-1], result, solutions, maxprob))
if result != 1:
  raise AssertionError('Something went wrong, invalid state.')
```

Experimenting with a few bit-widths:

```
def main(argv):
  [...]


  for nbits in range(3, 8):
    run_experiment(nbits)
```

Should produce results like these:

```
Got f((1, 0, 1)) = 1, want: 1, #:  1, p: 0.3906
Got f((1, 0, 1, 1)) = 1, want: 1, #:  1, p: 0.4542
Got f((1, 0, 1, 0, 0)) = 1, want: 1, #:  1, p: 0.4485
Got f((1, 0, 0, 1, 1, 1)) = 1, want: 1, #:  1, p: 0.4818
Got f((0, 1, 0, 1, 0, 0, 0)) = 1, want: 1, #:  1, p: 0.4710
```

6.8   Amplitude Amplification

How should we modify Grover's algorithm to account for multiple solutions? We have to adjust the phase inversion, inversion about the mean, and the iteration count.

Phase inversion for multiple solutions is easy to achieve. We modify the function make_f and give it a parameter solutions to indicate how many solutions to mark. We also thread this parameter through the code (not shown here, but available in the open-source repository):

```
def make_f(d: int = 3, solutions: int = 1):
  """Construct function that will return 1 for 'solutions' bits."""

  num_inputs = 2**d
  answers = np.zeros(num_inputs, dtype=np.int32)
  for i in range(solutions):
    idx = random.randint(0, num_inputs - 1)

    # Avoid collisions.
    while answers[idx] == 1:
      idx = random.randint(0, num_inputs - 1)
```

```
    # Found proper index. Populate 'answers' array.
    answers[idx] = 1

    # The actual function just returns an array elements.
    # pylint: disable=no-value-for-parameter
    def func(*bits):
        return answers[helper.bits2val(*bits)]

    # Return the function we just made.
    return func
```

We already derived the proper iteration count in the derivation for Grover's algorithm in Equation (6.11) as:

$$k = \frac{\pi}{4}\sqrt{\frac{N}{M}}.$$

We assumed $M = 1$ there (Section 6.7.6). To account for multiple solutions, we have to adjust the computation of the iteration count and divide by M, which is parameter `solutions` in the code:

```
iterations = int(math.pi / 4 * math.sqrt(2**nbits / solutions))
```

We add a test sequence to our main driver code to check whether any solution can be found, and with what maximal probability. For good performance, we fix the number of qubits at eight and gradually increase the number of solutions from 1 to 32:

```
for solutions in range(1, 33):
    run_experiment(8, solutions)
```

If we print the number of states with nonzero probability, we find that all of their probabilities are identical, and there are twice as many states with nonzero probability as there are solutions! This is an artifact of our oracle construction and the entanglement with the ancilla qubit. We should get output like the following:

```
Got f((1, 1, 0, 0, 1, 0, 0, 0)) = 1, want: 1, solutions:  1, found 1
↪   with P: 0.4913
Got f((1, 0, 1, 1, 1, 1, 0, 1)) = 1, want: 1, solutions:  2, found 1
↪   with P: 0.2355
Got f((1, 1, 1, 0, 0, 1, 1, 0)) = 1, want: 1, solutions:  3, found 1
↪   with P: 0.1624
Got f((0, 0, 1, 0, 0, 0, 1, 0)) = 1, want: 1, solutions:  4, found 1
↪   with P: 0.1204
Got f((0, 0, 1, 1, 1, 1, 1, 1)) = 1, want: 1, solutions:  5, found 1
↪   with P: 0.0908
Got f((1, 1, 1, 0, 1, 1, 1, 1)) = 1, want: 1, solutions:  6, found 1
↪   with P: 0.0804
```

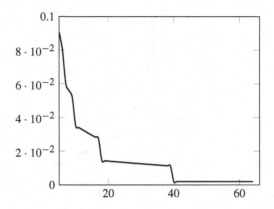

Figure 6.20 Probability of finding a solution when the total number of solutions ranges from 5 up to 64 in a state space of 128 elements.

Note how the probabilities decline rapidly. Let's visualize this with the graph in Figure 6.20. On the x-axis, we have the number of solutions ranging from 5 to 64. On the y-axis, we ignore the first few cases with high probability and set a maximum of 0.1. We can see how the probabilities decline rapidly and drop to 0 after the total number of solutions exceeds 40.

What if there are many more solutions, perhaps even a majority of the state space? To answer this question, Grover's algorithm has been generalized by Brassard et al. (2002) as *Quantum Amplitude Amplification* (QAA).

Grover expected just one special element and initialized the search with an equal superposition of all inputs by applying the algorithm $A = H^{\otimes n}$ to the input (note the unusual use of the term algorithm here). However, we might already have prior knowledge about the state of the system, which we can exploit by preparing the state differently. QAA supports any algorithm A to initialize the input and changes the Grover iteration to a more general form:

$$Q = AWA^{-1}U_f.$$

Operator U_f is the phase inversion operator for multiple solutions, and W is the inversion about the mean matrix we saw in Grover's algorithm. What changes is the derivation of the iteration count k, which has been shown to be proportional to the probability p_{good} of finding a solution (see Kaye et al., 2007, section 8.2), which was M/N (with $M = 1$ in the case of Grover):

$$k = \sqrt{\frac{1}{p_{good}}}.$$

Let us see how the probabilities improve with the new and improved iteration count. As an experiment,[7] we keep $A = H^{\otimes n}$ and compute the new iteration count as the

---

[7] Not in open-source, but can be obtained easily by modifying file `grover.py`.

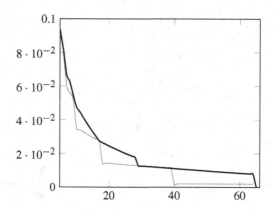

Figure 6.21 Probabilities for amplitude amplification finding 1 out of up to 64 solutions in a state space with 128 elements: (thick black line) amplitude amplification, (light gray line) and Grover's search

following, where we now divide by `solutions` to reflect the probability of finding a solution:

```
iterations = int(math.sqrt(2**nbits / solutions))
```

Figure 6.21 shows the probabilities for the two iterations, where the thick line represents the probabilities obtained with the new iteration count. We see that the situation improves markedly, but the probabilities still drop to 0 at more than 64 solutions. We have twice as many states with nonzero probabilities as there are solutions because of the ancilla entanglement. As soon as we hit half the size of the space, probabilities will drop to 0. A simple way to work around this problem is to just add another qubit. This additional qubit will double the size of the state space and eliminate the problem.

The technique of amplitude amplification requires knowledge of the number of good solutions, as well as their probability distribution. A general technique called *amplitude estimation* can help with this (see Kaye et al., 2007, section 8.2). In the next section, we detail a special case of amplitude estimation, *quantum counting*, which assumes an equal superposition of the search space with algorithm $A = H^{\otimes n}$, similar to Grover.

6.9   Quantum Counting

Quantum Counting is an interesting extension of the search problems we previously solved with Grover's algorithm and amplitude amplification. It combines these search algorithms with phase estimation in interesting ways to solve the problem of not knowing how many solutions M exist in a population of N elements. As we saw in the previous section, amplitude amplification requires knowledge of M to determine

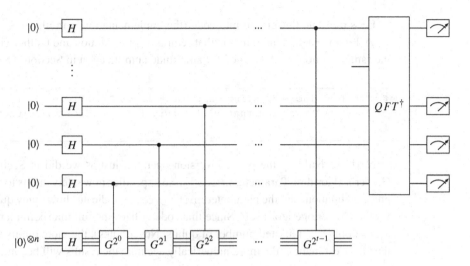

Figure 6.22 Phase estimation for the Grover operator G.

the right iteration count. Quantum counting is a special case of *amplitude estimation* that seeks to estimate this number M. Because it expects an equal superposition of the search space, similar to Grover, with algorithm $A = H^{\otimes n}$, we can reuse much of the Grover implementation in the code below.

As in Grover's algorithm, we partition the state space into a space with no solution $|\alpha\rangle$ and the space with only solutions $|\beta\rangle$:

$$|\psi\rangle = \sqrt{\frac{N - M}{N}}|\alpha\rangle + \sqrt{\frac{M}{N}}|\beta\rangle.$$

Applying the Grover operator amounts to a rotation by an angle ϕ towards the solution space $|\beta\rangle$. You may refer back to Figure 6.15 for a graphical illustration of this process. Since this a counterclockwise rotation, we can express the Grover operator as a standard rotation matrix:

$$G(\phi) = \begin{pmatrix} \cos\phi & -\sin\phi \\ \sin\phi & \cos\phi \end{pmatrix}.$$

Rotation matrices are unitary matrices with the eigenvalues:

$$\lambda_{0,1} = e^{\pm i\phi}.$$

We have also learned in the analysis of Grover's algorithm that Equation (6.9), replicated here, holds, with N being the number of elements and M being the number of solutions:

$$\sin\left(\frac{\phi}{2}\right) = \sqrt{\frac{M}{N}}.$$

If we find ϕ, we can estimate M because we already know N. We also know that we can use our friendly neighborhood phase estimator to find ϕ. For this, we build the circuit as shown in Figure 6.22.

Let's translate this circuit into code (the implementation is in file `src/counting` `.py`). First we define the function that returns 1 for a solution and 0 otherwise. This is the same function we developed for amplitude amplification in Section 6.8:

```
def make_f(d: int = 3, solutions: int = 1) -> Callable:
    """Construct function that will return 1 for 'solutions' bits."""
    [...]
```

Next, we build up the phase inversion operator, just as we did in Section 6.7 on Grover's algorithm. Parameter `nbits_phase` specifies how many qubits to use for the phase estimation, and the parameter `nbits_grover` indicates how many qubits to use for the Grover operator itself. Since this code utilizes the full matrix implementation, we can only use a limited number of qubits. Nevertheless, the more qubits we use for the phase estimation, the more numerically accurate the results will become.

```
def run_experiment(nbits_phase: int, nbits_grover: int,
                   solutions: int) -> None:
    """Run full experiment for a given number of solutions."""

    # Building the Grover operator.
    # A projector of all |00...0><0...00| is an all-0 matrix
    # with just element (1, 1) set to 1:
    #
    n = 2**nbits_grover
    zero_projector = np.zeros((n, n))
    zero_projector[0, 0] = 1
    op_zero = ops.Operator(zero_projector)

    # Construct function (with f(x*) = 1) and corresponding oracle:
    #
    f = make_f(nbits_grover, solutions)
    u = ops.OracleUf(nbits_grover + 1, f)
```

We build up the circuit as in Figure 6.22. Note that the Grover operator needs a $|1\rangle$ ancilla, which we also have to add to the state (not shown in the Figure). We apply a Hadamard to the inputs, including the ancilla:

```
    # The state for the counting algorithm.
    # We reserve nbits_phase for the phase estimation.
    # We also reserve nbits_grover for the Oracle.
    # These numbers could be adjusted to achieve better
    # accuracy.
    #
    # We also add the |1> for the Oracle.
    #
    psi = (state.zeros(nbits_phase) * state.zeros(nbits_grover)
           * state.ones(1))
```

```
# Apply Hadamard to all the qubits.
for i in range(nbits_phase + nbits_grover + 1):
  psi.apply(ops.Hadamard(), i)
```

Let us construct the Grover operator next. This, again, is very similar to the previous section on Grover's algorithm:

```
# Construct the Grover operator.
reflection = op_zero * 2.0 - ops.Identity(nbits_grover)
hn = ops.Hadamard(nbits_grover)
inversion = hn(reflection(hn)) * ops.Identity()
grover = inversion(u)
```

We follow this with the sequence of exponentiated gates and a final inverse QFT:

```
# Now that we have the Grover operator, we have to perform
# phase estimation. This loop is a copy from phase_estimation.py
# with more comments there.
#
for idx, inv in enumerate(range(nbits_phase - 1, -1, -1)):
  u2 = grover
  for _ in range(idx):
    u2 = u2(u2)
  psi = ops.ControlledU(inv, nbits_phase, u2)(psi, inv)

# Reverse QFT gives us the phase as a fraction of 2*pi.
psi = ops.Qft(nbits_phase).adjoint()(psi)
```

This completes the circuit. We measure and find the state with the highest probability. We reconstruct the phase from the binary fractions and then use Equation (6.9) to estimate M:

```
# Get the state with highest probability and compute the phase
# as a binary fraction. Note that the probability decreases
# as M, the number of solutions, gets closer and closer to N,
# the total number of states.
maxbits, maxprob = psi.maxprob()
phi_estimate = (sum(maxbits[i] * 2**(-i - 1)
                 for i in range(nbits_phase)))

# We know that after phase estimation, this holds:
#
#     sin(phi/2) = sqrt(M/N)
#              M = N * sin(phi/2)^2
#
# Hence we can compute M. We keep the result to 2 digit to visualize
# the errors. Note that the phi_estimate is a fraction of 2*pi, hence
```

```
# the 1/2 in above formula cancels out against the 2 and we compute:
M = round(n * math.sin(phi_estimate * math.pi)**2, 2)

print('Estimate: {:.4f} prob: {:5.2f}% --> M: {:5.2f}, want: {:2d}'
      .format(phi_estimate, maxprob * 100.0, M, solutions))
```

Let's run some experiments with seven qubits for the phase estimation, and five qubits for the Grover operator. In each experiment, we increase M by 1. For $N = 64$, we let M range from 1 to 10:

```
def main(argv):
    [...]
    for solutions in range(1, 11):
        run_experiment(7, 5, solutions)
```

Running this code should produce output like the following. We can see that our estimates are "in the ballpark" and will round to the correct solution. The solution probability also decreases significantly with higher values for M. It is instructional to experiment with all these parameters.

```
Estimate: 0.0547 prob: 10.05% --> M:  0.94, want:  1
Estimate: 0.0781 prob:  4.56% --> M:  1.89, want:  2
Estimate: 0.8984 prob:  2.85% --> M:  3.15, want:  3
Estimate: 0.8828 prob:  2.36% --> M:  4.14, want:  4
[...]
Estimate: 0.8203 prob:  1.16% --> M:  9.16, want:  9
Estimate: 0.1875 prob:  1.13% --> M:  9.88, want: 10
```

6.10   Quantum Random Walk

A *classical random walk* describes a process of random movement about a given topology, such as randomly moving left or right on a number line, left/right and up/down on a 2-dimensional grid, or moving along the edges of a graph. Random walks appear to accurately model an extensive range of real-world phenomena across disciplines as varied as physics, chemistry, economics, and sociology. In computer science, random walks are effectively used in randomized algorithms; for example, to determine the connectivity of vertices in a graph. Some of these algorithms have lower computational complexity than previously known, nonrandomized algorithms.

Random walks have fascinating properties. For example, assume two random walkers are starting their journey on a 2-dimensional grid. Will the walkers meet again in the future, and if so, how often? The answers are yes and infinitely often.

A *quantum random walk* is the quantum equivalent of a classical random walk (Kempe, 2003). Certain problems, such as the glued tree algorithm developed by

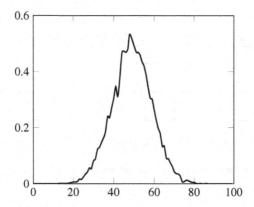

Figure 6.23 Results from a simulated classical random walk, plotting the likelihood of final position after starting in the middle of the range.

Childs et al. (2003, 2009), cannot be tractably computed on a classical machine. Herein lies the great interest in quantum random walks: some of these intractable problems become tractable on a quantum machine. In this section, we touch on basic principles, such as how probabilities propagate through a topology.

6.10.1   1D Walk

Let us start by considering a classical 1-dimensional walk on a number line. For each step, a coin toss determines whether to move left or right. After a number of moves, the probability distribution of the final location will be shaped like a classic bell curve, with the highest probability clustering around the origin of the journey. Figure 6.23 shows the result from a simple experiment,[8] which is available in the open-source repository in `tools/random_walk.py`.

The equivalent quantum walk operates in a similar fashion with coin tosses and movements. Because this is quantum, we exploit superposition and move in both directions at the same time. In short, a quantum random walk is the repeated application of an operator $U = CM$, with C being a coin toss and M being the move operator.

The most straightforward coin toss operator we can think of is, of course, a single Hadamard gate. In this context, the coin is called a *Hadamard coin*. The $|0\rangle$ part of the resulting superposition will control a movement to the left, and the $|1\rangle$ part, the move to the right.

The movement circuits can be constructed the following way, as shown by Douglas and Wang (2009). A number line is of length infinity, which cannot be properly represented. We should assume a circle with N states as underlying topology for the walk. Simple up- and down-counters with overflow and underflow between N and 0

---

[8] In fairness, the curve simply reflects the random number distribution chosen for the experiment.

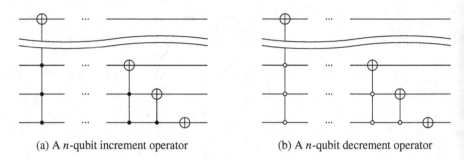

(a) A *n*-qubit increment operator   (b) A *n*-qubit decrement operator

Figure 6.24 Increment and decrement operators for quantum walks.

will work as movement operators. We can construct an *n*-qubit increment circuit as shown in Figure 6.24a, with the corresponding Python code (the full implementation is in file src/quantum_walk.py):

```
def incr(qc, idx: int, nbits: int, aux, controller=[]):
  """Increment-by-1 circuit."""

  #   -X--
  #   -o--X--
  #   -o--o--X--
  #   -o--o--o--X--
  #   ...
  for i in range(nbits):
    ctl=controller.copy()
    for j in range(nbits-1, i, -1):
      ctl.append(j+idx)
    qc.multi_control(ctl, i+idx, aux, ops.PauliX(), 'multi-1-X')
```

The analogous *n*-qubit decrement circuit is easy to construct as well, as shown in Figure 6.24b, with this code:

```
def decr(qc, idx: int, nbits: int, aux, controller=[]):
  """Decrement-by-1 circuit."""

  # Similar to incr, except controlled-by-0's are being used.
  #
  #   -X--
  #   -0--X--
  #   -0--0--X--
  #   -0--0--0--X--
  #   ...
  for i in range(nbits):
    ctl=controller.copy()
    for j in range(nbits-1, i, -1):
      ctl.append([j+idx])
    qc.multi_control(ctl, i+idx, aux, ops.PauliX(), 'multi-0-X')
```

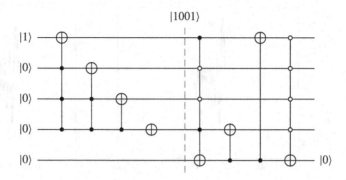

Figure 6.25 A increment modulo 9 operator.

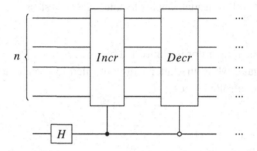

Figure 6.26 A single step for a quantum walk.

For both cases, N is a power of 2. We can construct other types of counters, for example, counters with step size larger than 1, or counters that increment modulo another number. For example, to construct a counter modulo 9, we add gates matching the binary representation of 9 to force a counter reset to 0, as shown in Figure 6.25.

With these tools, we can construct an initial n-qubit quantum circuit *step*, as shown in Figure 6.26. It has to be applied repeatedly to simulate a walk (consisting of more than just a single step).

We can see how to generalize this pattern to other topologies. For example, for a 2D walk across a grid, we can use two Hadamard coins: one for the left or right movement and one for movements up or down. For graph traversals, we would encode a graph's connectivity as an unitary operator. Several other examples can be found in Douglas and Wang (2009).

6.10.2   Walk the Walk

To simulate a given number of steps, we use the following driver code. We initialize the x register *in the middle* of the state's number range for n qubits, as binary $0b100\ldots0$. This way, we avoid immediate underflow below zero, and visualizations appear centered. Note how the increment operator is controlled by coin[0], while the

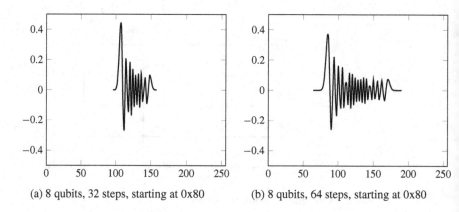

(a) 8 qubits, 32 steps, starting at 0x80   (b) 8 qubits, 64 steps, starting at 0x80

Figure 6.27 Propagating amplitudes after 32 and 64 steps.

decrement operator is controlled by `[coin[0]]`. The former is a standard controlled-by-1 gate, while the latter is a controlled-by-0 gate, as outlined in Section 4.3.7 on multi-controlled gates.

```python
def simple_walk():
  """Simple quantum walk."""

  nbits = 8
  qc = circuit.qc('simple_walk')
  qc.reg(nbits, 0x80)
  aux = qc.reg(nbits, 0)
  coin = qc.reg(1, 0)   # Add single coin qubit

  for _ in range(64):
    qc.h(coin[0])
    incr(qc, 0, nbits, aux, [coin[0]])     # ctrl-by-1
    decr(qc, 0, nbits, aux, [[coin[0]]])   # ctrl-by-0
```

What is really happening here? With n qubits, we can represent 2^n states with the corresponding number of probability amplitudes. As we perform step after step, nonzero amplitudes will start to *propagate out* over the state space. Looking at the examples in Figures 6.27b and 6.28b we see that, in contrast to a classical quantum walk, the amplitude distribution spreads out faster and with a very different shape. A series of 32 steps produces a nonzero amplitude in 64 states; the walk progresses in both directions at the same time. The farther away from the origin, the larger the amplitudes become. These are the key properties that quantum algorithms exploit to solve classically intractable problems, such as Childs' welded tree algorithm (Childs et al., 2003). To visualize the effect, we graph the resulting amplitudes:

```
for bits in helper.bitprod(nbits):
  idx_bits = bits
  for i in range(nbits+1):
      idx_bits = idx_bits + (0,)
  if qc.psi.ampl(*idx_bits) != 0.0:
      print('{:5.3f}'.format(qc.psi.ampl(*idx_bits0).real))
```

Let us experiment with eight qubits. The starting position should be in the middle of the range of states. With eight qubits, there are 256 possible states, and we initialize with 0x80, the middle of the range. It is possible to initialize with 0 of course, but that would lead to immediate wraparound effects. The amplitudes after 32, 64, and 96 steps are shown in Figure 6.27a, Figure 6.27b, and Figure 6.28a. The x-axis shows the state space (256 unique states for eight qubits). The y-axis shows each state's amplitude.

Notice how in the figures the amplitudes progress in a biased fashion. It is possible to create coin operators that are biased to the other side, or even balanced coin operators. Alternatively, we can start in a state different from |0⟩. In the example in Figure 6.28b, we simply initialize the coin state as |1⟩.

There are countless more experiments that you can perform with different coin operators, starting points, initial states, number of qubits, iteration counts, and more complex topologies beyond simple 1D and 2D walks.

It is exciting that if we can express a particular algorithmic reachability problem as a quantum walk circuit, the fast speed of quantum walks and the dense storage of states can lead to quantum algorithms with lower complexity than their corresponding classical algorithms. As an example, the 2010 IARPA program announcement set a challenge of eight complex algorithms to drive scalable quantum software and infrastructure development (IARPA, 2010). Three of these algorithms utilized quantum

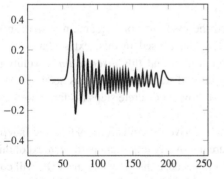 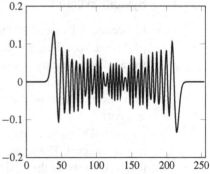

(a) 8 qubits, 96 steps, starting at 0x80, with initial state |0⟩

(b) 8 qubits, 96 steps, starting at 0x80, with initial state |1⟩

Figure 6.28 Propagating amplitudes with different initial states.

walks: the triangle finding algorithm (Buhrman et al., 2005; Magniez et al., 2005), the Boolean formula algorithm (Childs et al., 2009), and the welded tree algorithm (Childs et al., 2003).

6.11   Variational Quantum Eigensolver

This section represents a brief foray into the area of quantum simulation. We discuss the *variational quantum eigensolver* (VQE), an algorithm to estimate the ground state energy of a Hamiltonian.

It is possible to use quantum phase estimation (QPE) for this purpose. However, for realistic Hamiltonians, the number of gates required can reach millions, even billions, making it challenging to keep a physical quantum machine coherent long enough to run the computation. VQE, on the other hand, is a hybrid classical/quantum algorithm. The quantum part requires fewer gates and, therefore, much shorter coherence times when compared to QPE. This is why it created great interest in today's era of Noisy Intermediate Scale Quantum Computers (NISQ), which have limited resources and short coherence times (Preskill, 2018).

There cannot be a book about quantum computing without mentioning the Schrödinger equation at least once. This is that section in this book. So we begin by marveling at the beauty of the equation, although we will not solve it here. The purpose of showing it is to derive the composition of Hamiltonians from eigenvectors and how the variational principle enables the approximation of a minimum eigenvalue. This is followed by a discussion of measurement in different bases. We explain the variational principle next before we detail the hybrid classical/quantum algorithm itself.

6.11.1   System Evolution

In Section 2.15 we described the evolution of a quantum system in postulate 2 as $|\psi\rangle' = U|\psi\rangle$. This is what we have used in this text so far – to change a state we applied a unitary operator to it – and this *discrete time* evolution of a system is sufficient for all the algorithms discussed in previous sections. However, it is a simplification, as time does not move in discrete steps (as far as we know, or perhaps *suspect*).

The following few paragraphs derive a specific form of the time-independent Schrödinger equation. The details are not overly important in the context of this text, and we focus primarily on the final form because that is where the VQE will come into play.

The *time dependent* evolution of a system Ψ is described with the beautiful Schrödinger equation. We show the one-dimensional version only. Again, let's just marvel at this differential equation. We don't have to solve it here:

$$i\hbar \frac{\partial \Psi}{\partial t} = -\frac{\hbar^2}{2m} \frac{\partial^2 \Psi}{\partial x^2} + V\Psi. \tag{6.15}$$

This equation can be transformed into a *time-independent* form:

$$-\frac{\hbar^2}{2m}\frac{d^2\psi}{dx^2} + V\psi = E\psi. \tag{6.16}$$

In classical mechanics, the total energy of a system, which is the kinetic energy plus the potential V, is called the *Hamiltonian*, denoted as $\mathcal{H}$, not to be confused with our Hadamard operator H.

$$
\begin{aligned}
\mathcal{H}(x,p) &= \frac{mv^2}{2} + V(x) \\
&= \frac{(mv)^2}{2m} + V(x) \\
&= \frac{p^2}{2m} + V(x).
\end{aligned}
$$

As a side note, the factor $\hbar$ (the Planck constant) appears here from the famous Heisenberg uncertainty principle for a particle's position x and momentum p_x, with $\Delta x \Delta p_x \geq \hbar/2$. A *Hamiltonian operator* is obtained by the standard substitution with the momentum operator:

$$p \rightarrow -i\hbar\frac{\partial}{\partial x},$$

$$\hat{\mathcal{H}} = -\frac{\hbar^2}{2m}\frac{\partial^2}{\partial x^2} + V(x).$$

We use this result to rewrite Equation (6.16) as the following, with $\hat{\mathcal{H}}$ being the operator and E being an energy eigenvalue. Note the parallel to the definition of eigenvectors as $A\vec{x} = \lambda\vec{x}$:

$$\hat{\mathcal{H}}\psi = E\psi.$$

The expectation value for the total energy is then:

$$\langle\hat{\mathcal{H}}\rangle = E.$$

This Hamiltonian operator is Hermitian – on measurement, we obtain real values. Hence the eigenvalues must be real. It has a complete set of orthonormal eigenvectors:

$$|E_0\rangle, |E_1\rangle, \ldots, |E_{n-1}\rangle,$$

with corresponding real eigenvalues $\lambda_0, \lambda_1, \ldots, \lambda_{n-1}$. We can describe states as linear combinations of the eigenvectors

$$|\psi\rangle = c_0|E_0\rangle + c_1|E_1\rangle + \cdots + c_{n-1}|E_{n-1}\rangle. \tag{6.17}$$

This is the result we were looking for. It is important to note that the c_i are *complex* coefficients, similar to how we described a superposition between $|0\rangle$ and $|1\rangle$. In this case, however, the basis vectors are E_i. For a detailed derivation of the above, see for example Fleisch (2020).

6.11.2   The Variational Principle

Assume we are looking for the *ground state energy* E_0 of a system described by a given Hamiltonian. Knowing the ground state energy is important in many fields. For example, in thermodynamics, it describes behavior at temperatures close to absolute zero. In chemistry, it allows drawing conclusions about electron energy levels.

Let us now also assume that we cannot solve the time-independent Schrödinger Equation (6.16). We know that measurement will project the state onto an eigenvector, and the measurement result will be the corresponding eigenvalue. The *variational principle* will give an *upper bound* for E_0 with an expectation value for $\hat{\mathcal{H}}$ as:

$$E_0 \leq \langle \psi | \hat{\mathcal{H}} | \psi \rangle \equiv \langle \hat{\mathcal{H}} \rangle.$$

However, what is this state $|\psi\rangle$? The answer is, *any* state, as long as the state is capable, or close to being capable, of producing an eigenvector for $\hat{\mathcal{H}}$. This state will determine the remaining error for the estimation of E_0. We have to be smart about how to construct it. This is the key idea of the VQE algorithm.

To see how this principle works, let's take our assumed state from above and further assume that λ_0 is the smallest eigenvalue:

$$|\psi\rangle = c_0 |E_0\rangle + c_1 |E_1\rangle + \cdots + c_{n-1} |E_{n-1}\rangle.$$

Computing $\langle \psi | \hat{\mathcal{H}} | \psi \rangle$, as follows, demonstrates that *any* computed expectation value will be greater or equal to the minimum eigenvalue:

$$(c_0^* \langle E_0 | + c_1^* \langle E_1 | + \cdots + c_{n-1}^* \langle E_{n-1} |) \, \hat{\mathcal{H}} \, (c_0 |E_0\rangle + c_1 |E_1\rangle + \cdots + c_{n-1} |E_{n-1}\rangle)$$
$$= |c_0|^2 \lambda_0 + |c_1|^2 \lambda_1 + \cdots + |c_{n-1}|^2 \lambda_{n-1}$$
$$\geq \lambda_0.$$

The VQE algorithm works with Hamiltonians that can be written as a sum of a polynomial number of terms of Pauli operators and their tensor products (Peruzzo et al., 2014). This type of Hamiltonian is used in quantum chemistry, the Heisenberg Model, the quantum Ising Model, and other areas. For example, for a helium hydride ion (He-H$^+$) with bond distance 90 pm, the energy (Hamiltonian) is:

$$\hat{\mathcal{H}} = -3.851II - 0.229I\sigma_x - 1.047I\sigma_z - 0.229\sigma_x I + 0.261\sigma_x \sigma_x$$
$$+ 0.229\sigma_x \sigma_z - 1.0467\sigma_z I + 0.229\sigma_z \sigma_x + 0.236\sigma_z \sigma_z.$$

6.11.3   Measurement in Pauli Bases

So far in this book, we have described measurement as projecting a state onto the basis states $|0\rangle$ and $|1\rangle$. If we recall the Bloch sphere representation as shown in Figure 6.29, measurement projects the state to either the north or south pole of the Bloch sphere, corresponding to a measurement along the z-axis.

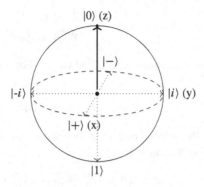

Figure 6.29 Bloch sphere representation with axes x, y, z.

However, what if the current state was aligned with a different axis, such as the x-axis from $|-\rangle$ to $|+\rangle$, or the y-axis pointing from $|-i\rangle$ to $|i\rangle$? In both cases, a measurement along the z-axis would result in a random toss between $|0\rangle$ and $|1\rangle$.

To measure in a different basis, we should *rotate* the state into the standard basis on the z-axis and perform a standard measurement there. The results can be interpreted along the original bases, and we get the added benefit that we only need a measurement apparatus in one direction.

To get a proper measurement along the x-axis, we could apply the Hadamard gate or rotate over the y-axis. Correspondingly, to get a measurement along the y-axis, we may rotate about the x-axis.

To compute expectation values for states composed of Pauli matrices, we remind ourselves of the basis states in the X, Y, and Z bases:

$$X: \quad |+\rangle = \frac{1}{\sqrt{2}}\begin{bmatrix}1\\1\end{bmatrix}, \quad |-\rangle = \frac{1}{\sqrt{2}}\begin{bmatrix}1\\-1\end{bmatrix},$$

$$Y: \quad |i\rangle = \frac{1}{\sqrt{2}}\begin{bmatrix}1\\i\end{bmatrix}, \quad |-i\rangle = \frac{1}{\sqrt{2}}\begin{bmatrix}1\\-i\end{bmatrix},$$

$$Z: \quad |0\rangle = \begin{bmatrix}1\\0\end{bmatrix}, \quad |1\rangle = \begin{bmatrix}0\\1\end{bmatrix}.$$

Pauli operators have eigenvalues of -1 and $+1$. Here are the operators applied to basis states with eigenvalues $+1$:

$$Z|0\rangle = |0\rangle,$$
$$X|+\rangle = |+\rangle,$$
$$Y|i\rangle = |i\rangle.$$

These are the same operators applied to basis states with eigenvalues -1:

$$Z|1\rangle = -|1\rangle,$$

$$X|-\rangle = -|-\rangle,$$
$$Y|-i\rangle = -|-i\rangle.$$

Let us now talk about expectation values. For a state in the Z-basis with amplitudes c_0^z and c_1^z:

$$|\psi\rangle = c_0^z|0\rangle + c_1^z|1\rangle.$$

Computing the expectation value for Z, in the Z-basis, yields the following, and similar for the X- and Y-bases:

$$\langle\psi|Z|\psi\rangle = \left(c_0^{z*}\langle 0| + c_1^{z*}\langle 1|\right) Z \left(c_0^z|0\rangle + c_1^z|1\rangle\right)$$
$$= |c_0^z|^2 - |c_1^z|^2$$

The values $|c_0^z|^2$ and $|c_1^z|^2$ are the measurement probabilities for $|0\rangle$ and $|1\rangle$. If we run N experiments and measure state $|0\rangle$ n_0 times and state $|1\rangle$ n_1 times:

$$|c_0^z|^2 = \frac{n_0}{N}, \quad |c_1^z|^2 = \frac{n_1}{N}.$$

Then this is the final expectation value for Z; please note the minus sign in this equation:

$$\langle Z\rangle = \frac{n_0 - n_1}{N}.$$

To give an example, let's assume we have a very simple circuit initialized with $|0\rangle$ and with just one Hadamard gate. The state after this gate will be $|+\rangle$, which is on the x-axis. If we now measure N times in the Z-basis, about 50% of the measurements will return $|0\rangle$, and 50% will return $|1\rangle$. The $|0\rangle$ corresponds to eigenvalue 1, the $|1\rangle$ corresponds to eigenvalue -1. Hence, the expectation value is 0:

$$\frac{(+1)N/2 + (-1)N/2}{N} = 0.$$

If we rotated the state into the Z-basis with another Hadamard gate, the expectation value of $|0\rangle$ in the Z-basis would now be 1.0, which corresponds to the expectation value of the state $|+\rangle$ originally in the X-basis.

In our infrastructure, we do not have to make measurements to compute probabilities because we can directly peek at the amplitudes of a state vector. To compute the expectation values for measurements made on Pauli operators with eigenvalues $+1$ and -1 corresponding to measuring $|0\rangle$ or $|1\rangle$, we add this function to our quantum circuit implementation qc:

```
def pauli_expectation(self, idx: int):
    """We can compute the Pauli expectation value from probabilities."""

    # Pauli eigenvalues are -1 and +1, hence we can compute the
    # expectation value like this:
    p0, _ = self.measure_bit(idx, 0, False)
    return p0 - (1 - p0)
```

Let's run a few experiments to familiarize ourselves with these concepts. What happens to the eigenvectors and eigenvalues for a Hamiltonian constructed from a single Pauli matrix multiplied with a factor? Is the result still unitary, or is it Hermitian?

```
factor = 0.6
H = factor * ops.PauliY()
eigvals = np.linalg.eigvalsh(H)
print(f'Eigenvalues of {factor} X = ', eigvals)
print(f'is_unitary: {H.is_unitary()}')
print(f'is_hermitian: {H.is_hermitian()}')
>>
Eigenvalues of 0.6 X =  [-0.6  0.6]
is_unitary: False
is_hermitian: True
```

Eigenvalues scale with the factor. Hamiltonians are Hermitian, but not necessarily unitary. Let's create a $|0\rangle$ state, show its Bloch sphere coordinates, and compute its expectation value in the Z-basis.

```
qc = circuit.qc('test')
qc.reg(1, 0)
qubit_dump_bloch(qc.psi)
print(f'Expectation value for 0 State: {qc.pauli_expectation(0)}')
>>
x: 0.00, y: 0.00, z: 1.00
Expectation value for 0 State: 1.0
```

As expected, the current position is on top of the north pole, corresponding to state $|0\rangle$. The expectation value is 1.0; there will be no measurements of the $|1\rangle$ state. Now, if we add just a single Hadamard gate, we will get:

```
x: 1.00, y: 0.00, z: -0.00
Expectation value for |0>: -0.00
```

The position on the Bloch sphere is now on the x-axis, and the corresponding expectation value in the Z-basis is 0; we will measure an equal amount of $|0\rangle$ and $|1\rangle$ states. Of course, to rotate this state back into the Z-basis, we only have to apply another Hadamard gate.

6.11.4 VQE Algorithm

The algorithm itself iterates over these steps:

1. **Ansatz.** Prepare a parameterized initial state $|\psi\rangle$. This is called the *ansatz*.
2. **Measurement.** Measure the expectation value $\langle\psi|\hat{\mathcal{H}}|\psi\rangle$.
3. **Minimize.** Tune the parameters of the ansatz to minimize the expectation value. The smallest value will be the best approximation of the minimum eigenvalue.

This is best explained by example. Let's focus on the single-qubit case first. We know that we can reach any point on the Bloch sphere with rotations about the x-axis and y-axis. Let's use this simple parameterized circuit as the ansatz:

$$|0\rangle \quad \boxed{R_x(\theta)} \quad \boxed{R_y(\phi)} \quad |\psi\rangle$$

We will construct multiple instances of ansatzes (which has a fun rhyme to it and is the proper English plural from; the correct German plural Ansätze does not sound quite as melodic). Let's wrap it into code (which is in file src/vqe_simple.py):

```
def single_qubit_ansatz(theta: float, phi: float) -> circuit.qc:
    """Generate a single qubit ansatz."""

    qc = circuit.qc('single-qubit ansatz Y')
    qc.qubit(1.0)
    qc.rx(0, theta)
    qc.ry(0, phi)
    return qc
```

Let's further assume a Hamiltonian of this form:

$$H = H_0 + H_1 + H_2 = 0.2X + 0.5Y + 0.6Z.$$

We can compute the minimum eigenvalue of -0.8062 with help from numpy:

```
H = 0.2 * ops.PauliX() + 0.5 * ops.PauliY() + 0.6 * ops.PauliZ()
# Compute known minimum eigenvalue.
eigvals = np.linalg.eigvalsh(H)
print(eigvals)
>>
[-0.8062258  0.8062258]
```

To compute the expectation value, let's create a state $|\psi\rangle$ and compute the expectation value $\langle\psi|\hat{\mathcal{H}}|\psi\rangle$ from two angles theta and phi:[9]

```
def run_single_qubit_experiment2(theta: float, phi: float):
    """Run experiments with single qubits."""

    # Construct Hamiltonian.
    H = 0.2 * ops.PauliX() + 0.5 * ops.PauliY() + 0.6 * ops.PauliZ()

    # Compute known minimum eigenvalue.
    eigvals = np.linalg.eigvalsh(H)
```

---

[9] This code segment is different from the open-source version. It is for illustration only.

```
# Build the ansatz with two rotation gates.
ansatz = single_qubit_ansatz(theta, phi)

# Compute <psi | H | psi>. Find smallest one, which will be
# the best approximation to the minimum eigenvalue from above.
val = np.dot(ansatz.psi.adjoint(), H(ansatz.psi))

# Result from computed approach:
print('Minimum: {:.4f}, Estimated: {:.4f}, Delta: {:.4f}'.format(
    eigvals[0], np.real(val), np.real(val - eigvals[0])))
```

Let's experiment with a few different values for `theta` and `phi`:

```
run_single_qubit_experiment2(0.1, -0.4)
run_single_qubit_experiment2(0.8, -0.1)
run_single_qubit_experiment2(0.9, -0.8)
>>
Minimum: -0.8062, Estimated: 0.4225, Delta: 1.2287
Minimum: -0.8062, Estimated: 0.0433, Delta: 0.8496
Minimum: -0.8062, Estimated: -0.2210, Delta: 0.5852
```

It appears we are moving in the right direction. We are getting closer to estimating the lowest eigenvalue, but we are still pretty far away. This particular ansatz is simple enough; we can incrementally iterate over both angles, approximating the minimum eigenvalue with good precision. Just picking random numbers would work as well, up to a certain degree. Obviously we can use techniques like gradient descent to find the best possible arguments more quickly (Wikipedia, 2021d). Let's run 10 experiments with random, single-qubit Hamiltonians, iterating over the angles ϕ and θ in increments of 10 degrees:

```
[...]
# iterate over all angles in increments of 10 degrees.
for i in range(0, 180, 10):
  for j in range(0, 180, 10):
    theta = np.pi * i / 180.0
    phi = np.pi * j / 180.0
[...]
# run 10 experiments with random H's.
[...]
>>
Minimum: -0.6898, Estimated: -0.6889, Delta: 0.0009
Minimum: -0.7378, Estimated: -0.7357, Delta: 0.0020
[...]
Minimum: -1.1555, Estimated: -1.1552, Delta: 0.0004
Minimum: -0.7750, Estimated: -0.7736, Delta: 0.0014
```

In the code above, we explicitly compute the expectation value with two dot products. The key to success here is that the ansatz is capable of creating the minimum eigenvalue's eigenvector (for two qubits). Shende et al. (2004) show how to construct a universal two-qubit gate. However, the challenge is to minimize gates for much larger Hamiltonians, especially on today's smaller machines. How to construct the ansatz is a research challenge. Which specific learning technique to use to accelerate the approximation is another subject of ongoing interest in the field, even though it appears that standard techniques from the field of machine learning work well enough.

6.11.5   Measuring Eigenvalues

In a physical setting, we cannot just multiply the state with the Hamiltonian. We have to measure along the Pauli bases and reconstruct the eigenvalues from the expectation values, as explained above. As mentioned earlier, we assume we can only measure in one direction. Let us once more assume a Hamiltonian of the following form. The factors are important; we have to remember them:

$$\hat{\mathcal{H}} = 0.2X + 0.5Y + 0.6Z.$$

We express the expectation values in the Z-basis with help of gate equivalences. Note how we isolate the Z in the last line, representing the measurement in the Z-basis:

$$\begin{aligned}
\langle\psi|\hat{\mathcal{H}}|\psi\rangle &= \langle\psi|0.2X + 0.5Y + 0.6Z|\psi\rangle \\
&= 0.2\langle\psi|X|\psi\rangle + 0.5\langle\psi|Y|\psi\rangle + 0.6\langle\psi|Z|\psi\rangle \\
&= 0.2\langle\psi|HZH|\psi\rangle + 0.5\langle\psi|HS^\dagger ZHS|\psi\rangle + 0.6\langle\psi|Z|\psi\rangle \\
&= 0.2\langle\psi H|Z|H\psi\rangle + 0.5\langle\psi HS^\dagger|Z|HS\psi\rangle + 0.6\langle\psi|Z|\psi\rangle.
\end{aligned}$$

In our experimental code, we first construct random Hamiltonians:

```
a = random.random()
b = random.random()
c = random.random()
H = (a * ops.PauliX() + b * ops.PauliY() + c * ops.PauliZ())
```

We have to build three circuits. The first is for $\langle\psi|X|\psi\rangle$, which requires an additional Hadamard gate:

```
# X-Basis
qc = single_qubit_ansatz(theta, phi)
qc.h(0)
val_a = a * qc.pauli_expectation(0)
```

Then one circuit for $\langle\psi|Y|\psi\rangle$, which requires a Hadamard gate and an $S^\dagger$ gate:

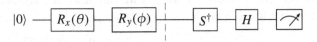

```
# Y-Basis
qc = single_qubit_ansatz(theta, phi)
qc.sdag(0)
qc.h(0)
val_b = b * qc.pauli_expectation(0)
```

Finally, a circuit for the measurement in the Z-basis $\langle\psi|Z|\psi\rangle$. In this basis we can measure as is, there is no need for additional gates:

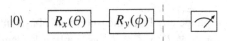

```
# Z-Basis
qc = single_qubit_ansatz(theta, phi)
val_c = c * qc.pauli_expectation(0)
```

As before, we iterate over the angles ϕ and θ in increments of, this time, 5 degrees. For each iteration, we take the expectation values `val_a`, `val_b`, and `val_c`, multiply them with the factors we noted above, add up the result, and look for the smallest value.

```
expectation = val_a + val_b + val_c
if expectation < min_val:
    min_val = expectation
```

This value `min_val` should be our estimate. The results are numerically accurate:

```
Minimum eigenvalue: -0.793, Delta: 0.000
Minimum eigenvalue: -0.986, Delta: 0.000
Minimum eigenvalue: -1.278, Delta: 0.000
Minimum eigenvalue: -0.937, Delta: 0.000
[...]
```

6.11.6 Multiple Qubits

How do we extend measurements to more than just one qubit? We begin with the simplest two-qubit Hamiltonians we can think of and extrapolate from there. Let's look at this tensor product and operator matrix:

$$Z \otimes I = \begin{bmatrix} 1 & 0 & 0 & 0 \\ 0 & 1 & 0 & 0 \\ 0 & 0 & -1 & 0 \\ 0 & 0 & 0 & -1 \end{bmatrix}.$$

We know that for diagonal matrices, the diagonal elements are eigenvalues, which are $+1$ and -1 in this case. This matrix has two subspaces, which map to these eigenvalues. On measurement, we would get a result of either $+1$ or -1.

Any unitary two-qubit transformation U on this matrix will map to a space with the same eigenvalues of $+1$ and -1. This means we can apply a similar trick as in the one-qubit case and apply the following transformations. Note that these are matrices; we have to multiply from both sides, as in:

$$U^{\dagger}(Z \otimes I)U.$$

We can change any Pauli measurement's basis into $Z \otimes I$. For example, to change the basis for $X \otimes I$ to $Z \otimes I$, we apply a Hadamard gate, just as above, with the operator $U = H \otimes I$. Let's verify this in code:

```
H = ops.Hadamard()
I = ops.Identity()
U = H * I
(ops.PauliZ() * I).dump('Z x I')
(ops.PauliX() * I).dump('X x I')
(U.adjoint() @ (ops.PauliX() * I)).dump('Udag(X x I)')
(U.adjoint() @ (ops.PauliX() * I) @ U).dump('Udag(X x I)U')
>>
Z x I (2-qubits operator)
  1.0        -          -          -
  -          1.0        -          -
  -          -         -1.0        -
  -          -          -         -1.0
X x I (2-qubits operator)
  -          -          1.0        -
  -          -          -          1.0
  1.0        -          -          -
  -          1.0        -          -
Udag(X x I) (2-qubits operator)
  0.7        -          0.7        -
  -          0.7        -          0.7
 -0.7        -          0.7        -
  -         -0.7        -          0.7
Udag(X x I)U (2-qubits operator)
  1.0        -          -          -
```

–	1.0	–	–
–	–	-1.0	–
–	–	–	-1.0

From this, it is straightforward to construct the operators for a first set of Pauli measurements containing at least one identity operator, as shown in Table 6.1.

But now it gets complicated. The operator for $Z \otimes Z$ is the Controlled-Not $U = CX_{1,0}$! How does this happen? Let look at the matrix $Z \otimes Z$:

$$Z \otimes Z = \begin{bmatrix} 1 & 0 & 0 & 0 \\ 0 & -1 & 0 & 0 \\ 0 & 0 & -1 & 0 \\ 0 & 0 & 0 & 1 \end{bmatrix}$$

It needs a few permutations to turn into the form we are looking for, which is $Z \otimes I$. If we apply the Controlled-Not from left and right:

$$CX_{1,0}^{\dagger}(Z \otimes Z)\, CX_{1,0} = (Z \otimes I),$$

we indeed get the result we are looking for:

```
(ops.Cnot(1, 0).adjoint() @ (ops.PauliZ() * ops.PauliZ()) @
               ops.Cnot(1, 0)).dump()
>>
1.0    –        –        –
 –     1.0      –        –
 –     –      -1.0       –
 –     –        –      -1.0
```

The operator matrices for $CX_{1,0}$ perform the required permutation; we should not think of this as an actually controlled operation. With these insights, we can now define the remaining 4×4 Pauli measurement operators as shown in Table 6.2.

From here, we can generalize the construction to more than two qubits, similar to Whitfield et al. (2011) for Hamiltonian simulation (which we don't cover here). All we have to do is to surround the multi-Z Hamiltonian with *cascading* Controlled-Not

Table 6.1 Operators for measurements containing an identity.

Pauli Measurement	Operator U
$Z \otimes I$	$I \otimes I$
$X \otimes I$	$H \otimes I$
$Y \otimes I$	$H S^{\dagger} \otimes I$
$I \otimes Z$	$(I \otimes I)\, SWAP$
$I \otimes X$	$(H \otimes I)\, SWAP$
$I \otimes Y$	$(H S^{\dagger} \otimes I)\, SWAP$

Table 6.2 Operators for measurements with no identity.

Pauli Measurement	Operator U
$Z \otimes Z$	$CX_{1,0}$
$X \otimes Z$	$CX_{1,0}\,(H \otimes I)$
$Y \otimes Z$	$CX_{1,0}\,(HS^{\dagger} \otimes I)$
$Z \otimes X$	$CX_{1,0}\,(I \otimes H)$
$X \otimes X$	$CX_{1,0}\,(H \otimes H)$
$Y \otimes X$	$CX_{1,0}\,(HS^{\dagger} \otimes H)$
$Z \otimes Y$	$CX_{1,0}\,(I \otimes HS^{\dagger})$
$X \otimes Y$	$CX_{1,0}\,(H \otimes HS^{\dagger})$
$Y \otimes Y$	$CX_{1,0}\,(HS^{\dagger} \otimes HS^{\dagger})$

gates. For example, for the three-qubit ZZZ, we write the code below (which could be simplified by recognizing that $CX_{1,0}^{\dagger} = CX_{1,0}$).

```
ZII = ops.PauliZ() * ops.Identity()* ops.Identity()
C10 = ops.Cnot(1, 0) * ops.Identity()
C21 = ops.Identity() * ops.Cnot(2, 1)
C10adj = C10.adjoint()
C21adj = C21.adjoint()
ZZZ = ops.PauliZ() * ops.PauliZ() * ops.PauliZ()

res = C10adj @ C21adj @ ZZZ @ C21 @ C10
self.assertTrue(res.is_close(ZII))
```

Note that the adjoint of the X-gate is identical to the X-gate and the adjoint of a Controlled-Not is a Controlled-Not as well. For $ZZZZ$, or even longer sequences of Z-gates, we build a cascading gate sequence in circuit notation, as shown in Figure 6.30. Now that we have this methodology available, we can measure in any Pauli measurement basis! And just to make sure, you can verify the construction for $ZZZZ$ with a short code sequence like the following:

```
op1 = ops.Cnot(1, 0) * ops.Identity() * ops.Identity()
op2 = ops.Identity() * ops.Cnot(2, 1) * ops.Identity()
op3 = ops.Identity() * ops.Identity() * ops.Cnot(3, 2)

bigop = op1 @ op2 @ op3 @ ops.PauliZ(4) @ op3 @ op2 @ op1
op = ops.PauliZ() * ops.Identity(3)
self.assertTrue(bigop.is_close(op))
```

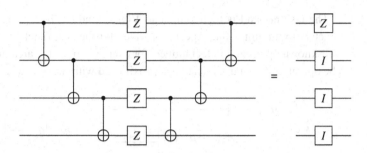

Figure 6.30 Measuring in the $ZZZZ$ basis.

6.12 Quantum Approximate Optimization Algorithm

In this section, we describe the *Quantum Approximate Optimization Algorithm*, or QAOA (pronounced "Quah-Wah"). It was first introduced in the seminal paper by Farhi et al. (2014), which also detailed using QAOA for an implementation of the Max-Cut algorithm. We explore Max-Cut in Section 6.13.

The QAOA technique is related to VQE, which could be considered a subroutine of QAOA. Here we provide only a short overview. There are two operators in QAOA, U_C and U_B. The first operator U_C applies a phase to pairs of qubits with a problem-specific cost function C, which is similar to the Ising formulation below in Section 6.13.1, with Z_i being the Pauli Z-gate applied to qubit i and l being the number of qubits or vertices involved:

$$C = \sum_{j,k}^{l} w_{jk} Z_j Z_k.$$

The operator itself depends on the phase angle γ:

$$U_C(\gamma) = e^{-i\gamma C} = \prod_{j,k} e^{i\gamma w_{jk} Z_j Z_k}.$$

This operator acts on two qubits and thus can be used for problems that can be expressed as weighted graphs.

The second operator U_B depends on a parameter β. It is problem-independent and applies rotations to each qubit with the following, where each X_j is a Pauli X-gate:

$$U_B(\beta) = e^{-i\beta B} = \prod_j e^{-i\beta X}, \quad \text{where } B = \sum_j X_j.$$

For problems with higher depth, these two operators U_C and U_B are applied repeatedly, each with their own set of hyperparameters γ_i and β_i, on an initial state of $|+\rangle^{\otimes n}$:

$$U_B(\beta_{n-1})U_C(\gamma_{n-1})\dots U_B(\beta_0)U_C(\gamma_0) \, |+\rangle^{\otimes n}.$$

The task at hand is then similar to VQE – find the best possible set of hyperparameters to minimize the expectation value for the cost function $\langle \gamma, \beta | C | \gamma, \beta \rangle$, using well-known optimization techniques, for example, from the area of machine learning. The operators U_C and U_B can be approximated with the following circuits:

We know from Section 6.11 on VQE how to implement this type of search, so we won't expand on this further.

The original QAOA paper showed that for 3-regular graphs, which are cubic graphs with each vertex having exactly three edges, the algorithm produces a cut that is at least 0.7 of the maximum cut, a number that we are roughly able to confirm in our experiments below. Together with VQE, QAOA is an attractive algorithm for today's NISQ machines with limited resources, as the corresponding circuits have a shallow depth (Preskill, 2018). At the same time, QAOA's utility for industrial-sized problems is still under debate (Harrigan et al., 2021).

6.13   Maximum Cut Algorithm

In the previous section, we saw how the VQE finds the minimum eigenvalue and eigenvector for a Hamiltonian. This is an exciting methodology because if we can successfully frame an optimization problem as a Hamiltonian, we can use a VQE to find an optimal solution. This section briefly describes how to construct a class of such Hamiltonians: the Ising spin glass model, representing a multivariate optimization problem. The treatment here is admittedly shallow but sufficient to implement examples – the Max-Cut and Min-Cut algorithms in this section and the Subset Sum problem in Section 6.14.

6.13.1   Ising Formulations of NP Algorithms

The construction of a Hamiltonian with the Pauli σ_z operators is based on Hamiltonians for Ising spin glass (Lucas, 2014). This type of Hamiltonian is written as an unconstrained quadratic programming problem (a multivariate optimization problem). In the Ising model of ferromagnetism, J_{ij} is the *interaction* between a pair i, j of neighboring spins. It takes the values $J_{ij} = 0$ for no interaction, $J_{ij} > 0$ for ferromagnetism, and $J_{ij} < 0$ for antiferromagnetism:

$$\sum_i^N h_i x_i + \sum_{i,j} J_{ij} x_i y_j,$$

which corresponds to this Hamiltonian:

$$H(x_0, x_1, \ldots, x_n) = -\sum_i^N h_i \sigma_i^z - \sum_{i,j} J_{ij} \sigma_i^z \sigma_j^z.$$

The term σ_i^z is the application of a Pauli Z-gate on qubit i. The minus sign explains that we can look for a minimum eigenvalue to find a maximum solution. For problems such as Max-Cut, we use σ^z because we want an operator with eigenvalues -1 and $+1$.

With this background, Lucas (2014) details several NP-complete or NP-hard problems for which this approach may work. The list of algorithms includes partitioning problems, graph coloring problems, covering and packing problems, Hamiltonian cycles (including the traveling salesman problem), and tree problems. In the next few sections, we develop a related problem, the graph Max-Cut problem. We will also explore a slightly modified formulation of the Subset Sum problem.

6.13.2   Max-Cut/Min-Cut

For a graph, a *cut* is a partition of the graph's vertices into two nonoverlapping sets L and R. A *maximum cut* is the cut that maximizes the number of edges between L and R. Assigning weights to the graph edges turns the problem into the more general *weighted maximum cut*, which aims to find the cut that maximizes the weights of edges between sets L and R. This is the *Max-Cut* problem we are trying to solve in this section.

Weights can be both positive and negative. The Max-Cut problem turns into a Min-Cut problem simply by changing the sign of each weight. As an example, the maximum cut in Figure 6.31a, a graph of four nodes, is between the sets $L = \{0, 2\}$ and $R = \{1, 3\}$. The nodes are colored white or gray, depending on which set they belong to.

For a graph with just 15 nodes, as shown in Figure 6.31b, the problem becomes unwieldy very quickly. General Max-Cut is NP-complete, we don't know of any polynomial time algorithm to find an optimal solution. This looks like a formidable challenge for a quantum algorithm!

6.13.3   Construct Graphs

We begin our exploration by constructing a random graph with n vertices with the help of the following code (the implementation is in file `src/max_cut.py`). As usual, the code is designed for simplicity. We number vertices from 0 to $n - 1$ and represent vertices as simple Python tuples (`from_node, to_node, weight`). A graph is then just a list of these tuples.

The code starts with a triangle of three nodes and then randomly adds new nodes up to limit `num`, ensuring that no double edges are generated.

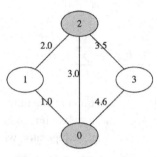

(a) A graph with 4 vertices

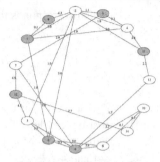

(b) A graph with 15 vertices

Figure 6.31 Example graphs with marked Max-Cut sets.

```python
def build_graph(num: int = 0) -> (int, List[int]):
    """Build a graph of num nodes."""

    if num < 3:
        raise app.UsageError('Must request graph of at least 3 nodes.')
    weight = 5.0
    nodes = [(0, 1, 1.0), (1, 2, 2.0), (0, 2, 3.0)]
    for i in range(num-3):
        l = random.sample(range(0, 3 + i - 1), 2)
        nodes.append((3 + i, l[0],
                      weight*np.random.random()))
        nodes.append((3 + i, l[1],
                      weight*np.random.random()))
    return num, nodes
```

For debugging and intuition, it helps to visualize the graph. The output of the routine below can be used to visualize the graphs with Graphviz (graphviz.org, 2021). The graphs in Figure 6.31 were produced this way.

```python
def graph_to_dot(n: int, nodes: List[int], max_cut) -> None:
    """Convert graph (up to 64 nodes) to dot file."""

    print('graph {')
    print('  {\n    node [ style=filled ]')
    pattern = bin(max_cut)[2:].zfill(n)
    for idx, val in enumerate(pattern):
        if val == '0':
            print(f'    "{idx}" [fillcolor=lightgray]')
    print('  }')
    for node in nodes:
        print('  "{}" -- "{}" [label="{:.1f}",weight="{:.2f}"];'
              .format(node[0], node[1], node[2], node[2]))
    print('}')
```

6.13.4   Compute Max-Cut

Graph nodes are numbered from 0 to $n - 1$. We use a binary representation to encode a cut. For example, nodes 0 and 2 in Figure 6.31a are in set L; nodes 1 and 3 are in set R. We align node 0 with index 0 in a binary bitstring (from left to right) and represent the cut as the binary string 1010. We extend this representation to quantum states, associating qubits q_i with graph nodes n_i:

$$| \underbrace{1}_{n_0} \ \underbrace{0}_{n_1} \ \underbrace{1}_{n_2} \ \underbrace{0}_{n_3} \rangle$$

We can compute the Max-Cut exhaustively, and quite inefficiently, given our choice of data structures. For n nodes, we generate all binary bitstrings from 0 to n. For each bitstring, we iterate over the individual bits and build two index sets: indices with a 0 in the bitstring, and indices with a 1 in the bitstring. For example, the bitstring 11001 would create set $L = \{0, 1, 4\}$ and set $R = \{2, 3\}$.

The calculation then iterates over all edges in the graph. For each edge, if one of the vertices is in L and the other in R, there is an edge between sets. We add the edge weight to the currently computed maximum cut and maintain the absolute maximum cut. Finally, we return the corresponding bit pattern as a decimal. For example, if the maximum cut was binary 11001, the routine returns 25 (this routine will only work with up to 64 bits or vertices).

```python
def compute_max_cut(n: int, nodes: List[int]) -> int:
    """Compute (inefficiently) the max cut, exhaustively."""

    max_cut = -1000
    for bits in helper.bitprod(n):
        # Collect in/out sets.
        iset = []
        oset = []
        for idx, val in enumerate(bits):
            iset.append(idx) if val == 0 else oset.append(idx)

        # Compute costs for this cut, record maximum.
        cut = 0
        for node in nodes:
            if node[0] in iset and node[1] in oset:
                cut += node[2]
            if node[1] in iset and node[0] in oset:
                cut += node[2]
        if cut > max_cut:
            max_cut_in, max_cut_out = iset.copy(), oset.copy()
            max_cut  = cut
            max_bits = bits

    state = bin(helper.bits2val(max_bits))[2:].zfill(n)
```

```
print('Max Cut. N: {}, Max: {:.1f}, {}  -  {}, |{}>'
      .format(n, np.real(max_cut), max_cut_in, max_cut_out,
              state))
return helper.bits2val(max_bits)
```

The performance of this code is, of course, quite horrible but perhaps indicative of the combinatorial character of the problem. On a standard workstation, computing the Max-Cut for 20 nodes takes about 10 seconds; for 23 nodes it takes about 110 seconds. Even considering performance differences between Python and C++ and the relatively poor choice of data structure, it is obvious that the runtime will quickly become intractable for larger graphs.

Note that the solution is symmetric. If a Max-Cut is $L = \{0, 1, 4\}$ and $R = \{2, 3\}$, then $L = \{2, 3\}$ and $R = \{0, 1, 4\}$ is a Max-Cut as well.

6.13.5   Construct Hamiltonian

To construct the Hamiltonian, we iterate over the graph's edges. We build the tensor product with identity matrices for nodes that are not part of the edge and Pauli σ_z matrices for the vertices connected by the edge. This follows the very brief methodology outlined above in Section 6.13.1. We may also use the intuition that Pauli σ_z are "easy" to measure, as we have outlined in Section 6.11 on measuring in the Pauli bases. The Pauli matrix σ_z has eigenvalues $+1$ and -1. An edge can *increase* or *decrease* the energy of the Hamiltonian, depending on which set vertices fall into. This construction *increases* the energy for vertices that are in the same set.

As an example for the construction, for the graph in Figure 6.31a we would build these tensor products for all edges $e_{from,to}$:

$$e_{0,1} = 1.0\,(Z \otimes Z \otimes I \otimes I),$$
$$e_{0,2} = 3.0\,(Z \otimes I \otimes Z \otimes I),$$
$$e_{0,3} = 4.6\,(Z \otimes I \otimes I \otimes Z),$$
$$e_{1,2} = 2.0\,(I \otimes Z \otimes Z \otimes I),$$
$$e_{2,3} = 3.5\,(I \otimes I \otimes Z \otimes Z).$$

We add up these partial operators to construct the final Hamiltonian, which mirrors Equation (6.17).

$$\mathcal{H} = e_{0,1} + e_{0,2} + e_{0,3} + e_{1,2} + e_{2,3}.$$

Here is the code to construct the Hamiltonian in full matrix form. It iterates over the edges and constructs the full tensor products as shown above:

```
def graph_to_hamiltonian(n: int, nodes: List[int]) -> ops.Operator:
    """Compute Hamiltonian matrix from graph."""

    # Full matrix.
    H = np.zeros((2**n, 2**n))
```

```
for node in nodes:
    idx1 = node[0]
    idx2 = node[1]
    if idx1 > idx2:
        idx1, idx2 = idx2, idx1
    op = 1.0
    for _ in range(idx1):
        op = op * ops.Identity()
    op = op * (node[2] * ops.PauliZ())
    for _ in range(idx1 + 1, idx2):
        op = op * ops.Identity()
    op = op * (node[2] * ops.PauliZ())
    for _ in range(idx2 + 1, n):
        op = op * ops.Identity()
    H = H + op
return ops.Operator(H)
```

As we have described so far, for a graph with n nodes, we would have to build operator matrices of size $2^n \times 2^n$, which does not scale well. Note, however, that both the identity matrix and σ_z are diagonal matrices. Tensor products of diagonal matrices result in diagonal matrices. For example:

$$I \otimes I \otimes Z = \begin{bmatrix} 1 & 0 & 0 & 0 & 0 & 0 & 0 & 0 \\ 0 & -1 & 0 & 0 & 0 & 0 & 0 & 0 \\ 0 & 0 & 1 & 0 & 0 & 0 & 0 & 0 \\ 0 & 0 & 0 & -1 & 0 & 0 & 0 & 0 \\ 0 & 0 & 0 & 0 & 1 & 0 & 0 & 0 \\ 0 & 0 & 0 & 0 & 0 & -1 & 0 & 0 \\ 0 & 0 & 0 & 0 & 0 & 0 & 1 & 0 \\ 0 & 0 & 0 & 0 & 0 & 0 & 0 & -1 \end{bmatrix}$$

$$= \mathrm{diag}(1, -1, 1, -1, 1, -1, 1, -1).$$

If we apply a factor to any individual operator, that factor multiplies across the whole diagonal. Let us look at what happens if we apply σ_z at index $0, 1, 2, \dots$ in the tensor products (from right to left):

$$I \otimes I \otimes Z = \mathrm{diag}(+1, -1, +1, -1, +1, -1, \underbrace{+1}_{2^0}, \underbrace{-1}_{2^0}),$$

$$I \otimes Z \otimes I = \mathrm{diag}(+1, +1, -1, -1, \underbrace{+1, +1}_{2^1}, \underbrace{-1, -1}_{2^1}),$$

$$Z \otimes I \otimes I = \mathrm{diag}(+1, +1, +1, +1, \underbrace{-1, -1, -1, -1}_{2^2}).$$

These are power-of-2 patterns, similar to those we have seen in the fast gate apply routines. This means we can optimize the construction of the diagonal Hamiltonian and only construct a diagonal tensor product! The full matrix code is very slow and can barely handle 12 graph nodes. The diagonal version below can easily handle twice as many nodes. C++ acceleration might help to further improve scalability, especially because the calls to `tensor_diag` can be parallelized.

```python
def tensor_diag(n: int, fr: int, to: int, w: float):
    """Construct a tensor product from diagonal I, Z matrices."""

    def tensor_product(w1:float, w2:float, diag):
        return [j for i in zip([x * w1 for x in diag],
                               [x * w2 for x in diag]) for j in i]

    diag = [w, -w] if (0 == fr or 0 == to) else [1, 1]
    for i in range(1, n):
        if i == fr or i == to:
            diag = tensor_product(w, -w, diag)
        else:
            diag = tensor_product(1, 1, diag)
    return diag

def graph_to_diagonal_h(n: int, nodes: List[int]) -> np.ndarray:
    """Construct diag(H)."""

    h = [0.0] * 2**n
    for node in nodes:
        diag = tensor_diag(n, node[0], node[1], node[2])
        for idx, val in enumerate(diag):
            h[idx] += val
    return h
```

6.13.6   VQE by Peek-A-Boo

After we constructed the Hamiltonian, we would typically run VQE (or QAOA) to find the minimum eigenvalue. The corresponding eigenstate would encode the Max-Cut in binary form. However, in our simulated case here we don't have to run the expensive VQE, we can just take a peek at the Hamiltonian's matrix. It is diagonal, meaning that the eigenvalues are on the diagonal. The corresponding eigenstate is a state vector with a single 1 at the same row or column in binary encoding as the minimum eigenvalue. For example, for the graph in Figure 6.32, the Hamiltonian is:

$$\mathcal{H} = \mathrm{diag}(49.91, -21.91, -18.67, -5.32, 10.67, -2.67, -41.91, 29.91,$$
$$29.91, -41.91, -2.67, 10.67, -5.32, -18.67, -21.91, 49.91).$$

The minimum value is -41.91 and appears in two places: at index 6, which is binary 0110, and the complementary index 9, which is binary 1001. This corresponds to state $|0110\rangle$ and the complementary $|1001\rangle$. This is precisely the Max-Cut pattern in Figure 6.32. We have found the Max-Cut by applying *VQE by peek-a-boo* on a properly prepared Hamiltonian!

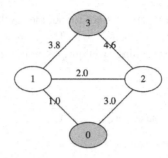

Figure 6.32 Graph with 4 nodes; Max-Cut is $\{0, 3\}, \{1, 2\}$, or 0110 in binary set encoding.

Here is the code to run experiments. It constructs the graph and computes the Max-Cut exhaustively. Then it computes the Hamiltonian and obtains the minimum value and its index off the diagonal.

```
def run_experiment(num_nodes: int):
    """Run an experiment, compute H, match against Max-Cut."""

    n, nodes = build_graph(num_nodes)
    max_cut  = compute_max_cut(n, nodes)
    #
    # These two lines are the basic implementation, where
    # a full matrix is being constructed. However, these
    # are diagonal, and can be constructed much faster.
    #   H      = graph_to_hamiltonian(n, nodes)
    #   diag   = H.diagonal()
    #
    diag      = graph_to_diagonal_h(n, nodes)
    min_idx   = np.argmin(diag)

    # Results...
    if flags.FLAGS.graph:
        graph_to_dot(n, nodes, max_cut)

    if min_idx == max_cut:
        print('SUCCESS: {:+10.2f} |{}>'.format(np.real(diag[min_idx]),
                        bin(min_idx)[2:].zfill(n)))
    else:
        print('FAIL    : {:+10.2f} |{}> '.format(np.real(diag[min_idx]),
                        bin(min_idx)[2:].zfill(n)), end='')
        print('Max-Cut: {:+10.2f} |{}>'.format(np.real(diag[max_cut]),
                        bin(max_cut)[2:].zfill(n)))
```

Running this code, we find that it does *not always* work; it fails in about 20–30% of the invocations. Our criteria is very strict; to mark a run as successful, we check whether the optimal cut was found. Anything else is considered a failure. However even if the optimal cut was not found, the results are still within 30% of optimal, and typically significantly below 20%. This matches the analysis from the QAOA paper.

For example, running over graphs with 12 nodes may produce output like the following:

```
Max Cut. N: 12, Max: 38.9, [0, 1, 4, 7, 9, 10]-[2, 3, 5, 6, 8, 11],
↪  |001101101001>
SUCCESS :     -129.39 |001101101001>
Max Cut. N: 12, Max: 39.5, [0, 1, 5, 6, 7, 9]-[2, 3, 4, 8, 10, 11],
↪  |001110001011>
SUCCESS :     -117.64 |001110001011>
Max Cut. N: 12, Max: 46.0, [0, 3, 5, 8, 11]-[1, 2, 4, 6, 7, 9, 10],
↪  |011010110110>
FAIL    :     -146.79 |001010110110>  Max-Cut:    -145.05 |011010110110>
[...]
Max Cut. N: 12, Max: 43.7, [0, 1, 3, 4, 7, 8, 9, 10]-[2, 5, 6, 11],
↪  |001001100001>
SUCCESS :     -124.69 |001001100001>
```

It is educational to experiment with the maximum degree of the graph, as it appears that this is one of the factors influencing the failure rate for this algorithm.

6.14   Subset Sum Algorithm

In Section 6.13, we saw how to use QAOA and VQE (by peek-a-boo) to solve an optimization problem. In this section, we explore another algorithm of this type, the so-called Subset Sum problem. Similar to Max-Cut, this problem is known to be NP-complete.

The problem can be stated the following way. Given a set S of integers, can S be divided into two sets, L and $R = S - L$, such that the sum of the elements in L equals the sum of the elements in R:

$$\sum_i^{|L|} l_i = \sum_j^{|R|} r_j.$$

We will also express this problem with a Hamiltonian constructed very similarly to Max-Cut, except that we will only introduce a single weighted Z-gate for each number in S. In Max-Cut we were looking for a minimal energy state. For this balanced sum problem, we have to look for a zero-energy state because this would indicate energy equilibrium, or equilibrium of the partial sums. Our implementation only decides whether or not a solution exists. It does not find a specific solution.

6.14.1   Implementation

To start, and since this algorithm is begging to be experimented with, we define relevant parameters as command line options (the implementation is in file `src/subset_sum.py`). The highest integer in S is specified with parameter `nmax`. We will encode integers as positions in a bitstring, or, correspondingly, a state. For integers up to `nmax`, we will need `nmax` qubits. The size $|S|$ of set S is specified with parameter `nnum`. And finally, the number of experiments to run is specified with parameter `iterations`.

```
flags.DEFINE_integer('nmax', 15, 'Maximum number')
flags.DEFINE_integer('nnum',  6,
                     'Maximum number of set elements [1-nmax]')
flags.DEFINE_integer('iterations', 20, 'Number of experiments')
```

The next step is to get `nnum` random, unique integers in the range from 1 to `nmax` inclusive. Other ranges are possible, including negative numbers, but given that we use integers as bit positions, we have to map any such range to the range of 0 to `nmax`.

```
def select_numbers(nmax: int, nnum: int) -> List[int]:
  """Select nnum random, unique numbers in range 1 to nmax."""

  while True:
    sample = random.sample(range(1, nmax), nnum)
    if sum(sample) % 2 == 0:
      return sample
```

The next step is to compute the diagonal tensor product. Note that we only have to check for a single number and a correspondingly weighted (by index i) Z-gate.

```
def tensor_diag(n: int, num: int):
  """Construct tensor product from diagonal matrices."""

  def tensor_product(w1: float, w2: float, diag):
    return [j for i in zip([x * w1 for x in diag],
                           [x * w2 for x in diag]) for j in i]

  diag = [1, -1] if num == 0 else [1, 1]
  for i in range(1, n):
    if i == num:
      diag = tensor_product(i, -i, diag)
    else:
      diag = tensor_product(1, 1, diag)
  return diag
```

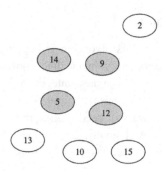

Figure 6.33 A subset partition for a set of eight integers. The partial sums of all elements in the white and gray sets are equal.

The final step for constructing the Hamiltonian is to add up all the diagonal tensor products from the step above. This function is identical to the same function in the Max-Cut algorithm, except for the invocation of the routine to compute the diagonal tensor product itself. If we implemented more algorithms of this type, we would clearly generalize the construction.

```
def set_to_diagonal_h(num_list: List[int],
                      nmax: int) -> np.ndarray:
    """Construct diag(H)."""

    h = [0.0] * 2**nmax
    for num in num_list:
        diag = tensor_diag(nmax, num)
        for idx, val in enumerate(diag):
            h[idx] += val
    return h
```

6.14.2   Experiments

Now on to experiments. We created a list of random numbers in the step above. The next step is to exhaustively compute potential partitions. Similar to Max-Cut, we divide the set of numbers into two sets with the help of binary bit patterns. For each division, we compute the two sums for these two sets. If the results match up, we add the corresponding bit pattern to the list of results. The routine then returns this list, which could be empty if no solution was found for a given set of numbers. A sample set partition is shown in Figure 6.33.

```
def compute_partition(num_list: List[int]):
    """Compute partitions that add up."""

    solutions = []
    for bits in helper.bitprod(len(num_list)):
```

```
    iset = []
    oset = []
    for idx, val in enumerate(bits):
        (iset.append(num_list[idx]) if val == 0 else
         oset.append(num_list[idx]))
    if sum(iset) == sum(oset):
        solutions.append(bits)
return solutions
```

Of course we need a small facility to print results:

```
def dump_solution(bits: List[int], num_list: List[int]):
    iset = []
    oset = []
    for idx, val in enumerate(bits):
        (iset.append(f'{num_list[idx]:d}') if val == 0 else
         oset.append(f'{num_list[idx]:d}'))
    return '+'.join(iset) + ' == ' + '+'.join(oset)
```

Finally, we run the experiments. For each experiment, we create a set of numbers, compute the solutions exhaustively, and compute the Hamiltonian.

```
def run_experiment() -> None:
    """Run an experiment, compute H, match against 0."""

    nmax = flags.FLAGS.nmax
    num_list = select_numbers(nmax, flags.FLAGS.nnum)
    solutions = compute_partition(num_list)
    diag = set_to_diagonal_h(num_list, nmax)
```

We perform VQE by peek-a-boo. For Max-Cut we plucked a defined index and value from the diagonal. But what is the right value to look for here? Ultimately, we are looking for a zero-energy state, because this would indicate a balance between sets L and R. Hence we look for zeros on the diagonal of the Hamiltonian. There can be multiple zeros, but as a long as a one single zero can be found, we know there should be a solution. If no solution was found exhaustively, but we still find a zero on the diagonal, we know that we have encountered a false positive. Conversely, if no zero was found on the diagonal, but the exhaustive search did identify a solution, we encountered a false negative. The code below checks for both conditions.

```
    non_zero = np.count_nonzero(diag)
    if non_zero != 2**nmax:
        print('Solution should exist...', end='')
        if solutions:
            print(' Found Solution:',
                  dump_solution(solutions[0], num_list))
            return True
```

```
      raise AssertionError('False positive found.')
   if solutions:
      raise AssertionError('False negative found.')
   return False
```

As we run the code, we should see a 100% success rate:

```
for i in range(flags.FLAGS.iterations):
    ret = run_experiment()
[...]
Solution should exist... Found Solution: 13+1+5+3 == 14+8
Solution should exist... Found Solution: 4+9+14 == 12+5+10
Solution should exist... Found Solution: 10+1+14 == 4+12+9
Solution should exist... Found Solution: 12+7+10 == 6+9+14
[...]
Solution should exist... Found Solution: 1+3+11+2 == 5+12
Solution should exist... Found Solution: 13+5+7 == 2+9+14
```

6.15   Solovay–Kitaev Theorem and Algorithm

We now switch gears and discuss the Solovay–Kitaev (SK) theorem and corresponding algorithm (Kitaev et al., 2002). It proves that *any* unitary gate can be approximated from a finite set of universal gates, which in the case of single-qubit gates, are just Hadamard and T-gates. This theorem is one of the key results in quantum computing. A version of the theorem that seems appropriate in our context is the following:

THEOREM 6.1 (Solovay–Kitaev theorem)   *Let G be a finite set of elements in SU(2) containing its own inverses, such that $\langle G \rangle$ is dense in SU(2). Let $\epsilon > 0$ be given. Then there is a constant c such that for any U in SU(2) there is a sequence of gates of a length $O(log^c(1/\epsilon))$ such that $||S - U|| < \epsilon$.*

In English, this theorem says that for a given unitary gate U, there is a finite sequence of universal gates that will approximate U up to any precision. To a degree, this should *not* surprise us because if this was not the case, the set of universal gates could hardly be called universal. The produced gate sequences can be quite long, and it appears the field has moved on (Ross and Selinger, 2016, 2021; Kliuchnikov et al., 2015). Nevertheless, the algorithm was seminal and is supremely elegant.

We will study it using the pedagogical review from Dawson and Nielsen (2006) as a guide. We start with a few important concepts and functions. Then we outline the high-level structure of the algorithm before diving deeper into the complex parts and implementation.

6.15.1   Universal Gates

For single qubits, a set of *universal* gates consists of the Hadamard gate H and the T-gate. We call this set "universal" because any point on a Bloch sphere can be reached by a sequence of just these two gates. We prove this below by showing that the SK algorithm, based on just these two gates, can approximate any unitary matrix up to arbitrary precision. We develop the implementation here in a piecemeal fashion, but the full code is available in the open-source repository src/solovay_kitaev.py.

6.15.2   SU(2)

One of the requirements for the SK algorithm is that the universal gates involved are part of the $SU(2)$ group, which is the group of all 2×2 unitary matrices with determinant 1. The determinants of both the Hadamard gate and the T-gate are not 1. In order to convert the gates to become members of $SU(2)$, we apply the simple transformation:

$$U' = \sqrt{\frac{1}{\det U}} U.$$

```
def to_su2(U):
    """Convert a 2x2 unitary to a unitary with determinant 1.0."""

    return np.sqrt(1 / np.linalg.det(U)) * U
```

We won't go deeper into $SU(2)$ and the related mathematics of Lie groups. For our purposes, we should simply think of $SU(2)$ in terms of rotations. For a given rotation V, the inverse rotation is $V^\dagger$, with $VV^\dagger = I$. For two rotations U and V, the inverse of UV is $V^\dagger U^\dagger$, with $UVV^\dagger U^\dagger = I$. However, similar to how two perpendicular sides on a Rubik's cube rotate against each other, $UVU^\dagger V^\dagger \neq I$.

6.15.3   Bloch Sphere Angle and Axis

Any 2×2 unitary matrix is of this form:

$$U = \begin{bmatrix} a & b \\ c & d \end{bmatrix}.$$

We can also write such a unitary operator the following way. The notation $\hat{n}$ refers to orthogonal, 3-dimensional axes. The symbol $\vec{\sigma}$ refers to the Pauli matrices:

$$U = e^{i\theta \hat{n}\frac{1}{2}\vec{\sigma}} = I \cos(\theta/2) + i\hat{n}\vec{\sigma} \sin(\theta/2).$$

This means that any unitary matrix can be constructed from a linear combination of the Pauli matrices in a specified coordinate system. Applying these unitary operators is equal to rotations about the axis $\hat{n}$ by angle θ. Only elements on the axis remain untouched by the rotation. With this, we can compute the angle and axis for a given unitary matrix with the following expansions:

$$U = e^{i\theta\hat{n}\cdot\frac{1}{2}\vec{\sigma}} = e^{i\theta/2\hat{n}\cdot\vec{\sigma}}$$

$$= I \cos(\theta/2) + \hat{n} \cdot i\vec{\sigma} \sin(\theta/2)$$

$$= I \cos(\theta/2) + n_1 i\sigma_1 \sin(\theta/2) + n_2 i\sigma_2 \sin(\theta/2) + n_3 i\sigma_3 \sin(\theta/2)$$

$$
= \begin{bmatrix} \cos(\theta/2) & 0 \\ 0 & \cos(\theta/2) \end{bmatrix} + \begin{bmatrix} 0 & n_1 i \sin(\theta/2) \\ n_1 i \sin(\theta/2) & 0 \end{bmatrix}
$$

$$
+ \begin{bmatrix} 0 & n_2 \sin(\theta/2) \\ -n_2 \sin(\theta/2) & 0 \end{bmatrix} + \begin{bmatrix} n_3 i \sin(\theta/2) & 0 \\ 0 & -n_3 i \sin(\theta/2) \end{bmatrix}
$$

$$
= \begin{bmatrix} \cos(\theta/2) + n_3 i \sin(\theta/2) & n_2 \sin(\theta/2) + n_1 i \sin(\theta/2) \\ -n_2 \sin(\theta/2) + n_1 i \sin(\theta/2) & \cos(\theta/2) - n_3 i \sin(\theta/2) \end{bmatrix} = \begin{bmatrix} a & b \\ c & d \end{bmatrix}.
$$

We compute the relevant parameters with simple algebraic transformations:

$$
\theta = 2 \arccos \frac{a+d}{2},
$$

$$
n_1 = \frac{b+c}{2i \sin(\theta/2)},
$$

$$
n_2 = \frac{b-c}{2 \sin(\theta/2)},
$$

$$
n_3 = \frac{a-d}{2i \sin(\theta/2)}.
$$

The corresponding (unoptimized) code is:

```python
def u_to_bloch(U):
    """Compute angle and axis for a unitary."""

    angle = np.real(np.arccos((U[0, 0] + U[1, 1])/2))
    sin = np.sin(angle)
    if sin < 1e-10:
        axis = [0, 0, 1]
    else:
        nx = (U[0, 1] + U[1, 0]) / (2j * sin)
        ny = (U[0, 1] - U[1, 0]) / (2 * sin)
        nz = (U[0, 0] - U[1, 1]) / (2j * sin)
        axis = [nx, ny, nz]
    return axis, 2 * angle
```

6.15.4 Similarity Metrics

The *trace distance* is a similarity measure for two states. Typically, this concept is applied for states that are expressed as density matrices, but we may as well adopt it here to measure similarity between operators. For two operators ρ and ϕ, the trace distance is defined as:

$$
T(\rho, \phi) = \frac{1}{2} \mathrm{tr} \left[\sqrt{(\rho - \phi)^\dagger (\rho - \phi)} \right].
$$

In code this looks straightforward:

```
def trace_dist(U, V):
    """Compute trace distance between two 2x2 matrices."""

    return np.real(0.5 * np.trace(np.sqrt((U - V).adjoint() @ (U - V))))
```

There are other similarity metrics. For example, *quantum fidelity*. It is instructive to experiment with these kind of measures to study their impact on the achieved accuracy of our implementation:

$$F(\rho, \phi) = \left(\text{tr} \left[\sqrt{\sqrt{\rho} \, \phi \, \sqrt{\rho}} \right] \right)^2.$$

6.15.5   Pre-computing Gates

The SK algorithm is recursive. At the innermost step, it maps a given unitary operator U against a library of pre-computed gate sequences, picking the resulting gate *closest* to U, as measured by the trace distance (or other similarity metrics).

The process of pre-computing gate sequences can be made quite simple. We only provide a most basic implementation, which is slow, but has the advantage of being easy to understand. There are only two base gates, as shown above. We generate all bitstrings up to a certain length, such as 0, 1, 00, 01, 10, 11, 000, 001, and so on. We initialize a temporary gate with the identity gate I and iterate through each bitstring, multiplying the temporary gate with one of the two basis gates, depending on whether a bit in the bitstring was set to 0 or 1. The function returns a list of all pre-computed gates. For simplicity, we throw away the actual gate sequences; we just keep the resulting unitary matrix, knowing that it was computed from the base gates.

```
def create_unitaries(base, limit):
    """Create all combinations of all base gates, up to length 'limit'."""

    # Create bitstrings up to bitstring length limit-1:
    #   0, 1, 00, 01, 10, 11, 000, 001, 010, ...
    #
    # Multiply together the 2 base operators, according to their index.
    # Note: This can be optimized, by remembering the last 2^x results
    # and multiplying them with base gates 0, 1.
    #
    gate_list = []
    for width in range(limit):
        for bits in helper.bitprod(width):
            U = ops.Identity()
            for bit in bits:
                U = U @ base[bit]
            gate_list.append(U)
    return gate_list
```

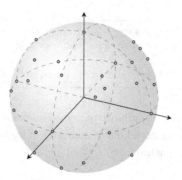

Figure 6.34 Distribution of 256 generated gate sequences applied to state |0⟩. There are many duplicates.

To look up the closest gate, we iterate over the list of gates, compute the trace distance to each one, and return the gate with the minimum distance. Again, this code is kept simple for illustrative purposes. It is horribly slow, but there are ways to speed it up significantly, for example, with KD-trees (Wikipedia, 2021a).

```
def find_closest_u(gate_list, u):
  """Find the one gate in the list closest to u."""

  min_dist, min_u = 10, ops.Identity()
  for gate in gate_list:
    tr_dist = trace_dist(gate, u)
    if tr_dist < min_dist:
      min_dist, min_u = tr_dist, gate
  return min_u
```

Note that the way we generate gate sequences here leads to duplicate gates. For example, when plotting the effects of the generated gates on state |0⟩, we see that the resulting distinct gates are quite sparse on the Bloch sphere, as shown in Figure 6.34.

6.15.6　Algorithm

Now we are ready to discuss the algorithm. We describe it in code, explaining it line by line. Inputs are the unitary operator U we seek to approximate and a maximum recursion depth n.

```
def sk_algo(U, gates, n):
  if n == 0:
    return find_closest_u(gates, U)
  else:
    U_next = sk_algo(U, gates, n-1)
    V, W   = gc_decomp(U @ U_next.adjoint())
```

```
V_next = sk_algo(V, gates, n-1)
W_next = sk_algo(W, gates, n-1)
return (V_next @ W_next @ V_next.adjoint() @ W_next.adjoint() @
        U_next)
```

The recursion is counting down from an initial value of n and stops as it reaches the termination case with n==0. At this point, the algorithm looks up the closest pre-computed gate it can find.

```
if n == 0:
    return find_closest_u(gates, U)
```

Starting with this basic approximation, the following steps further improve the approximation by applying sequences of other inaccurate gates. The magic of this algorithms is, of course, that this actually works!

The first recursive step tries to find an approximation of U. For example, if n==1, the recursion would reach the termination clause and return the closest pre-computed gate.

```
U_next = sk_algo(U, gates, n-1)
```

The next key steps are now to define $\Delta = UU_{n-1}^{\dagger}$ and to improve the approximation of Δ. We concatenate the two gate sequences for U and $U_{n-1}^{\dagger}$ to obtain the improved approximation. The interesting part here is that we use $U_{n-1}^{\dagger}$. The gate U_{n-1} got us closer to the target. The recursion wants to find out what we did *before* in order to arrive at this gate.

We decompose Δ as a *group commutator*, which is defined as $\Delta = VWV^{\dagger}W^{\dagger}$ with unitary gates V, W. There are an infinite number of such decompositions, but we apply an accuracy criterion to get a *balanced group commutator*. The math motivating this decomposition is beyond this book. We refer to Dawson and Nielsen (2006) and Kitaev et al. (2002) for details. Here we accept the result and show how to implement gc_decomp().

```
V, W    = gc_decomp(U @ U_next.adjoint())
```

The next recursive steps are then to get *improved* approximations for V, W with the same algorithm and to return a new and improved sequence $UU_{n-1}^{\dagger}$, as:

$$U_n = V_{n-1}W_{n-1}V_{n-1}^{\dagger}W_{n-1}^{\dagger}U_{n-1}.$$

```
V_next = sk_algo(V, gates, n-1)
W_next = sk_algo(W, gates, n-1)
return (V_next @ W_next @
        V_next.adjoint() @ W_next.adjoint() @ U_next
```

6.15.7   Balanced Group Commutator

There is an infinite set of group commutator decompositions for a unitary operator U. We are looking for one for which $VWV^\dagger W^\dagger = U$, but with the distance between I and both V and W being smaller than a certain error bound. The difference between U_n and U_{n-1} will then be close to the identity matrix in the algorithm above as well. This condition can be expressed as the following, with $d()$ being a similarity metric and c being a constant:

$$d(I, V), d(I, W) < c\sqrt{\epsilon}.$$

This can be accomplished by considering V as a rotation by angle ϕ about the x-axis of a Bloch sphere and W as a similar rotation about the y-axis. The group commutator $VWV^\dagger W^\dagger$ is then a rotation about the Bloch sphere around axis $\hat{n}$ by an angle θ, satisfying Equation 6.18:

$$\sin(\theta/2) = 2\sin^2(\phi/2)\sqrt{1 - \sin^4(\phi/2)}. \tag{6.18}$$

In the next few paragraphs, we will first derive Equation (6.18) and then solve for ϕ. Both V and W were defined as rotations about the x-axis and y-axis:

$$V = R_x(\phi),$$

$$V^\dagger = R_x(\phi)^\dagger = R_x(-\phi),$$

$$U = VWV^\dagger W^\dagger = R_x(\phi)R_y(\phi)R_x(-\phi)R_y(-\phi).$$

Similar to how we derived a unitary operator's Bloch sphere angle and axis, we express rotations as:

$$R_x(\phi) = \cos(\phi/2) I + i\sin(\phi/2) X,$$
$$R_y(\phi) = \cos(\phi/2) I + i\sin(\phi/2) Y.$$

We can multiply this out and only evaluate the diagonal elements as above as $\cos\left(\frac{\theta}{2}\right) = \frac{a+d}{2}$ to arrive at:

$$\cos(\theta/2) = \cos^4(\phi/2) + 2\cos^2(\phi/2)\sin^2(\phi/2) - \sin^4(\phi/2).$$

We can factor out $\cos^2(\phi/2) + \sin^2(\phi/2)$ for:

$$\cos(\theta/2) = \cos^4(\phi/2) + 2\cos^2(\phi/2)\sin^2(\phi/2) - \sin^4(\phi/2)$$

$$= \left(\cos^2(\phi/2) + \sin^2(\phi/2)\right)^2 - 2\sin^4(\phi/2)$$

$$= 1 - 2\sin^4(\phi/2).$$

Using Pythagoras' theorem, we get the form we were looking for:

$$\sin^2(\theta/2) = 1 - \cos^2(\theta/2)$$

$$= 1 - \left(1 - 2\sin^4(\phi/2)\right)^2$$

$$= 4\sin^4(\phi/2) - 4\sin^8(\phi/2)$$

$$= 4\sin^4(\phi/2)\left(1 - \sin^4(\phi/2)\right)$$

$$\Rightarrow \sin(\theta/2) = 2\sin^2(\phi/2)\sqrt{1 - \sin^4(\phi/2)}.$$

Now on to solving for ϕ. From what we've done so far, we know how to compute θ for an operator. We get rid of the square root in Equation (6.18) by squaring the whole equation. For ease of notation, we substitute x for the left side:

$$x = \left(\frac{\sin(\theta/2)}{2}\right)^2 = \left(\sin^2(\phi/2)\sqrt{1 - \sin^4(\phi/2)}\right)^2$$

$$x = \sin^4(\phi/2)\left(1 - \sin^4(\phi/2)\right)$$

$$= \sin^4(\phi/2) - \sin^8(\phi/2)$$

$$\Rightarrow 0 = \sin^4(\phi/2) - \sin^8(\phi/2) - x$$

$$= \sin^8(\phi/2) - \sin^4(\phi/2) + x.$$

This is a quadratic equation, which we can solve:

$$y^2 - y + x = 0$$

$$\Rightarrow \sin^4(\phi/2) = y = \frac{1 \pm \sqrt{1 - 4x}}{2}$$

$$\sin(\phi/2) = \sqrt{\sqrt{y}}$$

$$\phi = 2\arcsin\left(\sqrt[4]{y}\right). \tag{6.19}$$

Expand y (and remember that $\cos^2(\phi) + \sin^2(\phi) = 1$):

$$y = \frac{1 \pm \sqrt{1 - 4x}}{2}$$

$$= \frac{1 \pm \sqrt{1 - 4\sin^2(\theta/2)/4}}{2}$$

$$= \frac{1 \pm \cos(\theta/2)}{2}.$$

Substituting this into Equation (6.19) leads to the final result for ϕ. We ignore the $+$ case from the quadratic equation, as the goal was to arrive at Equation (6.18):[10]

$$\phi = 2\arcsin\left(\sqrt[4]{\frac{1 - \cos(\theta/2)}{2}}\right).$$

The construction proceeds as follows. We assumed that U is a rotation by angle θ about some axis $\hat{x}$. The angle ϕ is the solution to Equation (6.18). We define V, W to be rotations by ϕ, so U must be *conjugate* to the rotation by θ,

---

[10] We recommend that rigor-sensitive readers please hold their noses here.

with $U = S(VWV^{\dagger}W^{\dagger})S^{\dagger}$ for some unitary matrix S. We define $\hat{V} = SVS^{\dagger}$ and $\hat{W} = SWS^{\dagger}$ to obtain:

$$U = \hat{V}\hat{W}\hat{V}^{\dagger}\hat{W}^{\dagger}.$$

Let's write this in code. First we define the function `gc_decomp`, adding a helper function to diagonalize a unitary matrix. We compute θ and ϕ as described above:

```python
def gc_decomp(U):
  """Group commutator decomposition."""

  def diagonalize(U):
    _, V = np.linalg.eig(U)
    return ops.Operator(V)

  # Get axis and theta for the operator.
  axis, theta = u_to_bloch(U)
  # The angle phi comes from eq 6.21 above.
  phi = 2.0 * np.arcsin(np.sqrt(
      np.sqrt((0.5 - 0.5 * np.cos(theta) / 2))))
```

We compute the axis on the Bloch sphere as shown above and construct the rotation operators V and W:

```python
V = ops.RotationX(phi)
if axis[2] > 0:
  W = ops.RotationY(2 * np.pi - phi)
else:
  W = ops.RotationY(phi)
```

Finally, we compute S as the transformation from U to the commutator:

```python
Ud = diagonalize(U)
VWVdWd = diagonalize(V @ W @ V.adjoint() @ W.adjoint())
S = Ud @ VWVdWd.adjoint()
```

And compute the results as outlined above:

```python
V_hat = S @ V @ S.adjoint()
W_hat = S @ W @ S.adjoint()
return V_hat, W_hat
```

6.15.8   Evaluation

For a brief and anecdotal evaluation, we define key parameters and run a handful of experiments. The number of experiments to run is given by `num_experiments`.

Variable `depth` is the maximum length of the bitstrings we use to pre-compute gates. For a depth value x, $2^x - 1$ gates are pre-computed. Variable `recursion` is the recursion depth for the SK algorithm. It is instructive to experiment with these values to explore the levels of accuracy and performance you can achieve.

```
def main(argv):
  if len(argv) > 1:
    raise app.UsageError('Too many command-line arguments.')

  num_experiments = 10
  depth = 8
  recursion = 4
  print('SK algorithm - depth: {}, recursion: {}, experiments: {}'.
        format(depth, recursion, num_experiments))
```

Next we compute the $SU(2)$ base gates and create the pre-computed gates.

```
  base = [to_su2(ops.Hadamard()), to_su2(ops.Tgate())]
  gates = create_unitaries(base, depth)
  sum_dist = 0.0
```

Finally, we run the experiments. In each experiment, we create a unitary gate U from a randomly chosen combination of rotations. We apply the algorithm and compute and print distance metrics of the results. We also compare the impact of both original and approximated unitary gates on a $|0\rangle$ state. We compute the dot product between the resulting states and show how much it deviates from 1.0, expressed as a percentage. This may give an intuitive measure of the impact of the remaining approximation errors.

```
  for i in range(num_experiments):
    U = (ops.RotationX(2.0 * np.pi * random.random()) @
         ops.RotationY(2.0 * np.pi * random.random()) @
         ops.RotationZ(2.0 * np.pi * random.random()))

    U_approx = sk_algo(U, gates, recursion)
    dist = trace_dist(U, U_approx)
    sum_dist += dist

    phi1 = U(state.zero)
    phi2 = U_approx(state.zero)
    print('[{:2d}]: Trace Dist: {:.4f} State: {:6.4f}%'.
          format(i, dist,
                 100.0 * (1.0 - np.real(np.dot(phi1, phi2.conj())))))
  print('Gates: {}, Mean Trace Dist:: {:.4f}'.
        format(len(gates), sum_dist / num_experiments))
```

This should result in output like the following. With just 255 pre-computed gates (including many duplicates) and a recursion depth of 4, approximation accuracy falls consistently below 1%.

```
$ bazel run solovay_kitaev
[...]
SK algorithm, depth: 8, recursion: 4. experiments: 10
[ 0]: Trace Dist: 0.0063 State: 0.0048%
[ 1]: Trace Dist: 0.0834 State: 0.3510%
[ 2]: Trace Dist: 0.0550 State: 0.1557%
[...]
[ 8]: Trace Dist: 0.1114 State: 0.6242%
[ 9]: Trace Dist: 0.1149 State: 0.6631%
Gates: 255, Mean Trace Dist:: 0.0698
```

6.15.9   Random Gate Sequences

The following question is interesting. How well does this algorithm perform compared to picking the best approximation from *random* sequences of base gates? We could try to answer this analytically, but we could also run experiments, construct random sequences of basis gates, and find the resulting unitary operator with the minimum trace distance to the original gate. Let's try that.

```
def random_gates(min_length, max_length, num_experiments):
  """Just create random sequences, find the best."""

  base = [to_su2(ops.Hadamard()), to_su2(ops.Tgate())]

  U = (ops.RotationX(2.0 * np.pi * random.random()) @
       ops.RotationY(2.0 * np.pi * random.random()) @
       ops.RotationZ(2.0 * np.pi * random.random()))
  min_dist = 1000
  for i in range(num_experiments):
    seq_length = min_length + random.randint(0, max_length)
    U_approx = ops.Identity()
    for j in range(seq_length):
      g = random.randint(0, 1)
      U_approx = U_approx @ base[g]
    dist = trace_dist(U, U_approx)
    min_dist = min(dist, min_dist)
  phi1 = U(state.zero)
  phi2 = U_approx(state.zero)
  print('Trace Dist: {:.4f} State: {:6.4f}%'.
        format(min_dist,
               100.0 * (1.0 - np.real(np.dot(phi1, phi2.conj())))))
```

It is educational to experiment with this approach. You can find approximated gates with small trace distances, but it appears the impact on basis states is much larger than for the SK algorithm. With longer gate sequences and many more tries, gate sequences can reach low trace distance deltas. However, to reach accuracies as shown above for the SK algorithm, the runtime can be orders of magnitude longer. To answer the question above about how well the SK algorithm performs – it does *very* well! Here is an example output from a sequence of randomized experiments:

```
Random Experiment, seq length: 10 - 50, tries: 100
Trace Dist: 0.2218 State: 58.4058%
Trace Dist: 0.2742 State: 39.3341%
[...]
Trace Dist: 0.2984 State: 198.4319%
Trace Dist: 0.2866 State: 102.0065%
```

This concludes the section on complex quantum algorithms. For a deeper mathematical treatment of these algorithms and their derivatives, see the Bibliography and relevant publications. For further reading on known algorithms, Mosca (2008) provides a detailed taxonomy and categorization of algorithms. The Quantum Algorithm Zoo lists another large number of algorithms alongside an excellent bibliography (Jordan, 2021). Abhijith et al. (2020) offers high-level descriptions of about 50 algorithm implementations in Qiskit.

7 Quantum Error Correction

In this section, we discuss techniques for quantum error correction, which is an absolute necessity for the success of quantum computing, given the high likelihood of noise, errors, and decoherence in larger circuits. We have ignored this topic so far and assumed an ideal, error-free execution environment. For real machines, this assumption will not hold. Quantum error correction is a fascinating and wide-ranging topic. This section is mostly an introduction, with focus on just a few core principles.

7.1 Quantum Noise

Building a real, physical quantum computer big enough to perform useful computation presents an enormous challenge. On one hand, the quantum system must be isolated from the environment as much as possible to avoid entanglement with the environment and other perturbations, which may introduce errors. For example, molecules may bump into qubits and change their relative phase, even at temperatures of close to absolute zero. On the other hand, the quantum system cannot be entirely isolated because we want to program the machine, perhaps dynamically, and make measurements.

Here is a summary of available technologies, as presented in Nielsen and Chuang (2011). Table 7.1 shows the underlying technology, the time τ_Q the system may stay coherent before it starts entangling with the environment, the time τ_{op} it takes to apply a typical unitary gate, and the number n_{op} of operations that can be executed while still in a coherent state.

For several technologies, the number of coherently executable instructions is rather small and won't suffice to execute very large algorithms with potentially billions of gates.

Errors are inevitable, given the quantum scale and very high likelihood of the environment perturbing the system. To compare the expected quantum and classical error rates – for a modern CPU, a typical error rate is about one per year, or one error for every 10^{17} operations. The actual error rate might be higher, but mitigation strategies are in place. In contrast, data from 2020 from IBM shows an average single-qubit gate error rate of about one per 10^{-3} seconds, and one per 10^{-2} seconds for two-qubit gates. Based on frequency, this could reach up to one error for every 200 operations. This is a difference of almost 10 orders of magnitude!

Table 7.1 Estimates for decoherence times (secs), gate application latency (secs), and number of gates that can be applied while coherent. Data from Nielsen and Chuang (2011).

System	τ_Q	τ_{op}	n_{op}
Nuclear spin	$10^{-2} - 10^{-8}$	$10^{-3} - 10^{-6}$	$10^5 - 10^{14}$
Electron spin	10^{-3}	10^{-7}	10^4
Ion trap	10^{-1}	10^{-14}	10^{13}
Electron - Au	10^{-8}	10^{-14}	10^6
Electron - GaAs	10^{-10}	10^{-13}	10^3
Quantum dot	10^{-6}	10^{-9}	10^3
Optical cavity	10^{-5}	10^{-14}	10^9
Microwave cavity	10^0	10^{-4}	10^4

What are possible error conditions, and how do we model the likelihood of their occurrence?

Bit-Flip Error

The *bit-flip error* causes the probability amplitudes of a qubit to flip, similar to the effect of an X-gate:

$$\alpha|0\rangle + \beta|1\rangle \rightarrow \beta|0\rangle + \alpha|1\rangle.$$

This is also called a *dissipation-induced* bit-flip error. Dissipation is the process of losing energy to the environment. If we think of a qubit in state $|1\rangle$ as an electron's excited state, as it loses energy, it may fall to the lower energy $|0\rangle$ state and emit a photon. Correspondingly, it may jump from $|0\rangle$ to $|1\rangle$ by absorbing a photon (in which case it should probably be called an *excitation-induced* error).

Phase-Flip Error

The *phase-flip error* causes the relative phase to flip from $+1$ to -1, similar to the effect of a Z-gate:

$$\alpha|0\rangle + \beta|1\rangle \rightarrow \alpha|0\rangle - \beta|1\rangle.$$

This is also called a *decoherence-induced* phase shift error. In the example, we shifted the phase by π, but for decoherence we should also consider much smaller phase changes and their insidious tendency to compound over time.

Combined Phase/Bit-Flip Error

This is the combination of the two error conditions above:

$$\alpha|0\rangle + \beta|1\rangle \rightarrow \beta|0\rangle - \alpha|1\rangle.$$

This is equivalent to applying the Y-gate, as we've seen before, ignoring the global phase:

$$Y(\alpha|0\rangle + \beta|1\rangle) = \begin{bmatrix} 0 & -i \\ i & 0 \end{bmatrix} \begin{bmatrix} \alpha \\ \beta \end{bmatrix} = -i\beta|0\rangle + i\alpha|1\rangle = -i(\beta|0\rangle - \alpha|1\rangle).$$

No Error

We should mention this one for completeness; it's the equivalent effect of applying an identity gate to a qubit, or, equally, doing nothing.

These errors will occur with a certain probability. To model this properly, we will introduce the concept of quantum operations next, which allow the formalizing of the statistical distribution of error conditions in an elegant way.

7.1.1   Quantum Operations

So far we have mostly focused on describing quantum states as vectors of probability amplitudes. We indicated that states can also be described with density operators, which allow describing mixtures of states. In the following, we adopt the formalism proposed in Nielsen and Chuang (2011).

Similar to how a state evolves with $|\psi'\rangle = U|\psi\rangle$, a state's density operator $\rho = |\psi\rangle\langle\psi|$ evolves as:

$$\rho' = \mathcal{E}(\rho).$$

Where the $\mathcal{E}$ is called a *quantum operation*. The two types of operations discussed in this book are unitary transformations and measurements (note the matrix multiplication from both sides):

$$\mathcal{E}(\rho) = U\rho U^\dagger \quad \text{and} \quad \mathcal{E}_M(\rho) = M\rho M^\dagger. \tag{7.1}$$

In a *closed* quantum system, which has no interaction with the environment, the system evolves as:

$$\rho \quad\rule{2em}{0.4pt}\boxed{U}\rule{2em}{0.4pt}\quad U\rho U^\dagger$$

In an *open* system, we model the system as the tensor product of state and environment as $\rho \otimes \rho_{env}$. The system evolves as described in Equation (7.1) as:

$$U(\rho \otimes \rho_{env})\, U^\dagger.$$

We can visualize this with this conceptual circuit:

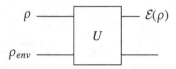

To describe the system without the environment, we trace out the environment using the methodology from Section 2.14:

$$\mathcal{E}(\rho) = \text{tr}_{env}\left[U(\rho \otimes \rho_{env})U^{\dagger}\right]. \tag{7.2}$$

Now, quantum operators can be expressed in the *operator-sum representation*, which describes the behavior of the principle system only, based on Equation (7.2). Let $|e_k\rangle$ be the orthonormal basis of the environment and $e_{env} = |e_0\rangle\langle e_0|$ the environment's initial state. It can be shown (see Nielsen and Chuang, 2011, section 8.2.3) that:

$$\mathcal{E}(\rho) = \sum_k E_k \rho E_k^{\dagger},$$

where $E_k = \langle e_k|U|e_0\rangle$. The E_k are the *operation elements* for the quantum operation $\mathcal{E}$. They are also called *Krauss operators*[1] and operate on the principal system only. Now let's see how we can use this formalism to describe the various error modes.

7.1.2   Bit Flip and Phase Flip Channels

The term *channel* is an abstraction in information theory to model noise and errors. It assumes that information must be conveyed from a source to a destination *somehow*. That "somehow" is commonly described as a channel. We can use this to describe the above error modes in the following way.

The *bit-flip channel* flips the states from $|0\rangle$ to $|1\rangle$ and vice versa with probability $1 - p$. It has the operation elements:

$$E_0 = \sqrt{p}\,I = \sqrt{p}\begin{bmatrix} 1 & 0 \\ 0 & 1 \end{bmatrix} \quad \text{and} \quad E_1 = \sqrt{1-p}\,X = \sqrt{1-p}\begin{bmatrix} 0 & 1 \\ 1 & 0 \end{bmatrix}.$$

The *phase-flip channel* flips the phase as described above with probability $1 - p$. It has the operation elements:

$$E_0 = \sqrt{p}\,I = \sqrt{p}\begin{bmatrix} 1 & 0 \\ 0 & 1 \end{bmatrix} \quad \text{and} \quad E_1 = \sqrt{1-p}\,Z = \sqrt{1-p}\begin{bmatrix} 1 & 0 \\ 0 & -1 \end{bmatrix}.$$

Finally, the *bit-flip phase-flip channel* has these operation elements:

$$E_0 = \sqrt{p}\,I = \sqrt{p}\begin{bmatrix} 1 & 0 \\ 0 & 1 \end{bmatrix} \quad \text{and} \quad E_1 = \sqrt{1-p}\,Y = \sqrt{1-p}\begin{bmatrix} 0 & -i \\ i & 0 \end{bmatrix}.$$

---

[1] This notation is sloppy, as U applies to both environment and state. Because this detail is not essential in our context, we tolerate it.

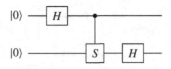

Figure 7.1 Circuit before noise injection.

7.1.3   Depolarization Channel

The *depolarization channel* is another standard way to describe quantum noise. Depolarization means that an original state is transformed into a completely mixed state $I/2$. We only briefly talked about pure and mixed states in Section 2.14, but in short, a maximally mixed state of $I/2$ means that the state is maximally entangled with something else, for example, the environment.

Quantum noise means that a state remains unmodified with probability $1 - p$. The state, expressed as its density matrix ρ, becomes the following in the presence of noise:

$$\rho' = p\frac{I}{2} + (1 - p)\rho.$$

For an arbitrary ρ, it can be shown that the following holds in operator-sum notation (see also the test `test_rho` in file `lib/ops_test.py`). This equation is related to Equation (2.5).

$$\frac{I}{2} = \frac{\rho + X\rho X + Y\rho Y + Z\rho Z}{4}$$

Suppose we assign a probability of $(1 - p)$ for a state to remain unmodified by noise, and we assign a probability of $1/3$ for each of the operators X, Y, and Z to introduce noise (other probability distributions are possible). In that case, the operator sum expression above can be transformed into:

$$\mathcal{E}(\rho) = (1 - p)\rho + \frac{p}{3}(X\rho X + Y\rho Y + Z\rho Z).$$

This is the result we were looking for. It allows us to model quantum noise by simply injecting Pauli gates with a given probability. Assume a gate E, which may be either of the Pauli matrices with probability as follows:

$$E = \begin{cases} X & \text{with } p_x, \\ Y & \text{with } p_y, \\ Z & \text{with } p_z, \\ I & \text{with } 1 - (p_x + p_y + p_z). \end{cases}$$

To model noise, we introduce error gates E with a given probability, injecting bit-flip and phase-flip errors. An example circuit before and after error injection is shown in Figures 7.1 and 7.2, respectively. It is very educational to inject these error gates and evaluate their impact on various algorithms. We will do just that in Section 7.2.

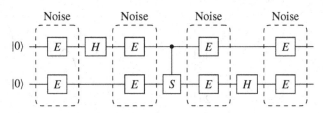

Figure 7.2 Circuit after noise injection.

7.1.4   Amplitude and Phase Damping

We mention amplitude damping and phase damping for completeness, but we will not elaborate further.

Amplitude damping seeks to model *energy dissipation*, the energy loss in a quantum system. It is described with these two operator elements, with γ (gamma) being the likelihood of energy loss, such as the emission of a photon in a physical system:

$$E_0 = \begin{bmatrix} 1 & 0 \\ 0 & \sqrt{1-\gamma} \end{bmatrix} \quad \text{and} \quad E_1 = \begin{bmatrix} 0 & \sqrt{\gamma} \\ 0 & 0 \end{bmatrix}.$$

Phase damping describes the process of a system losing relative phase between qubits, thus introducing errors in algorithms that rely on successful quantum interference. The operator elements are:

$$E_0 = \begin{bmatrix} 1 & 0 \\ 0 & \sqrt{1-\gamma} \end{bmatrix} \quad \text{and} \quad E_1 = \begin{bmatrix} 0 & 0 \\ 0 & \sqrt{\gamma} \end{bmatrix}.$$

Note that the factor γ might be expressed as an exponential function in more realistic modeling environments.

7.1.5   Imprecise Gates

Gates themselves may not be perfect. There could be issues with manufacturing, external influences, temperature, and other conditions, all influencing gate accuracy. Additionally, it is unlikely that all software gates we use in this text will be available on physical machines. Software gates will have to be decomposed into hardware gates or be approximated. Approximations have residual errors, as we detailed in Section 6.15 on the Solovay–Kitaev algorithm.

The impact of gate imprecision varies by algorithm. Since we wrote the algorithms in source, we can run experiments and inject various error distributions. In the following brief example, we modify the final inverse QFT in the phase estimation circuit by introducing errors in the R_k phase gates. To achieve this, we compute a random number in the range from 0.0 to 1.0 and scale a noise factor n_f with it. As an example, a factor of $n_f = 0.1$ means a *maximum* error of 10% can be introduced. The actual values will range randomly from 0% to the limit of 10%. This is a very simple model, but you can experiment with other error distributions.

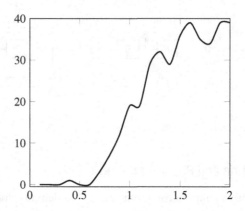

Figure 7.3 Phase estimation errors exceeding a threshold of 2% from increasing levels of noise, for N = 50 experiments per setting. The x-axis represents noise ranging from 0% to 200%, the y-axis represents the number of experiments exceeding the threshold.

```
def Rk(k):
  return Operator(np.array([[(1.0, 0.0),
              (0.0, cmath.exp((1 + (random.random() * flags.FLAGS.noise)) *
              (2.0 * cmath.pi * 1j / 2**k)))]]))
```

Then, for values of n_f ranging from 0.0 to 2.0, we run 50 experiments and count the number of experiments that result in a phase estimation error larger than 2%. Hence, we test the robustness of phase estimation against small to large errors in the inverse QFT rotation gates. Figure 7.3 shows the distribution.

We see that the inverse QFT is surprisingly robust against sizeable maximum errors in the rotation gates, but this is just an anecdote. The exact outcome would depend on the statistical distribution of the actual errors. We should also expect that each algorithm has different tolerances and sensitivities. For comparison, introducing depolarization with just 0.1% probability leads to significantly different outcomes in the order finding algorithm, which is very sensitive to this particular type of error.

7.2   Quantum Error Correction

We will need some form of error correction techniques to control the impact of noise. In classical computing, a large body of known error correction techniques exists. Error correction code memory, or ECC (Wikipedia, 2021b), may be one of the best known ones. There are many more techniques that prevent invalid data, missing data, or spurious data. NASA, in particular, has developed impressive techniques to communicate with their ever-more-distant exploratory vehicles.

A simple classical error correction technique is based on repetition codes and majority voting. For example, we could triple each binary digit:

Table 7.2 Majority voting for a simple repetition code.

Measured	Voted	Measured	Voted
000	0	111	1
001	0	110	1
010	0	101	1
100	0	011	1

$$0 \rightarrow 000$$
$$1 \rightarrow 111$$

As we receive data over a noisy channel, we measure it and perform majority voting with the scheme shown in Table 7.2. This simple scheme does not account for missing or erroneous bits, but it is good enough to explain the basic principles.

In quantum computing, the situation is generally more difficult:

- Physical quantum computers operate at the quantum level of atomic spins, photons, and electrons. There is a very high probability of encountering errors or decoherence, especially for longer-running computations.
- Errors can be more subtle than simple bit flips. There are multiple error modes.
- Errors, such as relative phase errors, compound during execution.
- Simple repetition codes will not work because of the no-cloning theorem.
- Most problematically, you cannot observe errors, as that would constitute a measurement that destroys the superposition and entanglement that algorithms rely upon.

Because of these difficulties, especially because of the inability to read a corrupted state, early speculation was that error correction code could not exist. Hence, it would be nearly impossible ever to produce a viable quantum computer (Haroche and Raimond, 1996; Rolf, 1995). This, fortunately, changed when Shor presented a viable nine-qubit error correction code (Shor, 1995). The principles of this approach underlie many quantum error correction techniques today.

7.2.1   Quantum Repetition Code

This circuit can be used to produce the quantum repetition code. Note its similarity to the GHZ circuit from Section 2.11.4:

$$|\psi\rangle = \alpha|0\rangle + \beta|1\rangle = \quad \alpha|000\rangle + \beta|111\rangle$$

In code, using a random qubit for demonstration:

```
    qbit = state.qubit(random.random())
    psi = qbit * state.zeros(2)
    psi = ops.Cnot(0, 2)(psi)
    psi = ops.Cnot(0, 1)(psi)
    psi.dump()
>>
|000> (|0>):  ampl: +0.78+0.00j prob: 0.61 Phase:     0.0
|111> (|7>):  ampl: +0.62+0.00j prob: 0.39 Phase:     0.0
```

Note again that these states do not violate the no-cloning theorem as we are not constructing $(\alpha|0\rangle + \beta|1\rangle)^{\otimes 3}$.

7.2.2   Correct Bit-Flip errors

Here is the main *trick* to error correction. It is related to quantum teleportation. First we introduce redundancy and triple each qubit into a GHZ state. We entangle this three-qubit state with two ancillae and measure *only* the ancillae, leaving the original state intact. Based on the measurement outcome, we apply gates to the original three-qubit state to correct it.

Figure 7.4 shows this procedure in circuit notation, assuming a single qubit-flip error in qubit 0, which we indicate on the left side of the circuit. The state $|\psi_1\rangle$ right before a measurement is this, where the bottom two qubits have been flipped to $|10\rangle$:

$$|\psi_1\rangle = \alpha|10010\rangle + \beta|01110\rangle,$$

which, right after measurement, turns into:

$$|\psi_2\rangle = (\alpha|100\rangle + \beta|011\rangle) \otimes |10\rangle.$$

The measurement outcome is called the *error syndrome*. Based on the syndrome, we know what to do next and which qubit to flip back with another X-gate.

- For a measurement result of $|00\rangle$, do nothing.
- For a measurement result of $|01\rangle$, apply X-gate to qubit 2.
- For a measurement result of $|10\rangle$, apply X-gate to qubit 0.
- For a measurement result of $|11\rangle$, apply X-gate to qubit 1.

The way Figure 7.4 is drawn is a bit sloppy because the function of gate R is different for each measurement outcome. Making physical measurements and reacting to the outcome is not a realistic scenario; it would be hard to achieve in practice, and even if it did, it would likely destroy a quantum computer's performance advantage because of Amdahl's law.[2] In larger circuits, we should also make sure to disentangle the ancillae.

---

[2] https://en.wikipedia.org/wiki/Amdahl%27s_law.

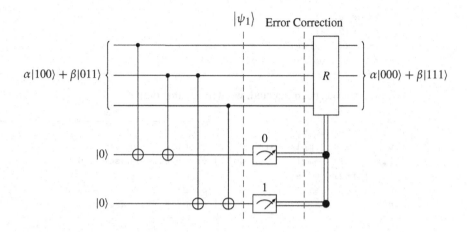

Figure 7.4 Bit-flip error correcting circuit.

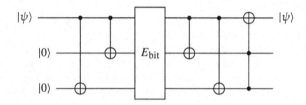

Figure 7.5 Error correction for bit-flip error.

A common construction to correct bit-flip errors can be found in the circuit in Figure 7.5. The noisy channel E, introduces errors according to Equation (7.3), the bit-flip error:

$$\varepsilon(\rho) = (1 - p)\rho + p(X\rho X). \tag{7.3}$$

In code, we can inject an error by introducing an X-gate, as in the following snippet:

```python
def test_x_error(self):
    qc = circuit.qc('x-flip / correction')
    qc.qubit(0.6)

    # Replication code setup.
    qc.reg(2, 0)
    qc.cx(0, 2)
    qc.cx(0, 1)
    qc.psi.dump('after setup')

    # Error insertion.
    qc.x(0)

    # Fix.
```

```
qc.cx(0, 1)
qc.cx(0, 2)
qc.ccx(1, 2, 0)
qc.psi.dump('after correction')
```

If no error has been injected, we will see this output:

```
|210> 'after setup'
|000> (|0>):  ampl: +0.60+0.00j prob: 0.36 Phase:    0.0
|111> (|7>):  ampl: +0.80+0.00j prob: 0.64 Phase:    0.0
|210> 'after correction'
|000> (|0>):  ampl: +0.60+0.00j prob: 0.36 Phase:    0.0
|100> (|4>):  ampl: +0.80+0.00j prob: 0.64 Phase:    0.0
```

If an error has indeed been injected, the state becomes:

```
|210> 'after setup'
|000> (|0>):  ampl: +0.60+0.00j prob: 0.36 Phase:    0.0
|111> (|7>):  ampl: +0.80+0.00j prob: 0.64 Phase:    0.0
|210> 'after correction'
|011> (|3>):  ampl: +0.60+0.00j prob: 0.36 Phase:    0.0
|111> (|7>):  ampl: +0.80+0.00j prob: 0.64 Phase:    0.0
```

Note the small difference in the final states with nonzero probabilities. In the case without an injected error, the state resumes to $|000\rangle$ and $|100\rangle$, the original input state. In the case with an injected error, the ancilla qubits are $|11\rangle$ for both resulting states.

7.2.3   Correct Phase-Flip Errors

We can use the same idea to correct phase-flip errors. Remember that applying uniform Hadamard gates puts a state in the Hadamard basis. A phase-flip error in the computational basis is the same as a bit-flip error in the Hadamard basis.

Correspondingly, we can use the circuit in Figure 7.6 to create a quantum repetition and error correction circuit, similar to Figure 7.5, but with surrounding Hadamard gates.

We use a similar code sequence for this as above, but we change it to the following for error injection:

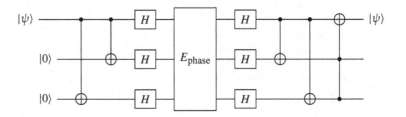

Figure 7.6 Error correction for phase-flip error.

```
[...]
qc.h(0)
qc.h(1)
qc.h(2)


qc.z(0)


qc.h(0)
qc.h(1)
qc.h(2)
[...]
```

The probability distribution of the resulting nonzero probability states is the same, but we get a few states with phases. For example, without error injection:

```
|210> 'after setup'
|000> (|0>):  ampl: +0.60+0.00j prob: 0.36 Phase:   0.0
|111> (|7>):  ampl: +0.80+0.00j prob: 0.64 Phase:   0.0
|210> 'after correction'
|000> (|0>):  ampl: +0.60+0.00j prob: 0.36 Phase:   0.0
|001> (|1>):  ampl: +0.00+0.00j prob: 0.00 Phase:   0.0
|010> (|2>):  ampl: -0.00+0.00j prob: 0.00 Phase: 180.0
|011> (|3>):  ampl: -0.00+0.00j prob: 0.00 Phase: 180.0
|100> (|4>):  ampl: +0.80+0.00j prob: 0.64 Phase:   0.0
|101> (|5>):  ampl: +0.00+0.00j prob: 0.00 Phase:   0.0
|110> (|6>):  ampl: +0.00+0.00j prob: 0.00 Phase:   0.0
```

7.3 Nine-Qubit Shor Code

All of this leads up to the final nine-qubit Shor code (Shor, 1995), which is a combination of the above. It combines the circuits to find bit-flip, phase-flip, and combined errors into one large circuit, as shown in Figure 7.7.

The Shor nine-qubit circuit is able to identify and correct one bit-flip error, one phase-flip error, or one of each on any of the nine qubits! Let's verify this in code and apply all Pauli gates to each of the qubits of this circuit. For this experiment, we construct a qubit with $\alpha = 0.60$ (the code can be found in file `lib/circuit_test.py`):

```
def test_shor_9_qubit_correction(self):
  for i in range(9):
    qc = circuit.qc('shor-9')
    print(f'Init qubit as 0.6|0> + 0.8|1>, error on qubit {i}')
    qc.qubit(0.6)
    qc.reg(8, 0)

    # Left Side.
    qc.cx(0, 3)
```

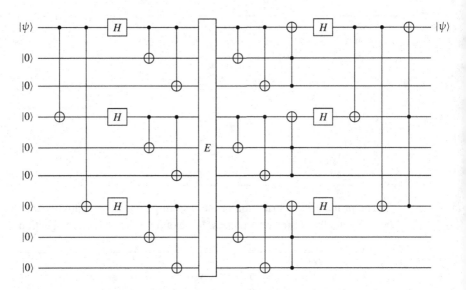

Figure 7.7 Shor's nine-qubit error correction circuit.

```
qc.cx(0, 6)
qc.h(0); qc.h(3); qc.h(6);
qc.cx(0, 1); qc.cx(0, 2)
qc.cx(3, 4); qc.cx(3, 5)
qc.cx(6, 7); qc.cx(6, 8)

# Error insertion, use x(i), y(i), or z(i)
qc.x(i)

# Fix.
qc.cx(0, 1); qc.cx(0, 2); qc.ccx(1, 2, 0)
qc.h(0)
qc.cx(3, 4); qc.cx(3, 5); qc.ccx(4, 5, 3)
qc.h(3)
qc.cx(6, 7); qc.cx(6, 8); qc.ccx(7, 8, 6)
qc.h(6)

qc.cx(0, 3); qc.cx(0, 6)
qc.ccx(6, 3, 0)

prob0, s = qc.measure_bit(0, 0)
prob1, s = qc.measure_bit(0, 1)
print('          Measured: {:.2f}|0> + {:.2f}|1>'.format(
    math.sqrt(prob0), math.sqrt(prob1)))
```

Indeed, we get the desired result:

```
Initialize qubit as 0.60|0> + 0.80|1>, error on qubit 0
        Measured: 0.60|0> + 0.80|1>
[...]
Initialize qubit as 0.60|0> + 0.80|1>, error on qubit 8
        Measured: 0.60|0> + 0.80|1>
```

There are several other techniques and formalisms for quantum information and quantum error correction. We only want to mention a small number of influential works. A good introduction and overview can be found in Devitt et al. (2013). Andrew Steane published the seven-qubit Steane code in Steane (1996). A five-qubit error correction code was discussed by Cory et al. (1998).

8 Quantum Languages, Compilers, and Tools

At this point, we understand the principles of quantum computing, the important foundational algorithms, and the basics of quantum error correction. We have developed a compact and reasonably fast infrastructure for exploration and experimentation with the presented material.

The infrastructure is working but still far away from enabling high programmer productivity. Composing algorithms is labor-intensive and error prone. Circuits with maybe 10^6 gates are supported, but some algorithms may require trillions of gates with orders of magnitude more qubits.

In classical computing, programs are being constructed at much higher levels of abstraction, which allows the targeting of several general-purpose architectures in a portable way. On a high-performance CPU, programs execute billions of instructions per second on a single core. Building quantum programs at that scale with a flat programming model like QASM stitching together individual gates does not scale. It is the equivalent of programming today's machines in assembly language, without looping constructs.

There are parallels to the 1950s, where assembly language was the trade of the day to program early computers. Just as FORTRAN emerged as one of the first compiled programming language and enabled major productivity gains, there are similar attempts today, trying to raise the abstraction level in the area of quantum computing.

In this chapter we discuss a representative cross-section of quantum programming languages, and briefly touch on tooling, such as simulators or entanglement analysis. There is also a discussion on quantum compiler optimizations, a fascinating topic with unique challenges. We write this chapter with the understanding that comparisons between toolchains are necessarily incomplete but nonetheless educational.

Section 8.5 on transpilation finishes the chapter; this is a powerful technique with many uses. It allows seamless porting of our circuits to other frameworks. This enables direct comparisons and the use of specific features of these platforms, such as advanced error models or distributed simulation. Transpilation can be used to produce circuit diagrams or LaTeX source code. The underlying compiler technology further enables implementation of several of the features found in various programming languages, such as uncomputation, entanglement analysis, and conditional blocks.

8.1 Challenges for Quantum Compilation

Quantum computing poses unique challenges for compiler design. In this section, we provide a brief overview of some of the main challenges. The next sections discuss additional details and proposed solutions.

Quantum computing needs a programming model – what will run, how, when, and where? Unlike classical coprocessors, such as graphics processing units (GPUs), quantum computers will not offer general-purpose functionality similar to a CPU. Instead, a classical machine will entirely control the quantum computer. A model called *QRAM* was proposed for this early in the history of quantum computing. We will discuss this model in Section 8.2.

A key question is how realistic this idealized model is, or can be. Quantum circuits operate at micro-Kelvin temperatures. It will be a challenge for standard CPU manufacturing processes to operate at this temperature, even though progress has been made (Patra et al., 2020). The CPU could alternatively operate away from the quantum circuit, but the bandwidth between classical and quantum circuits may be severely limited. Current work is presented in Xue et al. (2021).

Constructing quantum circuits gate by gate is tedious and prone to error. There are additional challenges, such as the no-cloning theorem and the need for automatic error correction. Programming languages offer a higher level of abstraction and will be essential for programmer productivity. But what is the *right* level of abstraction? We sample several existing approaches to quantum programming languages in Section 8.3. Compiler construction and intermediate representation (IR) design are challenges by themselves; it is apparent that a flat, QASM-like, linked-list IR will not scale to programs with trillions of gates.

The required precision of gates is an important design parameter. We will have to approximate certain unitaries by sequences of existing, physical gates, but this introduces inaccuracies and noise. Some algorithms are robust against noise, others not at all. The toolchain plays an essential role in this area as well.

Aspects of dynamic code generation may become necessary, for example, to approximate specific rotations dynamically or to reduce noise (Wilson et al., 2020). There are challenges in fast gate approximation, compile time, accuracy, and optimality of the approximating gate sequences. To give a taste of these problems, we already detailed the Solovay–Kitaev algorithm in Section 6.15.

Compiler optimization has a novel set of transformations to consider in an exponentially growing search space. We are currently in the era of physical machines with 50–100 physical qubits, the *Noisy Intermediate-Scale Quantum Computers* (Preskill, 2018). Future systems will have more qubits and qubits with likely different characteristics than today's qubits. Compiler optimizations and code generation techniques will have to evolve accordingly as well. We discuss several optimization techniques in Section 8.4.

8.2   Quantum Programming Model

As our standard model of computation, we assume the quantum random access model (QRAM) as proposed by Knill (1996). The model proposes connecting a general-purpose machine with a quantum computer in order to use it as an accelerator. Registers are explicitly quantum or classical. There are functions to initialize quantum registers, to program gate sequences into the quantum device, and to get results back via measurements.

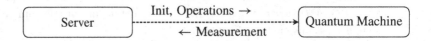

On the surface, this model is not much different from today's programming models for PCIe connected accelerators,[1] such as GPUs or storage devices, which are ubiquitous today. The elegant CUDA programming model for GPUs provides clear abstractions for code that is supposed to run on either device or server (Buck et al., 2004; Nickolls et al., 2008). Source code for the accelerator and host can be mixed in the same source file to enhance programmer productivity.

QRAM is an idealization. Communication between the classical and quantum parts of a program may be severely limited. There may either be a significant lack of compute power close to the quantum circuit, which operates at micro-Kelvin temperature, or bandwidth-limited communication to a CPU further away.

It is important to keep the separation between classical and quantum in mind. In QRAM, as in our simulation infrastructure, the separation of classical and quantum is muddled, running classical loops over applications of quantum gates interspersed with print statements. This might be a good approach for learning, but it is not realistic for a real machine. To a degree, the approach is more akin to an infrastructure such as the machine learning platform Tensorflow. It first builds up computation in the form of a graph before executing the graph in a distributed fashion on CPU, GPU, or TPU.

Another aspect of the QRAM model is the expectation of available *universal* gates on the target quantum machine. Several universal sets of gates have been described in the literature (see Nielsen and Chuang, 2011, section 4.5.3). We showed how any unitary gate can be approximated by universal gates in Section 6.15. With this, we assume that any gate may be used freely in our idealized infrastructure. On real machines, however, the number of gates is limited, and there are accuracy and noise concerns.

8.3   Quantum Programming Languages

In this section, we discuss a representative cross-section of quantum programming languages with corresponding compilers and tooling. The descriptions are brief and

---

[1] https://en.wikipedia.org/wiki/PCI_Express

necessarily incomplete. Most importantly, the selection does not judge the quality of the nonselected languages. Each attempt makes novel contributions over prior art, variations of which can be found in other related works.

In a hierarchy of abstractions, this is how to place quantum programming languages:

- The high abstraction level of programming languages. This level may provide automatic ancilla management, support correct program construction with advanced typing rules, offer libraries for standard operations (such as QFT), and perhaps offer meta-programming techniques.
- Programming at the level of gates. This is the level of this text. It is the construction and manipulation of individual qubits and gates.
- Direct machine control with pulses and wave forms to operate a physical device. We will not discuss related infrastructure, such as OpenPulse (Gokhale et al., 2020).

For each of the platforms, there is lots of material available online to experiment with. This section is meant to be educational – it should also inspire. For example, we could easily add several of the proposed features to our infrastructure. Also, despite all progress, the development of quantum programming languages and their compilers appears to still be in its infancy.

8.3.1 QASM

The quantum assembly language (QASM) was an early attempt to textually specify quantum circuits (Svore et al., 2006). We've already seen QASM code in Section 6.3 on quantum arithmetic, and we will see more of it in Section 8.5 on transpilation.

The structure of a QASM program is very simple. Qubits and registers are declared, and gate applications follow one by one. There are no looping constructs, function calls, or other constructs that would help to structure and densify the code. For example, a simple entangler circuit would read like this:

```
qubit x,y;
gate h;
gate cx;
h x;
cx x,y;
```

More capable variants emerged to augment QASM in a variety of ways. Open-QASM adds the ability to define new gates, control-flow constructs, and barriers (Cross et al., 2017). It also offers looping constructs. cQASM is one attempt to unify QASM dialects into a single form[2] (Khammassi et al., 2018). It offers additional language features, such as explicit parallelization, register mapping/renaming, and a

---

[2] See also xkcd cartoon #927.

variety of measurement types. An example implementation of a three-qubit Grover algorithm takes about 50 lines of code.

8.3.2   QCL

The *quantum computing language* (QCL) was an early attempt to use classical programming constructs to express quantum computation (Ömer, 2000, 2005; QCL Online). Algorithms are run on a classical machine controlling a quantum computer and might have to run multiple times until a solution is found. Quantum and classical code are intermixed. Qubits are defined as registers of a given length, and gates are applied directly to registers:

```
qureg q[1];
qureg f[1];
H(q);
Not(f);
const n=#q;    // length of q register
for i =1 to n {  // classical loop
   Phase(pi/2^(i));
}
```

QCL defines several quantum register types. There is the unrestricted `qureg`, `quconst` defines an invariant qubit, and `quvoid` specifies a register to be *empty*. It is guaranteed to be in state $|0\rangle$. The register type `quscratch` denotes ancillae.

Code is organized into *quantum functions*. Functions and operators are reversible. Prefixing a function with an exclamation point produces the inverse, as in this example from the Grover algorithm:[3]

```
operator diffuse(qureg q) {
  H(q);                  // Hadamard transform
  Not(q);                // Invert q
  CPhase(pi,q);          // Rotate if q=1111...
  !Not(q);               // Undo inversion
  !H(q);                 // Undo Hadamard transform
}
```

QCL defines several types of functions, such as the nonreversible `procedure`, which may contain classical code and allows side effects. Functions marked as `operator` and `qufunct` are side-effect free and reversible.

---

[3] Note that both the Hadamard and the NOT gates are their own inverses. This might not be the most convincing example.

To facilitate uncomputation, QCL supports a `fanout` operation. It restores scratch registers and auxiliary registers, while preserving the results, as outlined in Section 2.13 on uncomputation:

$$|x,0,0,0\rangle \rightarrow |x,0,f(x),g(x)\rangle$$
$$\rightarrow |x,g(x),f(x),g(x)\rangle$$
$$\rightarrow |x,g(x),0,0\rangle$$

The implementation of `fanout` is quite elegant: Assume a function $F(x,y,s)$ with x being the input, y being the output, and s being junk qubits. Allocate the ancilla t and transform F into the following, adding t to its signature:

$$F(x,y,s,t) = F^{\dagger}(x,t,s) \text{ fanout}(t,y) \ F(x,t,s).$$

What makes this elegant is the fact that `fanout` is written in QCL itself:

```
cond qufunct Fanout (quconst ancilla, quvoid b) {
    int i;
    for i=0 to #ancilla-1 {
        CNot (b[i], ancilla[i]);
    }
}
```

QCL supports conditionals in interesting ways. Standard controlled gates are supported as described in Section 2.7. If a function signature is marked with the keyword cond and has as parameter a `quconst` condition qubit, QCL automatically transforms the operators in the functions to controlled operators:

```
cond qufunct cinc (qureg x, quconst e) { . . . }
```

Additionally, QCL supports an `if` statement, where `if e { inc(x); }` is equivalent to a new function `cinc(x, e)` as shown above, with the if-then-else statement translating into:

```
    if e {
        inc (x);
    } else {
        !inc (x);
    }
=>
    cinc (x, e);
    Not (e);
    !cinc (x, e);
    Not (e)
```

As an example, here is the implementation of QFT in QCL, as found in the thesis (Ömer, 2000):

```
cond qufunct flip(qureg q) {
  int i;                   // declare loop counter
  for i=0 to #q/2-1 {      // swap 2 symmetric bits
    Swap(q[i],q[#q-i-1]);
  }
}

operator qft(qureg q) { // main operator
  const n=#q;             // set n to length of input
  int i; int j;          // declare loop counters
  for i=1 to n {
    for j=1 to i-1 {      // apply conditional phase gates
      V(pi/2^(i-j),q[n-i] & q[n-j]);
    }
    H(q[n-i]);           // qubit rotation
  }
  flip(q);               // swap bit order of the output
}
```

8.3.3   Scaffold

Scaffold takes a different approach (Javadi-Abhari et al., 2014). It *extends* the open-source LLVM compiler and its Clang-based front end for C/C++. Scaffold introduces data types *qbit* and *cbit* to distinguish quantum from classical data. Quantum gates, such as the X-gate or the Hadamard gate, are implemented as *built-ins*; the compiler recognizes them as such and can reason about them in transformation passes.

Scaffold supports hierarchical code structure via *modules*, which are specially marked functions. Quantum circuits do not support calls and returns, so modules representing subcircuits need to be *instantiated*, similar to, say, how Verilog modules are instantiated in a hardware design. Modules must be reversible, either by design or via automatic compiler transformations, such as full unrolling of classical loops.

Scaffold offers convenient functionality to convert classical circuits to quantum gates, via the Classical-To-Quantum-Circuit (CTQC) tool. This tool is of great utility for quantum algorithms that perform classical computation in the quantum domain. CQTC emits QASM assembly. To enable whole program optimization, Scaffold has a QASM to LLVM IR transpiler, which can be used to import QASM modules, enabling further cross-module optimization.

Modules are parameterized. This means the compiler has to manage module instantiation, for example, with IR duplication. This can lead to sizeable code bloat and correspondingly long compile times. The example given is the following code snippet, where the module `Oracle` would have to be instantiated $N = 3000$ times. Clearly, a parameterized IR would alleviate this problem considerably.

```
#define N 3000 // iteration count
module Oracle (qbit a[1], qbit b[1], int j) {
  double theta = (-1)*pow(2.0, j)/100;
  X(a[0]);
  Rz(b[0], theta);
}

module main () {
  qbit a[1], b[1];
  int i, j;
  for (i=1; i<=N; i++) {
    for (j=0; j<=3; j++) {
      Oracle(a, b, j);
    }
  }
}
```

As a result, Javadi-Abhari et al. (2014) reports compile times ranging from 24 hours to several days for a larger triangle finding problem with size $n = 15$ (see also Magniez et al., 2005).

Hierarchical QASM

Scaffold intends to scale to very large circuits. The existing QASM model, as shown above, is *flat*, which is not suitable for large circuits. One of the main contributions of Scaffold is the introduction of *hierarchical* QASM. Additionally, the compiler employs heuristics for what code sequences to flatten or keep in a hierarchical structure. For example, the compiler distinguishes between *forall* loops to apply a gate to all qubits in a register and *repeat* loops, such as those required for the Grover iterations.

Entanglement Analysis

Scaffold includes tooling for entanglement analysis. In the development of Shor's algorithm, we observed a certain ancilla qubit that was still entangled after modular addition. How does one reason about this?

Scaffold tracks entanglement-generating gates, such as Controlled-Not gates, on a stack. As inverse gates are executed in reverse order, items are popped off the stack. If, for a given qubit, no more entangling gates are found on the stack, the qubit is marked as *unentangled*. As a result of the analysis, the generated output can be decorated to show the estimated entanglement:

```
module EQxMark_1_1 ( qbit* b , qbit* t ) {
...
Toffoli ( x[0] , b[1] , b[0] );
// x0, b1, b0
Toffoli ( x[1] , x[0] , b[2] );
```

```
// x1, x0, b2, b1, b0
...
}
// Final entanglements:
// (t0, b4, b3, b2, b1, b0);
```

8.3.4   Q language

We can contrast this work with a pure C++-embedded approach, as presented in Bettelli et al. (2003). This approach consists of a library of C++ classes modeling quantum registers, operators, operator application, and other functions, such as reordering of quantum registers. The class library builds up an internal data structure to represent the computation, similar in nature to the infrastructure we developed here. It is interesting to ponder the question of which approach makes more sense:

- Extension of the C/C++ compiler with specific quantum types and operators, as in Scaffold.
- A C++ class library as in the *Q language*.

Both approaches appear equally powerful in principle. The compiler-based approach has the advantage of benefitting from a large set of established compiler passes, such as inlining, loop transformations, redundancy elimination, and many other scalar, loop, and inter-procedural optimizations. The C++ class library has the advantage that the management of the IR, all optimizations, and final code generation schemes are being maintained *outside* of the compiler. Since compilers can prove impenetrable for noncompiler experts, this approach might have a maintenance advantage, but at the cost of potentially having to re-implement many optimization passes.

8.3.5   Quipper

Haskell is a popular choice for programming language theorists and enthusiasts because of its powerful type system. An example of a Haskell-embedded implementation of a quantum programming system can be found with the Quantum IO Monad (Altenkirch and Green, 2013). Another even more rigid example is van Tonder's proposal for a λ-calculus to express quantum computation (van Tonder, 2004).

What these approaches have in common is the attempt to guarantee correctness by construction with support of the type system. This is also one of Quipper's core design ideas (Green et al., 2013; Quipper Online, 2021). Quipper is an embedded DSL in Haskell. At the time of Quipper's publication, Haskell lacked linear types, which could have guaranteed that objects were only referenced once, as well as dependent types, which are types combined with a value. Dependent types, for example, allow you to distinguish a QFT operator over n qubits from one over m qubits.

Quipper is designed to scale and handle large programs with up to 10^{12} operators. Quipper has a notion of ancilla scope, with an ability to reason about ancilla live ranges. Allocating ancilla qubits turns into a register allocation problem. Ancilla live ranges have to be marked explicitly by the programmer.

At the language level, qubits are held in variables and gates are applied to these variables. For example, to generate a Bell state:

```
bell :: Qubit -> Qubit -> Circ (Qubit, Qubit)
bell a b = do
  a <- hadamard a
  (a, b) <- controlled_not a b
  return (a, b)
```

To control an entire block of gates, Quipper offers a `with_controls` construct, similar in nature to QCL's `if` blocks. Another block-level construct allows managing ancillae explicitly via `with_ancilla`. Circuits defined this way are reversed with a `reverse_simple` construct. Quipper's type system distinguishes different types of quantum data, such as simple qubits, or fixed point interpretations of multiple qubits.

Automatic Oracles

Quipper offers tooling for the automatic construction of oracles. Typically, oracles are constructed with the following four manual steps. There are open-source implementations available for these techniques (Soeken et al., 2019).

1. Build a classical oracle, for example, a permutation matrix.
2. Translate the classic oracle into classical circuits.
3. Compile classical circuits to quantum circuits, potentially using additional ancillae. We saw examples of this in Section 3.3.1.
4. Finally, make the oracle reversible, typically with an XOR construction to another ancilla.

Quipper utilizes Template Haskell to automate steps two and three. The approach has high utility and has been used to synthesize millions of gates in a set of benchmarks. In direct comparison to QCL on the Binary Welded Tree algorithm, it appears that QCL generates significantly more gates and qubits than Quipper. On the other hand, Quipper appears to generate more ancillae.

Despite the tooling, type checks, automation of oracles, and utilization of the Haskell environment, it still took 55 man months to implement the 11 algorithms in a given benchmark set (IARPA, 2010). This is certainly a productivity improvement over manually constructing all the benchmarks at the gate level, but it still compares unfavorably against programmer productivity on classical infrastructure.

Quipper led to interesting follow-up work, such a Proto-Quipper-M (Rios and Selinger, 2018), Proto-Quipper-S (Ross, 2017), up to Proto-Quipper-D (Fu et al., 2020). These attempts are steeped in type theory and improve on program correctness by a variety of techniques, for example, using linear types to enforce the no-cloning theorem and linear *dependent* types to support the construction of type-safe families of circuits.

8.3.6   Silq

Based on a fork from the PSI probabilistic programming language (PSI Online, 2021), *Silq* is another step in the evolution of quantum programming languages, supporting safe and *automatic* uncomputation (Bichsel et al., 2020).

It explicitly distinguishes between the classical and quantum domains with syntactical constructs. Giving the responsibility for safe uncomputation to the compiler leads to two major benefits. First, the code becomes more compact. Direct comparisons against Quipper and Q# appear to show significant code size savings for Silq in the range of 30% to over 40%. Second, the compiler may choose an optimal strategy for uncomputation, minimizing the required number of ancillae. As an added benefit, the compiler may choose to skip uncomputation for simulation altogether and just renormalize states and unentangle ancillae.

Many of the Haskell embedded DSLs bemoan either the absence of linear types or difficulties handling constants. Silq resolves this by using linear types for nonconstant values and a standard type system for constants. This leads to safe semantics, even across function calls, and the no-cloning theorem falls out naturally. Function type annotations are used to aid the type checker:

- The annotation `qfree` indicates that a function can be classically computed. For example, the quantum X-gate is considered `qfree`, while the superposition-inducing Hadamard gate is not.
- Function parameters marked as `const` are preserved and not *consumed* by a function. They continue to be accessible after a function call. Parameters not marked as `const` are no longer available after the function call. Functions with only `const` parameters are called `lifted`.
- Functions marked as `mfree` promise not to perform measurements and are reversible.

Silq supports other quantum language features, such as function calls, measurement, explicit reversing of an operator via `reverse`, and an `if-then-else` construct that can be classical or quantum, similar to other quantum languages. Looping constructs must be classical. As an improvement over prior approaches, Silq supports Oracle construction with quantum gates.

With the annotations and the corresponding operational semantics, Silq can safely deduce which operations are safe to reverse and uncompute, even across function calls. The paper provides many examples of potentially hazardous corner cases that are being handled correctly (Bichsel et al., 2020).

As a program example, the code snippet below solves one of the challenges in Microsoft's Q# Summer 2018 coding contest:[4] *Given classical binary string* $b \in \{0,1\}^n$ *with* $b[0] = 1$, *return state* $1/\sqrt{2}(|b\rangle + |0\rangle)$, *where* $|0\rangle$ *is represented using* n *qubits.*

The code iself demonstrates several of Silq's features, for example, the use of ! to denote classical values and types.

```
def solve[n:|N|](bits:||!B|^n){
  // prepare superposition between 0 and 1
  x:=H(0:||!B|);
  // prepare superposition between bits and 0
  qs := if x then bits else (0:int[n]) as ||!B|^n;
  // uncompute x
  forget(x=qs[0]); // valid because bits[0]==1
  return qs;
}

def main(){
  // example usage for bits=1, n=2
  x := 1:||!||int[2];
  y := x as ||!B|^2;
  return solve(y);
}
```

8.3.7 Commercial Systems

Commercial systems are open-source infrastructures that are maintained by commercial entities. The most important systems appear to be Microsoft's Q# (Microsoft Q#, 2021), IBM's Qiskit (Gambetta et al., 2019), Google's Cirq (Google, 2021c), and ProjectQ (Steiger et al., 2018). Microsoft's Q# is a functional stand-alone language and a part of the Quantum Developer Kit (QDK). Qiskit, Cirq, and ProjectQ all provide Python embeddings. By the time you read this, others might have become more popular.

These ecosystems are vast, fast evolving, and provide excellent learning materials that we do not have to cover here. For further reading, we recommend (Garhwal et al., 2021), which details Q#, Cirq, ProjectQ, and Qiskit, or Chong et al. (2017), which describes some of the major challenges for quantum tool flows in general.

8.4 Compiler Optimization

Compiler optimization is a fascinating topic in classical compiler construction. For quantum compilers, it gets even more exciting, given the exponential complexity

---

[4] http://codeforces.com/blog/entry/60209.

and novelty of transformations. Compiler optimizations play an important role in several areas:

- **Ancilla management**. As we use higher-level abstractions and programming languages, ancilla qubits should be managed automatically, in a manner similar to register allocation for classical compilers. The compiler can trade off circuit depth against the number of ancilla bits, supporting the goal of squeezing a circuit into limited resources. Minimizing ancillae in the general case appears to be an unsolved problem.
- **Noise reduction**. The application of quantum gates is subject to noise. Some gates introduce more noise than others. Hence, the role of the optimizer is to minimize gates as a whole and emit gate sequences to actively contain noise.
- **Gate mapping to physical machines**. Real quantum computers only support a small number of gate types. The compiler must decompose logical gates and map them to available physical gates. Furthermore, at least in the short term, the number of available qubits is extremely limited. It is one of the compiler's main roles to map circuits onto those limited resources.
- **Logical to physical register mapping**. Quantum computers have topological constraints on how qubits can interact with each other. For example, only next neighbor interactions may be possible in some cases. Multi-qubit gates spanning nonneighboring qubits thus must be decomposed into two-qubit gates between neighboring qubits.
- **Accuracy tuning**. Individual gates may not be accurate enough for a given algorithm, and multiple gates may be necessary to achieve the desired result. The compiler plays a central role in determining the required accuracy and the corresponding generation of approximating circuits.
- **Error correction**. Automatic insertion of minimal error-correcting circuitry is an important task for the compiler.
- **Tooling**. The compiler sees the whole circuit and can apply whole-program analyses, such as the entanglement analysis that we saw in Section 8.3.3.
- **Performance**. Optimization should also target circuit depth and complexity. Given the short coherence times of real machines, the shorter a circuit has to run, the fewer gates it needs to execute, the higher the chances of reliable outcomes.

The space is large and complex, and we won't be able to cover it exhaustively. Instead, we again provide representative examples of key principles and techniques, hoping to give a taste of the challenges.

8.4.1   Classic(al) Compiler Optimizations

In our infrastructure and many other platforms we described in Section 8.3, classical code is freely intermixed with quantum code. This means that classical optimizations, such as loop unrolling, function inlining, redundancy elimination, constant propagation, and many other scalar, loop- and inter-procedural optimizations still apply. This is necessary because all classical constructs must be eliminated before sending a circuit to the quantum accelerator. Additionally, classical techniques like the elimination of dead code and constant folding equally apply to quantum circuitry.

Scaffold is a great example of the mix of the classical and quantum worlds and the impact of classical optimizations on the performance of a quantum circuit (Javadi-Abhari et al., 2014). Scaffold represents quantum operations in a classical compiler's intermediate representation (IR) and directly benefit from the rich library of available optimization passes in LLVM (Lattner and Adve, 2004).

Other known classical techniques also apply. Analysis of communication overhead and routing strategies developed for distributed systems work with modifications for quantum computing (Ding et al., 2018). Register allocation can lead to optimal allocation and reuse of quantum registers (Ding et al., 2020).

8.4.2   Simple Gate Transformations

The most basic optimization is to eliminate gates that will have no effect. For example, two X-gates in a row, or two other involutory matrices in sequence acting on the same qubit, or two rotations adding up to 0; all of these can be eliminated:

$$Z_i \; \underbrace{X_i X_i}_{redundant} \; Y_i = Z_i Y_i.$$

Sequences like this can be found as a result of higher-level transformations which chain together independent circuit fragments. For example, take the four-qubit decrement circuit which we detailed in Section 6.10 on quantum random walks:

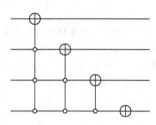

The circuit expands the multi-control gates into this much longer sequence of gates (don't worry, you are not expected to be able to decipher this):

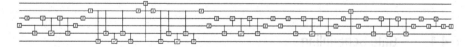

Zooming in at the right, we can see the opportunity to eliminate redundant X-gates:

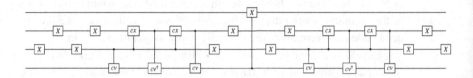

In general, for a single-qubit operator U, if the compiler can prove that the input state is an eigenstate of U with an eigenvalue of 1 (which means $U|\psi\rangle = |\psi\rangle$)), it can simply remove the gate. For example, if the qubit is in the $|+\rangle$ state, the X-gate has no effect, as $X|+\rangle = |+\rangle$.

Depending on the numerical conditioning of an algorithm, the compiler may also decide to remove gates that have only small effects. As an example, we have seen the effectiveness of this technique in the approximate QFT (Coppersmith, 2002).

8.4.3   Gate Fusion

For simulation, and perhaps for physical machines with a suitable gate set, we can *fuse* consecutive gates via simple matrix multiplies. Some of the high-performance simulators apply this technique. Fusion can happen at several levels and across a varying number of qubits. The resulting gates may not be available on a physical machine, in which case the compiler will have to approximate the fused gates. This can nullify the benefits of the fusion, but in cases where two gates X and Y both have to be approximated, it may be beneficial to approximate the combined gate YX:

$$-\boxed{X}-\boxed{Y}- \quad = \quad -\boxed{YX}-$$

The compiler can also exploit the fact that qubits may be unentangled. For example, assume qubits $|\psi\rangle$ and $|\phi\rangle$ are known to be unentangled and must be swapped, potentially by a Swap gate spanning multiple qubits. Since the gates are unentangled and in a pure state, we may be able to classically find a unitary operator U such that $U|\psi\rangle = |\phi\rangle$ and $U^\dagger|\phi\rangle = |\psi\rangle$. In circuit notation:

$$
\begin{array}{ccc}
|\psi\rangle \longrightarrow\!\!\!\times\!\!\!- |\phi\rangle & & |\psi\rangle -\boxed{U}- |\phi\rangle \\
& = & \\
|\phi\rangle \longrightarrow\!\!\!\times\!\!\!- |\psi\rangle & & |\phi\rangle -\boxed{U^\dagger}- |\psi\rangle
\end{array}
$$

8.4.4   Gate Scheduling

We have described many gate equivalences, and there are even more available in the literature. Which specific gate sequence to use will depend on what a specific quantum computer can support, topological constraints, and also on the relative cost of specific gates. For example, T-gates might be an order of magnitude slower than other gates and may have to be avoided.

In order to find the best equivalences, pattern matching can be used. To maximize the number of possible matches, you may have to reorder and reschedule gates. Valid and efficient recipes for reordering are hence a rich area of research. As a simple example, single-qubit gates applied to different qubits can be reordered and parallelized, as:

$$(U \times I)(I \times V) = (I \times V)(U \times I) = (U \times V)$$

There are many other opportunities to reorder. For example, if a gate is followed by a controlled gate of the same type, the two gates can be re-ordered:

$$Y_i CY_{ji} = CY_{ji} Y_i.$$

Rotations are a popular target for reordering. For example, the S-gate, T-gate, and Phase-gate all represent rotations, which can be applied in any order. Nam et al. (2018) provide many recipes, rewrite rules, and examples, such as the following:

In simulation, it may not help to parallelize gates, at least in our implementation. On a physical quantum computer, however, it is safe to assume that multiple gates will be able to operate in parallel. Mapping gates to parallel running qubits will improve device utilization and has the potential to reduce circuit depth. Shorter depth means shorter runtime and a higher probability to conclude an execution before decoherence.

Measurements typically happen at the end of a circuit execution. Qubits have a limited lifetime, so it is a good strategy to initialize qubits as late as possible. This is achieved with a policy to schedule gates *as late as possible* (ALAP), working backward from the measurement. This is also the default policy in IBM's Qiskit compiler. Ding and Chong (2020) detail other scheduling policies and additional techniques to minimize communication costs.

8.4.5 Peephole Optimization

Peephole optimization gets its name from the fact that it looks at only a small sliding window over code or circuitry, hoping to find exploitable patterns in this small

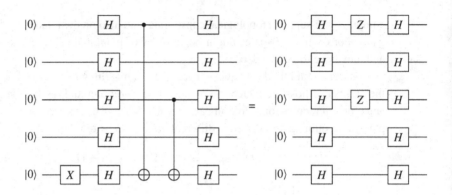

Figure 8.1 Optimized Bernstein-Vazirani circuit.

window. This is a standard technique in classical computing, but it applies to quantum computing as well (McKeeman, 1965).

Limited window pattern matching approaches have in common that, for a given gate replacement, the underlying unitary operator must not change. This guarantees correctness of a transformation.

With *relaxed peephole optimization*, this constraint can be, well, *relaxed* (Liu et al., 2021). For example, if a controlling qubit is known to be in state $|0\rangle$ as shown above, we can eliminate the controlled gate. The circuit is still logically equivalent, but the underlying operator has changed.

We can exploit this insight. A Controlled-U operation with a controlling $|0\rangle$ qubit has no effect and can be eliminated (the compiler has to *ascertain* that the controller will be $|0\rangle$):

$$
\begin{array}{c}
|0\rangle \;\;\bullet \\
\;\;\;\;\;\;| \\
|\psi\rangle \;\;\oplus
\end{array}
\quad = \quad
\begin{array}{c}
\;\;\;\;\; \\
\;\;\;\;\;
\end{array}
$$

We can also squeeze the Swap gate if one of the inputs is known to be $|0\rangle$:

$$
\begin{array}{c}
|0\rangle \;\;\bullet\;\;\oplus\;\;\bullet \\
|\psi\rangle \;\;\oplus\;\;\bullet\;\;\oplus
\end{array}
\quad = \quad
\begin{array}{c}
\;\;\oplus\;\;\bullet\;\; |\psi\rangle \\
\;\;\bullet\;\;\oplus\;\; |0\rangle
\end{array}
$$

The Controlled-Not gates in the Bernstein–Vazirani oracle circuit can be replaced by simple Z-gates because the leading Hadamard gates put the qubits into the $|+\rangle$ basis. This is shown in Figure 8.1. The techniques can be generalized to multi-controlled gates as well. More examples of this technique, along with a full evaluation, can be found in (Liu et al., 2021).

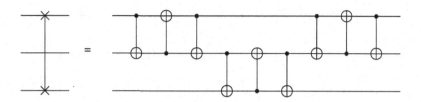

Figure 8.2 Decomposition of a Swap gate spanning three qubits into next-neighbor controlled gates.

8.4.6   High-Performance Pattern Libraries

The efficient matching of patterns to gate sequences is a challenge. A possible approach is to precompute a library of high-performance subcircuits and then transpile nonoptimal and permuted subcircuits into known high-performance circuits. This approach is similar to the end-game library in a chess-playing computer. McKeeman (1965) gives an example of building up a library of thousands of highly optimized four-qubit subcircuits, which were found with an elaborate automated search.

8.4.7   Logical to Physical Mapping

We have already seen many gate equivalences in Section 3.2. Choosing which ones to apply will depend on the physical constraints of an underlying architecture. In this context, logical to physical qubit mapping presents an optimization challenge.

For example, Swap gates may only be applied to neighboring physical qubits. If there is a swap between qubits 0 and (very large) n, it might be better to place physical qubit n right next to qubit 0. Otherwise, the *communication overhead* will be very high. For example, a construction like the following is needed to swap qubits 0 and 2 in a three-qubit circuit. The circuit as presented is not very efficient; it simply stitches together a series of two-qubit Swap gates. To bridge longer distance swaps, this ladder must be extended to more qubits, all the way down and back up as shown in the example in Figure 8.2 for a swap gate spanning over 3 qubits.

If the physical qubit assignment has been decided, gates may have to be further deconstructed to fit the topological constraints. In the example shown in Figure 8.3, a Controlled-Not from a qubit 0 to qubit 2 is being decomposed into next-neighbor controlled gates. Several other types of Controlled-Not deconstructions deconstructions are presented in Garcia-Escartin and Chamorro-Posada (2011).

A related proposed technique is *wire optimization* (Paler et al., 2016). It uses qubit lifetime analysis to *recycle* wires and qubits, with the insight being that not all qubits are needed during the execution of a full circuit. Under the assumption that we can measure and reuse qubits, this work shows drastic reductions in the number of required qubits for an algorithm, up to 90%. This mirrors the results we find with our sparse implementation. However, at the time of this writing, it does not appear that intermittent measurement and reinitialization of qubits can be performed efficiently.

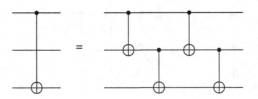

Figure 8.3 A Controlled-Not from qubit 0 to qubit 2 is decomposed into next-neighbor Controlled-Not gates.

8.4.8   Physical Gate Decomposition

Finally, an important step for compiler and optimizer is to decompose higher level gates to actually available, physical gates, respecting connectivity constraints. For example, the IBMQX5 has five qubits and the gates u_1, u_2, u_3, as well as a CNOT gate (IBM, 2021a), which can only be applied to neighboring gates.

$$u_1(\lambda) = \begin{bmatrix} 1 & 0 \\ 0 & e^{i\lambda} \end{bmatrix},$$

$$u_2(\phi, \lambda) = \frac{1}{\sqrt{2}} \begin{bmatrix} 1 & -e^{i\lambda} \\ e^{i\phi} & e^{i(\phi+\lambda)} \end{bmatrix}$$

$$= R_z(\phi + \pi/2) R_x(\pi/2) R_z(\lambda - \pi/2),$$

$$u_3(\theta, \phi, \lambda) = \begin{bmatrix} \cos(\theta/2) & -i\sin(\theta/2) \\ e^{i\phi}\sin(\theta/2) & e^{i(\lambda+\phi)}\cos(\theta/2) \end{bmatrix}.$$

Other architectures offer different available gates on differently-shaped topologies. Mapping idealized gates to physical gates is challenging, especially if the physical gates have unusual structure. A broader analysis and taxonomy can be found in Murali et al. (2019).

We also discussed earlier, in Section 8.2, that in an idealized programming model we may use any gate, knowing that gates can be approximated. The key questions are:

1. What is the *best* set of gates to realize in hardware?
2. What is the impact of this choice on gate approximation or other design parameters and circuit depth?
3. What is the accuracy impact of approximations on an algorithm?
4. If approximation would require an exponentially growing set of gates, would this not nullify the complexity advantage of quantum algorithms?

Some abstract gates will be easier to approximate than others on a given physical instruction set, such as the IBM machine above. Each target and algorithm will hence require targeted methodology and compilation techniques.

8.5 Transpilation

Transpilation is an interesting modulation of the term *compilation*. Typically, transpilation describes the process of translating a program written in one programming language to another, for example, translating Java to Javascript, where still another compilation step is needed to run the code on an actual machine. In quantum computing, the term is typically used to describe the process of mapping a circuit onto a physical quantum computer, in which case it should be called compilation. Naming is difficult.

In our context, we use the term transpilation as the compiler gods intended: to describe the process of taking a circuit written in our infrastructure and transpiling it to another platform, such as IBM's Qiskit, Google's Cirq, or our sparse representation libq. It is not compilation because the translation from the input onto the target machine still has to be done by the respective platforms. Transpilation appears to be the accurate term in our context, but we may also refer to the various levels of compilation as *staged compilation*. Did we mention yet that naming is hard?

In this section, we introduce a simple data structure that allows transpilation (!) of our algorithms to other formats, including QASM (Cross et al., 2017), which is supported by many platforms, including IBM's Qiskit. Other transpilers are in development; you can find them in the open-source repository. The code generators are quite simple and mostly of prototype quality. We show them in great detail to encourage experimentation and the development of additional transpilers.

8.5.1 Intermediate Representation (IR)

To compile a program into another form, we need a data structure to represent the input. In compilers, this data structure is typically called an *intermediate representation* (IR). Our IR will be very simple – just a list of nodes corresponding to the gates as they were added to the circuit. As described earlier, quantum computing has no classical control flow, which enables the use of this simple data structure for a number of purposes.

There are only three meaningful operation types in our infrastructure: the undefined operation UNK, a single-qubit gate SINGLE, and a controlled gate CTL. We define them all with the enumeration type class Op(enum.Enum). For debugging and better formatting of generated outputs, we also introduce the notion of a *section*, but we ignore this for now.

8.5.2 IR Nodes

A node will hold all information available for the operations, such as target qubit or intended rotation angle. The nodes themselves are represented by a simple Python class with all the relevant parameters passed to its constructor. One class is enough to represent all possible node types. Again, we keep it very simple in this prototype implementation.

```
class Node:
    """Single node in the IR."""

    def __init__(self, opcode, name, idx0=0, idx1=None, val=None):
        self._opcode = opcode
        self._name = name
        self._idx0 = idx0
        self._idx1 = idx1
        self._val = val
```

We add functions to check for node properties:

```
def is_single(self):
    return self._opcode == Op.SINGLE

def is_ctl(self):
    return self._opcode == Op.CTL

def is_gate(self):
    return self.is_single() or self.is_ctl()
```

Then, based on the specific node type, the transpilers will query the properties to get the node attributes:

```
@property
def opcode(self):
    return self._opcode

@property
def name(self):
    if not self._name:
        return '*unk*'
    return self._name

@property
def desc(self):
    return self._name
[...]
```

8.5.3   IR Base Class

The IR itself is now fairly straightforward. It is just a list of nodes, functions to add nodes for single gates and controlled gates, and a function to manage quantum registers.

```
class Ir:
  """Compiler IR."""

  def __init__(self):
    self._ngates = 0   # gates in this IR
    self.gates = []    # [] of gates
    self.regs = []     # [] of tuples (global reg index, name, reg index)
    self.nregs = 0     # number of registers
    self.regset = []   # [] of tuples (name, size, reg) for registers


  def reg(self, size, name, register):
    self.regset.append((name, size, register))
    for i in range(size):
      self.regs.append((self.nregs + i, name, i))
    self.nregs += size

  def single(self, name, idx0, val=None):
    self.gates.append(Node(Op.SINGLE, name, idx0, None, val))
    self._ngates += 1

  def controlled(self, name, idx0, idx1, val=None):
    self.gates.append(Node(Op.CTL, name, idx0, idx1, val))
    self._ngates += 1

  @property
  def ngates(self):
    return self._ngates
```

8.5.4 Quantum Circuit Extensions

To construct the IR, we moderately extend the quantum circuit class. An *eager* mode executes the circuit as it is being constructed. This is the default behavior. Setting eager to `False` will only construct the IR and not execute the circuit. We also add the IR to the quantum circuit by extending the constructor:

```
def __init__(self, name=None, eager=True):
  self.name = name
  self.psi = 1.0
  self.ir = ir.Ir()
  self.eager = eager
  state.reset()
```

There are only two functions in the `qc` class that *apply* gates. We have to add IR-construction calls to those two functions. This is one of the benefits of having this abstraction, as alluded to in Section 4.3:

```
def apply1(self, gate, idx, name=None, *, val=None):
    if isinstance(idx, state.Reg):
        for reg in range(idx.nbits):
            self.ir.single(name, idx[reg], val)
            if self.eager:
                xgates.apply1(self.psi, gate.reshape(4), self.psi.nbits,
                              idx[reg], tensor.tensor_width)
        return
    self.ir.single(name, idx, val)
    if self.eager:
        xgates.apply1(self.psi, gate.reshape(4), self.psi.nbits, idx,
                      tensor.tensor_width)

[...] similar for apply_controlled
```

Registers are also supported. As a matter of fact, at the time of writing, *only* quantum registers are supported for code generation. In other words, to generate valid output, the qubits have to be generated and initialized as registers.

8.5.5   Circuits of Circuits

The IR enables a few other powerful capabilities for circuits. It allows the storing away of subcircuits and then combining them later in flexible ways. This makes it easy to invert a circuit, which can be helpful for uncomputation. Furthermore, with just minor changes, we could introduce control for whole subcircuits, similar to the constructs in QCL from Section 8.3.2.

We can create multiple circuits and add them to build even larger circuits. For example, we can create a main circuit, a subcircuit, and replay this subcircuit three times with code like this:

```
main = circuit.qc('main circuit, eager execution')
[... add gates to main]

sub1 = circuit.qc('sub circuit', eager=False)
[... gates to sub1, non-eager]

# Now add three copies of sub1 to main (eager),
# all at a different offset:
main.qc(sub1, 0)
main.qc(sub1, 1)
main.qc(sub1, 2)
```

It is important to note that as the subcircuit is being constructed, it is not yet executed. The gates and their order are recorded for replay later. This is achieved with the `eager` parameter set to `False`.

The second useful capability of this IR is that gate sequences can be inverted. To achieve this, the stored list of gates is reverted. In the process, each gate is replaced by its adjoint, and the gate names get decorated with `"^-1"`. To reverse the application of the three subcircuits in the code example above, the following code could be used. Note how using inverses can be used for uncomputation in an elegant way.

```
# Create an inverse copy of sub1 (which is still non-eager)
sub1_inv = sub1.inverse()

# Now add three copies of sub1 to main (eagar),
# at the reverted list of offsets:
main.qc(sub1_inv, 2)
main.qc(sub1_inv, 1)
main.qc(sub1_inv, 0)
```

8.5.6   Code Generation

We now briefly discuss several transpilers. There is not a lot of magic to them; the compilation from one infrastructure to the next is mostly linear, gate application by gate application, just generating different syntax. To invoke any of the code generators, we define a flag for each of them:

```
flags.DEFINE_string('libq', '', 'Generate libq output file')
flags.DEFINE_string('qasm', '', 'Generate qasm output file')
flags.DEFINE_string('cirq', '', 'Generate cirq output file')
```

For example, to produce a QASM output file, the following flag will generate this format and write it to `/tmp/test.qasm`:

```
> ... --qasm=/tmp/test.qasm
```

To enable this, we add the following functions to the quantum circuit class. The function `dump_to_file` checks for any of the flags. If one is present, it passes the flag and a corresponding code generator function to `dump_with_dumper`, which will call this function on the IR and produce the output:

```
def dump_with_dumper(self, flag: bool,
                     dumper_func: Callable[ir.Ir]) -> None:
  if flag:
    result = dumper_func(self.ir)
```

```
    with open(flag, 'w') as f:
        print(result, file=f)

def dump_to_file(self):
    self.dump_with_dumper(flags.FLAGS.libq, dumpers.libq)
    self.dump_with_dumper(flags.FLAGS.qasm, dumpers.qasm)
    self.dump_with_dumper(flags.FLAGS.cirq, dumpers.cirq)
```

There are, of course, better ways to structure this, especially when many more code generators and options become available. For this text, the simple implementation will do. The various code generators below also use a small number of helper functions, which can be found in the open-source repository as well.

Fractions of Pi

As we produce textual output, it greatly improves readability to print fractions of π as a fraction such as $3\pi/2$ instead of 4.71238898038. For example, the complex algorithms use the quantum Fourier transform with lots of rotations. Showing them as fractions of π makes debug prints and generated code easier to read.

```
def pi_fractions(val, pi='pi') -> str:
    """Convert a value in fractions of pi."""

    if val is None:
        return ''
    if val == 0:
        return '0'
    for pi_multiplier in range(1, 4):
        for denom in range(-128, 128):
            if denom and math.isclose(val, pi_multiplier * math.pi / denom):
                pi_str = ''
                if pi_multiplier != 1:
                    pi_str = f'{abs(pi_multiplier)}*'
                if denom == -1:
                    return f'-{pi_str}{pi}'
                if denom < 0:
                    return f'-{pi_str}{pi}/{-denom}'
                if denom == 1:
                    return f'{pi_str}{pi}'
                return f'{pi_str}{pi}/{denom}'
    # Couldn't find fractional, just return original value.
    return f'{val}'
```

8.5.7   QASM

The first dumper we present is the simplest one: QASM. It just traverses the list of nodes and outputs the nodes with their names as found. Conveniently, the names chosen for the operators already match the QASM specification. Not a coincidence.

```
def qasm(ir) -> str:
  """Dump IR in QASM format."""

  res = 'OPENQASM 2.0;\n'
  for regs in ir.regset:
    res += f'qreg {regs[0]}[{regs[1]}];\n'
  res += '\n'

  for op in ir.gates:
    if op.is_gate():
      res += op.name
      if op.val is not None:
        res += '({})'.format(helper.pi_fractions(op.val))
      if op.is_single():
        res += f' {reg2str(ir, op.idx0)};\n'
      if op.is_ctl():
        res += f' {reg2str(ir, op.ctl)},{reg2str(ir, op.idx1)};\n'
  return res
```

That's it! It is really that simple. Here is an output example:

```
OPENQASM 2.0;
qreg q2[4];
qreg q1[8];
qreg q0[6];
creg c0[8];
h q1[0];
h q1[1];
h q1[2];
[. . .]
cu1(-pi/64) q1[7],q1[1];
cu1(-pi/128) q1[7],q1[0];
h q1[7];
measure q1[0] -> c0[0];
measure q1[1] -> c0[1];
[...]
```

QASM is fairly simple and supported by other infrastructures. Hence, it is very useful for debugging the complex algorithms and comparing the results to those other infrastructures produce.

8.5.8   LIBQ

The generation of sparse `libq` C++ code is similarly trivial. It produces C++, which requires a bit more scaffolding in the beginning and end, but the core function is similar: iterate over all nodes and convert IR nodes to C++. Compiling C++ requires proper include paths and initialization. Those are stubbed out below and must be set to the specifics of a given build system:

```python
def libq(ir) -> str:
  """Dump IR to a compilable C++ program with libq."""

  # Configure: This code needs to change for specific build/run envs.
  res = ('// This file was generated by qc.dump_to_file()\n\n' +
        '#include <math.h>\n' +
        '#include <stdio.h>\n\n' +
        <setup specific headers>
        <setup specific dir>'quantum/libq/libq.h"\n\n' +

        'int main(int argc, char* argv[]) \n' +
        '  <specific init code>\n\n')

  total_regs = 0
  for regs in ir.regset:
    total_regs += regs[1]
  res += f'  libq::qureg* q = libq::new_qureg(0, {total_regs});\n\n'

  total_regs = 0
  for regs in ir.regset:
    for r in regs[2].val:
      if r == 1:
        res += f'  libq::x({total_regs}, q);\n'
      total_regs += 1
  res += '\n'

  for op in ir.gates:
    if op.is_gate():
      res += f'  libq::{op.name}('
      if op.is_single():
        res += f'{op.idx0}'
        if op.val is not None:
          res += ', {}'.format(helper.pi_fractions(op.val, 'M_PI'))
        res += ', q);\n'
      if op.is_ctl():
        res += f'{op.ctl}, {op.idx1}'
        if op.val is not None:
          res += ', {}'.format(helper.pi_fractions(op.val, 'M_PI'))
        res += ', q);\n'
  [...]
```

Here is an example of generated output:

```cpp
int main(int argc, char* argv[]) {
  [...]

  libq::qureg* q = libq::new_qureg(0, 26);
```

```
libq::x(1,  q);
libq::x(13,  q);
libq::cu1(11, 12, M_PI/2, q);
[...]
libq::cu1(11, 12, -M_PI/2, q);
libq::h(12,  q);

libq::flush(q);
libq::print_qureg(q);
libq::delete_qureg(q);
return EXIT_SUCCESS;
}
```

8.5.9   Cirq

The last example is the converter to Google's Cirq. This one is interesting: Because Cirq doesn't support certain gates, we have to construct workarounds as we traverse the IR. Also, the operators need to be renamed (see op_map below):

```python
def cirq(ir) -> str:
"""Dump IR to a Cirq Python file."""

  res = ('# This file was generated by qc.dump_to_file()\n\n' +
         'import cirq\n' +
         'import cmath\n' +
         'from cmath import pi\n' +
         'import numpy as np\n\n')

  res += 'qc = cirq.Circuit()\n\n'
  res += f'r = cirq.LineQubit.range({ir.nregs})\n'
  res += '\n'

  # Map to translate gate names:
  op_map = {'h': 'H', 'x': 'X', 'y': 'Y', 'z': 'Z',
            'cx': 'CX', 'cz': 'CZ'}

  for op in ir.gates:
    if op.is_gate():
      if op.name == 'u1':
        res += 'm = np.array([[(1.0, 0.0), (0.0, '
        res += f'cmath.exp(1j * {helper.pi_fractions(op.val)})]])\n'
        res += f'qc.append(cirq.MatrixGate(m).on(r[{op.idx0}]))\n'
        continue

      # [... similar for cu1, cv, cv_adj]

      op_name = op_map[op.name]
      res += f'qc.append(cirq.{op_name}('
```

```
    if op.is_single():
      res += f'r[{op.idx0}]'
      if op.val is not None:
        res += ', {}'.format(helper.pi_fractions(op.val))
      res += '))\n'
    if op.is_ctl():
      res += f'r[{op.ctl}], r[{op.idx1}]'
      if op.val is not None:
        res += ', {}'.format(helper.pi_fractions(op.val))
      res += '))\n'

  res += 'sim = cirq.Simulator()\n'
  res += 'print(\'Simulate...\')\n'
  res += 'result = sim.simulate(qc)\n'
  res += 'res_str = str(result)\n'
  res += 'print(res_str.encode(\'utf-8\'))\n'
  return res
```

Writing a transpiler does not appear overly complicated.[5] At the time of writing, other transpilers are gestating in open-source, such as one for LATEX. They were used for a few of the circuits in this book, both to evaluate performance and to generate circuit diagrams.

8.5.10   Open-Source Simulators

We discussed the basic principles of how to construct an efficient, but still bare-bones simulator. With the help of our transcoding facilities, we can now target other available simulators, for example, to utilize simulators that support distributed computation or advanced noise models. In this section, we provide a cross-section of the most cited and well-developed simulators. A more exhaustive list of simulators can be found in Quantiki (2021).

The full-state simulator qHipster implements threading, vectorization, and distributed computation via MPI and OpenMP (Smelyanskiy et al., 2016). It also uses highly optimized libraries on Intel platforms. At the time of writing, the simulator was rebranded as Intel Quantum Simulator (Guerreschi et al., 2020), available on Github (Intel, 2021). This simulator also allows the modeling of quantum noise processes, which enables the simulation of quantum hardware subject to these noise processes. This also mimics the sampling process that real quantum hardware requires.

The only sparse implementation we are aware of is libquantum (Butscher and Weimer, 2013). We used it as the foundation for our libq. The library is no longer actively maintained (the last release was in 2013). It offers excellent single-thread performance for circuits where the maximum number of states with non-zero amplitudes is only a small fraction of all possible states. It also makes provisions for quantum error correction and allows modeling of decoherence effects.

---

[5] A sentence likely falling in the category of "famous last words."

QX is an open-source, high-performance simulator implementation (Khammassi et al., 2017). It accepts as input *quantum code*, which is a variation on QASM that supports explicit parallelism between gates, debug print statements, and looping constructs. It performs aggressive optimizations but still appears to store the full state vector. QX also supports noisy execution using a variety of error models. It is part of a larger quantum development environment from the University of Delft.

ProjectQ is a Python-embedded, compiler-supported framework for quantum computing (Steiger et al., 2018). It allows targeting of both real hardware and the simulator included in the distribution. The simulator allows "shortcuts" by setting the expected result of an expensive computation without simulating it. ProjectQ's distribution contains transpilers to several other available frameworks. It can call into RevKit (Soeken et al., 2012) to automatically construct reversible oracles from classical gates, a function of great utility.

QuEST, the Quantum Exact Simulation Toolkit, is a full state, multithreaded, distributed, and GPU-accelerated simulator (Jones et al., 2019). It hybridizes MPI and OpenMP and has demonstrated impressive scaling on large supercomputers. It supports state-vector and density matrix simulation, general decoherence channels of any size, general unitaries with any number of control and target qubits, and other advanced facilities like Pauli gadgets and higher-order Trotterisation. The related QuESTlink (Jones and Benjamin, 2020) system allows use of the QuEST features from within the Mathematica package.

Recently, Cirq published two high-performance simulators, qsim and qsimh (Google, 2021d). The former, qsim, targets single machines, while qsimh allows distributed computation via OpenMP. The implementations are vectorized and perform several optimizations, such as gate fusion. The qsim simulator is a full state Schrödinger simulator. The qsimh simulator is a Schrödinger-Feynman simulator (Markov et al., 2018), which trades performance for reduced memory requirements.

Microsoft's quantum development kit offers several simulators, including a full state simulator, several resource estimators, and an accelerated simulator for Clifford gates, which can handle millions of gates (Microsoft QDK Simulators, 2021).

The Qiskit ecosystem offers a range of simulators spanning full state simulators, resource estimation tools, noisy simulations, as well as QASM simulators (Qiskit, 2021).

Appendix: Sparse Implementation

This appendix details the implementation of `libq`, including some optimization successes and failures. The full source code can be found online in directory `src/libq` in the open-source repository. It is about 500 lines of C++ code. Correspondingly, this section is very code heavy.

A.1 Register File

The register file, which holds the qubits, is defined in `libq.h` in the type `qureg_t`. Again, we use similar names in `libq` as found in libquantum to enable line-by-line comparisons. This structure will hold an array with complex amplitudes and an array with the state bitmasks.

```
typedef uint64 state_t;

struct qureg_t {
 cmplx* amplitude;
 state_t* state;
 }
```

Interesting tidbit: in an earlier version of this library that was included in the SPEC 2006 benchmarks, those two arrays were written as an array of structures, which is not good for performance, as iterations over the array to, say, flip a bit in all states has to iterate over more memory than necessary. This author implemented a quite involved data layout transformation in the HP compilers for Itanium to transform the array of `struct`s into a `struct` of arrays (Hundt et al., 2006). A later version of the library then modified the source code itself, erasing the need and benefit of the complex compiler transformation.

The member `width`, which probably deserves a better name, holds the number of qubits in this register. The member `size` holds the number of nonzero probabilities, and `hash` is the actual hash table, with `hashw` being the allocation size of the hash table.

```
int width; /* number of qubits in the qureg */
int size;  /* number of non-zero vectors */

int hashw; /* width of the hash array */
int* hash; /* hash table */
```

The operations to check whether a bit is set and to XOR a specific bit with a value
are common, so we extract them into member functions:

```
bool bit_is_set(int index, int target) __attribute__ ((pure)) {
  return state[index] & (static_cast<state_t>(1) << target);
}
void bit_xor(int index, int target) {
  state[index] ^= (static_cast<state_t>(1) << target);
}

typedef struct qureg_t qureg;
```

The following operations are allowed for this quantum register.

Create a new quantum register of a given size `width` and initialize an initial single
state with bitmask `initval` with probability 1.0 (one state must be defined). The
function's main job is to `calloc()` the various arrays and make sure there are no
out-of-memory errors.

```
qureg *new_qureg(state_t initval, int width);

.cc:
   libq::qureg* q = libq::new_qureg(0, 2);
```

Free all allocated data structures, set relevant pointers to `nullptr`.

```
void delete_qureg(qureg *reg);
```

Print a textual representation of the current state by listing all states with non-zero
probability.

```
void print_qureg(qureg *reg);
```

Display statistics, such as how many qubits were stored, how often the hash table
was recomputed, and, another important metric, the maximum number of non-zero
probability states reached during the execution of an algorithm:

```
void print_qureg_stats(qureg *reg);
```

For certain experiments, we cache internal state. This next function ensures that all remaining states will be flushed. This could mean a computation is completed or some pending prints are flushed to stdout.

```
void flush(qureg* reg);
```

A.2   Superposition-Preserving Gates

These are gates that do not create or destroy superposition. They represent the "easy" case in this sparse representation. Let us look at a few representative gates; the full implementation is in libq/gates.cc.

To apply the X-gate to a specific qubit, the bit corresponding to the qubit index must be flipped. Recall that the gate's function is determined by:

$$\begin{bmatrix} 0 & 1 \\ 1 & 0 \end{bmatrix} \begin{bmatrix} \alpha \\ \beta \end{bmatrix} = \begin{bmatrix} \beta \\ \alpha \end{bmatrix}.$$

If there are n states with nonzero probabilities in the system, we will have n tuples. To flip one qubit's probability according to the gate, we have to flip the bit for that qubit in each of those tuples, as that represents the operation of this gate on all the states. The probability amplitudes for that qubit are flipped by just flipping the bit; there is no other data movement. The code is remarkably simple:

```
void x(int target, qureg *reg) {
    for (int i = 0; i < reg->size; ++i) {
        reg->bit_xor(i, target);
    }
}
```

For another class of operators, we must check whether a bit is set before applying a transformation. For example, applying the Z-gate to a state acts like this:

$$\begin{bmatrix} 1 & 0 \\ 0 & -1 \end{bmatrix} \begin{bmatrix} \alpha \\ \beta \end{bmatrix} = \begin{bmatrix} \alpha \\ -\beta \end{bmatrix}.$$

The gate only has effect if β is nonzero. In the sparse representation, this means that there must be a tuple representing a nonzero probability that has a 1 at the intended qubit location. We iterate over all state tuples, check for the condition, and only negate the amplitude if that bit was set:

```
void z(int target, qureg *reg) {
    for (int i = 0; i < reg->size; ++i) {
        if (reg->bit_is_set(i, target)) {
            reg->amplitude[i] *= -1;
        }
    }
}
```

Recall that if the qubit is in superposition, there will be two tuples: one with the corresponding bit set to 0 and the amplitude set to α, and the other with the bit set to 1 and the amplitude set to β. For the Z-gate, we only need to change the second tuple. A related example is the T-gate, there are a few more gates of this nature:

```
void t(int target, qureg *reg) {
    static cmplx z = cexp(M_PI / 4.0);
    for (int i = 0; i < reg->size; ++i) {
        if (reg->bit_is_set(i, target)) {
            reg->amplitude[i] *= z;
        }
    }
}
```

The Y-gate is moderately more complex, using a combination of the methods shown above.

$$\begin{bmatrix} 0 & -i \\ i & 0 \end{bmatrix} \begin{bmatrix} \alpha \\ \beta \end{bmatrix} = \begin{bmatrix} -i\beta \\ i\alpha \end{bmatrix}.$$

First, we flip the bit, similar to the X-gate, and then we apply i or $-i$, depending on whether or not the qubit's bit is set after being flipped:

```
void y(int target, qureg *reg) {
    for (int i = 0; i < reg->size; ++i) {
        reg->bit_xor(i, target);
        if (reg->bit_is_set(i, target))
            reg->amplitude[i] *= cmplx(0, 1.0);
        else
            reg->amplitude[i] *= cmplx(0, -1.0);
    }
}
```

A.3   Controlled Gates

Controlled gates are a logical extension of the above. In order to make a gate controlled, we only have to check whether the corresponding control bit is set to 1. For example, for the Controlled-X gate:

```
void cx(int control, int target, qureg *reg) {
    for (int i = 0; i < reg->size; ++i) {
        if (reg->bit_is_set(i, control)) {
            reg->bit_xor(i, target);
        }
    }
}
```

For the Controlled-Z gate:

```
void cz(int control, int target, qureg *reg) {
    for (int i = 0; i < reg->size; ++i) {
        if (reg->bit_is_set(i, control)) {
            if (reg->bit_is_set(i, target)) {
                reg->amplitude[i] *= -1;
            }
        }
    }
}
```

This even works for double-controlled gates, where we only have to check for both control bits to be set. Here is the implementation of a double-controlled X-gate:

```
void ccx(int control0, int control1, int target, qureg *reg) {
    for (int i = 0; i < reg->size; ++i) {
        if (reg->bit_is_set(i, control0)) {
            if (reg->bit_is_set(i, control1)) {
                reg->bit_xor(i, target);
            }
        }
    }
}
```

A.4   Superpositioning Gates

The difficult case is for gates that create or destroy superposition. We provide a single implementation in `apply.cc` for this in function `libq_gate1`. The function expects the 2×2 gate to be passed in.

For example, for the Hadamard gate:

```
void h(int target, qureg *reg) {
    static cmplx mh[4] = {sqrt(1.0/2), sqrt(1.0/2), sqrt(1.0/2),
                          -sqrt(1.0/2)};
    libq_gate1(target, mh, reg);
}
```

The implementation itself applies the same technique we saw earlier in Section 4.5 on accelerated gates: a linear traversal over the states, except it is adapted to the sparse representation. Additionally, it manages memory by filtering out close-to-zero states. Let's dive into it. The implementation is about 175 lines of code.

A.5   Hash Table

First, as indicated above, states are maintained in a hash table with the following hash function:

```
static inline unsigned int hash64(state_t key, int width) {
    unsigned int k32 = (key & 0xFFFFFFFF) ^ (key >> 32);
    k32 *= 0x9e370001UL;
    k32 = k32 >> (32 - width);
    return k32;
}
```

The hash lookup function `get_state` checks whether a given state exists with nonzero probability. It computes the hash index for a state *a* and iterates over the dense array, hoping to find the actual state. If a 0 state was found (the marker for a unpopulated entry) or if the search wraps around, no state was found and -1 is returned; otherwise, the position in the hash table is returned:

```
state_t get_state(state_t a, qureg *reg) {
    unsigned int i = hash64(a, reg->hashw);
    while (reg->hash[i]) {
        if (reg->state[reg->hash[i] - 1] == a) {
            return reg->hash[i] - 1;
        }
        i++;
        if (i == (1 << reg->hashw)) {
            break;
        }
    }
    return -1;
}
```

There is, of course, a function to add a state to the hash table:

```
void libq_add_hash(state_t a, int pos, qureg *reg) {
    int mark = 0;

    int i = hash64(a, reg->hashw);
    while (reg->hash[i]) {
        i++;
        if (i == (1 << reg->hashw)) {
            if (!mark) {
                i = 0;
                mark = 1;
            }
```

```
    }
  }
  reg->hash[i] = pos + 1;
  // -- Optimization will happen here (later).
}
```

The most interesting function from a performance perspective is the one to reconstruct the hash table. Since the gate apply function will filter out states with probabilities close to 0.0, after gate application, we have to reconstruct the hash table to ensure it only contains valid entries. This is the most expensive operation of the whole libq implementation. We show some optimizations below, where the first loop is being replaced with a memset(), and also in Section A.8.

```
void libq_reconstruct_hash(qureg *reg) {
    reg->hash_computes += 1;    // count invocations.

    for (int i = 0; i < (1 << reg->hashw); ++i) {
        reg->hash[i] = 0;
    }
    for (int i = 0; i < reg->size; ++i) {
        libq_add_hash(reg->state[i], i, reg);
    }
}
```

The first thing to note is the first loop, which resets the hash array to all zeros:

```
    for (int i = 0; i < (1 << reg->hashw); ++i) {
        reg->hash[i] = 0;
    }
```

You might expect that the compiler transforms this loop to a vectorized memset operation. However, it does not. The loop-bound reg->hashw aliases with the loop body, meaning that the compiler cannot infer whether or not the loop body would modify the loop bound. Manually changing this to a memset speeds up the whole simulation by about 20%.

```
    memset(reg->hash, 0, (1 << reg->hashw) * sizeof(int));
```

This memset is still the slowest part of the implementation. Later, we will show how to optimize it further.

A.6   Gate Application

Here is the routine to apply a gate. It assumes that something changed since last invocation, so the first task is to reconstruct the hash table:

```
void libq_gate1(int target, cmplx m[4], qureg *reg) {
    int addsize = 0;
    libq_reconstruct_hash(reg);
    [...]
}
```

Superposition on a given qubit means that both the states with a 0 and a 1 at a given bit position must exist. So the function iterates, and counts how many of those states are missing and need to be added:

```
/* calculate the number of basis states to be added */
for (int i = 0; i < reg->size; ++i) {
    /* determine whether XORed basis state already exists */
    if (get_state(reg->state[i] ^
        (static_cast<state_t>(1) << target), reg) == -1)
        addsize++;
}
```

If new states need to be added, the function reallocates the arrays. It also does some bookkeeping and remembers the largest number of states with nonzero probability:

```
/* allocate memory for the new basis states */
if (addsize) {
    reg->state = static_cast<state_t *>(
        realloc(reg->state, (reg->size + addsize) * sizeof(state_t)));
    reg->amplitude = static_cast<cmplx *>(
        realloc(reg->amplitude, (reg->size + addsize) * sizeof(cmplx)));

    memset(&reg->state[reg->size], 0, addsize * sizeof(int));
    memset(&reg->amplitude[reg->size], 0, addsize * sizeof(cmplx));
    if (reg->size + addsize > reg->maxsize) {
        reg->maxsize = reg->size + addsize;
    }
}
```

This is all for state and memory management. Now on to applying the gates. We allocate an array done to remember which states we've already handled. The limit variable will be used at the end of the function to remove states with close to zero probability.

```
char *done =
    static_cast<char *>(calloc(reg->size + addsize, sizeof(char)));
int next_state = reg->size;
float limit = (1.0 / (static_cast<state_t>(1) << reg->width))
              * 1e-6;
```

We then we iterate over all states and check if a state has not been handled. We check whether a target bit has been set and obtain the other base state's index in variable `xor_index`. The amplitudes for the $|0\rangle$ and $|1\rangle$ basis states are stored in `tnot` and `t`.

```
/* perform the actual matrix multiplication */
for (int i = 0; i < reg->size; ++i) {
    if (!done[i]) {
        /* determine if the target of the basis state is set */
        int is_set = reg->state[i] & (static_cast<state_t>(1) <<
        ↪ target);
        int xor_index =
            get_state(reg->state[i] ^
            (static_cast<state_t>(1) << target), reg);
        cmplx tnot = xor_index >= 0 ? reg->amplitude[xor_index] : 0;
        cmplx t = reg->amplitude[i];
    }
    [...]
}
```

The matrix multiplication follows the patterns we've seen before for the fast gate application in Section 4.5. If states are found, we apply the gate. If the XOR'ed state was not found, this means we have to add a new state and perform the multiplication:

```
if (is_set) {
    reg->amplitude[i] = m[2] * tnot + m[3] * t;
} else {
    reg->amplitude[i] = m[0] * t + m[1] * tnot;
}

if (xor_index >= 0) {
    if (is_set) {
        reg->amplitude[xor_index] = m[0] * tnot + m[1] * t;
    } else {
        reg->amplitude[xor_index] = m[2] * t + m[3] * tnot;
    }
} else { /* new basis state will be created */
    if (abs(m[1]) == 0.0 && is_set) break;
    if (abs(m[2]) == 0.0 && !is_set) break;

    reg->state[next_state] =
        reg->state[i] ^ (static_cast<state_t>(1) << target);
    reg->amplitude[next_state] = is_set ? m[1] * t : m[2] * t;
    next_state += 1;
}
```

```
    if (xor_index >= 0) {
        done[xor_index] = 1;
    }
```

As a final step, we filter out the states with a probability close to 0. This code densifies the array by moving up all nonzero elements before finally reallocating the amplitude and state arrays to a smaller size (which is actually a redundant operation):

```
reg->size += addsize;
free(done);

/* remove basis states with extremely small amplitude */
if (reg->hashw) {
    int decsize = 0;
    for (int i = 0, j = 0; i < reg->size; ++i) {
        if (probability(reg->amplitude[i]) < limit) {
            j++;
            decsize++;
        } else if (j) {
            reg->state[i - j] = reg->state[i];
            reg->amplitude[i - j] = reg->amplitude[i];
        }
    }

    if (decsize) {
        reg->size -= decsize;

        # Note that these 2 realloc's are redundant and not needed.
        // reg->amplitude = static_cast<cmplx *>(
        //    realloc(reg->amplitude, reg->size * sizeof(cmplx)));
        // reg->state = static_cast<state_t *>(
        //    realloc(reg->state, reg->size * sizeof(state_t)));
    }
}
```

A.7 Premature Optimization, Second Act

Here is an anecdote that might serve as a lesson. After implementing the code and running initial benchmarks, it appeared obvious that the repeated iteration over the memory just had to be a bottleneck. Some form of mini-JIT (Just-In-Time compilation) should be helpful, which first collects all the operations and then fuses gate applications into the same loop iteration. The goal would be to significantly reduce repeated iterations over the states to avoid the memory traffic which, again, just had to be the problem. The code is available online. It might become valuable in the future, as other performance bottlenecks are being resolved.

The goal of the main routine was to execute something like the following, with just one outer loop and a switch statement over all superposition-preserving gates:

```
[...]
void Execute(qureg *reg) {
    for (int i = 0; i < reg->size; ++i) {
      for (auto op : op_list_) {
        switch (op.op()) {
          case op_t::X:
            reg->bit_xor(i, op.target());
            break;

          case op_t::Y:
            reg->bit_xor(i, op.target());
            if (reg->bit_is_set(i, op.target()))
              reg->amplitude[i] *= cmplx(0, 1.0);
            else
              reg->amplitude[i] *= cmplx(0, -1.0);
            break;

          case op_t::Z:
            if (reg->bit_is_set(i, op.target())) {
              reg->amplitude[i] *= -1;
            }
            Break;
    [...] }}}}
```

As a complete surprise, running the JIT'ed version produced a performance improvement of 0%. Simple profiling then revealed that about 96% of the execution time was spent in reconstructing the hash table. Gate application wasn't a performance bottleneck at all. Lesson learned – intuition is good; validation is better. Didn't we mention this before?

A.8   Actual Performance Optimization

As noted above, reconstructing the hash table is the most expensive operation in this library. The hash table is sized to hold all potential states, given the number of qubits. However, even for complex algorithms, the actual maximal number of states with nonzero probability can be quite small. For example, for two benchmarks we extract from quantum arithmetic (Arith) and order finding (Order), we show the maximum number of nonzero states reached (8,192) and, given the number of qubits involved, the theoretical maximal number of states. The percentage is 3.125% for Order, and only 0.012% for Arith. It has a lot more qubits and, hence, a very large potential number of states.

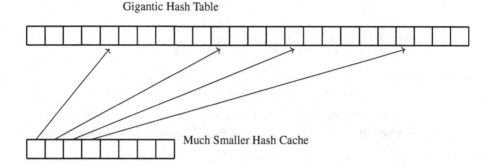

Gigantic Hash Table

Much Smaller Hash Cache

Figure A.1 A caching scheme to accelerate hash table zeroing.

```
Arith:  Maximum of states: 8192, theoretical: 67108864, 0.012%
Order:  Maximum of states: 8192, theoretical: 262144, 3.125%
```

During execution, the number of states changes dynamically in powers of two as libq removes states that are very close to 0.0. Therefore, there is an opportunity to augment the hash table and track, or cache, the addresses of elements that have been set, up to a given threshold, for example, up to 64K elements.

To reset the hash table, we iterate over this *hash cache* and zero out the populated elements in the hash table, as shown in Figure A.1. There will be a crossover point. For some size of the hash cache, just linearly sweeping the hash table will be faster than the random memory access patterns from the cache because of hardware prefetching dynamics. We picked 64K as cache size, which, for our given examples, improves the runtime significantly. This is an interesting space to experiment in, trying to find better heuristics and data structures.

In function libq_reconstruct_hash, we additionally maintain an array called hash_hits which holds the addresses of states in the main hash table, along with a counter reg->hits of those. Then, we selectively zero out only those memory addresses in the hash table that we cached. If the hash cache was not big enough, we have to resort to zeroing out the full hash table:

```
void libq_reconstruct_hash(qureg *reg) {
  reg->hash_computes += 1;

  if (reg->hash_caching && reg->hits < HASH_CACHE_SIZE) {
    for (int i = 0; i < reg->hits; ++i) {
      reg->hash[reg->hash_hits[i]] = 0;
      reg->hash_hits[i] = 0;
    }
    reg->hits = 0;
  } else {
    memset(reg->hash, 0, (1 << reg->hashw) * sizeof(int));
    memset(reg->hash_hits, 0, reg->hits * sizeof(int));
```

```
    reg->hits = 0;
  }
  for (int i = 0; i < reg->size; ++i) {
    libq_add_hash(reg->state[i], i, reg);
  }
}
```

All that's left to do is to fill in this array hash_hits whenever we add a new element in libq_add_hash using the following code at the very bottom:

```
[...]
reg->hash[i] = pos + 1;
 if (reg->hash_caching && reg->hits < HASH_CACHE_SIZE) {
   reg->hash_hits[reg->hits] = i;
   reg->hits += 1;
 }
```

The performance gains from this optimization can be substantial, depending on the characteristics of an algorithm. Anecdotal evidence points to improvements in the range of 20–30% for Arith and Order, as long as the nonzero states fit in the hash cache.

References

S. Aaronson and D. Gottesman. Improved simulation of stabilizer circuits. *Physical Review A*, 70(5), 2004. doi: 10.1103/physreva.70.052328.

J. Abhijith, A. Adetokunbo, J. Ambrosiano, et al. Quantum algorithm implementations for beginners, 2020. arXiv:1804.03719v2 [cs.ET].

T. Altenkirch and A. Green. The quantum IO monad. *Semantic Techniques in Quantum Computation*, 2013. doi: 10.1017/CBO9781139193313.006.

E. Altman, K. R. Brown, G. Carleo, et al. Quantum simulators: Architectures and opportunities. *PRX Quantum*, 2(1), 2021. doi: 10.1103/prxquantum.2.017003.

S. Anders and H. J. Briegel. Fast simulation of stabilizer circuits using a graph-state representation. *Physical Review A*, 73(2), 2006. doi: 10.1103/physreva.73.022334.

D. L. Applegate, R. E. Bixby, V. Chvátal, and W. J. Cook. The Traveling Salesman Problem: A Computational Study. Princeton University Press, 2006. URL www.jstor.org/stable/j.ctt7s8xg.

F. Arute, K. Arya, R. Babbush, et al. Quantum supremacy using a programmable superconducting processor. *Nature*, 574(7779):505–510, 2019. doi: 10.1038/s41586-019-1666-5.

F. Arute, K. Arya, R, Babbush, et al. Supplementary information: Quantum supremacy using a programmable superconducting processor. https://arxiv.org/pdf/1910.11333.pdf, 2020.

A. Barenco, C. H. Bennett, R. Cleve, et al. Elementary gates for quantum computation. *Physical Review A*, 52(5):3457–3467, 1995. doi: 10.1103/physreva.52.3457.

S. Beauregard. Circuit for Shor's algorithm using 2n+3 qubits. *Quantum Information and Compututation*, 3(2):175–185, 2003.

J. S. Bell. On the Einstein Podolsky Rosen paradox. *Physics Physique Fizika*, 1:195–200, 1964. doi: 10.1103/PhysicsPhysiqueFizika.1.195.

C. H. Bennett. Logical reversibility of computation. *IBM Journal of Research and Development*, 17(6):525–532, 1973. doi: 10.1147/rd.176.0525.

C. H. Bennett, G. Brassard, C. Crépeau, R. Jozsa, A. Peres, and W. K. Wootters. Teleporting an unknown quantum state via dual classical and Einstein–Podolsky–Rosen channels. *Physical Review Letters*, 70:1895–1899, 1993. doi: 10.1103/PhysRevLett.70.1895.

D. W. Berry and B. C. Sanders. Quantum teleportation and entanglement swapping for systems of arbitrary spin. In *2002 Summaries of Papers Presented at the Quantum Electronics and Laser Science Conference*, pp. 265–, 2002. doi: 10.1109/QELS.2002.1031404.

S. Bettelli, T. Calarco, and L. Serafini. Toward an architecture for quantum programming. *The European Physical Journal D – Atomic, Molecular and Optical Physics*, 25(2):181–200, 2003. doi: 10.1140/epjd/e2003-00242-2.

B. Bichsel, M. Baader, T. Gehr, and M. T. Vechev. Silq: a high-level quantum language with safe uncomputation and intuitive semantics. In A. F. Donaldson and E. Torlak, eds., *Proceedings of the 41st ACM SIGPLAN International Conference on Programming Language Design and Implementation, PLDI 2020, London, UK, June 15–20, 2020,* pp. 286–300. ACM, 2020. doi: 10.1145/3385412.3386007.

S. Boixo, S. V. Isakov, V. N. Smelyanskiy, et al. Characterizing quantum supremacy in near-term devices. *Nature Physics,* 14(6):595–600, 2018. doi: 10.1038/s41567-018-0124-x.

G. Brassard, P. Høyer, M. Mosca, and A. Tapp. Quantum amplitude amplification and estimation. *Quantum Computation and Information,* pp. 53–74, 2002. doi: 10.1090/conm/305/05215.

I. Buck, T. Foley, D. Horn, et al. Brook for GPUs: Stream computing on graphics hardware. *ACM Transactions on Graphics,* 23:777–786, 2004. doi: 10.1145/1186562.1015800.

H. Buhrman, R. Cleve, J. Watrous, and R. de Wolf. Quantum fingerprinting. *Physical Review Letters,* 87(16), 2001. doi: 10.1103/physrevlett.87.167902.

H. Buhrman, C. Dürr, M. Heiligman, et al. Quantum algorithms for element distinctness. *SIAM Journal on Computing,* 34(6):1324–1330, 2005. doi: 10.1137/s0097539702402780.

B. Butscher and H. Weimer. libquantum. www.libquantum.de/, 2013. Accessed: 2021-02-10.

A. M. Childs, R. Cleve, E. Deotto, E. Farhi, S. Gutmann, and D. A. Spielman. Exponential algorithmic speedup by a quantum walk. *Proceedings of the Thirty-Fifth ACM Symposium on Theory of Computing – STOC '03,* 2003. doi: 10.1145/780542.780552.

A.M. Childs, R. Cleve, S. P. Jordan, and D. Yonge-Mallo. Discrete-query quantum algorithm for nand trees. *Theory of Computing,* 5(1):119–123, 2009. doi: 10.4086/toc.2009.v005a005.

F. T. Chong, D. Franklin, and M. Martonosi. Programming languages and compiler design for realistic quantum hardware. *Nature,* 549(7671):180–187, 2017. doi: 10.1038/nature23459.

D. Coppersmith. An approximate Fourier transform useful in quantum factoring. *arXiv e-prints,* art. quant-ph/0201067, Jan. 2002.

D. G. Cory, M. D. Price, W. Maas, et al. Experimental quantum error correction. *Physical Review Letters,* 81(10):2152–2155, 1998. doi: 10.1103/physrevlett.81.2152.

A. W. Cross, L. S. Bishop, J. A. Smolin, and J. M. Gambetta. Open quantum assembly language, 2017. arXiv:1707.03429.

C. M. Dawson and M. A. Nielsen. The Solovay–Kitaev algorithm. *Quantum Information and Computation,* 6(1):81–95, 2006.

H. De Raedt, F. Jin, D. Willsch, et al. Massively parallel quantum computer simulator, eleven years later. *Computer Physics Communications,* 237:47–61, 2019. doi: 10.1016/j.cpc.2018.11.005.

W. Dean. Computational complexity theory. In E. N. Zalta, ed., *The Stanford Encyclopedia of Philosophy.* Metaphysics Research Lab, Stanford University, 2016.

D. Deutsch. Quantum theory, the Church–Turing principle and the universal quantum computer. *Proceedings of the Royal Society of London Series A,* 400(1818):97–117, 1985. doi: 10.1098/rspa.1985.0070.

D. Deutsch and R. Jozsa. Rapid solution of problems by quantum computation. *Proceedings of the Royal Society of London. Series A,* 439(1907):553–558, 1992. doi: 10.1098/rspa.1992.0167.

S. J. Devitt, W. J. Munro, and K. Nemoto. Quantum error correction for beginners. *Reports on Progress in Physics,* 76(7):076001, 2013. doi: 10.1088/0034-4885/76/7/076001.

Y. Ding and F. T. Chong. Quantum computer systems: Research for noisy intermediate-scale quantum computers. *Synthesis Lectures on Computer Architecture,* 15(2):1–227, 2020. doi: 10.2200/S01014ED1V01Y202005CAC051.

Y. Ding, A. Holmes, A. Javadi-Abhari, D. Franklin, M. Martonosi, and F. Chong. Magic-state functional units: Mapping and scheduling multi-level distillation circuits for fault-tolerant quantum architectures. *2018 51st Annual IEEE/ACM International Symposium on Microarchitecture (MICRO)*, 2018. doi: 10.1109/micro.2018.00072.

Y. Ding, X.-C. Wu, A. Holmes, A. Wiseth, D. Franklin, M. Martonosi, and F. T. Chong. Square: Strategic quantum ancilla reuse for modular quantum programs via cost-effective uncomputation. *2020 ACM/IEEE 47th Annual International Symposium on Computer Architecture (ISCA)*, 2020. doi: 10.1109/isca45697.2020.00054.

B. L. Douglas and J. B. Wang. Efficient quantum circuit implementation of quantum walks, *Physical Review A*, 79:1050–2947, 2009. doi: 10.1103/PHYSREVA.79.052335.

T. G. Draper. Addition on a quantum computer. *arXiv e-prints*, art. quant-ph/0008033, 2000.

A. Einstein, B. Podolsky, and N. Rosen. Can quantum-mechanical description of physical reality be considered complete? *Physical Review*, 47:777–780, 1935. doi: 10.1103/PhysRev.47.777.

E. Farhi, J. Goldstone, and S. Gutmann. A quantum approximate optimization algorithm, 2014. URL https://arxiv.org/abs/1411.4028.

J. Faye. Copenhagen interpretation of quantum mechanics. In E. N. Zalta, ed., *The Stanford Encyclopedia of Philosophy*. Metaphysics Research Lab, Stanford University, 2019.

R. Feynman. *The Character of Physical Law*. MIT Press, 1965.

D. A. Fleisch. *A Student's Guide to the Schroedinger Equation*. Cambridge University Press, 2020.

M. P. Frank, U. H. Meyer-Baese, I. Chiorescu, L. Oniciuc, and R. A. van Engelen. Space-efficient simulation of quantum computers. *Proceedings of the 47th Annual Southeast Regional Conference on – ACM-SE 47*, 2009. doi: 10.1145/1566445.1566554.

P. Fu, K. Kishida, N. J. Ross, and P. Selinger. A tutorial introduction to quantum circuit programming in dependently typed Proto-Quipper, 2020. URL https://arxiv.org/abs/2005.08396.

J. Gambetta, D. M. Rodríguez, A. Javadi-Abhari, et al. Qiskit/qiskit-terra: Qiskit Terra 0.7.2, 2019. URL https://doi.org/10.5281/zenodo.2656592.

J. C. Garcia-Escartin and P. Chamorro-Posada. Equivalent quantum circuits, 2011. https://arxiv.org/abs/1110.2998.

S. Garhwal, M. Ghorani, and A. Ahmad. Quantum programming language: A systematic review of research topic and top cited languages. *Archives of Computational Methods in Engineering*, 28(2):289–310, 2021. doi: 10.1007/s11831-019-09372-6.

G. Ghirardi and A. Bassi. Collapse theories. In E. N. Zalta, ed., *The Stanford Encyclopedia of Philosophy*. Metaphysics Research Lab, Stanford University, 2020.

C. Gidney. Asymptotically Efficient Quantum Karatsuba Multiplication, 2019. https://arxiv.org/abs/1904.07356.

C. Gidney. Quirk online quantum simulator. https://algassert.com/quirk, 2021a. Accessed: 2021-02-10.

C. Gidney. Breaking down the quantum swap. https://algassert.com/post/1717, 2021b. Accessed: 2021-02-10.

P. Gokhale, A. Javadi-Abhari, N. Earnest, Y. Shi, and F. T. Chong. Optimized quantum compilation for near-term algorithms with OpenPulse. In *2020 53rd Annual IEEE/ACM International Symposium on Microarchitecture (MICRO)*, pp. 186–200, 2020. doi: 10.1109/MICRO50266.2020.00027.

Google. Quantum supremacy using a programmable superconducting processor. https://ai
.googleblog.com/2019/10/quantum-supremacy-using-programmable.html, 2019. Accessed:
2021-02-10.

Google. C++ style guide. http://google.github.io/styleguide/cppguide.html, 2021a. Accessed:
2021-02-10.

Google. Python style guide. http://google.github.io/styleguide/pyguide.html, 2021b. Accessed:
2021-02-10.

Google. Cirq. https://cirq.readthedocs.io/en/stable/, 2021c. Accessed: 2021-02-10.

Google. qsim and qsimh. https://quantumai.google/qsim, 2021d. Accessed: 2021-02-10.

Graphviz.org. Graphviz, 2021. Accessed: 2021-02-10.

A. S. Green, P. L. Lumsdaine, N. J. Ross, P. Selinger, and B. Valiron. Quipper: A scalable
quantum programming language. In *Proceedings of the 34th ACM SIGPLAN Conference
on Programming Language Design and Implementation*, p. 333–342, Seattle, Washington,
USA, 2013. Association for Computing Machinery. doi: 10.1145/2491956.2462177.

D. M. Greenberger, M. A. Horne, and A. Zeilinger. Going beyond Bell's theorem, 2008. doi:
10.1007/978-94-017-0849-4_10.

L. K. Grover. A fast quantum mechanical algorithm for database search. In *Proceedings of the
Twenty-Eighth Annual ACM Symposium on Theory of Computing*, STOC '96, pp. 212–219,
New York, NY, 1996. Association for Computing Machinery. doi: 10.1145/237814.237866.

G. G. Guerreschi, J. Hogaboam, F. Baruffa, and N. P. D. Sawaya. Intel quantum simulator:
A cloud-ready high-performance simulator of quantum circuits. *Quantum Science and
Technology*, 5(3):034007, 2020. doi: 10.1088/2058-9565/ab8505.

T. Häner and D. S. Steiger. 0.5 petabyte simulation of a 45-qubit quantum circuit. *Proceedings
of the International Conference for High Performance Computing, Networking, Storage and
Analysis*, Nov 2017. doi: 10.1145/3126908.3126947.

S. Haroche and J.-M. Raimond. Quantum computing: Dream or nightmare? *Physics Today*,
49:51–52, 1996.

M. P. Harrigan, K. J. Sung, M. Neeley, et al. Quantum approximate optimization of non-planar
graph problems on a planar superconducting processor. *Nature Physics*, 17(3):332–336,
2021. doi: 10.1038/s41567-020-01105-y.

A. W. Harrow and A. Montanaro. Quantum computational supremacy. *Nature*, 549(7671):
203–209, 2017. doi: 10.1038/nature23458.

R. Hundt, S. Mannarswamy, and D. Chakrabarti. Practical structure layout optimization and
advice. In *International Symposium on Code Generation and Optimization, CGO 2006*,
2006. doi: 10.1109/CGO.2006.29.

IARPA. Quantum Computer Science (QCS) Program Broad Agency Announcement (BAA).
https://beta.sam.gov/opp/637e87ac1274d030ce2ab69339ccf93c/view, 2010. Accessed:
2021-02-10.

IBM. IBM Q 16 Rueschlikon V1.x.x. https://github.com/Qiskit/ibmq-device-information/tree/
master/backends/rueschlikon/V1, 2021a. Accessed: 2021-02-10.

IBM. Quantum Computation Center. www.ibm.com/blogs/research/2019/09/quantum-
computation-center/, 2021b. Accessed: 2021-02-10.

Intel. Intel quantum simulator. https://github.com/iqusoft/intel-qs, 2021. Accessed: 2021-02-10.

A. Javadi-Abhari, S. Patil, D. Kudrow, et al. ScaffCC: A framework for compilation and analysis
of quantum computing programs. In *Proceedings of the 11th ACM Conference on Computing
Frontiers*, CF '14, New York, NY, 2014. Association for Computing Machinery. doi: 10.
1145/2597917.2597939.

T. Jones and S. Benjamin. QuESTlink—Mathematica embiggened by a hardware-optimised quantum emulator. *Quantum Science and Technology*, 5(3):034012, 2020. doi: 10.1088/ 2058-9565/ab8506.

T. Jones, A. Brown, I. Bush, and S. C. Benjamin. Quest and high performance simulation of quantum computers. *Scientific Reports*, 9(1):10736, 2019. doi: 10.1038/ s41598-019-47174-9.

S. Jordan. Quantum algorithm zoo. https://quantumalgorithmzoo.org/, 2021. Accessed: 2021-02-10.

P. Kaye, R. Laflamme, and M. Mosca. *An Introduction to Quantum Computing*. Oxford University Press, Inc., 2007.

J. Kempe. Quantum random walks: An introductory overview. *Contemporary Physics*, 44(4):307–327, 2003. doi: 10.1080/00107151031000110776.

N. Khammassi, I. Ashraf, X. Fu, C. G. Almudever, and K. Bertels. QX: A high-performance quantum computer simulation platform. In *Design, Automation Test in Europe Conference Exhibition, 2017*, pp. 464–469, 2017. doi: 10.23919/DATE.2017.7927034.

N. Khammassi, G. G. Guerreschi, I. Ashraf, et al. cQASM v1.0: Towards a common quantum assembly language, 2018.

A. Y. Kitaev, A. H. Shen, and M. N. Vyalyi. *Classical and Quantum Computation*. American Mathematical Society, 2002.

V. Kliuchnikov, A. Bocharov, M. Roetteler, and J. Yard. A framework for approximating qubit unitaries, 2015. arXiv:1510.03888v1 [quant-ph]

E. Knill. Conventions for quantum pseudocode, 1996. doi: 10.2172/366453.

D. E. Knuth. Computer science and its relation to mathematics. *The American Mathematical Monthly*, 81(4):323–343, 1974. doi: 10.1080/00029890.1974.11993556.

D. Landauer. Wikipedia: Landauer's principle, 1973. URL https://en.wikipedia.org/wiki/ Landauer's%27s%95principle. [Online; accessed 09-Jan-2021].

C. Lattner and V. Adve. LLVM: A compilation framework for lifelong program analysis & transformation. In *Proceedings of the International Symposium on Code Generation and Optimization: Feedback-Directed and Runtime Optimization*, CGO '04, p. 75, 2004. IEEE Computer Society.

T. Leao. Shor's algorithm in Qiskit. https://github.com/ttlion/ShorAlgQiskit, 2021. Accessed: 2021-02-10.

J. Liu, L. Bello, and H. Zhou. Relaxed peephole optimization: A novel compiler optimization for quantum circuits. *2021 IEEE/ACM International Symposium on Code Generation and Optimization (CGO)*, 2021, pp. 301–314, doi: 10.1109/CGO51591.2021.9370310.

A. Lucas. Ising formulations of many NP problems. *Frontiers in Physics*, 2, 2014. doi: 10.3389/ fphy.2014.00005.

F. Magniez, M. Santha, and M. Szegedy. Quantum algorithms for the triangle problem. In *Proceedings of SODA'05*, pp. 1109–1117, 2005.

I. L. Markov, A. Fatima, S. V. Isakov, and S. Boixo. Quantum supremacy is both closer and farther than it appears, 2018. arXiv:1807.10749v3 [quant-ph]

W. M. McKeeman. Peephole optimization. *Communications of the ACM*, 8(7):443–444, 1965. doi: 10.1145/364995.365000.

Mermin, N. David. What's wrong with this pillow? *Physics Today*, 42(4):9, 1989. doi: 10.1063/ 1.2810963.

N. D. Mermin. *Quantum Computer Science: An Introduction*. Cambridge University Press, 2007. doi: 10.1017/CBO9780511813870.

Microsoft Q#. Q#. https://docs.microsoft.com/en-us/quantum/, 2021. Accessed: 2021-02-10.

Microsoft QDK Simulators. Microsoft QDK Simulators. https://docs.microsoft.com/en-us/azure/quantum/user-guide/machines/, 2021. Accessed: 2021-02-10.

M. Mosca. Quantum algorithms, 2008. arXiv:0808.0369v1 [quant-ph]

P. Murali, N. M. Linke, M. Martonosi, et al. Full-stack, real-system quantum computer studies: Architectural comparisons and design insights, Association for Computing Machinery, New York, NY, USA 2019. doi: 10.1145/3307650.3322273.

Y. Nam, N. J. Ross, Y. Su, A. M. Childs, and D. Maslov. Automated optimization of large quantum circuits with continuous parameters. *npj Quantum Information*, 4(1), 2018. doi: 10.1038/s41534-018-0072-4.

J. Nickolls, I. Buck, M. Garland, and K. Skadron. Scalable parallel programming with CUDA: Is CUDA the parallel programming model that application developers have been waiting for? *Queue*, 6(2):40–53, 2008. doi: 10.1145/1365490.1365500.

M. A. Nielsen and I. L. Chuang. *Quantum Computation and Quantum Information: 10th Anniversary Edition*. Cambridge University Press, 10th edition, 2011.

T. Norsen. *Foundations of Quantum Mechanics*. Springer International Publishing, 2017.

Oak Ridge National Laboratory. Summit Supercomputer. www.olcf.ornl.gov/summit/, 2021. Accessed: 2021-02-10.

B. Ömer. QCL – A programming language for quantum computers, Unpublished Master's thesis, Technical University of Vienna, 2000. http://tph.tuwien.ac.at/~oemer/doc/quprog.pdf.

B. Ömer. Classical concepts in quantum programming. *International Journal of Theoretical Physics*, 44(7):943–955, 2005. doi: 10.1007/s10773-005-7071-x.

A. Paler, R. Wille, and S. J. Devitt. Wire recycling for quantum circuit optimization. *Physical Review A*, 94(4), 2016. doi: 10.1103/physreva.94.042337.

F. Pan and P. Zhang. Simulating the Sycamore quantum supremacy circuits, 2021. arXiv:2103.03074v1 [quant-ph].

R. B. Patel, J. Ho, F. Ferreyrol, T. C. Ralph, and G. J. Pryde. A quantum Fredkin gate. *Science Advances*, 2(3), 2016. doi: 10.1126/sciadv.1501531.

B. Patra, J. P. G. van Dijk, S. Subramanian, et al. A scalable cryo-CMOS 2-to-20GHz digitally intensive controller for 4x32 frequency multiplexed spin qubits/transmons in 22nm FinFET technology for quantum computers. In *2020 IEEE International Solid-State Circuits Conference – (ISSCC)*, pp. 304–306, 2020. doi: 10.1109/ISSCC19947.2020.9063109.

E. Pednault, J. A. Gunnels, G. Nannicini, L. Horesh, and R. Wisnieff. Leveraging secondary storage to simulate deep 54-qubit Sycamore circuits, 2019. arXiv:1910.09534.

A. Peruzzo, J. McClean, P. Shadbolt, et al. A variational eigenvalue solver on a photonic quantum processor. *Nature Communications*, 5(1):4213, 2014. doi: 10.1038/ncomms5213.

J. Preskill. Quantum computing and the entanglement frontier, 2012. arXiv:1203.5813v3 [quant-ph].

J. Preskill. Quantum computing in the NISQ era and beyond. *Quantum*, 2:79, 2018. doi: 10.22331/q-2018-08-06-79.

PSI Online. PSI. http://psilang.org/, 2021. Accessed: 2021-02-10.

QCL Online. QCL. http://tph.tuwien.ac.at/~oemer/qcl.html, 2021.

I. Qiskit. IBM qiskit simulators. https://qiskit.org/documentation/tutorials/simulators/1_aer_provider.html, 2021. Accessed: 2021-02-10.

Quantiki. List of simulators. https://quantiki.org/wiki/list-qc-simulators, 2021. Accessed: 2021-02-10.

Quipper Online. Quipper. www.mathstat.dal.ca/~selinger/quipper/, 2021. Accessed: 2021-02-10.

F. Rios and P. Selinger. A categorical model for a quantum circuit description language (extended abstract). *Electronic Proceedings in Theoretical Computer Science*, 266:164–178, 2018. doi: 10.4204/eptcs.266.11.

R. L. Rivest, A. Shamir, and L. Adleman. A method for obtaining digital signatures and public-key cryptosystems. *Communications of the ACM*, 21:120–126, 1978.

L. Rolf. Is quantum mechanics useful? *Philosophical Transactions of the Royal Society of London. Series A: Physical and Engineering Sciences*, 353:367–376, 1995. doi: 10.1098/rsta.1995.0106.

N. J. Ross. Algebraic and logical methods in quantum computation, 2017. URL https://arxiv.org/abs/1510.02198.

N. J. Ross and P. Selinger. Optimal ancilla-free Clifford+T approximation of z-rotations. *Quantum Information and Computation*, 11–12:901–953, 2016.

N. J. Ross and P. Selinger. Exact and approximate synthesis of quantum circuits. www.mathstat.dal.ca/~selinger/newsynth/, 2021. Accessed: 2021-02-10.

B. Rudiak-Gould. The sum-over-histories formulation of quantum computing. *arXiv e-prints*, art. quant-ph/0607151, 2006.

V. V. Shende, I. L. Markov, and S. S. Bullock. Minimal universal two-qubit controlled-NOT-based circuits. *Physical Review A*, 69(6):062321, 2004. doi: 10.1103/physreva.69.062321.

P. W. Shor. Algorithms for quantum computation: Discrete logarithms and factoring. In *Proceedings 35th Annual Symposium on Foundations of Computer Science*, pp. 124–134, 1994. doi: 10.1109/SFCS.1994.365700.

P. W. Shor. Scheme for reducing decoherence in quantum computer memory. *Physics Review A*, 52:R2493–R2496, 1995. doi: 10.1103/PhysRevA.52.R2493.

D. Simon. On the power of quantum computation. In *Proceedings 35th Annual Symposium on Foundations of Computer Science*, pp. 116–123, 1994. doi: 10.1109/SFCS.1994.365701.

M. Smelyanskiy, N. P. D. Sawaya, and A. Aspuru-Guzik. qHiPSTER: The quantum high performance software testing environment, 2016. arXiv:1601.07195v2 [quant-ph].

M. Soeken, S. Frehse, R. Wille, and R. Drechsler. RevKit: An open source toolkit for the design of reversible circuits. In *Reversible Computation 2011*, vol. 7165 of *Lecture Notes in Computer Science*, pp. 64–76, 2012. RevKit is available at www.revkit.org.

M. Soeken, H. Riener, W. Haaswijk, et al. The EPFL logic synthesis libraries, 2019. arXiv:1805.05121v2.

A. Steane. Multiple particle interference and quantum error correction. *Proceedings of the Royal Society of London. Series A: Mathematical, Physical and Engineering Sciences*, 452(1954):2551–2577, 1996. doi: 10.1098/rspa.1996.0136.

D. S. Steiger, T. Häner, and M. Troyer. ProjectQ: An open source software framework for quantum computing. *Quantum*, 2:49, 2018. doi: 10.22331/q-2018-01-31-49.

K. M. Svore, A. V. Aho, A. W. Cross, I. Chuang, and I. L. Markov. A layered software architecture for quantum computing design tools. *Computer*, 39(1):74–83, 2006. doi: 10.1109/MC.2006.4.

A. van Tonder. A lambda calculus for quantum computation. *SIAM Journal on Computing*, 33(5):1109–1135, 2004. doi: 10.1137/s0097539703432165.

J. D. Whitfield, J. Biamonte, and A. Aspuru-Guzik. Simulation of electronic structure Hamiltonians using quantum computers. *Molecular Physics*, 109(5):735–750, 2011. doi: 10.1080/00268976.2011.552441.

Wikipedia. KD-Trees. https://en.wikipedia.org/wiki/K-d_tree, 2021a. Accessed: 2021-02-10.

Wikipedia. ECC, Error correction code memory. https://en.wikipedia.org/wiki/ECC_memory, 2021b. Accessed: 2021-02-10.

Wikipedia. Extended Euclidean algorithm. https://en.wikipedia.org/wiki/Extended_Euclidean_algorithm, 2021c. Accessed: 2021-02-10.

Wikipedia. Gradient descent. https://en.wikipedia.org/wiki/Gradient_descent, 2021d. Accessed: 2021-02-10.

C. P. Williams. *Explorations in Quantum Computing*. Springer-Verlag, London, 2011. doi: 10.1007/978-1-84628-887-6.

E. Wilson, S. Singh, and F. Mueller. Just-in-time quantum circuit transpilation reduces noise, 2020. DOI: 10.1109/QCE49297.2020.00050.

W. K. Wootters and W. H. Zurek. A single quantum cannot be cloned. *Nature*, 299(5886):802–803, 1982. doi: 10.1038/299802a0.

X. Xue, B. Patra, J. P. G. van Dijk, et al. Cmos-based cryogenic control of silicon quantum circuits. *Nature*, 593(7858):205–210, 2021. doi: 10.1038/s41586-021-03469-4.

Index

$\oplus$ symbol, controlled qubit in quantum circuit
notation, 53
$\otimes$ Kronecker product
operator, 16
$\star$ operator for Kronecker
product, 11, 16
@ operator for matrix multiplication, 11
5-qubit error correction code, 291
7-qubit Steane code, 291
9-qubit Shor error correction code, 285, 289

Addition
Constants, 179
Increment operator, 236
Quantum arithmetic, 172–177
Quantum gates, 172–174
qc data structure, 134
Testing quantum arithmetic, 178
Adjoint gates
adjoint() function for gates, 26
qc data structure, 130
Conjugate synonym, 6
Adjoint operators
adjoint() function for operators, 85
ALAP Scheduling, 307
Algorithm references, 277
Amdahl's law, 286
Amplitude amplification, 227–230
Amplitude damping, 283
Amplitude estimation, 230–234
Quantum counting, 230–234
Ancilla qubits (ancillae)
About, 66
Ancilla registers, 124
Code to create and initialize, 125
Compiler optimization and, 304
Entanglement, 66, 86
Error correction trick, 286
Multi-controlled gates, 66
Quantum computation, 66
Quipper programming language, 300
Silq programming language, 302
AND logic gates, 92

Ansatz, 245
Arithmetic via quantum gates
Decrement circuit, 236
Full adder, 89–91
Code, 90
Constants, 179
qc data structure, 134
Quantum arithmetic, 172–177
Increment circuit, 236
Multiplication, 177
Powers, 208
Subtraction, 177
Testing quantum arithmetic, 178
Arute, Frank, 150
at (@) operator for matrix multiplication, 11

Basis states of qubits, 13
Constructing a qubit, 15
Density matrices
Diagonal elements, 24
Density matrix diagonal elements, 23
Measurement, 73
Orthonormal set of basis vectors, 13, 15
Superposition as orthonormal basis, 44
Projection operators extracting amplitude, 42
State as superposition, 17
Superposition via Hadamard gates, 44
Hadamard basis, 44
Bell measurement, 98, 99
Bell states, 63
Code, 63
Measurement example, 77
Quipper programming language, 301
Tracing out qubits, 71
Bell, John S., 60, 63
Benchmarking
Benchmark gaming, 150
Cross entropy benchmarking, 150
Gate fast application, 139
Gate faster application in C++, 143
Quantum random circuits, 150
Quantum versus classical computers,
150–152
Sparse representation, 147

Bernstein–Vazirani algorithm
  Oracle form
    Compiler optimization, 308
Bernstein-Vazirani algorithm, 105–108
  Oracle form, 117
  Phase kick rotation gates, 162
Beyond Classical, 149
  About algorithm types, 160
  Computational complexity theory, 122, 149, 159
  Google Sycamore processor, 150
    Benchmarking, 150
    Benchmarking quantum versus classical computers, 150–152
  Quantum random circuits, 150
    Simulation design, 152
    Simulation evaluation, 158
    Simulation implementation, 154
    Simulation metric, 157
    Simulation run estimation, 155–158
Binary fractions, 163
Binary interpretation, 18
Birthday paradox, 191
Bit conversion, 24
Bit index notation for states, 136
Bit iteration, 25
Bit order
  Binary interpretation, 18
  Qubit order, 18
  States, 17
    Two tensored states, 18
Bit-flip errors
  Bit-flip channel, 281
  Bit-flip phase-flip channel, 281
  Combined phase/bit-flip error, 279
  Dissipation-induced error, 279
  Error correction, 286–288
    Shor's 9-qubit code, 289
Bits to binary fractions, 163
Bits-decimal conversion functions, 24
bits2frac() for binary fractions, 163
bits2val() for binary to decimal, 24
bitstring() function, 22
Bloch sphere, 55–60
  About, 35, 55, 242
  Expectation values, 59, 74, 244
  Minus sign as global phase, 59
  Qubit described by, 55–56
    Computing coordinates for given state, 58
  Quirk online simulator, 171
  Relative phase, 35
  Rotation operators, 35
  Single-qubit states only, 59
  Solovay–Kitaev algorithm, 267
  Two degrees of freedom for superdense coding, 102
  Universal gates, 266

Bloch, Felix, 55
Boolean formulas with quantum gates, 92
Born rule, 72
  About projective measurement, 72
BPP (complexity), 149, 159
BQP (complexity), 149, 159
Bra(c)kets, 3
Brakets, 3
Branching, see Controlled gates
Bras
  Dirac notation, 3
  Inner products, 3
    Bra-Ket notation, 3
  Tensor products, 5

C++
  Accelerated gate application, 139–145
    Execution speed, 139, 145
  Extending Python with, 140
  Q language C++ class library, 300
    Transpiler code generation flag, 315
  Sparse representation, 145
    Benchmarking, 147
"Can Quantum-Mechanical Description of Physical Reality Be Considered Complete?" (Einstein, Podolsky, and Rosen), 60
Cartesian coordinates for Bloch sphere, 58
Channels in information theory, 281
  Bit-flip channel, 281
  Bit-flip phase-flip channel, 281
  Depolarization channel, 282
  Phase-flip channel, 281
Circuits
  About function calls and returns, 298
    Scaffold programming language, 298
    Silq programming language, 302
  Compiler optimization and, 304
  Decrement circuit, 236
  Entangler circuits, 61
  Grover's algorithm implemented, 224–227
  Increment circuit, 236
  Intermediate representation capabilities, 314
  Libraries of compiler optimization patterns, 309
  Logic circuits, 91
    Fan-out in QCL, 296
    Gan-out circuits, 92
  Phase kick circuit, 161
  Quantum circuit data structure, 126
    Constructor, 127
    Gates, 129–133
    Gates applied, 128
    Measurements, 131
    Multi-Controlled gates, 132
    Quantum registers, 127
    Qubits added, 128
    Swap and controlled swap gates, 131

Quantum random circuits, 150
  Simulation design, 152
  Simulation evaluation, 158
  Simulation implementation, 154
  Simulation metric, 157
  Simulation run estimation, 155–158
  Qubits
    Ordering of qubits, 18
    qc data structure, 128
    Quantum circuit notation, 52
  Shor's 9-qubit error correction, 289
Cirq commercial system (Google), 303
  Simulators, 321
  Transpilation
    Code generation flag, 315
    Dumper function, 319
Classical arithmetic, *see* Arithmetic via quantum
    gates
Classical computers versus quantum, 150–152
  Summit simulating quantum random circuits,
    158
Clifford gates, 124
Closed quantum systems, 280
CNOT, *see* Controlled-Not gate
CNOT0, *see* Controlled-Not-by-0 gates
Coin toss operator, 235
Column vectors
  Inner products, 3
  Kets
    Dirac notation, 2
    Hermitian conjugate of, 2
  Qubits and states as, 2
Combined phase/bit-flip error, 279
Commercial systems, 303
Compiler design challenges, 293, 309
  About transpilation, 311
  Intermediate representation, 311
  Staged compilation, 311
Compiler optimization, 303
  About, 303
  Classical for classical constructs, 304
  Constant propagation, 304
  Gate approximation, 310
  Gate elimination, 305
  Gate fusion, 306
  Gate parallelization, 307
  Gate scheduling, 306
  High-performance pattern libraries, 309
  Inlining, 304
  Logical to physical mapping, 304, 309
    Resource for information, 310
  Loop unrolling, 304
  Peephole optimization, 307
    Libraries of compiler optimization patterns,
      309
    Relaxed peephole optimization, 308

Physical gate decomposition, 310
  Unentangled qubits, 306
Complex numbers
  2D plane, 2
    Polar coordinates, 55–56
  About, 1
  Conjugates, 1
  Exponentiation, 2
  Modulus, 2
  Norm, 1
  Python, 2
  Qubits as column vectors of, 2
  States as column vectors of, 2
  Tensor comparisons to values, 12
  tensor_type() abstraction, 10
Complexity classes
  BPP, 149, 159
  BQP, 149, 159
  NP, 149
  NP-complete, 149
  NP-hard, 149
  P, 149
Complexity of simulation, 151, 155
Composite kets inner products, 5
Computation reversed, 66
Computational complexity theory, 122,
    149, 159
Conditional execution, *see* Controlled gates
Congruency between numbers, 189
Conjugate Rotations, 274
Conjugates
  Adjoint synonymous with conjugate, 6
  Complex numbers, 1
  Denotation not explicit, 3
  Hermitian conjugate matrix, 6
  Operator adjoint() function, 26
Conjugation
  conjugate() with complex numbers, 2
  Involutivity, 3
Constants in quantum addition, 179
Control register, 124
Controlled gates
  About, 46
  About QCL programming language, 297
  Controlled rotation gates additive, 161
  Controlled-Controlled gates, 48, 85
    Toffoli gates, 49, 85
  Controlled-Controlled-Not gates, 49
    Sets of universal gates, 49
  Controlled-Not gates, 46–49
  Controlled-Not-by-0 gates, 49
  Controlled-U1 gate for quantum arithmetic,
    172
  Controlled-Z gates, 81
    Multi-Controlled-Z gates, 82
  Function of, 46–49

Controlled gates (Cont.)
  Multi-Controlled gates, 86
    Ancilla qubits, 86
    Multi-Controlled-Z gates, 82
    qc data structure, 132
  Multi-controlled gates
    Ancilla qubits, 66
  Nonadjacent controller and controlled qubits, 47
  Notation for gates involved, 46
  qc data structure
    Fast application of gates, 137
    Faster application with C++, 141
    Multi-Controlled gates, 132
  Quantum circuit notation
    Controlled-X gates, 53
    Controlled-Not-by-0 gates built, 53
  Scalability, 48
  Swap gates, 50, 88
    Compiler optimization, 308
    Controlled-Controlled Swap gates, 51
    qc data structure, 131
    Quantum circuit notation, 53
Controlled modular multiplication, 207
Controlled-Controlled gates, 85
  Toffoli gates, 49, 85
    Logic circuits from, 92
Controlled-Controlled-Not gates (CCX-gate), 49
Controlled-Not gates (CNOT; CX)
  Compiler optimization, 308
  Constructor function, 49
  Controlled-Z with Hadamard gates, 82
  Entangler circuits, 62
  Function, 46–49
  GHZ states, 64
  Inverted Controlled-Not gate, 80
  Logic circuits from, 92
  Quantum registers for result storage, 67
  Swap gate action, 51
Controlled-Not-by-0 gates (CNOT0), 49
  Quantum circuit notation, 53
Controlled-U gates under compiler optimization, 308
Controlled-Z gates, 81
  Controlled-Not gates via, 82
  Multi-Controlled-Z gates, 82
Copenhagen interpretation of quantum mechanics, 61
Counters
  Decrement operator, 236
  Increment operator, 236
cQASM, 295
Cross entropy benchmarking (XEB), 150
Cut on graph, 255
CX, *see* Controlled-Not gate

Data registers, 124
  Code to create and initialize, 125
Data structure, *see* Quantum circuit (qc) data structure
Debugging
  Operator matrices for, 81
  qc data structure abstraction, 126
  Reduced density operator, 68
  Tensors compared to values, 12
Decoherence times of technologies, 278
Decoherence-induced phase shift error, 279
Decrement circuit, 236
Density matrices
  About, 9, 68
  Bloch sphere coordinate computation, 58
    Cartesian coordinates, 58
  Outer product of state with itself, 23, 68
  Partial trace derivation, 68
    Code, 69
    Tracing out other qubits, 69
  Probabilities of measuring a basis state, 24
  Quantum computing theory as, 24, 68
  Trace of, 24, 70
Depolarization, 282
Depolarization channel, 282
  Depolarization definition, 282
Deutsch algorithm, 108–117
Deutsch–Jozsa algorithm, 118–121
Diagonal matrices
  Tensor products, 5
Diffusion Operator, 220
Dirac notation
  Bras, 3
  Kets, 2
  Qubits
    0-state and 1-state, 13
    Two tensored states, 18
Discrete phase gates, 39, 164
Dissipation-induced error, 279
Dot products, *see* Inner products
Dual vectors for a ket, 3
Dumper function for all relevant info, 21
  Transpilation, 315

EGCD, *see* Extended Euclidean algorithm
Eigenstates
  About, 7
  Compiler optimization of gates, 306
Eigenvalues, 7
  About, 7
  Compiler optimization of gates, 306
  Hamiltonians, 240, 248
  Hermitian and Pauli matrices, 35
  Phase estimation, 180
  Trace of a matrix, 8
  variational quantum eigensolver, 248

Eigenvectors
  About, 7
  Hamiltonians in Schrödinger equation, 240
  Phase estimation, 180
Einstein, Albert
  Hidden state, 60
  Spooky action at a distance, 60
Electron decoherence time
  Electron spin, 278
  Gallium arsenide, 278
  Gold, 278
Entanglement, 60–65
  About, 60
  Analysis by Scaffold, 299
  Ancilla qubits, 66, 86
  Bell states, 63
    Code, 63
    Tracing out qubits, 71
  Code
    Bell states, 63
    Entangler circuit, 62
    GHZ states, 64
  Compiler optimization and, 306
  Copenhagen interpretation, 61
  Entangler circuits, 61
    Code, 62
  GHZ states, 64
    Code, 64
    Error correction trick, 286
  Maximal entanglement, 64
  Mixed states, 68
    Depolarization, 282
  Product states, 61
  Quantum teleportation, 97–102
  Superdense coding, 102–105
  Swapping, 102
  Teleportation, 97–102
  Tracing out qubits, 71
Entangler circuits, 61
Environmental challenges of quantum computing,
  278–284
Closed versus open quantum systems, 280
Equal superposition of adjacent qubits, 45
Erasure of information resulting in heat dissipation,
  66
Error correction
  About, 278, 284
  Bit-flip errors, 286–288
    Shor's 9-qubit code, 289
  Channels, 281
  Compiler optimization and, 304
  Error correction code memory, 284
  Error syndrome, 286
  Phase-flip errors, 288
    Shor's 9-qubit code, 289
  Quantum computing challenges, 285
  Quantum noise, 278–284

Repetition code, 284
    Majority voting, 285
    No-cloning theorem, 285
    Quantum repetition code, 285
  Resources for information, 291
  Shor's 9-qubit error correction code, 285, 289
Error correction code memory (ECC), 284
Error injection to model quantum noise, 282
  Checking bit-flip error correction, 287
  Gates as quantum noise source, 283
Error syndrome, 286
Euler's formula
  Complex exponentiation, 2
  Phase gate derivation, 38, 165
Euler's identity, 37
Expectation values, 74
  Bloch sphere, 59
  Variational quantum eigensolver, 244
Exponentiation
  Complex numbers, 2
  Operators, 36
Extended Euclidean algorithm, 202

Factorization, 190
Fan-out circuits, 92
  QCL programming language, 296
Fast Gate Application, 134
Feynman, R., xi
Fidelity, 269
Flexible phase gates
  Discrete phase gates, 39
  U1(lambda) gates, 40
Fourier transform, *see* Quantum Fourier transform
    (QFT)
Fractions
  Binary fractions, 163
  π fractions transpilation output, 316
Fredkin gates, 51
Full adder, 89–91
  Code, 90
    qc data structure, 134
  Quantum arithmetic, 172–177
Fused gates, 306

Gallium arsenide (GaAs) electron decoherence
    time, 278
Gate equivalences
  About, 79
  Compiler optimization, 306, 309
  Controlled gate equivalencies listed, 87
    Code to validate, 88
  Controlled-phase symmetry, 82
  Controlled-Z gates, 81
    Controlled-Not gates via, 82
  Inverted Controlled-Not, 80
  Multi-Controlled gates, 86

Gate equivalences (Cont.)
Negate Y-gate, 83
Pauli matrices, 83
Rotation axis changed, 84
Squaring root of gate equals gate, 80
Gates
About operators as gates, 25
About ordering of gate applications, 54
About Scaffold built-ins, 298
Classical-To-Quantum-Circuit tool, 298
Adjoint gates, 130
Application, 27–29
apply() function, 32, 128, 142
Density matrices, 68
Fast application, 134–139
Fast application generalized, 137–139
Faster application with C++, 139–145
Fastest Benchmarked, 147
Fastest with sparse representation, 145–147
Multiple operators in sequence, 31
Multiple qubits, 29–31
Noise reduction via compiler optimization,
304
Norm preserving, 6, 25
Notation for qubit index applied to, 31
Padding operators, 31, 48
Projection operators extracting subspace, 73
Quantum computation, 66
to state ψ at qubit index, 32
Compiler optimization
Gate approximation, 310
Gate elimination, 305
Gate fusion, 306
Gate parallelization, 307
Gate scheduling, 306
Logical to physical mapping, 304, 309
Logical to physical mapping resource for
information, 310
Noise reduction, 304
Physical gate decomposition, 310
Unentangled qubits, 306
Controlled gates, *see* Controlled gates
Equivalences, *see* Gate equivalences
Flexible phase gates
Discrete phase gates, 39
Phase shift or kick gate, 40
Hadamard gates, 44–45
Identity gates, 26, 33
Applied to multiple qubits, 30
Multi-qubit gates
Controlled gates, 46–51
Hadamard gates, 44–45
Single-qubit constructors for, 33
Outer product representation of operator, 43
Phase gates, 38
Discrete phase gates, 39

Phase inversion operator, 219
Phase shift or kick gates, 40
Phases via various gates, 40
Square root of as T-gate, 41
Projection operators, 42
qc data structure, 129
Gates applied, 128
libq implementation, 324–326
Quantum circuit notation, 53
About ordering of gate applications, 54
Applying operator, 52
Quantum noise source, 283
Qubit on Bloch sphere, 56–58
Rk gates, 39
RotationZ-gates versus phase gates, 38
Sets of universal gates, 49
Single-qubit gates, 33–45
Solovay–Kitaev theorem, 266
T-gates
Phases via, 40, 165
Rotation axis changed, 84
Square root of phase gates, 41
Universal gates, 266
U1(lambda) gates, 40
V-gates
Square root of X-gates, 85
V-gates as square roots of X-gates, 41
X-gates, 26, 34
Y-gates, 34
Negate Y-gate, 83
Square root of, 41
Yroot gates, 41
GCD, *see* Greatest common divisor
GHZ states, 64
Error correction trick, 286
Global phase, 59
Bloch sphere, 59
Phase invariance, 59
Relative phase versus, 60
Rotation axis changed, 84
"Going Beyond Bell's Theorem" (Greenberger,
Horne, and Zeilinger), 64
Gold (Au) electron decoherence time, 278
Google
Cirq commercial system, 303
Simulators, 321
Transpilation, 315, 319
Coding style, 12
Underscore in function names, 12
Quantum random circuits, 150, 158
Simulation design, 152
Simulation evaluation, 158
Simulation implementation, 154
Simulation metric, 157
Simulation run estimation, 155–158
Sycamore processor supremacy, 150–152

Gradient descent, 247
Greatest common divisor (GCD), 190
Greenberger, Daniel M., 64
Ground state energy
   About variational quantum eigensolver, 240
   Variational principle, 242–245
Grover's algorithm
   About, 210
   Examples
      Simple numerical, 214
      Two-qubit, 214
   Grover operator, 211, 217
      Constructing, 233
      Implementing, 226
      Quantum counting, 231
   High-level overview, 211
   Implementation, 224–227
   Inversion about the mean, 213
      Implementation, 219–223
      Operator, 223
   Iteration count, 216–218
      Multiple solutions, 228–230
   Multiple solutions, 227–230
   Phase inversion, 212
      Implementation, 218
      Multiple solutions, 227–230
      Operator, 219, 232
   Quantum amplitude amplification, 227–230
   Quantum counting, 230–234

Hadamard basis, 44
   Measuring in, 104
Hadamard gates, 44–45
   Entangler circuits, 61
   Function call syntax via Pauli matrices, 83
   Hadamard basis, 44
      Measuring in, 104
   Hadamard coin, 235
   Its own inverse, 45
   Quantum circuit notation
      Gate applied, 52
   Qubit on Bloch sphere, 56–58
   Random number generator, 78
   Rotation axis changed, 84
   Universal gates, 266
Hamiltonian
   Definition, 241
   Eigenvalues
      About VQE algorithm, 160, 240, 242
      Schrödinger equation derivation, 240
      Variational principle, 242–245
      Variational principle measurements, 248
   Ising spin glass model, 254
      Hamiltonian constructed, 258–260
   Operator, 241
      Hermitian, 241

Hash table in libq, 327, 332
Haskell programming language, 300
   Quipper as embedded DSL, 300
      Oracle automatic construction, 301
   Silq as embedded DSL, 302
Heisenberg uncertainty principle, 241
Helper functions
   Bit conversion, 24
   Bit iteration, 25
Hermitian conjugate vector, 2
Hermitian matrices
   About, 6
   Checking if tensor is Hermitian, 12
   Eigenvalues as real, 7
   Hermitian adjoint matrices, 6
      Expressions, 6
   Hermitian conjugate matrices
      Adjoint synonymous with conjugate, 6
   Projection operators as, 43
   Real vector space basis, 35
   Trace of, 8
Hermitian projector, 43
Hidden state, 60, 63
Hierarchical QASM, 299
High-Performance Computing (HPC) techniques,
   124
Horne, Michael A., 64

IBM
   Qiskit commercial system, 303
      ALAP scheduling of gates, 307
      Algorithm reference, 277
      QASM support, 311
      Simulators, 321
   Sycamore supremacy challenged, 150
   Summit supercomputer, 158
Idempotent projection operators, 43
Identity gates, 26, 33
   Applied to multiple qubits, 30
   Controller and controlled qubits not adjacent,
      47
   Hermitian matrix real vector space, 35
   Phases via, 40
Increment circuit, 236
Increment modulo 9 circuit, 237
Indirect measures of similarity between states,
   93–97
   Swap test code, 96
Information
   Erasure resulting in heat dissipation, 66
   Quantum circuit double lines, 54
   Quantum teleportation, 97–102
   Superdense coding, 102–105
   Teleportation, 97–102
Inner products
   About, 3
   Tensors, 5

Instruction Set Architecture (ISA) of quantum computers, 25
Intel Quantum Simulator, 320
Intermediate representation (IR)
　About circuit capabilities, 314
　Scaffold, 298
　　Classic and quantum mix, 305
　Scalability, 293
　Transpilation, 311
　　About transpilation, 311
　　IR base class, 312
　　IR nodes, 311
　　Quantum circuit extensions, 313
　　Uncomputation, 315
Inversion about the mean, 213
　Implementation, 219–223
　Operator, 223
Involutivity, 3
　Hadamard gates, 45
　Pauli matrices, 35
　Rotations, 36
Ion trap decoherence time, 278
IR, *see* Intermediate representation (IR)
ISA (Instruction Set Architecture) of quantum computers, 25
Ising
　Hamiltonian, 254
　Spin Glass, 254

Junk qubits
　Quantum computation, 66

KD-Tree, 270
Kets
　About, 72
　Composite kets inner products, 5
　Dirac notation, 2
　Dual vectors for, 3
　Hermitian conjugate of, 2
　Inner products, 3
　　Bra-Ket notation, 3
　　Composite kets, 5
　Outer products, 4
　　Trace of, 8
　Tensor products, 5
Knuth, D. E., xi
Krauss operators, 281
Kronecker power function (kpow), 11
Kronecker product, 5, 10
　⊗ operator symbol, 16
　⋆ operator for, 11, 16

Landauer's principle, 66
Landauer, D., 66
Least significant bit, *see* Bit order
Libq, 145

Implementation
　About, 322
　Controlled gates, 325
　Gate application, 328
　Hash table, 327, 332
　Register file, 322
　Superposition-preserving gates, 324
　Superpositioning gates, 326
　libquantum basis, 145
　Transpilation
　　Code generation flag, 315
　　Dumper function, 317
libquantum, 145
　Library for sparse representation, 145
Libquantum library for sparse representation
　Simulation, 320
Libraries of compiler optimization patterns, 309
Logic circuits, 91
　Fan-out circuits, 92
　QCL programming language, 296
"Logical Reversibility of Computation" (Bennett), 66

Majority voting for repetition code, 285
Mathematical notation of gate application, 55
Matrices
　⋆ operator for Kronecker product, 11
　2-dimensional index via projection operators, 43
　Density matrices, 23
　Diagonalization function, 274
　Eigenvalues, 7, 180
　Hermitian, *see* Hermitian matrices
　Matrix multiplication ordering of gate application, 55
　Pauli matrices, 34
　　Hermitian matrix real vector space, 35
　　Involutivity, 35
　Permutation matrices, 12
　Scalability, 122
　Tensoring together, 11
　Trace of matrix, 8
　Transposition, 2
　Unitary, 6
Maximal entanglement, 64
Maximally mixed state, 64
Maximum cut algorithm
　About, 254
　Cut definition, 255
　Ising formulations of NP algorithms, 254
　Maximum cut definition, 255
　Quantum approximate optimization algorithm, 253
　Variational quantum eigensolver, 260
　Weighted maximum cut, 255
　　Computing maximum cut, 257

Graphs constructed, 255
Hamiltonian constructed, 258–260
Measurement gates, 54
Measurements
By peek-a-boo, 131
By peek-a-boo, Grover's algorithm, 226
Entanglement, 60
Error detection challenges, 285
Expectation values, 59, 74, 244
Implementation, 75
Indirect measures of similarity between states, 93–97
Measuring in Hadamard basis, 104
Pauli bases, 242
Projective, 72
Examples, 76
Implementation, 75
qc data structure, 131
Statistical sampling function, 131
Quantum circuit notation, 54
Quantum Fourier transform and, 169
Quantum mechanics postulates, 72
States collapsing on measurement, 13, 60
Born rule, 72
Measurement definition, 72
Renormalization, 74
Mermin, David, 61
Microsoft Q# commercial system, 303
Quantum Developer Kit, 303
Simulators, 321
Microwave cavity decoherence time, 278
Minimum cut problems, 255
Mixed states, 68
Depolarization, 282
Tracing out qubits, 71
MLPerf benchmarks, 150
Modular arithmetic, 189
Controlled modular multiplication, 207
Modular addition, 205–207
Modular inverse, 202
Modulus of complex numbers, 2
Most significant bit, *see* Bit order
Multi-Controlled gates, 86
Ancilla qubits, 86
qc data structure, 132
Multi-qubit gates
About controlled gates, 46
About single-qubit constructors, 33
Hadamard gates, 44–45
Multiplication, 177
Testing quantum arithmetic, 178

NAND logic gates, 92
nbits property of Tensor class, 16
qc data structure, 128

No-cloning theorem, 65
Fan-out circuits and, 92
Repetition code for error control, 285
Uncomputation not violating, 67
Node class for transpilation, 311
Noise, *see* Quantum noise
Noisy Intermediate Scale Quantum Computers (NISQ), 240, 293
Norm
Complex numbers, 1
Product of two states, 16
Unitary matrices as norm preserving, 6, 25
Vectors
Normalization, 20
Not-gates, *see also* X-gates
Logic circuits from, 92
Nuclear spin decoherence time, 278
numpy
★ operator for Kronecker product, 11
About, 9
adjoint() function for operators, 26
allclose() for Tensor comparisons, 12
Complex number support, 10
Eigenvalues of matrices, 180
ndarray, 10
Base for Tensor, 9
ndarray base for Tensor, 9
Instantiating, 10
Path to, 140
print configuration, 27

"On the Einstein Podolsky Rosen paradox" (Bell), 60, 63
Open quantum systems, 280
Open-source simulators, 320
OpenPulse, 295
OpenQASM, 295
Transpilation
About QASM, 311
Code generation flag, 315
Dumper function, 316
Operator class
adjoint() function, 26
Dumper function for matrix structure, 26
Gate applied to state ψ at qubit index, 32
Gate function returning Operator object, 32
Tensor class parent, 26
Operator-sum representation, 281
Operators
About, 9, 25
Application, 27–29
apply() function, 32, 128, 142
Density matrices, 68
Fast application, 134–139
Fast application generalized, 137–139
Faster application with C++, 139–145

Operators (Cont.)
  Fastest benchmarked, 147
  Fastest with sparse representation, 145–147
  Multiple operators in sequence, 31
  Multiple qubits, 29–31
  Noise reduction via compiler optimization, 304
  Norm preserving, 6, 25
  Notation for qubit index applied to, 31
  Padding operators, 31, 48
  Projection operators extracting subspace, 73
  Quantum computation, 66
  To state ψ at qubit index, 32
Cloning qubits impossible, 65
Outer product representation, 43
qc data structure, 129
  Gates applied, 128
Quantum Fourier transform operator, 169
  Inverse, 170
Tensor class parent, 26
Unitary, 25
  Invertable, 26
Optical cavity decoherence time, 278
Optimization
  Gate application iteration lesson, 331
  Gate application special cases, 143–145
  Hamiltonians constructed for, 254
  Hash table reconstruction, 332
OR logic gates, 92
Oracles
  Bernstein–Vazirani algorithm, 106, 117
  Deutsch algorithm, 108–117
  Deutsch-Jozsa algorithm, 118–121
  General oracle operator, 117
  Phase inversion implementation, 218
  Quipper automatic construction of, 301
  RevKit for constructing reversible, 321
  Silq construction of, 302
Oracles–Bernstein-Vazirani algorithm
  Compiler optimization, 308
Order finding, 192
  About, 192
  Order finding quantum algorithm, 196–200
    Continued fractions, 208
    Experimentation, 209
    Main program, 200
    Modular addition, 205–207
    Support routines, 202–205
Orthogonal vectors, 4
Outer product representation, 43
Outer products
  About, 4
  Density matrices as, 23, 68
  Outer product representation of operator, 43
  Projection operators, 42
  Trace of
    State vectors, 70

Two kets, 8
Overloading ⋆ operator, 11

Parallelism, *see* Quantum parallelism
Partial-trace procedure
  Bloch spheres in many-qubit system, 59
  Code, 69
    Experimenting with, 70
  Derivation for reduced density operator, 68
  Maximal entanglement, 64
  Tracing out other qubits, 69
    Entangled states, 71
    Environment traced out, 281
    Experimenting with, 70
    Mixed states, 71
    Pure states, 71
    Quirk qubits on Bloch sphere, 171
Path to numpy, 140
Pauli commutators, 83
Pauli matrices
  About, 34
  Eigenvalues, 180
  Function call syntax via Hadamard gates, 83
    Pauli commutators, 83
  Hermitian matrix real vector space, 35
  Involutivity, 35
  Measurement in Pauli bases, 242
  Pauli X-gates, *see also* X-gates
  Pauli Y-gates, 34
  Pauli Z-gates
    Phase-flip gates, 34, 37
  Quantum noise modeling, 282
  Rotation operators via exponentiation, 35
Peephole optimization, 307
  Libraries of compiler optimization patterns, 309
  Relaxed peephole optimization, 308
Performance
  Compiler optimization and, 304
  Quantum versus classical computers, 150–152
Period of function, 192
  Order finding quantum algorithm, 208
  Period finding quantum algorithm, 196–200
    Experimentation, 209
    Main program, 200
    Modular addition, 205–207
    Support routines, 202–205
Permutation matrices
  About, 12
  Checking if tensor is permutation, 12
  Controlled-Not gate, 46, 47
Phase damping, 283
Phase estimation, *see* Quantum phase estimation (QPE)
Phase gates, 38, 164

Discrete phase gates, 39, 164
Phase inversion operator, 219
Phase shift or kick gates, 40, 164
Phases via various gates, 40
RotationZ-gates versus, 38
Square root of as T-gate, 41
U1(lambda) gates, 40, 164
    Controlled-U1 gate for quantum arithmetic, 172
Phase invariance, 59
Phase inversion, 212
    Implementation, 218
    Multiple solutions, 227–230
    Operator, 219
        Quantum counting, 232
Phase kick circuit, 161
Phase of qubits, 21
Phase shift error, decoherence-induced, 279
Phase-flip errors, 279
    Bit-flip phase-flip channel, 281
    Error correction, 288
        Shor's 9-qubit code, 289
    Phase-flip channel, 281
Phase-flip gates, 37
Phase/bit-flip errors, 279
π (pi) fractions transpilation output, 316
Planck constant, 241
Podolsky, B., 60
Polar coordinates for qubit, 55–56
    Moving about sphere, 56
Postulates of quantum mechanics, 72
Power arithmetic, 208
Power function via Kronecker products, 11
Preskill, John, 149
Probabilistic Turing machines, 149
Probability amplitudes, 13
    Binary addressing, 19
    Ket definition, 72
    Maximally mixed state, 64
    Measurement, 72, 73
    Qubits as states, 15, 16
        Equal superposition with same amplitude, 45
        Projection operators extracting amplitude, 42
    State class code, 19
    State collapsing on measurement, 13, 72
    State vectors and unitary operators, 25
    Swap gates, 50
Product states, 61
Programming languages
    About hierarchy of abstractions, 295
    FORTRAN, 292
    Haskell, 300
        Quipper as embedded DSL, 300
        Quipper oracle automatic construction, 301

Silq as embedded DSL, 302
PSI probabilistic, 302
Q language C++ class library, 300
Q#, 303
    Silq comparison, 302
QASM tool, 295
    Addition via QFT circuit, 173
QCL, 296–298
    Quipper comparison, 301
Quipper, 300
    Oracle automatic construction, 301
    Proto-Quipper follow-ups, 301
    QCL comparison, 301
    Silq comparison, 302
Resources for information, 303
Scaffold, 298
    Classical and quantum constructs, 305
    Entanglement analysis, 299
    Hierarchical QASM, 299
    Transpiler, 298
Silq, 302
    Code snippet showcasing, 303
    Oracle construction, 302
Projection operators, 42
    2-dimensional index into matrix, 43
    Controller and controlled qubits not adjacent, 47
    Hermitian, 43
    Not unitary or reversible, 43
    Outer product representation, 43
    Projective measurements and, 73
Projective measurements, 72
    About projective, 73
ProjectQ commercial system, 303
    Simulator, 321
ψ as qubit state space, 13
    operator applied to ψ at qubit index, 32
PSI probabilistic programming language, 302
Pure states, 68
    Compiler optimization, 306
    Trace of density matrix, 24
    Tracing out qubits, 71
Python
    About numpy, 9
    About ordering of gate applications, 54
    C++
        Accelerated gate application, 139–145
        Execution speed, 139, 145
        Extending Python with, 140
        Sparse representation, 145
        Sparse representation benchmarked, 147
    Complex numbers, 2
    conjugate() function, 2
    Operator application, 27–29
    Tensor class
        About, 9

Q language C++ class library, 300
    Transpiler code generation flag, 315
Q# commercial system (Microsoft), 303
    Q# programming language, 303
        Silq comparison, 302
    Quantum Developer Kit, 303
QASM tool, 295
    Addition via QFT circuit, 173
    cQASM, 295
    Hierarchical QASM, 299
    OpenQASM, 295
    Transpilation
        About QASM, 311
        Code generation flag, 315
        Dumper function, 316
qc (quantum circuit) data structure
    About abstraction, 126, 134
    Constructor, 127
    Full adder example, 134
    Gates, 129
        Adjoint, 130
        Applying, 128, 142
        Fast application, 134–139
        Fast application generalized, 137–139
        Faster application with C++, 139–145
        Multi-Controlled gates, 132
        Swap and controlled swap gates, 131
    Measurements, 131
        Statistical sampling function, 131
    nbits property, 128
    Quantum registers, 127
    Qubits added, 128
    Sparse representation, 145–147
        Benchmarking, 147
    Transpilation extension of, 313
        Code generation flags, 315
        Eager mode, 313, 314
QCL programming language, 296–298
    Quipper comparison, 301
QFT, *see* Quantum Fourier transform
qHipster simulator, 320
Qiskit commercial system (IBM), 303
    ALAP scheduling of gates, 307
    Algorithm reference, 277
    QASM support, 311
    Simulators, 321
QPE, *see* Quantum phase estimation
QRAM model of quantum computing, 293, 294
    Gate approximation, 310
qsim simulator (Google), 321
qsimh simulator (Google), 321
Quadratic programming problem, 254
Quantum advantage, 149
Quantum algorithm zoo, 277
Quantum amplitude amplification (QAA), 227–230
Quantum approximate optimization algorithm
    (QAOA), 253

Quantum circuit (qc) data structure
    About abstraction, 126, 134
    Constructor, 127
    Full adder example, 134
    Gates, 129
        Adjoint, 130
        Applying, 128, 142
        Fast application, 134–139
        Fast application generalized, 137–139
        Faster application with C++, 139–145
        Multi-Controlled gates, 132
        Swap and controlled swap gates, 131
    Measurements, 131
        Statistical sampling function, 131
    nbits property, 128
    Quantum registers, 127
    Qubits added, 128
    Sparse representation, 145–147
        Benchmarking, 147
    Transpilation extension of, 313
        Code generation flags, 315
        Eager mode, 313, 314
Quantum circuit notation
    About ordering of gate applications, 54
    Controlled gates
        Controlled-X gates, 53
        Controlled-Z gates, 53
        Controlled-Not-by-0 gates, 53
        More than one qubit controlling, 54
    Entangler circuits, 61
    Fan-out circuits, 92
    Full adder, 89
    Information flow double lines, 54
    Logic circuits, 92
    Measurement, 54
    Oracle for Bernstein-Vazirani algorithm, 106
    Qubit order, 51
    Single-qubit operator applied, 52, 53
    State as tensor product combined state, 52
    State change depiction, 52
    State initialization, 52
    Swap test, 93
    X-gates, 53
Quantum computers
    Arithmetic via full adder, 89–91
        Quantum arithmetic, 172–177
    Classical computers controlling, 293, 294
    Classical computers simulated by, 149
    Commercial systems, 303
    Compiler design challenges, 293
    Density matrices for theory of, 24, 68
    Environmental challenges, 278–284
    Error correction challenges, 285
    Flow control via controlled gates, 46
        QCL programming language, 297
        Silq programming language, 302

Logic circuits, 91
Noisy Intermediate Scale Quantum Computers
    era, 240, 293
Operators as ISA of, 25
QRAM model, 293, 294
    Gate approximation, 310
Quantum computation, 66
    λ-calculus to express, 300
Quantum registers, 67, 124–126
Simulation, 124
Uncomputation, 66
    QCL programming language, 296
    Silq programming language, 302
    Transpilation intermediate representation,
        315
    Trick for saving result, 67
Quantum counting, 230–234
Quantum Developer Kit (QDK), 303
    Simulators, 321
Quantum dot decoherence time, 278
Quantum error conditions, 279
Quantum error correction
    About, 278, 284
    Bit-flip errors, 286–288
        Shor's 9-qubit code, 289
    Channels, 281
    Compiler optimization and, 304
    Error correction code memory, 284
    Error syndrome, 286
    Phase-flip errors, 288
        Shor's 9-qubit code, 289
    Quantum computing challenges, 285
    Quantum noise, 278–284
    Repetition code, 284
        Majority voting, 285
        No-cloning theorem, 285
        Quantum repetition code, 285
    Resources for information, 291
    Shor's 9-qubit error correction code, 285, 289
Quantum fidelity, 269
Quantum Fourier transform (QFT)
    About, 169
    Algorithm detail
        About, 163
        Binary fractions, 163
        Quantum Fourier transform, 165–167
        Two-qubit QFT, 167–169
        Two-qubit QFT online simulation, 170
    Measurement, 169
    Online simulation, 170
    Phase kick circuits, 161
    QCL programming language, 298
    QFT operator, 169
        Inverse, 170
    Quantum arithmetic
        Addition, 172–177

Multiplication, 177
Subtraction, 177
Testing, 178
Quantum information, *see* Information
Quantum IO Monad, 300
Quantum mechanics
    Copenhagen interpretation, 61
    Hidden state, 60, 63
    Postulates, 72
Quantum noise, 278–284
    Amplitude damping, 283
    Channels, 281
        Bit flip and phase flip, 281
        Depolarization, 282
    Compiler optimization and noise reduction, 304
    Error correction, 284–291
    Error injection to model, 282
        Checking bit-flip error correction, 287
        Gates as quantum noise source, 283
    Gates imprecise, 283
    Phase damping, 283
    Quantum operations, 280
        Operation element, 281
        Operator-sum representation, 281
    Simulation, 320, 321
Quantum operations
    Operation element, 281
    Operator-sum representation, 281
Quantum parallelism, 108, 112
Quantum phase estimation (QPE)
    Detailed derivation, 182–186
    Eigenvalues and eigenvectors, 180
    Hamiltonian eigenvalues, 240
    Implementation, 186–189
    Phase estimation, 181
        Definition, 181
    Quantum counting, 231
Quantum programming languages
    About hierarchy of abstractions, 295
    Haskell, 300
        Quipper as embedded DSL, 300
        Quipper oracle automatic construction, 301
        Silq as embedded DSL, 302
    PSI probabilistic, 302
    Q language C++ class library, 300
    Q#, 303
        Silq comparison, 302
    QASM tool, 295
        Addition via QFT circuit, 173
    QCL, 296–298
        Quipper comparison, 301
    Quipper, 300
        Oracle automatic construction, 301
        Proto-Quipper follow-ups, 301
        QCL comparison, 301
        Silq comparison, 302
    Resources for information, 303

Quantum programming languages (Cont.)
  Scaffold, 298
    Classical and quantum constructs, 305
    Entanglement analysis, 299
    Hierarchical QASM, 299
    Transpiler, 298
  Silq, 302
    Code snippet showcasing, 303
    Oracle construction, 302
Quantum random circuits (QRC), 150
  Simulation design, 152
  Simulation evaluation, 158
  Simulation implementation, 154
  Simulation metric, 157
  Simulation run estimation, 155–158
Quantum random walk, 234–240
  1D walk, 235
  2D walk, 237
  About, 234, 238
  Coin toss, 235
  Walking the walk, 237
Quantum registers, 124–126
  Code to create and initialize, 125
    qc data structure, 127
  Compiler optimization and, 304
  For result storage, 67
  QCL programming language, 296
  Reg class, 124
Quantum supremacy, 149
"Quantum supremacy using a programmable
    superconducting processor" (Arute et
    al.), 150
Quantum teleportation, 97–102
  Error correction trick, 286
Quantum Turing machines, 149
Qubits
  About the state of a qubit, 13
    Basis states, 13, 15
    Basis states orthonormal, 15
    Collapsing on measurement, 13, 60, 72
    Communicating state of two with one,
      102–105
    Equal superposition of adjacent qubits, 45
    Measurement, 75
    Measurement examples, 76
    Probability amplitudes, 13, 15, 16
    State class constructors, 22
    Superposition via Hadamard gates, 44
    Tensor product combined state, 52
  Ancilla qubits, 66
  Binary addressing, 19
  Bloch sphere describing, 55–56
    Computing coordinates for given state, 58
  Cloning or copying impossible, 65
  Column vectors of complex numbers, 2, 15
  Compiler optimization via recycling, 309

Complexity of scaling up, 122
Constructing in code, 14
  Data structure, 14
Entanglement, 60–65
Junk qubits, 66
Operator application, 27–29
  Applied at index specified, 31
  Controller and controlled qubits, 46–51, 53
  Multiple operators in sequence, 31
  Multiple qubits, 29–31
  Nonadjacent controller and controlled
    qubits, 47
  Norm preserving, 6, 25
  Notation for qubit index applied to, 31
  Projection operators extracting subspace,
    73
  Quantum computation, 66
  Qubit ordering, 137
Order of qubits, 18
  Operator application, 137
  Quantum circuit notation, 51
Phase, 21
Polar coordinates describing
  Moving about sphere, 56
Tensors constructing, 9, 14
  Code, 15
  nbits property, 16
  n qubits, 16
QuEST (Quantum Exact Simulation Toolkit),
    321
Quipper programming language, 300
  Oracle automatic construction, 301
  Proto-Quipper follow-ups, 301
  QCL comparison, 301
  Silq comparison, 302
Quirk online simulations, 170
QX Simulator, 320

Random circuits, see Quantum random circuits
    (QRC)
Random number generator, 78
  Coin toss, 235
  Random combination of 0 or 1 states, 23
Random walk, 234–240
  1D walk, 235
  2D walk, 237
  About, 234, 238
  Coin toss, 235
  Walking the walk, 237
Reduced density operator, 68
  Debugging tool for inspecting states, 68
  Partial trace derivation, 68
    Code, 69
  Quirk qubits on Bloch sphere, 171
Reg class, 124
Registers, 67, 124–126
  Code to create and initialize, 125

libq implementation, 322
qc data structure, 127
Compiler optimization and, 304
QCL programming language, 296
Reg class, 124
Relative phase, 35
Global phase versus, 60
Relaxed peephole optimization, 308
Renormalization
States collapsing on measurement
Renormalization, 74
Repetition code, 284
Majority voting, 285
No-cloning theorem, 285
Quantum repetition code, 285
Resources for information
Algorithms, 277
Computational complexity theory, 149
Logical to physical mapping, 310
Quantum error correction, 291
Quantum programming languages, 303
Quirk online simulator, 170
Schrödinger equation, 241
Simulators available, 320
RevKit for reversible oracles, 321
Rk gates, 39
Phases via various gates, 40
Roots of gates, 41
Square roots of gates
About, 41
Rosen, N., 60
Rotation Axis, 37
Rotation operators, 35
Axis of rotation, 37
Controlled rotation gates additive, 161
Discrete phase gates, 39
Quantum counting, 231
Qubit on Bloch sphere, 56
Rotation axis changed, 84
Square roots of, 41
Row vectors
Bras in Dirac notation, 3
Inner products, 3
RSA encryption algorithm, 189

S-gates, *see also* Phase gates, 165
Scaffold programming language, 298
Classical and quantum constructs, 305
Entanglement analysis, 299
Hierarchical QASM, 299
transpiler, 298
Scalability
About, 122
Complexity of scaling up, 122, 293
Controlled gates, 48
Gate fast application, 134–139
Hierarchical QASM, 299

Quipper programming language, 300
Scalar products, *see* Inner products
Scheduling of gates, 306
Schrödinger–Feynman Simulation, 124
Schrödinger equation
qsim simulator, 321
Resource for more information, 241
Time-independent for state evolving, 72
Drivation, 240
Variational principle, 242–245
Schrödinger–Feynman path histories, 145,
151, 159
qsimh simulator, 321
scipy
Installing, 42
sqrtm() function, 42
Sets of universal gates, 49
Shor's 9-qubit error correction code, 285, 289
Shor's integer factorization algorithm
About, 189
About phase estimation, 163
Classical
Experimentation, 193
Factorization, 190
Greatest common divisor, 190
Modular arithmetic, 189
Period finding, 192
Period finding quantum algorithm, 196–200
Continued fractions, 208
Controlled modular multiplication, 207
Experimentation, 209
Main program, 200
Modular addition, 205–207
Support routines, 202–205
Sparse representation Benchmarked, 147
Silq programming language, 302
Code snippet showcasing, 303
Oracle construction, 302
Simon's algorithm, 121
Simon's generalized algorithm, 121
Simulation
About scalability, 122
Available simulators, 320
Complexity, 122, 151, 155
Online simulators, 170
Open-source simulators, 320
Parallelization of gates, 307
Quantum Fourier transform online simulation,
170
Quantum random circuits
Google team, 151, 158
Metric, 157
Simulation design, 152
Simulation evaluation, 158
Simulation implementation, 154
Simulation run estimation, 155–158

Simulation (Cont.)
Quantum registers, 124–126
Quantum simulating classical computers,
149
Single-qubit gates, 33–45
About constructing multi-qubit operators, 33
About operators, 9
Applying operator, 52
Hadamard gates, 44–45
Identity gates, 26, 33
Applied to multiple qubits, 30
Phase gates, 38
Discrete phase gates, 39
Phase shift or kick gates, 40
Phases via various gates, 40
Projection operators, 42
Reversed by conjugate transpose, 26
Rk gates, 40
Rotation operators, 35
RotationZ-gates versus phase gates, 38
Square roots of gates, 41
T-gates, 40
Phases via, 40
U1(lambda) gates, 40
X-gates, 26, 34
Applied to multiple qubits, 30
State initialization to 0- or 1-state, 22
Y-gates, 34
Z-gates, 34
Sleator-Weinfurter construction, 85
Solovay–Kitaev (SK) theorem, 266
Solovay–Kitaev (SK) algorithm
About, 266
Algorithm, 270–272
Balanced group commutator, 272–274
Matrix diagonalization function, 274
Bloch sphere angle and axis, 267
Evaluation, 274
Pre-computing gates, 269
Random gate sequences, 276
Similarity metrics
Quantum fidelity, 269
Trace distance, 268
Theorem, 266
Universal gates, 266
SU(2) group, 267
Sparse representation, 145–147
About, 122
Benchmarking, 147
libquantum library, 145
Simulation, 320
SPEC benchmarks, 150
Spooky action at a distance, 60, 63
Quantum teleportation, 97–102
sqrtm() function of scipy, 42
Square roots of gates

scipy sqrtm() function, 42
Squaring root of gate equals gate, 80
State class
Constructing qubits in code, 14
Qubit data structure, 14
Constructors, 22
All 0-states or 1-states, 22
density() function, 23
Member functions, 19–21
Dumper function for all relevant info, 21
Probability and amplitudes, 19
Tensor class parent, 15
nbits property, 16
States
About, 9
About bit order, 17, 18
Binary interpretation, 18
Bit index notation, 136
Basis states of qubits, *see* Basis states
Cloning, 65
Collapsing on measurement, 13, 60
Born rule, 72
Measurement definition, 72
Renormalization, 74
Density matrices, 68
Entanglement, 60–65
Kets representing state of system, 72
State evolving via operators, 72
Maximally mixed state, *see also* Probability
amplitudes
Operator application, 27–29
Multiple qubits, 29–31
Projection operators extracting amplitude, 42
Quantum circuit notation
Single-qubit operators applied, 52
State change depiction, 52
State initialization, 52
Quantum operations, 280
Similarity via swap test, 93–97
Code, 96
Single-qubit 0 and 1 state constants, 23
Tensors constructing, 9
Tensors constructing qubits, 14
Code, 15
Qubit data structure, 14
n qubits, 16
Tensor product combined state, 52
Vectors
Binary interpretation, 18
Column vectors of complex numbers, 2, 14
Complexity of scaling up, 122
Kets representing state of system, 72
Normalization, 13, 20
Normalized vectors and, 4
Operator application, 27–29, 72
Unitary operators as norm preserving, 25
Steane code, 291

Steane, Andrew, 291
SU(2) group, 267
Subset-sum algorithm
  About, 262
  Experiments, 264
  Implementation, 263
Subtraction, 177
  Decrement operator, 236
  Testing quantum arithmetic, 178
Summit supercomputer simulating quantum
        random circuits, 158
Superdense coding, 102–105
Superposition
  About, 44
  About measurement, 72
  Hadamard gates on qubits, 44
    Equal superposition of adjacent qubits,
        45
  Linear combination of basis states, 13
  Maximally mixed state, 64
  State after operator applied, 52
Swap gates, 50, 88
  Compiler optimization, 308
  Controlled-controlled Swap gates, 51
  qc data structure, 131
Swap test, 93–97
  Code, 96
Sycamore processor, 150

T-gates
  Phases via, 40, 165
  Rotation axis changed, 84
  Square root of phase gates, 41
  Universal gates, 266
Teleportation, 97–102
  Error correction trick, 286
Tensor class
  About array behavior, 9
  Comparing to values, 12
  Instantiating, 10
    tensor_type() abstraction, 10
  Kronecker product member function, 11
  Operators derived from, 26
  Qubit states
    Code, 15
  State class derived from, 15
    nbits property, 16
Tensor products, 5
  Binary interpretation, 19
  Distributive, 5
  Kronecker product as, 10
  Multiplication with scalar, 5
  Operators applied to multiple qubits, 29–31
    Multiple operators in sequence, 31
  Product states, 61
  State of two or more qubits, 16
  Trace of matrix, 8

Tensors, 9
  About array behavior, 9
  Checking if Hermitian or unitary, 12
  Comparing to values, 12
  Inner products, 5
  Instantiating, 10
    tensor_type() abstraction, 10
  Kronecker product, 10
Testing
  Benchmarking, *see* Benchmarking
    Gate fast application, 139
  Controlled gate equivalencies validated, 88
  Debugging, 12
  Quantum arithmetic, 178
  Tracing out state of one qubit, 70
Toffoli gates, 49, 85
  Logic circuits from, 92
  Multi-Controlled X-gates, 86
Trace distance, 268
Trace of matrix, 8
  Hermitian matrices, 8
  Partial-trace procedure, 59
  Tensor product, 8
  Trace of outer product two kets, 8
Transpilation
  About, 292, 311
  Code generation flags, 315
  Dumper function, 315
    Cirq, 319
    libq, 317
    QASM, 316
  Intermediate representation, 311
    Circuit capabilities of, 314
    IR base class, 312
    IR nodes, 311
    Quantum circuit extensions, 313
    Uncomputation, 315
    π fractions output, 316
  Scaffold transpiler, 298
Transposition
  Involutivity, 3
  Matrix, 2
Two-qubit quantum Fourier transform, 167–169
  Online simulator, 170

U1(lambda) gates, 40, 164
  Controlled-U1 gate for quantum arithmetic, 172
Uncomputation, 66, 315
  QCL programming language, 296
  Silq programming language, 302
  Transpilation intermediate representation, 315
  Trick for saving result, 67
Underscore in function names, 12
Unitary matrices
  About, 6
  Checking if tensor is unitary, 12

Unitary matrices (Cont.)
  Norm preserving, 6, 25
  Tensoring together, 11
Unitary operators, *see also* Gates; Operators
  Invertable, 26
Universal gates, 49
  Definition, 266
  QRAM model of quantum computing,
      294
  Solovay–Kitaev theorem, 266
    SU(2) group, 267
Universal gates in quantum computing, 49

V-gates
  Square root of X-gates, 41, 85
val2bits() for decimal to binary, 24
Variational quantum eigensolver (VQE)
  About, 160, 240
  Algorithm, 245–248
  Expectation values, 244
  Hamiltonian type, 242
  Measurement in Pauli bases, 242
  Measuring eigenvalues, 248
  Multiple qubits, 250–252
  Quantum phase estimation, 240
  Schrödinger equation, 240
  Variational principle, 242–245
Vectors
  Binary interpretation, 18
  Complex numbers, 2
  Norm, 4
  Orthogonal, 4
  States
    Basis states of qubits, 13
    Complexity of scaling up, 122
    Initializing with normalized vector, 23
    Kets representing state of system, 72
    Operator application, 27–29, 72
    Unitary operators as norm preserving, 25

Tensor products, 5
  Unitary matrices as norm preserving, 6, 25
VQE, *see* Variational quantum eigensolver
    algorithm

Weighted maximum cut, 255
Wilczek, F., xi
Wire optimization, 309

X-gates, 26, 34
  Applied to multiple qubits, 30, 135
  Controlled-Controlled X-gates (CCX-gates),
      49, 85
  Logic circuits from, 92
  Multi-Controlled X-gates, 86
  Not-gate, 34
  Quantum circuit notation
    Controlled-X gates, 53
    Controlled-Not-by-0 gates built, 53
    X-gates, 53
  Qubit on Bloch sphere, 56
  Square root of as V-gate, 41, 85
  State initialization to 0- or 1-state, 22

Y-gates, 34
  Negate Y-gate, 83
  Square root of, 41

Z-gates, 34
  Controlled-Z gates, 81
    Controlled-Not gates via, 82
    Multi-Controlled-Z gates, 82
  Phase-flip gates, 34, 37
  Phases via, 40
  Quantum circuit notation, 53
    Controlled Z-gates, 53
  Qubit on Bloch sphere, 56–58
Z90-gates, *see also* Phase gates
Zeilinger, Anton, 64

Printed in the United States
by Baker & Taylor Publisher Services